The GnuTLS 3.6.1 Manual

This document includes text contributed by Nikos Mavrogiannopoulos, Simon Josefsson, Daiki Ueno, Carolin Latze, Alfredo Pironti, Ted Zlatanov and Andrew McDonald. Several corrections are due to Patrick Pelletier and Andreas Metzler.

ISBN 978-1-326-00266-4

Contents

Contents

Contents

Contents

List of Tables

List of Figures

Preface

This document demonstrates and explains the GnuTLS library API. A brief introduction to the protocols and the technology involved is also included so that an application programmer can better understand the GnuTLS purpose and actual offerings. Even if GnuTLS is a typical library software, it operates over several security and cryptographic protocols which require the programmer to make careful and correct usage of them. Otherwise it is likely to only obtain a false sense of security. The term of security is very broad even if restricted to computer software, and cannot be confined to a single cryptographic library. For that reason, do not consider any program secure just because it uses GnuTLS; there are several ways to compromise a program or a communication line and GnuTLS only helps with some of them.

Although this document tries to be self contained, basic network programming and public key infrastructure (PKI) knowledge is assumed in most of it. A good introduction to networking can be found in [40], to public key infrastructure in [15] and to security engineering in [5].

Updated versions of the GnuTLS software and this document will be available from http://www.gnutls.org/.

Introduction to GnuTLS

In brief GnuTLS can be described as a library which offers an API to access secure communication protocols. These protocols provide privacy over insecure lines, and were designed to prevent eavesdropping, tampering, or message forgery.

Technically GnuTLS is a portable ANSI C based library which implements the protocols ranging from SSL 3.0 to TLS 1.2 (see chapter 2, for a detailed description of the protocols), accompanied with the required framework for authentication and public key infrastructure. Important features of the GnuTLS library include:

- Support for TLS 1.2, TLS 1.1, TLS 1.0 and SSL 3.0 protocols.

- Support for Datagram TLS 1.0 and 1.2.

- Support for handling and verification of X.509 certificates.

- Support for password authentication using TLS-SRP.

- Support for keyed authentication using TLS-PSK.

- Support for TPM, PKCS #11 tokens and smart-cards.

The GnuTLS library consists of three independent parts, namely the "TLS protocol part", the "Certificate part", and the "Cryptographic back-end" part. The "TLS protocol part" is the actual protocol implementation, and is entirely implemented within the GnuTLS library. The "Certificate part" consists of the certificate parsing, and verification functions and it uses functionality from the libtasn1 library. The "Cryptographic back-end" is provided by the nettle and gmplib libraries.

1.1. Downloading and installing

GnuTLS is available for download at: http://www.gnutls.org/download.html

GnuTLS uses a development cycle where even minor version numbers indicate a stable release and a odd minor version number indicate a development release. For example, GnuTLS 1.6.3 denote a stable release since 6 is even, and GnuTLS 1.7.11 denote a development release since 7 is odd.

GnuTLS depends on `nettle` and `gmplib`, and you will need to install it before installing GnuTLS. The `nettle` library is available from http://www.lysator.liu.se/~nisse/nettle/, while `gmplib` is available from http://www.gmplib.org/. Don't forget to verify the cryptographic signature after downloading source code packages.

The package is then extracted, configured and built like many other packages that use Autoconf. For detailed information on configuring and building it, refer to the "INSTALL" file that is part of the distribution archive. Typically you invoke `./configure` and then `make check install`. There are a number of compile-time parameters, as discussed below.

Several parts of GnuTLS require ASN.1 functionality, which is provided by a library called libtasn1. A copy of libtasn1 is included in GnuTLS. If you want to install it separately (e.g., to make it possibly to use libtasn1 in other programs), you can get it from http://www.gnu.org/software/libtasn1/.

The compression library, `libz`, the PKCS #11 helper library `p11-kit`, the TPM library `trousers`, as well as the IDN library `libidn`[1] are optional dependencies. Check the README file in the distribution on how to obtain these libraries.

A few `configure` options may be relevant, summarized below. They disable or enable particular features, to create a smaller library with only the required features. Note however, that although a smaller library is generated, the included programs are not guaranteed to compile if some of these options are given.

```
--disable-srp-authentication
--disable-psk-authentication
--disable-anon-authentication
--disable-dhe
--disable-ecdhe
--disable-openssl-compatibility
--disable-dtls-srtp-support
--disable-alpn-support
--disable-heartbeat-support
--disable-libdane
--without-p11-kit
--without-tpm
--without-zlib
```

For the complete list, refer to the output from `configure --help`.

1.2. Installing for a software distribution

When installing for a software distribution, it is often desirable to preconfigure GnuTLS with the system-wide paths and files. There two important configuration options, one sets the trust store in system, which are the CA certificates to be used by programs by default (if they

---

[1]Needed to use RFC6125 name comparison in internationalized domains.

don't override it), and the other sets to DNSSEC root key file used by unbound for DNSSEC verification.

For the latter the following configuration option is available, and if not specified GnuTLS will try to auto-detect the location of that file.

```
--with-unbound-root-key-file
```

To set the trust store the following options are available.

```
--with-default-trust-store-file
--with-default-trust-store-dir
--with-default-trust-store-pkcs11
```

The first option is used to set a PEM file which contains a list of trusted certificates, while the second will read all certificates in the given path. The recommended option is the last, which allows to use a PKCS #11 trust policy module. That module not only provides the trusted certificates, but allows the categorization of them using purpose, e.g., CAs can be restricted for e-mail usage only, or administrative restrictions of CAs, for examples by restricting a CA to only issue certificates for a given DNS domain using NameConstraints. A publicly available PKCS #11 trust module is p11-kit's trust module[2].

1.3. Overview

In this document we present an overview of the supported security protocols in chapter 2, and continue by providing more information on the certificate authentication in section 3.1, and shared-key as well anonymous authentication in section 3.3. We elaborate on certificate authentication by demonstrating advanced usage of the API in section 3.2. The core of the TLS library is presented in chapter 5 and example applications are listed in chapter 6. In chapter 7 the usage of few included programs that may assist debugging is presented. The last chapter is chapter 8 that provides a short introduction to GnuTLS' internal architecture.

---

[2]http://p11-glue.freedesktop.org/doc/p11-kit/trust-module.html

2

Introduction to TLS and DTLS

TLS stands for "Transport Layer Security" and is the successor of SSL, the Secure Sockets Layer protocol [13] designed by Netscape. TLS is an Internet protocol, defined by IETF[1], described in [10]. The protocol provides confidentiality, and authentication layers over any reliable transport layer. The description, above, refers to TLS 1.0 but applies to all other TLS versions as the differences between the protocols are not major.

The DTLS protocol, or "Datagram TLS" [33] is a protocol with identical goals as TLS, but can operate under unreliable transport layers such as UDP. The discussions below apply to this protocol as well, except when noted otherwise.

2.1. TLS Layers

TLS is a layered protocol, and consists of the record protocol, the handshake protocol and the alert protocol. The record protocol is to serve all other protocols and is above the transport layer. The record protocol offers symmetric encryption, and data authenticity[2]. The alert protocol offers some signaling to the other protocols. It can help informing the peer for the cause of failures and other error conditions. section 2.4, for more information. The alert protocol is above the record protocol.

The handshake protocol is responsible for the security parameters' negotiation, the initial key exchange and authentication. section 2.5, for more information about the handshake protocol. The protocol layering in TLS is shown in Figure 2.1.

2.2. The Transport Layer

TLS is not limited to any transport layer and can be used above any transport layer, as long as it is a reliable one. DTLS can be used over reliable and unreliable transport layers. GnuTLS supports TCP and UDP layers transparently using the Berkeley sockets API. However, any

---

[1]IETF, or Internet Engineering Task Force, is a large open international community of network designers, operators, vendors, and researchers concerned with the evolution of the Internet architecture and the smooth operation of the Internet. It is open to any interested individual.

[2]In early versions of TLS compression was optionally available as well. This is no longer the case in recent versions of the protocol.

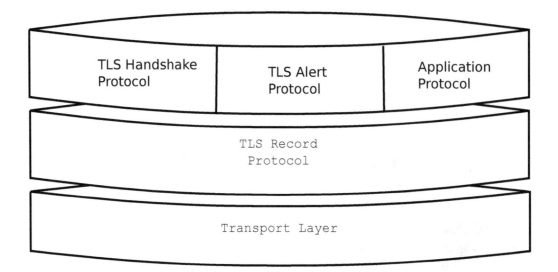

Figure 2.1.: The TLS protocol layers.

transport layer can be used by providing callbacks for GnuTLS to access the transport layer (for details see section 5.5).

2.3. The TLS record protocol

The record protocol is the secure communications provider. Its purpose is to encrypt, and authenticate packets. The record layer functions can be called at any time after the handshake process is finished, when there is need to receive or send data. In DTLS however, due to re-transmission timers used in the handshake out-of-order handshake data might be received for some time (maximum 60 seconds) after the handshake process is finished.

The functions to access the record protocol are limited to send and receive functions, which might, given the importance of this protocol in TLS, seem awkward. This is because the record protocol's parameters are all set by the handshake protocol. The record protocol initially starts with NULL parameters, which means no encryption, and no MAC is used. Encryption and authentication begin just after the handshake protocol has finished.

2.3.1. Encryption algorithms used in the record layer

Confidentiality in the record layer is achieved by using symmetric ciphers like AES or CHACHA20. Ciphers are encryption algorithms that use a single, secret, key to encrypt and decrypt data. Early versions of TLS separated between block and stream ciphers and had message authentication plugged in to them by the protocol, though later versions switched to using authenticated-encryption (AEAD) ciphers. The AEAD ciphers are defined to combine encryption and authentication, and as such they are not only more efficient, as the primitives used are designed to interoperate nicely, but they are also known to interoperate in a secure way.

The supported in GnuTLS ciphers and MAC algorithms are shown in Table 2.1 and Table 2.2.

Algorithm	Type	Description
AES-128-GCM, AES-256-GCM	AEAD	This is the AES algorithm in the authenticated encryption GCM mode. This mode combines message authentication and encryption and can be extremely fast on CPUs that support hardware acceleration.
AES-128-CCM, AES-256-CCM	AEAD	This is the AES algorithm in the authenticated encryption CCM mode. This mode combines message authentication and encryption and is often used by systems without AES or GCM acceleration support.
AES-128-CCM-8, AES-256-CCM-8	AEAD	This is the AES algorithm in the authenticated encryption CCM mode with a truncated to 64-bit authentication tag. This mode is for communication with restricted systems.
CAMELLIA-128-GCM, CAMELLIA-256-GCM	AEAD	This is the CAMELLIA algorithm in the authenticated encryption GCM mode.
CHACHA20-POLY1305	AEAD	CHACHA20-POLY1305 is an authenticated encryption algorithm based on CHACHA20 cipher and POLY1305 MAC. CHACHA20 is a refinement of SALSA20 algorithm, an approved cipher by the European ESTREAM project. POLY1305 is Wegman-Carter, one-time authenticator. The combination provides a fast stream cipher suitable for systems where a hardware AES accelerator is not available.
AES-128-CBC, AES-256-CBC	Legacy (block)	AES or RIJNDAEL is the block cipher algorithm that replaces the old DES algorithm. It has 128 bits block size and is used in CBC mode.
CAMELLIA-128-CBC, CAMELLIA-256-CBC	Legacy (block)	This is an 128-bit block cipher developed by Mitsubishi and NTT. It is one of the approved ciphers of the European NESSIE and Japanese CRYPTREC projects.
3DES-CBC	Legacy (block)	This is the DES block cipher algorithm used with triple encryption (EDE). Has 64 bits block size and is used in CBC mode.
ARCFOUR-128	Legacy (stream)	ARCFOUR-128 is a compatible algorithm with RSA's RC4 algorithm, which is considered to be a trade secret. It is a considered to be broken, and is only used for compatibility purposed. For this reason it is not enabled by default.

Table 2.1.: Supported ciphers in TLS.

Algorithm	Description
MAC-MD5	This is an HMAC based on MD5 a cryptographic hash algorithm designed by Ron Rivest. Outputs 128 bits of data.
MAC-SHA1	An HMAC based on the SHA1 cryptographic hash algorithm designed by NSA. Outputs 160 bits of data.
MAC-SHA256	An HMAC based on SHA2-256. Outputs 256 bits of data.
MAC-SHA384	An HMAC based on SHA2-384. Outputs 384 bits of data.
MAC-AEAD	This indicates that an authenticated encryption algorithm, such as GCM, is in use.

Table 2.2.: Supported MAC algorithms in TLS.

2.3.2. Compression algorithms and the record layer

In early versions of TLS the record layer supported compression. However, that proved to be problematic in many ways, and enabled several attacks based on traffic analysis on the transported data. For that newer versions of the protocol no longer offer compression, and GnuTLS since 3.6.0 no longer implements any support for compression.

2.3.3. Weaknesses and countermeasures

Some weaknesses that may affect the security of the record layer have been found in TLS 1.0 protocol. These weaknesses can be exploited by active attackers, and exploit the facts that

1. TLS has separate alerts for "decryption_failed" and "bad_record_mac"

2. The decryption failure reason can be detected by timing the response time.

3. The IV for CBC encrypted packets is the last block of the previous encrypted packet.

Those weaknesses were solved in TLS 1.1 [9] which is implemented in GnuTLS. For this reason we suggest to always negotiate the highest supported TLS version with the peer[3]. For a detailed discussion of the issues see the archives of the TLS Working Group mailing list and [27].

2.3.4. On record padding

The TLS protocol allows for extra padding of records in CBC ciphers, to prevent statistical analysis based on the length of exchanged messages (see [10] section 6.2.3.2). GnuTLS appears to be one of few implementations that take advantage of this feature: the user can provide some plaintext data with a range of lengths she wishes to hide, and GnuTLS adds extra padding to make sure the attacker cannot tell the real plaintext length is in a range smaller than the user-provided one. Use `gnutls_record_send_range` to send length-hidden messages and `gnutls_record_can_use_length_hiding` to check whether the current session supports length hiding. Using the standard `gnutls_record_send` will only add minimal padding.

---

[3]If this is not possible then please consult subsection 5.12.7.

The TLS implementation in the Symbian operating system, frequently used by Nokia and Sony-Ericsson mobile phones, cannot handle non-minimal record padding. What happens when one of these clients handshake with a GnuTLS server is that the client will fail to compute the correct MAC for the record. The client sends a TLS alert (`bad_record_mac`) and disconnects. Typically this will result in error messages such as 'A TLS fatal alert has been received', 'Bad record MAC', or both, on the GnuTLS server side.

If compatibility with such devices is a concern, not sending length-hidden messages solves the problem by using minimal padding.

If you implement an application that has a configuration file, we recommend that you make it possible for users or administrators to specify a GnuTLS protocol priority string, which is used by your application via `gnutls_priority_set`. To allow the best flexibility, make it possible to have a different priority string for different incoming IP addresses.

2.4. The TLS alert protocol

The alert protocol is there to allow signals to be sent between peers. These signals are mostly used to inform the peer about the cause of a protocol failure. Some of these signals are used internally by the protocol and the application protocol does not have to cope with them (e.g. `GNUTLS_A_CLOSE_NOTIFY`), and others refer to the application protocol solely (e.g. `GNUTLS_A_USER_CANCELLED`). An alert signal includes a level indication which may be either fatal or warning. Fatal alerts always terminate the current connection, and prevent future re-negotiations using the current session ID. All alert messages are summarized in the table below.

The alert messages are protected by the record protocol, thus the information that is included does not leak. You must take extreme care for the alert information not to leak to a possible attacker, via public log files etc.

Alert	ID	Description
GNUTLS_A_CLOSE_NOTIFY	0	Close notify
GNUTLS_A_UNEXPECTED_MESSAGE	10	Unexpected message
GNUTLS_A_BAD_RECORD_MAC	20	Bad record MAC
GNUTLS_A_DECRYPTION_FAILED	21	Decryption failed
GNUTLS_A_RECORD_OVERFLOW	22	Record overflow
GNUTLS_A_DECOMPRESSION_FAILURE	30	Decompression failed
GNUTLS_A_HANDSHAKE_FAILURE	40	Handshake failed
GNUTLS_A_SSL3_NO_CERTIFICATE	41	No certificate (SSL 3.0)
GNUTLS_A_BAD_CERTIFICATE	42	Certificate is bad
GNUTLS_A_UNSUPPORTED_CERTIFICATE	43	Certificate is not supported
GNUTLS_A_CERTIFICATE_REVOKED	44	Certificate was revoked
GNUTLS_A_CERTIFICATE_EXPIRED	45	Certificate is expired
GNUTLS_A_CERTIFICATE_UNKNOWN	46	Unknown certificate
GNUTLS_A_ILLEGAL_PARAMETER	47	Illegal parameter

GNUTLS_A_UNKNOWN_CA	48	CA is unknown
GNUTLS_A_ACCESS_DENIED	49	Access was denied
GNUTLS_A_DECODE_ERROR	50	Decode error
GNUTLS_A_DECRYPT_ERROR	51	Decrypt error
GNUTLS_A_EXPORT_RESTRICTION	60	Export restriction
GNUTLS_A_PROTOCOL_VERSION	70	Error in protocol version
GNUTLS_A_INSUFFICIENT_SECURITY	71	Insufficient security
GNUTLS_A_INTERNAL_ERROR	80	Internal error
GNUTLS_A_INAPPROPRIATE_FALLBACK	86	Inappropriate fallback
GNUTLS_A_USER_CANCELED	90	User canceled
GNUTLS_A_NO_RENEGOTIATION	100	No renegotiation is allowed
GNUTLS_A_UNSUPPORTED_EXTENSION	110	An unsupported extension was sent
GNUTLS_A_CERTIFICATE_UNOBTAINABLE	111	Could not retrieve the specified certificate
GNUTLS_A_UNRECOGNIZED_NAME	112	The server name sent was not recognized
GNUTLS_A_UNKNOWN_PSK_IDENTITY	115	The SRP/PSK username is missing or not known
GNUTLS_A_NO_APPLICATION_PROTOCOL	120	No supported application protocol could be negotiated

Table 2.3.: The TLS alert table

2.5. The TLS handshake protocol

The handshake protocol is responsible for the ciphersuite negotiation, the initial key exchange, and the authentication of the two peers. This is fully controlled by the application layer, thus your program has to set up the required parameters. The main handshake function is **gnutls_handshake**. In the next paragraphs we elaborate on the handshake protocol, i.e., the ciphersuite negotiation.

2.5.1. TLS ciphersuites

The handshake protocol of TLS negotiates cipher suites of a special form illustrated by the **TLS_DHE_RSA_WITH_3DES_CBC_SHA** cipher suite name. A typical cipher suite contains these parameters:

- The key exchange algorithm. **DHE_RSA** in the example.

- The Symmetric encryption algorithm and mode **3DES_CBC** in this example.

- The MAC[4] algorithm used for authentication. **MAC_SHA** is used in the above example.

---

[4]MAC stands for Message Authentication Code. It can be described as a keyed hash algorithm. See RFC2104.

The cipher suite negotiated in the handshake protocol will affect the record protocol, by enabling encryption and data authentication. Note that you should not over rely on TLS to negotiate the strongest available cipher suite. Do not enable ciphers and algorithms that you consider weak.

All the supported ciphersuites are listed in Appendix C.

2.5.2. Authentication

The key exchange algorithms of the TLS protocol offer authentication, which is a prerequisite for a secure connection. The available authentication methods in GnuTLS follow.

- Certificate authentication: Authenticated key exchange using public key infrastructure and X.509 certificates.

- SRP authentication: Authenticated key exchange using a password.

- PSK authentication: Authenticated key exchange using a pre-shared key.

- Anonymous authentication: Key exchange without peer authentication.

2.5.3. Client authentication

In the case of ciphersuites that use certificate authentication, the authentication of the client is optional in TLS. A server may request a certificate from the client using the `gnutls_certificate_server_set_request` function. We elaborate in subsection 5.4.1.

2.5.4. Resuming sessions

The TLS handshake process performs expensive calculations and a busy server might easily be put under load. To reduce the load, session resumption may be used. This is a feature of the TLS protocol which allows a client to connect to a server after a successful handshake, without the expensive calculations. This is achieved by re-using the previously established keys, meaning the server needs to store the state of established connections (unless session tickets are used – subsection 2.6.3).

Session resumption is an integral part of GnuTLS, and subsection 5.12.1, subsection 6.1.9 illustrate typical uses of it.

2.6. TLS extensions

A number of extensions to the TLS protocol have been proposed mainly in [6]. The extensions supported in GnuTLS are discussed in the subsections that follow.

2.6.1. Maximum fragment length negotiation

This extension allows a TLS implementation to negotiate a smaller value for record packet maximum length. This extension may be useful to clients with constrained capabilities. The functions shown below can be used to control this extension.

---

size_t **gnutls_record_get_max_size** (*gnutls_session_t* **session**)

ssize_t **gnutls_record_set_max_size** (*gnutls_session_t* **session**, *size_t* **size**)

2.6.2. Server name indication

A common problem in HTTPS servers is the fact that the TLS protocol is not aware of the hostname that a client connects to, when the handshake procedure begins. For that reason the TLS server has no way to know which certificate to send.

This extension solves that problem within the TLS protocol, and allows a client to send the HTTP hostname before the handshake begins within the first handshake packet. The functions `gnutls_server_name_set` and `gnutls_server_name_get` can be used to enable this extension, or to retrieve the name sent by a client.

---

int **gnutls_server_name_set** (*gnutls_session_t* **session**, *gnutls_server_name_type_t* **type**, *const void* * **name**, *size_t* **name_length**)

int **gnutls_server_name_get** (*gnutls_session_t* **session**, *void* * **data**, *size_t* * **data_length**, *unsigned int* * **type**, *unsigned int* **indx**)

2.6.3. Session tickets

To resume a TLS session, the server normally stores session parameters. This complicates deployment, and can be avoided by delegating the storage to the client. Because session parameters are sensitive they are encrypted and authenticated with a key only known to the server and then sent to the client. The Session Tickets extension is described in RFC 5077 [38].

A disadvantage of session tickets is that they eliminate the effects of forward secrecy when a server uses the same key for long time. That is, the secrecy of all sessions on a server using tickets depends on the ticket key being kept secret. For that reason server keys should be rotated and discarded regularly.

Since version 3.1.3 GnuTLS clients transparently support session tickets, unless forward secrecy is explicitly requested (with the PFS priority string).

2.6.4. HeartBeat

This is a TLS extension that allows to ping and receive confirmation from the peer, and is described in [31]. The extension is disabled by default and **gnutls_heartbeat_enable** can be used to enable it. A policy may be negotiated to only allow sending heartbeat messages or sending and receiving. The current session policy can be checked with **gnutls_heartbeat_-allowed**. The requests coming from the peer result to GNUTLS_E_HEARTBEAT_PING_RECEIVED being returned from the receive function. Ping requests to peer can be send via **gnutls_-heartbeat_ping**.

---

unsigned **gnutls_heartbeat_allowed** (*gnutls_session_t* **session,** *unsigned int* **type**)

void **gnutls_heartbeat_enable** (*gnutls_session_t* **session,** *unsigned int* **type**)

---

int **gnutls_heartbeat_ping** (*gnutls_session_t* **session,** *size_t* **data_size,** *unsigned int* **max_tries,** *unsigned int* **flags**)

int **gnutls_heartbeat_pong** (*gnutls_session_t* **session,** *unsigned int* **flags**)

void **gnutls_heartbeat_set_timeouts** (*gnutls_session_t* **session,** *unsigned* *int* **retrans_timeout,** *unsigned int* **total_timeout**)

unsigned int **gnutls_heartbeat_get_timeout** (*gnutls_session_t* **session**)

2.6.5. Safe renegotiation

TLS gives the option to two communicating parties to renegotiate and update their security parameters. One useful example of this feature was for a client to initially connect using anonymous negotiation to a server, and the renegotiate using some authenticated ciphersuite. This occurred to avoid having the client sending its credentials in the clear.

However this renegotiation, as initially designed would not ensure that the party one is renegotiating is the same as the one in the initial negotiation. For example one server could forward all renegotiation traffic to an other server who will see this traffic as an initial negotiation attempt.

This might be seen as a valid design decision, but it seems it was not widely known or understood, thus today some application protocols use the TLS renegotiation feature in a manner that enables a malicious server to insert content of his choice in the beginning of a TLS session.

The most prominent vulnerability was with HTTPS. There servers request a renegotiation to enforce an anonymous user to use a certificate in order to access certain parts of a web site. The attack works by having the attacker simulate a client and connect to a server, with server-only authentication, and send some data intended to cause harm. The server will then require renegotiation from him in order to perform the request. When the proper client attempts to contact the server, the attacker hijacks that connection and forwards traffic to the initial server that requested renegotiation. The attacker will not be able to read the data exchanged between the client and the server. However, the server will (incorrectly) assume that the initial request sent by the attacker was sent by the now authenticated client. The result is a prefix plain-text injection attack.

The above is just one example. Other vulnerabilities exists that do not rely on the TLS renegotiation to change the client's authenticated status (either TLS or application layer).

While fixing these application protocols and implementations would be one natural reaction, an extension to TLS has been designed that cryptographically binds together any renegotiated handshakes with the initial negotiation. When the extension is used, the attack is detected and the session can be terminated. The extension is specified in [34].

GnuTLS supports the safe renegotiation extension. The default behavior is as follows. Clients will attempt to negotiate the safe renegotiation extension when talking to servers. Servers will accept the extension when presented by clients. Clients and servers will permit an initial handshake to complete even when the other side does not support the safe renegotiation extension. Clients and servers will refuse renegotiation attempts when the extension has not been negotiated.

Note that permitting clients to connect to servers when the safe renegotiation extension is not enabled, is open up for attacks. Changing this default behavior would prevent interoperability against the majority of deployed servers out there. We will reconsider this default behavior in the future when more servers have been upgraded. Note that it is easy to configure clients to always require the safe renegotiation extension from servers.

To modify the default behavior, we have introduced some new priority strings (see section 5.10). The %UNSAFE_RENEGOTIATION priority string permits (re-)handshakes even when the safe renegotiation extension was not negotiated. The default behavior is %PARTIAL_RENEGOTIATION that will prevent renegotiation with clients and servers not supporting the extension. This is secure for servers but leaves clients vulnerable to some attacks, but this is a trade-off between security and compatibility with old servers. The %SAFE_RENEGOTIATION priority string makes clients and servers require the extension for every handshake. The latter is the most secure option for clients, at the cost of not being able to connect to legacy servers. Servers will also deny clients that do not support the extension from connecting.

It is possible to disable use of the extension completely, in both clients and servers, by using the %DISABLE_SAFE_RENEGOTIATION priority string however we strongly recommend you to only do this for debugging and test purposes.

The default values if the flags above are not specified are:

- Server: %PARTIAL_RENEGOTIATION

- Client: %PARTIAL_RENEGOTIATION

For applications we have introduced a new API related to safe renegotiation. The `gnutls_-safe_renegotiation_status` function is used to check if the extension has been negotiated on a session, and can be used both by clients and servers.

2.6.6. OCSP status request

The Online Certificate Status Protocol (OCSP) is a protocol that allows the client to verify the server certificate for revocation without messing with certificate revocation lists. Its drawback is that it requires the client to connect to the server's CA OCSP server and request the status of the certificate. This extension however, enables a TLS server to include its CA OCSP server response in the handshake. That is an HTTPS server may periodically run `ocsptool` (see subsection 3.2.7) to obtain its certificate revocation status and serve it to the clients. That way a client avoids an additional connection to the OCSP server.

See subsection 3.2.4 for further information.

Since version 3.1.3 GnuTLS clients transparently support the certificate status request.

2.6.7. SRTP

The TLS protocol was extended in [26] to provide keying material to the Secure RTP (SRTP) protocol. The SRTP protocol provides an encapsulation of encrypted data that is optimized for voice data. With the SRTP TLS extension two peers can negotiate keys using TLS or DTLS and obtain keying material for use with SRTP. The available SRTP profiles are listed below.

enum gnutls_srtp_profile_t :	
GNUTLS_SRTP_AES128_CM_HMAC_-SHA1_80	`128 bit AES with a 80 bit HMAC-SHA1`
GNUTLS_SRTP_AES128_CM_HMAC_-SHA1_32	`128 bit AES with a 32 bit HMAC-SHA1`
GNUTLS_SRTP_NULL_HMAC_SHA1_80	`NULL cipher with a 80 bit HMAC-SHA1`
GNUTLS_SRTP_NULL_HMAC_SHA1_32	`NULL cipher with a 32 bit HMAC-SHA1`

Table 2.4.: Supported SRTP profiles

To enable use the following functions.

---

int **gnutls_srtp_set_profile** (*gnutls_session_t* **session**, *gnutls_srtp_profile_t* **profile**)

int **gnutls_srtp_set_profile_direct** (*gnutls_session_t* **session**, *const char* * **profiles**, *const char* ** **err_pos**)

To obtain the negotiated keys use the function below.

---

int **gnutls_srtp_get_keys** (*gnutls_session_t* **session**, *void* * **key_material**, *unsigned int* **key_material_size**, *gnutls_datum_t* * **client_key**, *gnutls_datum_t* * **client_salt**, *gnutls_datum_t* * **server_key**, *gnutls_datum_t* * **server_salt**)

Description: This is a helper function to generate the keying material for SRTP. It requires the space of the key material to be pre-allocated (should be at least 2x the maximum key size and salt size). The **client_key**, **client_salt**, **server_key** and **server_salt** are convenience datums that point inside the key material. They may be **NULL**.

Returns: On success the size of the key material is returned, otherwise, **GNUTLS_E_-SHORT_MEMORY_BUFFER** if the buffer given is not sufficient, or a negative error code. Since 3.1.4

Other helper functions are listed below.

---

int **gnutls_srtp_get_selected_profile** (*gnutls_session_t* **session**, *gnutls_srtp_profile_t* * **profile**)

const char * **gnutls_srtp_get_profile_name** (*gnutls_srtp_profile_t* **profile**)

int **gnutls_srtp_get_profile_id** (*const char* * **name**, *gnutls_srtp_profile_t* * **profile**)

2.6.8. False Start

The TLS protocol was extended in [22] to allow the client to send data to server in a single round trip. This change however operates on the borderline of the TLS protocol security guarantees and should be used for the cases where the reduced latency outperforms the risk of an adversary intercepting the transferred data. In GnuTLS applications can use the GNUTLS_ENABLE_FALSE_START as option to `gnutls_init` to request an early return of the `gnutls_handshake` function. After that early return the application is expected to transfer any data to be piggybacked on the last handshake message.

After handshake's early termination, the application is expected to transmit data using **gnutls_record_send**, and call **gnutls_record_recv** on any received data as soon, to ensure that handshake completes timely. That is, especially relevant for applications which set an explicit time limit for the handshake process via **gnutls_handshake_set_timeout**.

Note however, that the API ensures that the early return will not happen if the false start requirements are not satisfied. That is, on ciphersuites which are not whitelisted for false start or on insufficient key sizes, the handshake process will complete properly (i.e., no early return). To verify that false start was used you may use **gnutls_session_get_flags** and check for the GNUTLS_SFLAGS_FALSE_START flag. For GnuTLS the false start is whitelisted for the following key exchange methods (see [22] for rationale)

- DHE

- ECDHE

but only when the negotiated parameters exceed **GNUTLS_SEC_PARAM_HIGH** –see Table 5.8, and when under (D)TLS 1.2 or later.

2.6.9. Application Layer Protocol Negotiation (ALPN)

The TLS protocol was extended in RFC7301 to provide the application layer a method of negotiating the application protocol version. This allows for negotiation of the application protocol during the TLS handshake, thus reducing round-trips. The application protocol is described by an opaque string. To enable, use the following functions.

---

int **gnutls_alpn_set_protocols** (*gnutls_session_t* **session**, *const gnutls_datum_t* * **protocols**, *unsigned* **protocols_size**, *unsigned int* **flags**)

int **gnutls_alpn_get_selected_protocol** (*gnutls_session_t* **session**, *gnutls_datum_t* * **protocol**)

Note that these functions are intended to be used with protocols that are registered in the Application Layer Protocol Negotiation IANA registry. While you can use them for other protocols (at the risk of collisions), it is preferable to register them.

2.6.10. Extensions and Supplemental Data

It is possible to transfer supplemental data during the TLS handshake, following [39]. This is for "custom" protocol modifications for applications which may want to transfer additional data (e.g. additional authentication messages). Such an exchange requires a custom extension to be registered. The provided API for this functionality is low-level and described in section 8.4.

2.7. How to use TLS in application protocols

This chapter is intended to provide some hints on how to use TLS over simple custom made application protocols. The discussion below mainly refers to the TCP/IP transport layer but may be extended to other ones too.

2.7.1. Separate ports

Traditionally SSL was used in application protocols by assigning a new port number for the secure services. By doing this two separate ports were assigned, one for the non-secure sessions, and one for the secure sessions. This method ensures that if a user requests a secure session then the client will attempt to connect to the secure port and fail otherwise. The only possible attack with this method is to perform a denial of service attack. The most famous example of this method is "HTTP over TLS" or HTTPS protocol [32].

Despite its wide use, this method has several issues. This approach starts the TLS Handshake procedure just after the client connects on the —so called— secure port. That way the TLS protocol does not know anything about the client, and popular methods like the host advertising in HTTP do not work[5]. There is no way for the client to say "I connected to YYY server" before the Handshake starts, so the server cannot possibly know which certificate to use.

Other than that it requires two separate ports to run a single service, which is unnecessary complication. Due to the fact that there is a limitation on the available privileged ports, this approach was soon deprecated in favor of upward negotiation.

2.7.2. Upward negotiation

Other application protocols[6] use a different approach to enable the secure layer. They use something often called as the "TLS upgrade" method. This method is quite tricky but it is more flexible. The idea is to extend the application protocol to have a "STARTTLS" request, whose purpose it to start the TLS protocols just after the client requests it. This approach does not require any extra port to be reserved. There is even an extension to HTTP protocol to support this method [19].

The tricky part, in this method, is that the "STARTTLS" request is sent in the clear, thus is vulnerable to modifications. A typical attack is to modify the messages in a way that the client is fooled and thinks that the server does not have the "STARTTLS" capability. See a typical conversation of a hypothetical protocol:

> (client connects to the server)
>
> CLIENT: HELLO I'M MR. XXX
>
> SERVER: NICE TO MEET YOU XXX

---

[5]See also the Server Name Indication extension on subsection 2.6.2.

[6]See LDAP, IMAP etc.

CLIENT: PLEASE START TLS

SERVER: OK

*** TLS STARTS

CLIENT: HERE ARE SOME CONFIDENTIAL DATA

And an example of a conversation where someone is acting in between:

(client connects to the server)

CLIENT: HELLO I'M MR. XXX

SERVER: NICE TO MEET YOU XXX

CLIENT: PLEASE START TLS

(here someone inserts this message)

SERVER: SORRY I DON'T HAVE THIS CAPABILITY

CLIENT: HERE ARE SOME CONFIDENTIAL DATA

As you can see above the client was fooled, and was naïve enough to send the confidential data in the clear, despite the server telling the client that it does not support "STARTTLS".

How do we avoid the above attack? As you may have already noticed this situation is easy to avoid. The client has to ask the user before it connects whether the user requests TLS or not. If the user answered that he certainly wants the secure layer the last conversation should be:

(client connects to the server)

CLIENT: HELLO I'M MR. XXX

SERVER: NICE TO MEET YOU XXX

CLIENT: PLEASE START TLS

(here someone inserts this message)

SERVER: SORRY I DON'T HAVE THIS CAPABILITY

CLIENT: BYE

(the client notifies the user that the secure connection was not possible)

This method, if implemented properly, is far better than the traditional method, and the security properties remain the same, since only denial of service is possible. The benefit is that the server may request additional data before the TLS Handshake protocol starts, in order to send the correct certificate, use the correct password file, or anything else!

2.8. On SSL 2 and older protocols

One of the initial decisions in the GnuTLS development was to implement the known security protocols for the transport layer. Initially TLS 1.0 was implemented since it was the latest at that time, and was considered to be the most advanced in security properties. Later the SSL 3.0 protocol was implemented since it is still the only protocol supported by several servers and there are no serious security vulnerabilities known.

One question that may arise is why we didn't implement SSL 2.0 in the library. There are several reasons, most important being that it has serious security flaws, unacceptable for a modern security library. Other than that, this protocol is barely used by anyone these days since it has been deprecated since 1996. The security problems in SSL 2.0 include:

- Message integrity compromised. The SSLv2 message authentication uses the MD5 function, and is insecure.

- Man-in-the-middle attack. There is no protection of the handshake in SSLv2, which permits a man-in-the-middle attack.

- Truncation attack. SSLv2 relies on TCP FIN to close the session, so the attacker can forge a TCP FIN, and the peer cannot tell if it was a legitimate end of data or not.

- Weak message integrity for export ciphers. The cryptographic keys in SSLv2 are used for both message authentication and encryption, so if weak encryption schemes are negotiated (say 40-bit keys) the message authentication code uses the same weak key, which isn't necessary.

Other protocols such as Microsoft's PCT 1 and PCT 2 were not implemented because they were also abandoned and deprecated by SSL 3.0 and later TLS 1.0.

3

Authentication methods

The initial key exchange of the TLS protocol performs authentication of the peers. In typical scenarios the server is authenticated to the client, and optionally the client to the server.

While many associate TLS with X.509 certificates and public key authentication, the protocol supports various authentication methods, including pre-shared keys, and passwords. In this chapter a description of the existing authentication methods is provided, as well as some guidance on which use-cases each method can be used at.

3.1. Certificate authentication

The most known authentication method of TLS are certificates. The PKIX [17] public key infrastructure is daily used by anyone using a browser today. GnuTLS provides a simple API to use the X.509 certificates [17].

The key exchange algorithms supported by certificate authentication are shown in Table 3.1.

3.1.1. X.509 certificates

The X.509 protocols rely on a hierarchical trust model. In this trust model Certification Authorities (CAs) are used to certify entities. Usually more than one certification authorities exist, and certification authorities may certify other authorities to issue certificates as well, following a hierarchical model.

One needs to trust one or more CAs for his secure communications. In that case only the certificates issued by the trusted authorities are acceptable. The framework is illustrated on Figure 3.1.

X.509 certificate structure

An X.509 certificate usually contains information about the certificate holder, the signer, a unique serial number, expiration dates and some other fields [17] as shown in Table 3.2.

The certificate's *subject or issuer name* is not just a single string. It is a Distinguished name and in the ASN.1 notation is a sequence of several object identifiers with their corresponding

Key exchange	Description
RSA	The RSA algorithm is used to encrypt a key and send it to the peer. The certificate must allow the key to be used for encryption.
DHE_RSA	The RSA algorithm is used to sign ephemeral Diffie-Hellman parameters which are sent to the peer. The key in the certificate must allow the key to be used for signing. Note that key exchange algorithms which use ephemeral Diffie-Hellman parameters, offer perfect forward secrecy. That means that even if the private key used for signing is compromised, it cannot be used to reveal past session data.
ECDHE_RSA	The RSA algorithm is used to sign ephemeral elliptic curve Diffie-Hellman parameters which are sent to the peer. The key in the certificate must allow the key to be used for signing. It also offers perfect forward secrecy. That means that even if the private key used for signing is compromised, it cannot be used to reveal past session data.
DHE_DSS	The DSA algorithm is used to sign ephemeral Diffie-Hellman parameters which are sent to the peer. The certificate must contain DSA parameters to use this key exchange algorithm. DSA is the algorithm of the Digital Signature Standard (DSS).
ECDHE_ECDSA	The Elliptic curve DSA algorithm is used to sign ephemeral elliptic curve Diffie-Hellman parameters which are sent to the peer. The certificate must contain ECDSA parameters (i.e., EC and marked for signing) to use this key exchange algorithm.

Table 3.1.: Supported key exchange algorithms.

Field	Description
version	The field that indicates the version of the certificate.
serialNumber	This field holds a unique serial number per certificate.
signature	The issuing authority's signature.
issuer	Holds the issuer's distinguished name.
validity	The activation and expiration dates.
subject	The subject's distinguished name of the certificate.
extensions	The extensions are fields only present in version 3 certificates.

Table 3.2.: X.509 certificate fields.

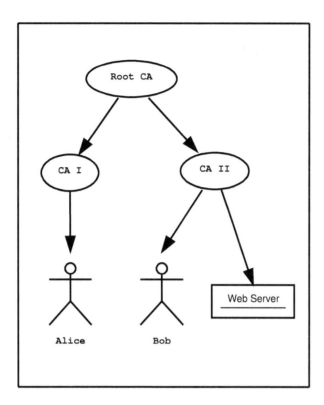

Figure 3.1.: An example of the X.509 hierarchical trust model.

values. Some of available OIDs to be used in an X.509 distinguished name are defined in "**gnutls/x509.h**".

The *Version* field in a certificate has values either 1 or 3 for version 3 certificates. Version 1 certificates do not support the extensions field so it is not possible to distinguish a CA from a person, thus their usage should be avoided.

The *validity* dates are there to indicate the date that the specific certificate was activated and the date the certificate's key would be considered invalid.

In GnuTLS the X.509 certificate structures are handled using the **gnutls_x509_crt_t** type and the corresponding private keys with the **gnutls_x509_privkey_t** type. All the available functions for X.509 certificate handling have their prototypes in "**gnutls/x509.h**". An example program to demonstrate the X.509 parsing capabilities can be found in subsection 6.4.2.

Importing an X.509 certificate

The certificate structure should be initialized using **gnutls_x509_crt_init**, and a certificate structure can be imported using **gnutls_x509_crt_import**.

> *int* **gnutls_x509_crt_init** (*gnutls_x509_crt_t* * **cert**)
>
> *int* **gnutls_x509_crt_import** (*gnutls_x509_crt_t* **cert**, *const gnutls_datum_t* * **data**, *gnutls_x509_crt_fmt_t* **format**)
>
> *void* **gnutls_x509_crt_deinit** (*gnutls_x509_crt_t* **cert**)

In several functions an array of certificates is required. To assist in initialization and import the following two functions are provided.

> *int* **gnutls_x509_crt_list_import** (*gnutls_x509_crt_t* * **certs**, *unsigned int* * **cert_max**, *const gnutls_datum_t* * **data**, *gnutls_x509_crt_fmt_t* **format**, *unsigned int* **flags**)
>
> *int* **gnutls_x509_crt_list_import2** (*gnutls_x509_crt_t* ** **certs**, *unsigned int* * **size**, *const gnutls_datum_t* * **data**, *gnutls_x509_crt_fmt_t* **format**, *unsigned int* **flags**)

In all cases after use a certificate must be deinitialized using `gnutls_x509_crt_deinit`. Note that although the functions above apply to `gnutls_x509_crt_t` structure, similar functions exist for the CRL structure `gnutls_x509_crl_t`.

X.509 certificate names

X.509 certificates allow for multiple names and types of names to be specified. CA certificates often rely on X.509 distinguished names (see section 3.1.1) for unique identification, while end-user and server certificates rely on the 'subject alternative names'. The subject alternative names provide a typed name, e.g., a DNS name, or an email address, which identifies the owner of the certificate. The following functions provide access to that names.

> *int* **gnutls_x509_crt_get_subject_alt_name2** (*gnutls_x509_crt_t* **cert**, *unsigned int* **seq**, *void* * **san**, *size_t* * **san_size**, *unsigned int* * **san_type**, *unsigned int* * **critical**)
>
> *int* **gnutls_x509_crt_set_subject_alt_name** (*gnutls_x509_crt_t* **crt**, *gnutls_x509_subject_alt_name_t* **type**, *const void* * **data**, *unsigned int* **data_size**, *unsigned int* **flags**)

---

int **gnutls_subject_alt_names_init** (*gnutls_subject_alt_names_t* * **sans**)

int **gnutls_subject_alt_names_get** (*gnutls_subject_alt_names_t* **sans,** *unsigned int* **seq,** *unsigned int* * **san_type,** *gnutls_datum_t* * **san,** *gnutls_datum_t* * **othername_oid**)

int **gnutls_subject_alt_names_set** (*gnutls_subject_alt_names_t* **sans,** *unsigned int* **san_type,** *const gnutls_datum_t* * **san,** *const char* * **othername_oid**)

Note however, that server certificates often used the Common Name (CN), part of the certificate DistinguishedName to place a single DNS address. That practice is discouraged (see [36]), because only a single address can be specified, and the CN field is free-form making matching ambiguous.

X.509 distinguished names

The "subject" of an X.509 certificate is not described by a single name, but rather with a distinguished name. This in X.509 terminology is a list of strings each associated an object identifier. To make things simple GnuTLS provides **gnutls_x509_crt_get_dn2** which follows the rules in [47] and returns a single string. Access to each string by individual object identifiers can be accessed using **gnutls_x509_crt_get_dn_by_oid**.

---

int **gnutls_x509_crt_get_dn2** (*gnutls_x509_crt_t* **cert,** *gnutls_datum_t* * **dn**)

Description: This function will allocate buffer and copy the name of the Certificate. The name will be in the form "C=xxxx,O=yyyy,CN=zzzz" as described in RFC4514. The output string will be ASCII or UTF-8 encoded, depending on the certificate data. This function does not output a fully RFC4514 compliant string, if that is required see gnutls_x509_crt_get_dn3().

Returns: On success, **GNUTLS_E_SUCCESS** (0) is returned, otherwise a negative error value.

---

int **gnutls_x509_crt_get_dn** (*gnutls_x509_crt_t* **cert**, *char* * **buf**, *size_t* * **buf_size**)

int **gnutls_x509_crt_get_dn_by_oid** (*gnutls_x509_crt_t* **cert**, *const char* * **oid**, *unsigned* **indx**, *unsigned int* **raw_flag**, *void* * **buf**, *size_t* * **buf_size**)

int **gnutls_x509_crt_get_dn_oid** (*gnutls_x509_crt_t* **cert**, *unsigned* **indx**, *void* * **oid**, *size_t* * **oid_size**)

Similar functions exist to access the distinguished name of the issuer of the certificate.

---

int **gnutls_x509_crt_get_issuer_dn** (*gnutls_x509_crt_t* **cert**, *char* * **buf**, *size_t* * **buf_size**)

int **gnutls_x509_crt_get_issuer_dn2** (*gnutls_x509_crt_t* **cert**, *gnutls_datum_t* * **dn**)

int **gnutls_x509_crt_get_issuer_dn_by_oid** (*gnutls_x509_crt_t* **cert**, *const char* * **oid**, *unsigned* **indx**, *unsigned int* **raw_flag**, *void* * **buf**, *size_t* * **buf_size**)

int **gnutls_x509_crt_get_issuer_dn_oid** (*gnutls_x509_crt_t* **cert**, *unsigned* **indx**, *void* * **oid**, *size_t* * **oid_size**)

int **gnutls_x509_crt_get_issuer** (*gnutls_x509_crt_t* **cert**, *gnutls_x509_dn_t* * **dn**)

The more powerful `gnutls_x509_crt_get_subject` and `gnutls_x509_dn_get_rdn_ava` provide efficient but low-level access to the contents of the distinguished name structure.

---

int **gnutls_x509_crt_get_subject** (*gnutls_x509_crt_t* **cert**, *gnutls_x509_dn_t* * **dn**)

int **gnutls_x509_crt_get_issuer** (*gnutls_x509_crt_t* **cert**, *gnutls_x509_dn_t* * **dn**)

X.509 extensions

X.509 version 3 certificates include a list of extensions that can be used to obtain additional information on the subject or the issuer of the certificate. Those may be e-mail addresses, flags that indicate whether the belongs to a CA etc. All the supported X.509 version 3 extensions are shown in Table 3.3.

---

int **gnutls_x509_dn_get_rdn_ava** (*gnutls_x509_dn_t* **dn**, *int* **irdn**, *int* **iava**, *gnutls_x509_ava_st* * **ava**)

Description: Get pointers to data within the DN. The format of the ava structure is shown below. struct gnutls_x509_ava_st gnutls_datum_t oid; gnutls_datum_t value; unsigned long value_tag; ; The X.509 distinguished name is a sequence of sequences of strings and this is what the **irdn** and **iava** indexes model. Note that ava will contain pointers into the dn structure which in turns points to the original certificate. Thus you should not modify any data or deallocate any of those. This is a low-level function that requires the caller to do the value conversions when necessary (e.g. from UCS-2).

Returns: Returns 0 on success, or an error code.

The certificate extensions access is split into two parts. The first requires to retrieve the extension, and the second is the parsing part.

To enumerate and retrieve the DER-encoded extension data available in a certificate the following two functions are available.

---

int **gnutls_x509_crt_get_extension_info** (*gnutls_x509_crt_t* **cert**, *unsigned* **indx**, *void* * **oid**, *size_t* * **oid_size**, *unsigned int* * **critical**)

int **gnutls_x509_crt_get_extension_data2** (*gnutls_x509_crt_t* **cert**, *unsigned* **indx**, *gnutls_datum_t* * **data**)

int **gnutls_x509_crt_get_extension_by_oid2** (*gnutls_x509_crt_t* **cert**, *const char* * **oid**, *unsigned* **indx**, *gnutls_datum_t* * **output**, *unsigned int* * **critical**)

After a supported DER-encoded extension is retrieved it can be parsed using the APIs in x509-ext.h. Complex extensions may require initializing an intermediate structure that holds the parsed extension data. Examples of simple parsing functions are shown below.

---

int **gnutls_x509_ext_import_basic_constraints** (*const gnutls_datum_t* * **ext**, *unsigned int* * **ca**, *int* * **pathlen**)

int **gnutls_x509_ext_export_basic_constraints** (*unsigned int* **ca**, *int* **pathlen**, *gnutls_datum_t* * **ext**)

int **gnutls_x509_ext_import_key_usage** (*const gnutls_datum_t* * **ext**, *unsigned int* * **key_usage**)

int **gnutls_x509_ext_export_key_usage** (*unsigned int* **usage**, *gnutls_datum_t* * **ext**)

More complex extensions, such as Name Constraints, require an intermediate structure, in that case `gnutls_x509_name_constraints_t` to be initialized in order to store the parsed extension data.

---

int **gnutls_x509_ext_import_name_constraints** (*const gnutls_datum_t* * **ext**, *gnutls_x509_name_constraints_t* **nc**, *unsigned int* **flags**)

int **gnutls_x509_ext_export_name_constraints** (*gnutls_x509_name_constraints_t* **nc**, *gnutls_datum_t* * **ext**)

After the name constraints are extracted in the structure, the following functions can be used to access them.

---

int **gnutls_x509_name_constraints_get_permitted** (*gnutls_x509_name_constraints_t* **nc**, *unsigned* **idx**, *unsigned* * **type**, *gnutls_datum_t* * **name**)

int **gnutls_x509_name_constraints_get_excluded** (*gnutls_x509_name_constraints_t* **nc**, *unsigned* **idx**, *unsigned* * **type**, *gnutls_datum_t* * **name**)

int **gnutls_x509_name_constraints_add_permitted** (*gnutls_x509_name_constraints_t* **nc**, *gnutls_x509_subject_alt_name_t* **type**, *const gnutls_datum_t* * **name**)

int **gnutls_x509_name_constraints_add_excluded** (*gnutls_x509_name_constraints_t* **nc**, *gnutls_x509_subject_alt_name_t* **type**, *const gnutls_datum_t* * **name**)

---

unsigned **gnutls_x509_name_constraints_check** (*gnutls_x509_name_constraints_t* **nc**, *gnutls_x509_subject_alt_name_t* **type**, *const gnutls_datum_t* * **name**)

unsigned **gnutls_x509_name_constraints_check_crt** (*gnutls_x509_name_constraints_t* **nc**, *gnutls_x509_subject_alt_name_t* **type**, *gnutls_x509_crt_t* **cert**)

Other utility functions are listed below.

---

int **gnutls_x509_name_constraints_init** (*gnutls_x509_name_constraints_t* * **nc**)

void **gnutls_x509_name_constraints_deinit** (*gnutls_x509_name_constraints_t* **nc**)

Similar functions exist for all of the other supported extensions, listed in Table 3.3.

Note, that there are also direct APIs to access extensions that may be simpler to use for non-complex extensions. They are available in **x509.h** and some examples are listed below.

---

int **gnutls_x509_crt_get_basic_constraints** (*gnutls_x509_crt_t* **cert**, *unsigned int* * **critical**, *unsigned int* * **ca**, *int* * **pathlen**)

int **gnutls_x509_crt_set_basic_constraints** (*gnutls_x509_crt_t* **crt**, *unsigned int* **ca**, *int* **pathLenConstraint**)

int **gnutls_x509_crt_get_key_usage** (*gnutls_x509_crt_t* **cert**, *unsigned int* * **key_usage**, *unsigned int* * **critical**)

int **gnutls_x509_crt_set_key_usage** (*gnutls_x509_crt_t* **crt**, *unsigned int* **usage**)

Accessing public and private keys

Each X.509 certificate contains a public key that corresponds to a private key. To get a unique identifier of the public key the **gnutls_x509_crt_get_key_id** function is provided. To export the public key or its parameters you may need to convert the X.509 structure to a **gnutls_pubkey_t**. See subsection 4.1.1 for more information.

The private key parameters may be directly accessed by using one of the following functions.

Extension	OID	Description
Subject key id	2.5.29.14	An identifier of the key of the subject.
Key usage	2.5.29.15	Constraints the key's usage of the certificate.
Private key usage period	2.5.29.16	Constraints the validity time of the private key.
Subject alternative name	2.5.29.17	Alternative names to subject's distinguished name.
Issuer alternative name	2.5.29.18	Alternative names to the issuer's distinguished name.
Basic constraints	2.5.29.19	Indicates whether this is a CA certificate or not, and specify the maximum path lengths of certificate chains.
Name constraints	2.5.29.30	A field in CA certificates that restricts the scope of the name of issued certificates.
CRL distribution points	2.5.29.31	This extension is set by the CA, in order to inform about the location of issued Certificate Revocation Lists.
Certificate policy	2.5.29.32	This extension is set to indicate the certificate policy as object identifier and may contain a descriptive string or URL.
Extended key usage	2.5.29.54	Inhibit any policy extension. Constraints the any policy OID (`GNUTLS_X509_OID_POLICY_ANY`) use in the policy extension.
Authority key identifier	2.5.29.35	An identifier of the key of the issuer of the certificate. That is used to distinguish between different keys of the same issuer.
Extended key usage	2.5.29.37	Constraints the purpose of the certificate.
Authority information access	1.3.6.1.5.5.7.1.1	Information on services by the issuer of the certificate.
Proxy Certification Information	1.3.6.1.5.5.7.1.14	Proxy Certificates includes this extension that contains the OID of the proxy policy language used, and can specify limits on the maximum lengths of proxy chains. Proxy Certificates are specified in [42].

Table 3.3.: Supported X.509 certificate extensions.

int **gnutls_x509_crt_get_key_id** (*gnutls_x509_crt_t* **crt**, *unsigned int* **flags**, *unsigned char** **output_data**, *size_t** **output_data_size**)

Description: This function will return a unique ID that depends on the public key parameters. This ID can be used in checking whether a certificate corresponds to the given private key. If the buffer provided is not long enough to hold the output, then *output_data_size is updated and GNUTLS_E_SHORT_MEMORY_BUFFER will be returned. The output will normally be a SHA-1 hash output, which is 20 bytes.

Returns: In case of failure a negative error code will be returned, and 0 on success.

---

int **gnutls_x509_privkey_get_pk_algorithm2** (*gnutls_x509_privkey_t* **key**, *unsigned int** **bits**)

int **gnutls_x509_privkey_export_rsa_raw2** (*gnutls_x509_privkey_t* **key**, *gnutls_datum_t** **m**, *gnutls_datum_t** **e**, *gnutls_datum_t** **d**, *gnutls_datum_t** **p**, *gnutls_datum_t** **q**, *gnutls_datum_t** **u**, *gnutls_datum_t** **e1**, *gnutls_datum_t** **e2**)

int **gnutls_x509_privkey_export_ecc_raw** (*gnutls_x509_privkey_t* **key**, *gnutls_ecc_curve_t** **curve**, *gnutls_datum_t** **x**, *gnutls_datum_t** **y**, *gnutls_datum_t** **k**)

int **gnutls_x509_privkey_export_dsa_raw** (*gnutls_x509_privkey_t* **key**, *gnutls_datum_t** **p**, *gnutls_datum_t** **q**, *gnutls_datum_t** **g**, *gnutls_datum_t** **y**, *gnutls_datum_t** **x**)

int **gnutls_x509_privkey_get_key_id** (*gnutls_x509_privkey_t* **key**, *unsigned int* **flags**, *unsigned char** **output_data**, *size_t** **output_data_size**)

Verifying X.509 certificate paths

Verifying certificate paths is important in X.509 authentication. For this purpose the following functions are provided.

The verification function will verify a given certificate chain against a list of certificate authorities and certificate revocation lists, and output a bit-wise OR of elements of the **gnutls_-certificate_status_t** enumeration shown in Table 3.4. The **GNUTLS_CERT_INVALID** flag is always set on a verification error and more detailed flags will also be set when appropriate.

An example of certificate verification is shown in subsection 6.1.7. It is also possible to have a set of certificates that are trusted for a particular server but not to authorize other certificates. This purpose is served by the functions **gnutls_x509_trust_list_add_named_crt** and **gnutls_-x509_trust_list_verify_named_crt**.

int **gnutls_x509_trust_list_add_cas** (*gnutls_x509_trust_list_t* **list**, *const gnutls_x509_crt_t* * **clist**, *unsigned* **clist_size**, *unsigned int* **flags**)

Description: This function will add the given certificate authorities to the trusted list. The list of CAs must not be deinitialized during this structure's lifetime. If the flag **GNUTLS_TL_NO_DUPLICATES** is specified, then the provided **clist** entries that are duplicates will not be added to the list and will be deinitialized.

Returns: The number of added elements is returned.

---

int **gnutls_x509_trust_list_add_named_crt** (*gnutls_x509_trust_list_t* **list**, *gnutls_x509_crt_t* **cert**, *const void* * **name**, *size_t* **name_size**, *unsigned int* **flags**)

Description: This function will add the given certificate to the trusted list and associate it with a name. The certificate will not be be used for verification with gnutls_x509_trust_list_verify_crt() but with gnutls_x509_trust_list_verify_named_crt() or gnutls_x509_trust_list_verify_crt2() - the latter only since GnuTLS 3.4.0 and if a hostname is provided. In principle this function can be used to set individual "server" certificates that are trusted by the user for that specific server but for no other purposes. The certificate must not be deinitialized during the lifetime of the trusted list.

Returns: On success, **GNUTLS_E_SUCCESS** (0) is returned, otherwise a negative error value.

---

int **gnutls_x509_trust_list_add_crls** (*gnutls_x509_trust_list_t* **list**, *const gnutls_x509_crl_t* * **crl_list**, *unsigned* **crl_size**, *unsigned int* **flags**, *unsigned int* **verification_flags**)

Description: This function will add the given certificate revocation lists to the trusted list. The list of CRLs must not be deinitialized during this structure's lifetime. This function must be called after gnutls_x509_trust_list_add_cas() to allow verifying the CRLs for validity. If the flag **GNUTLS_TL_NO_DUPLICATES** is given, then any provided CRLs that are a duplicate, will be deinitialized and not added to the list (that assumes that gnutls_x509_trust_list_deinit() will be called with all=1). If GNUTLS_TL_-VERIFY_CRL is given the CRLs will be verified before being added.

Returns: The number of added elements is returned.

---

int **gnutls_x509_trust_list_verify_crt** (*gnutls_x509_trust_list_t* **list**, *gnutls_x509_crt_t* * **cert_list**, *unsigned int* **cert_list_size**, *unsigned int* **flags**, *unsigned int* * **voutput**, *gnutls_verify_output_function* **func**)

Description: This function will try to verify the given certificate and return its status. The **voutput** parameter will hold an OR'ed sequence of **gnutls_certificate_status_t** flags. The details of the verification are the same as in gnutls_x509_trust_list_verify_-crt2().

Returns: On success, **GNUTLS_E_SUCCESS** (0) is returned, otherwise a negative error value.

---

int **gnutls_x509_trust_list_verify_crt2** (*gnutls_x509_trust_list_t* **list**, *gnutls_x509_crt_t* * **cert_list**, *unsigned int* **cert_list_size**, *gnutls_typed_vdata_st* * **data**, *unsigned int* **elements**, *unsigned int* **flags**, *unsigned int* * **voutput**, *gnutls_verify_output_function* **func**)

Description: This function will attempt to verify the given certificate chain and return its status. The **voutput** parameter will hold an OR'ed sequence of **gnutls_certificate_-status_t** flags. When a certificate chain of **cert_list_size** with more than one certificates is provided, the verification status will apply to the first certificate in the chain that failed verification. The verification process starts from the end of the chain (from CA to end certificate). The first certificate in the chain must be the end-certificate while the rest of the members may be sorted or not. Additionally a certificate verification profile can be specified from the ones in **gnutls_certificate_verification_profiles_t** by ORing the result of GNUTLS_PROFILE_TO_VFLAGS() to the verification flags. Additional verification parameters are possible via the **data** types; the acceptable types are **GNUTLS_DT_DNS_-HOSTNAME, GNUTLS_DT_IP_ADDRESS** and **GNUTLS_DT_KEY_PURPOSE_OID**. The former accepts as data a null-terminated hostname, and the latter a null-terminated object identifier (e.g., **GNUTLS_KP_TLS_WWW_SERVER**). If a DNS hostname is provided then this function will compare the hostname in the end certificate against the given. If names do not match the **GNUTLS_CERT_UNEXPECTED_OWNER** status flag will be set. In addition it will consider certificates provided with gnutls_x509_trust_list_add_named_crt(). If a key purpose OID is provided and the end-certificate contains the extended key usage PKIX extension, it will be required to match the provided OID or be marked for any purpose, otherwise verification will fail with **GNUTLS_CERT_PURPOSE_MISMATCH** status.

Returns: On success, **GNUTLS_E_SUCCESS** (0) is returned, otherwise a negative error value. Note that verification failure will not result to an error code, only **voutput** will be updated.

33

int **gnutls_x509_trust_list_verify_named_crt** (*gnutls_x509_trust_list_t* **list**, *gnutls_x509_crt_t* **cert**, *const void* * **name**, *size_t* **name_size**, *unsigned int* **flags**, *unsigned int* * **voutput**, *gnutls_verify_output_function* **func**)

Description: This function will try to find a certificate that is associated with the provided name --see gnutls_x509_trust_list_add_named_crt(). If a match is found the certificate is considered valid. In addition to that this function will also check CRLs. The voutput parameter will hold an OR'ed sequence of gnutls_certificate_status_t flags. Additionally a certificate verification profile can be specified from the ones in gnutls_certificate_verification_profiles_t by ORing the result of GNUTLS_PROFILE_TO_VFLAGS() to the verification flags.

Returns: On success, **GNUTLS_E_SUCCESS** (0) is returned, otherwise a negative error value.

---

int **gnutls_x509_trust_list_add_trust_file** (*gnutls_x509_trust_list_t* **list**, *const char* * **ca_file**, *const char* * **crl_file**, *gnutls_x509_crt_fmt_t* **type**, *unsigned int* **tl_flags**, *unsigned int* **tl_vflags**)

Description: This function will add the given certificate authorities to the trusted list. PKCS #11 URLs are also accepted, instead of files, by this function. A PKCS #11 URL implies a trust database (a specially marked module in p11-kit); the URL "pkcs11:" implies all trust databases in the system. Only a single URL specifying trust databases can be set; they cannot be stacked with multiple calls.

Returns: The number of added elements is returned.

---

int **gnutls_x509_trust_list_add_trust_mem** (*gnutls_x509_trust_list_t* **list**, *const gnutls_datum_t* * **cas**, *const gnutls_datum_t* * **crls**, *gnutls_x509_crt_fmt_t* **type**, *unsigned int* **tl_flags**, *unsigned int* **tl_vflags**)

Description: This function will add the given certificate authorities to the trusted list.

Returns: The number of added elements is returned.

---

int **gnutls_x509_trust_list_add_system_trust** (*gnutls_x509_trust_list_t* **list**, *unsigned int* **tl_flags**, *unsigned int* **tl_vflags**)

Description: This function adds the system's default trusted certificate authorities to the trusted list. Note that on unsupported systems this function returns GNUTLS_-E_UNIMPLEMENTED_FEATURE. This function implies the flag GNUTLS_TL_NO_-DUPLICATES.

Returns: The number of added elements or a negative error code on error.

Verifying a certificate in the context of TLS session

When operating in the context of a TLS session, the trusted certificate authority list may also be set using:

---

int **gnutls_certificate_set_x509_trust_file** (*gnutls_certificate_credentials_t* **cred**, *const char* * **cafile**, *gnutls_x509_crt_fmt_t* **type**)

int **gnutls_certificate_set_x509_trust_dir** (*gnutls_certificate_credentials_t* **cred**, *const char* * **ca_dir**, *gnutls_x509_crt_fmt_t* **type**)

int **gnutls_certificate_set_x509_crl_file** (*gnutls_certificate_credentials_t* **res**, *const char* * **crlfile**, *gnutls_x509_crt_fmt_t* **type**)

int **gnutls_certificate_set_x509_system_trust** (*gnutls_certificate_credentials_t* **cred**)

These functions allow the specification of the trusted certificate authorities, either via a file, a directory or use the system-specified certificate authorities. Unless the authorities are application specific, it is generally recommended to use the system trust storage (see **gnutls_-certificate_set_x509_system_trust**).

Unlike the previous section it is not required to setup a trusted list, and there are two approaches to verify the peer's certificate and identity. The recommended in GnuTLS 3.5.0 and later is via the **gnutls_session_set_verify_cert**, but for older GnuTLS versions you may use an explicit callback set via **gnutls_certificate_set_verify_function** and then utilize **gnutls_certificate_verify_peers3** for verification. The reported verification status is identical to the verification functions described in the previous section.

Note that in certain cases it is required to check the marked purpose of the end certificate (e.g. GNUTLS_KP_TLS_WWW_SERVER); in these cases the more advanced **gnutls_session_set_verify_-cert2** and **gnutls_certificate_verify_peers** should be used instead.

There is also the possibility to pass some input to the verification functions in the form of flags.

For `gnutls_x509_trust_list_verify_crt2` the flags are passed directly, but for `gnutls_-certificate_verify_peers3`, the flags are set using `gnutls_certificate_set_verify_flags`. All the available flags are part of the enumeration `gnutls_certificate_verify_flags` shown in Table 3.5.

Verifying a certificate using PKCS #11

Some systems provide a system wide trusted certificate storage accessible using the PKCS #11 API. That is, the trusted certificates are queried and accessed using the PKCS #11 API, and trusted certificate properties, such as purpose, are marked using attached extensions. One example is the p11-kit trust module[1].

These special PKCS #11 modules can be used for GnuTLS certificate verification if marked as trust policy modules, i.e., with `trust-policy: yes` in the p11-kit module file. The way to use them is by specifying to the file verification function (e.g., `gnutls_certificate_set_-x509_trust_file`), a pkcs11 URL, or simply `pkcs11:` to use all the marked with trust policy modules.

The trust modules of p11-kit assign a purpose to trusted authorities using the extended key usage object identifiers. The common purposes are shown in Table 3.6. Note that typically according to [8] the extended key usage object identifiers apply to end certificates. Their application to CA certificates is an extension used by the trust modules.

With such modules, it is recommended to use the verification functions `gnutls_x509_trust_-list_verify_crt2`, or `gnutls_certificate_verify_peers`, which allow to explicitly specify the key purpose. The other verification functions which do not allow setting a purpose, would operate as if `GNUTLS_KP_TLS_WWW_SERVER` was requested from the trusted authorities.

3.1.2. OpenPGP certificates

Previous versions of GnuTLS supported limited OpenPGP key authentication. That functionality has been deprecated and is no longer made available. The reason is that, supporting alternative authentication methods, when X.509 and PKIX were new on the Internet and not well established, seemed like a good idea, in today's Internet X.509 is unquestionably the main container for certificates. As such supporting more options with no clear use-cases, is a distraction that consumes considerable resources for improving and testing the library. For that we have decided to drop this functionality completely in 3.6.0.

3.1.3. Advanced certificate verification

The verification of X.509 certificates in the HTTPS and other Internet protocols is typically done by loading a trusted list of commercial Certificate Authorities (see `gnutls_certificate_-set_x509_system_trust`), and using them as trusted anchors. However, there are several examples (eg. the Diginotar incident) where one of these authorities was compromised. This risk

---

[1]see `http://p11-glue.freedesktop.org/trust-module.html`.

can be mitigated by using in addition to CA certificate verification, other verification methods. In this section we list the available in GnuTLS methods.

Verifying a certificate using trust on first use authentication

It is possible to use a trust on first use (TOFU) authentication method in GnuTLS. That is the concept used by the SSH programs, where the public key of the peer is not verified, or verified in an out-of-bound way, but subsequent connections to the same peer require the public key to remain the same. Such a system in combination with the typical CA verification of a certificate, and OCSP revocation checks, can help to provide multiple factor verification, where a single point of failure is not enough to compromise the system. For example a server compromise may be detected using OCSP, and a CA compromise can be detected using the trust on first use method. Such a hybrid system with X.509 and trust on first use authentication is shown in subsection 6.1.2.

See subsection 5.12.2 on how to use the available functionality.

Verifying a certificate using DANE (DNSSEC)

The DANE protocol is a protocol that can be used to verify TLS certificates using the DNS (or better DNSSEC) protocols. The DNS security extensions (DNSSEC) provide an alternative public key infrastructure to the commercial CAs that are typically used to sign TLS certificates. The DANE protocol takes advantage of the DNSSEC infrastructure to verify TLS certificates. This can be in addition to the verification by CA infrastructure or may even replace it where DNSSEC is fully deployed. Note however, that DNSSEC deployment is fairly new and it would be better to use it as an additional verification method rather than the only one.

The DANE functionality is provided by the `libgnutls-dane` library that is shipped with GnuTLS and the function prototypes are in `gnutls/dane.h`. See subsection 5.12.2 for information on how to use the library.

Note however, that the DANE RFC mandates the verification methods one should use in addition to the validation via DNSSEC TLSA entries. GnuTLS doesn't follow that RFC requirement, and the term DANE verification in this manual refers to the TLSA entry verification. In GnuTLS any other verification methods can be used (e.g., PKIX or TOFU) on top of DANE.

3.1.4. Digital signatures

In this section we will provide some information about digital signatures, how they work, and give the rationale for disabling some of the algorithms used.

Digital signatures work by using somebody's secret key to sign some arbitrary data. Then anybody else could use the public key of that person to verify the signature. Since the data may be arbitrary it is not suitable input to a cryptographic digital signature algorithm. For this reason and also for performance cryptographic hash algorithms are used to preprocess the input to the signature algorithm. This works as long as it is difficult enough to generate two different messages with the same hash algorithm output. In that case the same signature could be used as a proof for both messages. Nobody wants to sign an innocent message of donating 1 euro to Greenpeace and find out that they donated 1.000.000 euros to Bad Inc.

For a hash algorithm to be called cryptographic the following three requirements must hold:

1. Preimage resistance. That means the algorithm must be one way and given the output of the hash function $H(x)$, it is impossible to calculate x.

2. 2nd preimage resistance. That means that given a pair x, y with $y = H(x)$ it is impossible to calculate an x' such that $y = H(x')$.

3. Collision resistance. That means that it is impossible to calculate random x and x' such $H(x') = H(x)$.

The last two requirements in the list are the most important in digital signatures. These protect against somebody who would like to generate two messages with the same hash output. When an algorithm is considered broken usually it means that the Collision resistance of the algorithm is less than brute force. Using the birthday paradox the brute force attack takes 2 *textasciicircum*(hash size)/2 operations. Today colliding certificates using the MD5 hash algorithm have been generated as shown in [24].

There has been cryptographic results for the SHA-1 hash algorithms as well, although they are not yet critical. Before 2004, MD5 had a presumed collision strength of 2 *textasciicircum*64, but it has been showed to have a collision strength well under 2 *textasciicircum*50. As of November 2005, it is believed that SHA-1's collision strength is around 2 *textasciicircum*63. We consider this sufficiently hard so that we still support SHA-1. We anticipate that SHA-256/386/512 will be used in publicly-distributed certificates in the future. When 2 *textasciicircum*63 can be considered too weak compared to the computer power available sometime in the future, SHA-1 will be disabled as well. The collision attacks on SHA-1 may also get better, given the new interest in tools for creating them.

Trading security for interoperability

If you connect to a server and use GnuTLS' functions to verify the certificate chain, and get a `GNUTLS_CERT_INSECURE_ALGORITHM` validation error (see section 3.1.1), it means that somewhere in the certificate chain there is a certificate signed using `RSA-MD2` or `RSA-MD5`. These two digital signature algorithms are considered broken, so GnuTLS fails verifying the certificate. In some situations, it may be useful to be able to verify the certificate chain anyway, assuming an attacker did not utilize the fact that these signatures algorithms are broken. This section will give help on how to achieve that.

It is important to know that you do not have to enable any of the flags discussed here to be able to use trusted root CA certificates self-signed using `RSA-MD2` or `RSA-MD5`. The certificates in the trusted list are considered trusted irrespective of the signature.

If you are using `gnutls_certificate_verify_peers3` to verify the certificate chain, you can call `gnutls_certificate_set_verify_flags` with the flags:

- GNUTLS_VERIFY_ALLOW_SIGN_RSA_MD2

- GNUTLS_VERIFY_ALLOW_SIGN_RSA_MD5

- GNUTLS_VERIFY_ALLOW_SIGN_WITH_SHA1

- GNUTLS_VERIFY_ALLOW_BROKEN

as in the following example:

```
gnutls_certificate_set_verify_flags (x509cred,
                                     GNUTLS_VERIFY_ALLOW_SIGN_RSA_MD5);
```

This will signal the verifier algorithm to enable `RSA-MD5` when verifying the certificates.

If you are using `gnutls_x509_crt_verify` or `gnutls_x509_crt_list_verify`, you can pass the `GNUTLS_VERIFY_ALLOW_SIGN_RSA_MD5` parameter directly in the `flags` parameter.

If you are using these flags, it may also be a good idea to warn the user when verification failure occur for this reason. The simplest is to not use the flags by default, and only fall back to using them after warning the user. If you wish to inspect the certificate chain yourself, you can use `gnutls_certificate_get_peers` to extract the raw server's certificate chain, `gnutls_x509_crt_list_import` to parse each of the certificates, and then `gnutls_x509_crt_get_signature_algorithm` to find out the signing algorithm used for each certificate. If any of the intermediary certificates are using GNUTLS_SIGN_RSA_MD2 or GNUTLS_SIGN_RSA_MD5, you could present a warning.

3.2. More on certificate authentication

Certificates are not the only structures involved in a public key infrastructure. Several other structures that are used for certificate requests, encrypted private keys, revocation lists, GnuTLS abstract key structures, etc., are discussed in this chapter.

3.2.1. PKCS #10 certificate requests

A certificate request is a structure, which contain information about an applicant of a certificate service. It typically contains a public key, a distinguished name and secondary data such as a challenge password. GnuTLS supports the requests defined in PKCS #10 [29]. Other formats of certificate requests are not currently supported by GnuTLS.

A certificate request can be generated by associating it with a private key, setting the subject's information and finally self signing it. The last step ensures that the requester is in possession of the private key.

int **gnutls_x509_crq_set_version** (*gnutls_x509_crq_t* **crq**, *unsigned int* **version**)

int **gnutls_x509_crq_set_dn** (*gnutls_x509_crq_t* **crq**, *const char* * **dn**, *const char* ** **err**)

int **gnutls_x509_crq_set_dn_by_oid** (*gnutls_x509_crq_t* **crq**, *const char* * **oid**, *unsigned int* **raw_flag**, *const void* * **data**, *unsigned int* **sizeof_data**)

int **gnutls_x509_crq_set_key_usage** (*gnutls_x509_crq_t* **crq**, *unsigned int* **usage**)

int **gnutls_x509_crq_set_key_purpose_oid** (*gnutls_x509_crq_t* **crq**, *const void* * **oid**, *unsigned int* **critical**)

int **gnutls_x509_crq_set_basic_constraints** (*gnutls_x509_crq_t* **crq**, *unsigned int* **ca**, *int* **pathLenConstraint**)

The `gnutls_x509_crq_set_key` and `gnutls_x509_crq_sign2` functions associate the request with a private key and sign it. If a request is to be signed with a key residing in a PKCS #11 token it is recommended to use the signing functions shown in section 4.1.

int **gnutls_x509_crq_set_key** (*gnutls_x509_crq_t* **crq**, *gnutls_x509_privkey_t* **key**)

Description: This function will set the public parameters from the given private key to the request.

Returns: On success, **GNUTLS_E_SUCCESS** (0) is returned, otherwise a negative error value.

The following example is about generating a certificate request, and a private key. A certificate request can be later be processed by a CA which should return a signed certificate.

```
1  /* This example code is placed in the public domain. */
2
3  #ifdef HAVE_CONFIG_H
4  #include <config.h>
5  #endif
6
7  #include <stdio.h>
8  #include <stdlib.h>
9  #include <string.h>
10 #include <gnutls/gnutls.h>
11 #include <gnutls/x509.h>
12 #include <gnutls/abstract.h>
13 #include <time.h>
14
15 /* This example will generate a private key and a certificate
```

---

int **gnutls_x509_crq_sign2** (*gnutls_x509_crq_t* **crq**, *gnutls_x509_privkey_t* **key**, *gnutls_digest_algorithm_t* **dig**, *unsigned int* **flags**)

Description: This function will sign the certificate request with a private key. This must be the same key as the one used in gnutls_x509_crt_set_key() since a certificate request is self signed. This must be the last step in a certificate request generation since all the previously set parameters are now signed. A known limitation of this function is, that a newly-signed request will not be fully functional (e.g., for signature verification), until it is exported an re-imported. After GnuTLS 3.6.1 the value of **dig** may be **GNUTLS_DIG_UNKNOWN**, and in that case, a suitable but reasonable for the key algorithm will be selected.

Returns: **GNUTLS_E_SUCCESS** on success, otherwise a negative error code. **GNUTLS_E_ASN1_VALUE_NOT_FOUND** is returned if you didn't set all information in the certificate request (e.g., the version using gnutls_x509_crq_set_version()).

```
16   * request.
17   */
18
19  int main(void)
20  {
21          gnutls_x509_crq_t crq;
22          gnutls_x509_privkey_t key;
23          unsigned char buffer[10 * 1024];
24          size_t buffer_size = sizeof(buffer);
25          unsigned int bits;
26
27          gnutls_global_init();
28
29          /* Initialize an empty certificate request, and
30           * an empty private key.
31           */
32          gnutls_x509_crq_init(&crq);
33
34          gnutls_x509_privkey_init(&key);
35
36          /* Generate an RSA key of moderate security.
37           */
38          bits =
39              gnutls_sec_param_to_pk_bits(GNUTLS_PK_RSA,
40                                          GNUTLS_SEC_PARAM_MEDIUM);
41          gnutls_x509_privkey_generate(key, GNUTLS_PK_RSA, bits, 0);
42
43          /* Add stuff to the distinguished name
44           */
45          gnutls_x509_crq_set_dn_by_oid(crq, GNUTLS_OID_X520_COUNTRY_NAME,
46                                        0, "GR", 2);
47
48          gnutls_x509_crq_set_dn_by_oid(crq, GNUTLS_OID_X520_COMMON_NAME,
49                                        0, "Nikos", strlen("Nikos"));
```

```
50
51      /* Set the request version.
52       */
53      gnutls_x509_crq_set_version(crq, 1);
54
55      /* Set a challenge password.
56       */
57      gnutls_x509_crq_set_challenge_password(crq,
58                              "something to remember here");
59
60      /* Associate the request with the private key
61       */
62      gnutls_x509_crq_set_key(crq, key);
63
64      /* Self sign the certificate request.
65       */
66      gnutls_x509_crq_sign2(crq, key, GNUTLS_DIG_SHA1, 0);
67
68      /* Export the PEM encoded certificate request, and
69       * display it.
70       */
71      gnutls_x509_crq_export(crq, GNUTLS_X509_FMT_PEM, buffer,
72                      &buffer_size);
73
74      printf("Certificate Request: \n%s", buffer);
75
76
77      /* Export the PEM encoded private key, and
78       * display it.
79       */
80      buffer_size = sizeof(buffer);
81      gnutls_x509_privkey_export(key, GNUTLS_X509_FMT_PEM, buffer,
82                      &buffer_size);
83
84      printf("\n\nPrivate key: \n%s", buffer);
85
86      gnutls_x509_crq_deinit(crq);
87      gnutls_x509_privkey_deinit(key);
88
89      return 0;
90
91  }
```

3.2.2. PKIX certificate revocation lists

A certificate revocation list (CRL) is a structure issued by an authority periodically containing a list of revoked certificates serial numbers. The CRL structure is signed with the issuing authorities' keys. A typical CRL contains the fields as shown in Table 3.7. Certificate revocation lists are used to complement the expiration date of a certificate, in order to account for other reasons of revocation, such as compromised keys, etc.

Each CRL is valid for limited amount of time and is required to provide, except for the current issuing time, also the issuing time of the next update.

The basic CRL structure functions follow.

---

int **gnutls_x509_crl_init** (*gnutls_x509_crl_t* * **crl**)

int **gnutls_x509_crl_import** (*gnutls_x509_crl_t* **crl**, *const gnutls_datum_t* * **data**, *gnutls_x509_crt_fmt_t* **format**)

int **gnutls_x509_crl_export** (*gnutls_x509_crl_t* **crl**, *gnutls_x509_crt_fmt_t* **format**, *void* * **output_data**, *size_t* * **output_data_size**)

int **gnutls_x509_crl_export** (*gnutls_x509_crl_t* **crl**, *gnutls_x509_crt_fmt_t* **format**, *void* * **output_data**, *size_t* * **output_data_size**)

Reading a CRL

The most important function that extracts the certificate revocation information from a CRL is `gnutls_x509_crl_get_crt_serial`. Other functions that return other fields of the CRL structure are also provided.

---

int **gnutls_x509_crl_get_crt_serial** (*gnutls_x509_crl_t* **crl**, *unsigned* **indx**, *unsigned char* * **serial**, *size_t* * **serial_size**, *time_t* * **t**)

Description: This function will retrieve the serial number of the specified, by the index, revoked certificate. Note that this function will have performance issues in large sequences of revoked certificates. In that case use gnutls_x509_crl_iter_crt_serial().

Returns: On success, **GNUTLS_E_SUCCESS** (0) is returned, otherwise a negative error value.

43

---

int **gnutls_x509_crl_get_version** (*gnutls_x509_crl_t* **crl**)

int **gnutls_x509_crl_get_issuer_dn** (*gnutls_x509_crl_t* **crl**, *char* * **buf**, *size_t* * **sizeof_buf**)

int **gnutls_x509_crl_get_issuer_dn2** (*gnutls_x509_crl_t* **crl**, *gnutls_datum_t* * **dn**)

time_t **gnutls_x509_crl_get_this_update** (*gnutls_x509_crl_t* **crl**)

time_t **gnutls_x509_crl_get_next_update** (*gnutls_x509_crl_t* **crl**)

int **gnutls_x509_crl_get_crt_count** (*gnutls_x509_crl_t* **crl**)

Generation of a CRL

The following functions can be used to generate a CRL.

---

int **gnutls_x509_crl_set_version** (*gnutls_x509_crl_t* **crl**, *unsigned int* **version**)

int **gnutls_x509_crl_set_crt_serial** (*gnutls_x509_crl_t* **crl**, *const void* * **serial**, *size_t* **serial_size**, *time_t* **revocation_time**)

---

int **gnutls_x509_crl_set_crt** (*gnutls_x509_crl_t* **crl**, *gnutls_x509_crt_t* **crt**, *time_t* **revocation_time**)

int **gnutls_x509_crl_set_next_update** (*gnutls_x509_crl_t* **crl**, *time_t* **exp_time**)

int **gnutls_x509_crl_set_this_update** (*gnutls_x509_crl_t* **crl**, *time_t* **act_time**)

The `gnutls_x509_crl_sign2` and `gnutls_x509_crl_privkey_sign` functions sign the revocation list with a private key. The latter function can be used to sign with a key residing in a PKCS #11 token.

Few extensions on the CRL structure are supported, including the CRL number extension and the authority key identifier.

---

int **gnutls_x509_crl_sign2** (*gnutls_x509_crl_t* **crl**, *gnutls_x509_crt_t* **issuer**, *gnutls_x509_privkey_t* **issuer_key**, *gnutls_digest_algorithm_t* **dig**, *unsigned int* **flags**)

Description: This function will sign the CRL with the issuer's private key, and will copy the issuer's information into the CRL. This must be the last step in a certificate CRL since all the previously set parameters are now signed. A known limitation of this function is, that a newly-signed CRL will not be fully functional (e.g., for signature verification), until it is exported an re-imported. After GnuTLS 3.6.1 the value of **dig** may be **GNUTLS_DIG_UNKNOWN**, and in that case, a suitable but reasonable for the key algorithm will be selected.

Returns: On success, **GNUTLS_E_SUCCESS** (0) is returned, otherwise a negative error value.

---

int **gnutls_x509_crl_privkey_sign** (*gnutls_x509_crl_t* **crl**, *gnutls_x509_crt_t* **issuer**, *gnutls_privkey_t* **issuer_key**, *gnutls_digest_algorithm_t* **dig**, *unsigned int* **flags**)

Description: This function will sign the CRL with the issuer's private key, and will copy the issuer's information into the CRL. This must be the last step in a certificate CRL since all the previously set parameters are now signed. A known limitation of this function is, that a newly-signed CRL will not be fully functional (e.g., for signature verification), until it is exported an re-imported. After GnuTLS 3.6.1 the value of **dig** may be **GNUTLS_DIG_UNKNOWN**, and in that case, a suitable but reasonable for the key algorithm will be selected.

Returns: On success, **GNUTLS_E_SUCCESS** (0) is returned, otherwise a negative error value. Since 2.12.0

---

int **gnutls_x509_crl_set_number** (*gnutls_x509_crl_t* **crl**, *const void* * **nr**, *size_t* **nr_size**)

int **gnutls_x509_crl_set_authority_key_id** (*gnutls_x509_crl_t* **crl**, *const void* * **id**, *size_t* **id_size**)

3.2.3. OCSP certificate status checking

Certificates may be revoked before their expiration time has been reached. There are several reasons for revoking certificates, but a typical situation is when the private key associated with a certificate has been compromised. Traditionally, Certificate Revocation Lists (CRLs) have been used by application to implement revocation checking, however, several problems with

CRLs have been identified [35].

The Online Certificate Status Protocol, or OCSP [28], is a widely implemented protocol which performs certificate revocation status checking. An application that wish to verify the identity of a peer will verify the certificate against a set of trusted certificates and then check whether the certificate is listed in a CRL and/or perform an OCSP check for the certificate.

Applications are typically expected to contact the OCSP server in order to request the certificate validity status. The OCSP server replies with an OCSP response. This section describes this online communication (which can be avoided when using OCSP stapled responses, for that, see subsection 3.2.4).

Before performing the OCSP query, the application will need to figure out the address of the OCSP server. The OCSP server address can be provided by the local user in manual configuration or may be stored in the certificate that is being checked. When stored in a certificate the OCSP server is in the extension field called the Authority Information Access (AIA). The following function extracts this information from a certificate.

---

int **gnutls_x509_crt_get_authority_info_access** (*gnutls_x509_crt_t* **crt**, *unsigned int* **seq**, *int* **what**, *gnutls_datum_t * * **data**, *unsigned int * * **critical**)

There are several functions in GnuTLS for creating and manipulating OCSP requests and responses. The general idea is that a client application creates an OCSP request object, stores some information about the certificate to check in the request, and then exports the request in DER format. The request will then need to be sent to the OCSP responder, which needs to be done by the application (GnuTLS does not send and receive OCSP packets). Normally an OCSP response is received that the application will need to import into an OCSP response object. The digital signature in the OCSP response needs to be verified against a set of trust anchors before the information in the response can be trusted.

The ASN.1 structure of OCSP requests are briefly as follows. It is useful to review the structures to get an understanding of which fields are modified by GnuTLS functions.

```
 1  OCSPRequest       ::=       SEQUENCE {
 2      tbsRequest                TBSRequest,
 3      optionalSignature  [0]    EXPLICIT Signature OPTIONAL }
 4
 5  TBSRequest        ::=       SEQUENCE {
 6      version           [0]     EXPLICIT Version DEFAULT v1,
 7      requestorName     [1]     EXPLICIT GeneralName OPTIONAL,
 8      requestList               SEQUENCE OF Request,
 9      requestExtensions [2]     EXPLICIT Extensions OPTIONAL }
10
11  Request           ::=       SEQUENCE {
12      reqCert                   CertID,
13      singleRequestExtensions   [0] EXPLICIT Extensions OPTIONAL }
14
15  CertID            ::=       SEQUENCE {
16      hashAlgorithm             AlgorithmIdentifier,
```

```
17    issuerNameHash          OCTET STRING, -- Hash of Issuer's DN
18    issuerKeyHash           OCTET STRING, -- Hash of Issuers public key
19    serialNumber            CertificateSerialNumber }
```

The basic functions to initialize, import, export and deallocate OCSP requests are the following.

---

int **gnutls_ocsp_req_init** (*gnutls_ocsp_req_t* * **req**)

void **gnutls_ocsp_req_deinit** (*gnutls_ocsp_req_t* **req**)

int **gnutls_ocsp_req_import** (*gnutls_ocsp_req_t* **req**, *const gnutls_datum_t* * **data**)

int **gnutls_ocsp_req_export** (*gnutls_ocsp_req_t* **req**, *gnutls_datum_t* * **data**)

int **gnutls_ocsp_req_print** (*gnutls_ocsp_req_t* **req**, *gnutls_ocsp_print_formats_t* **format**, *gnutls_datum_t* * **out**)

To generate an OCSP request the issuer name hash, issuer key hash, and the checked certificate's serial number are required. There are two interfaces available for setting those in an OCSP request. The is a low-level function when you have the issuer name hash, issuer key hash, and certificate serial number in binary form. The second is more useful if you have the certificate (and its issuer) in a `gnutls_x509_crt_t` type. There is also a function to extract this information from existing an OCSP request.

---

int **gnutls_ocsp_req_add_cert_id** (*gnutls_ocsp_req_t* **req**, *gnutls_digest_algorithm_t* **digest**, *const gnutls_datum_t* * **issuer_name_hash**, *const gnutls_datum_t* * **issuer_key_hash**, *const gnutls_datum_t* * **serial_number**)

int **gnutls_ocsp_req_add_cert** (*gnutls_ocsp_req_t* **req**, *gnutls_digest_algorithm_t* **digest**, *gnutls_x509_crt_t* **issuer**, *gnutls_x509_crt_t* **cert**)

int **gnutls_ocsp_req_get_cert_id** (*gnutls_ocsp_req_t* **req**, *unsigned* **indx**, *gnutls_digest_algorithm_t* * **digest**, *gnutls_datum_t* * **issuer_name_hash**, *gnutls_datum_t* * **issuer_key_hash**, *gnutls_datum_t* * **serial_number**)

Each OCSP request may contain a number of extensions. Extensions are identified by an Object Identifier (OID) and an opaque data buffer whose syntax and semantics is implied by the OID. You can extract or set those extensions using the following functions.

---

int **gnutls_ocsp_req_get_extension** (*gnutls_ocsp_req_t* **req**, *unsigned* **indx**, *gnutls_datum_t* * **oid**, *unsigned int* * **critical**, *gnutls_datum_t* * **data**)

int **gnutls_ocsp_req_set_extension** (*gnutls_ocsp_req_t* **req**, *const char* * **oid**, *unsigned int* **critical**, *const gnutls_datum_t* * **data**)

A common OCSP Request extension is the nonce extension (OID 1.3.6.1.5.5.7.48.1.2), which is used to avoid replay attacks of earlier recorded OCSP responses. The nonce extension carries a value that is intended to be sufficiently random and unique so that an attacker will not be able to give a stale response for the same nonce.

---

int **gnutls_ocsp_req_get_nonce** (*gnutls_ocsp_req_t* **req**, *unsigned int* * **critical**, *gnutls_datum_t* * **nonce**)

int **gnutls_ocsp_req_set_nonce** (*gnutls_ocsp_req_t* **req**, *unsigned int* **critical**, *const gnutls_datum_t* * **nonce**)

int **gnutls_ocsp_req_randomize_nonce** (*gnutls_ocsp_req_t* **req**)

The OCSP response structures is a complex structure. A simplified overview of it is in Table 3.8. Note that a response may contain information on multiple certificates.

We provide basic functions for initialization, importing, exporting and deallocating OCSP responses.

---

int **gnutls_ocsp_resp_init** (*gnutls_ocsp_resp_t* * **resp**)

void **gnutls_ocsp_resp_deinit** (*gnutls_ocsp_resp_t* **resp**)

int **gnutls_ocsp_resp_import** (*gnutls_ocsp_resp_t* **resp**, *const gnutls_datum_t* * **data**)

int **gnutls_ocsp_resp_export** (*gnutls_ocsp_resp_t* **resp**, *gnutls_datum_t* * **data**)

int **gnutls_ocsp_resp_print** (*gnutls_ocsp_resp_t* **resp**, *gnutls_ocsp_print_formats_t* **format**, *gnutls_datum_t* * **out**)

The utility function that extracts the revocation as well as other information from a response is shown below.

---

int **gnutls_ocsp_resp_get_single** (*gnutls_ocsp_resp_t* **resp**, *unsigned* **indx**, *gnutls_digest_algorithm_t* * **digest**, *gnutls_datum_t* * **issuer_name_hash**, *gnutls_datum_t* * **issuer_key_hash**, *gnutls_datum_t* * **serial_number**, *unsigned int* * **cert_status**, *time_t* * **this_update**, *time_t* * **next_update**, *time_t* * **revocation_time**, *unsigned int* * **revocation_reason**)

Description: This function will return the certificate information of the indx'ed response in the Basic OCSP Response resp. The information returned corresponds to the OCSP SingleResponse structure except the final singleExtensions. Each of the pointers to output variables may be NULL to indicate that the caller is not interested in that value.

Returns: On success, **GNUTLS_E_SUCCESS** (0) is returned, otherwise a negative error code is returned. If you have reached the last CertID available **GNUTLS_E_-REQUESTED_DATA_NOT_AVAILABLE** will be returned.

The possible revocation reasons available in an OCSP response are shown below.

Note, that the OCSP response needs to be verified against some set of trust anchors before it can be relied upon. It is also important to check whether the received OCSP response corresponds to the certificate being checked.

---

int **gnutls_ocsp_resp_verify** (*gnutls_ocsp_resp_t* **resp**, *gnutls_x509_trust_list_t* **trustlist**, *unsigned int* * **verify**, *unsigned int* **flags**)

int **gnutls_ocsp_resp_verify_direct** (*gnutls_ocsp_resp_t* **resp**, *gnutls_x509_crt_t* **issuer**, *unsigned int* * **verify**, *unsigned int* **flags**)

int **gnutls_ocsp_resp_check_crt** (*gnutls_ocsp_resp_t* **resp**, *unsigned* *int* **indx**, *gnutls_x509_crt_t* **crt**)

3.2.4. OCSP stapling

To avoid applications contacting the OCSP server directly, TLS servers can provide a "stapled" OCSP response in the TLS handshake. That way the client application needs to do nothing more. GnuTLS will automatically consider the stapled OCSP response during the TLS certificate verification (see `gnutls_certificate_verify_peers2`). The stapled response can be obtained using `gnutls_ocsp_status_request_get`.

In addition, since GnuTLS 3.5.1 the client will consider the [16] OCSP-Must-staple certificate extension, and will consider it while checking for stapled OCSP responses. If the extension is present and no OCSP staple is found the certificate verification will fail and the status code `GNUTLS_CERT_MISSING_OCSP_STATUS` will returned from the verification function.

GnuTLS servers can provide this response to their clients using the following functions.

---

void **gnutls_certificate_set_ocsp_status_request_function**
(*gnutls_certificate_credentials_t* **sc**, *gnutls_status_request_ocsp_func* **ocsp_func**, *void* * **ptr**)

int **gnutls_certificate_set_ocsp_status_request_file** (*gnutls_certificate_credentials_t* **sc**, *const char* * **response_file**, *unsigned* **idx**)

Note: *the ability to set multiple OCSP responses per credential structure via the index* **idx** *was added in version 3.5.6. To keep backwards compatibility, it requires using gnutls_-certificate_set_flags() with the* **GNUTLS_CERTIFICATE_API_V**2 *flag to make the set certificate functions return an index usable by this function.*

int **gnutls_ocsp_status_request_is_checked** (*gnutls_session_t* **session**, *unsigned int* **flags**)

The simplest approach is for a server to provide the OCSP server's response using the `gnutls_-certificate_set_ocsp_status_request_file`. The response may be updated periodically using the following command (see also subsection 3.2.7).

```
1  ocsptool --ask --load-cert server_cert.pem --load-issuer the_issuer.pem
2          --load-signer the_issuer.pem --outfile ocsp.response
```

3.2.5. Managing encrypted keys

Transferring or storing private keys in plain may not be a good idea, since any compromise is irreparable. Storing the keys in hardware security modules (see section 4.3) could solve the storage problem but it is not always practical or efficient enough. This section describes ways to store and transfer encrypted private keys.

There are methods for key encryption, namely the PKCS #8, PKCS #12 and OpenSSL's custom encrypted private key formats. The PKCS #8 and the OpenSSL's method allow encryption of the private key, while the PKCS #12 method allows, in addition, the bundling of accompanying data into the structure. That is typically the corresponding certificate, as well as a trusted CA certificate.

High level functionality

Generic and higher level private key import functions are available, that import plain or encrypted keys and will auto-detect the encrypted key format.

Any keys imported using those functions can be imported to a certificate credentials structure using `gnutls_certificate_set_key`, or alternatively they can be directly imported using

---

int **gnutls_privkey_import_x509_raw** (*gnutls_privkey_t* **pkey**, *const gnutls_datum_t* * **data**, *gnutls_x509_crt_fmt_t* **format**, *const char* * **password**, *unsigned int* **flags**)

Description: This function will import the given private key to the abstract *gnutls_privkey_t* type. The supported formats are basic unencrypted key, PKCS8, PKCS12, and the openssl format.

Returns: On success, **GNUTLS_E_SUCCESS** (0) is returned, otherwise a negative error value.

---

int **gnutls_x509_privkey_import2** (*gnutls_x509_privkey_t* **key**, *const gnutls_datum_t* * **data**, *gnutls_x509_crt_fmt_t* **format**, *const char* * **password**, *unsigned int* **flags**)

Description: This function will import the given DER or PEM encoded key, to the native *gnutls_x509_privkey_t* format, irrespective of the input format. The input format is auto-detected. The supported formats are basic unencrypted key, PKCS8, PKCS12, and the openssl format. If the provided key is encrypted but no password was given, then **GNUTLS_E_DECRYPTION_FAILED** is returned. Since GnuTLS 3.4.0 this function will utilize the PIN callbacks if any.

Returns: On success, **GNUTLS_E_SUCCESS** (0) is returned, otherwise a negative error value.

---

gnutls_certificate_set_x509_key_file2.

PKCS #8 structures

PKCS #8 keys can be imported and exported as normal private keys using the functions below. An addition to the normal import functions, are a password and a flags argument. The flags can be any element of the **gnutls_pkcs_encrypt_flags_t** enumeration. Note however, that GnuTLS only supports the PKCS #5 PBES2 encryption scheme. Keys encrypted with the obsolete PBES1 scheme cannot be decrypted.

---

int **gnutls_x509_privkey_import_pkcs8** (*gnutls_x509_privkey_t* **key**, *const gnutls_datum_t* * **data**, *gnutls_x509_crt_fmt_t* **format**, *const char* * **password**, *unsigned int* **flags**)

int **gnutls_x509_privkey_export_pkcs8** (*gnutls_x509_privkey_t* **key**, *gnutls_x509_crt_fmt_t* **format**, *const char* * **password**, *unsigned int* **flags**, *void* * **output_data**, *size_t* * **output_data_size**)

int **gnutls_x509_privkey_export2_pkcs8** (*gnutls_x509_privkey_t* **key**, *gnutls_x509_crt_fmt_t* **format**, *const char* * **password**, *unsigned int* **flags**, *gnutls_datum_t* * **out**)

PKCS #12 structures

A PKCS #12 structure [20] usually contains a user's private keys and certificates. It is commonly used in browsers to export and import the user's identities. A file containing such a key can be directly imported to a certificate credentials structure by using **gnutls_certificate_set_x509_simple_pkcs12_file**.

In GnuTLS the PKCS #12 structures are handled using the **gnutls_pkcs12_t** type. This is an abstract type that may hold several **gnutls_pkcs12_bag_t** types. The bag types are the holders of the actual data, which may be certificates, private keys or encrypted data. A bag of type encrypted should be decrypted in order for its data to be accessed.

To reduce the complexity in parsing the structures the simple helper function **gnutls_pkcs12_simple_parse** is provided. For more advanced uses, manual parsing of the structure is required using the functions below.

---

int **gnutls_pkcs12_get_bag** (*gnutls_pkcs12_t* **pkcs12**, *int* **indx**, *gnutls_pkcs12_bag_t* **bag**)

int **gnutls_pkcs12_verify_mac** (*gnutls_pkcs12_t* **pkcs12**, *const char* * **pass**)

int **gnutls_pkcs12_bag_decrypt** (*gnutls_pkcs12_bag_t* **bag**, *const char* * **pass**)

int **gnutls_pkcs12_bag_get_count** (*gnutls_pkcs12_bag_t* **bag**)

---

int **gnutls_pkcs12_simple_parse** (*gnutls_pkcs12_t* **p12**, *const char* * **password**, *gnutls_x509_privkey_t* * **key**, *gnutls_x509_crt_t* ** **chain**, *unsigned int* * **chain_len**, *gnutls_x509_crt_t* ** **extra_certs**, *unsigned int* * **extra_certs_len**, *gnutls_x509_crl_t* * **crl**, *unsigned int* **flags**)

Description: This function parses a PKCS12 structure in pkcs12 and extracts the private key, the corresponding certificate chain, any additional certificates and a CRL. The structures in key, chain crl, and extra_certs must not be initialized. The extra_certs and extra_certs_len parameters are optional and both may be set to **NULL**. If either is non-**NULL**, then both must be set. The value for extra_certs is allocated using gnutls_-malloc(). Encrypted PKCS12 bags and PKCS8 private keys are supported, but only with password based security and the same password for all operations. Note that a PKCS12 structure may contain many keys and/or certificates, and there is no way to identify which key/certificate pair you want. For this reason this function is useful for PKCS12 files that contain only one key/certificate pair and/or one CRL. If the provided structure has encrypted fields but no password is provided then this function returns **GNUTLS_E-DECRYPTION_FAILED**. Note that normally the chain constructed does not include self signed certificates, to comply with TLS' requirements. If, however, the flag **GNUTLS_-PKCS12_SP_INCLUDE_SELF_SIGNED** is specified then self signed certificates will be included in the chain. Prior to using this function the PKCS #12 structure integrity must be verified using gnutls_pkcs12_verify_mac().

Returns: On success, **GNUTLS_E_SUCCESS** (0) is returned, otherwise a negative error value.

---

int **gnutls_pkcs12_bag_get_data** (*gnutls_pkcs12_bag_t* **bag**, *unsigned* **indx**, *gnutls_datum_t* * **data**)

int **gnutls_pkcs12_bag_get_key_id** (*gnutls_pkcs12_bag_t* **bag**, *unsigned* **indx**, *gnutls_datum_t* * **id**)

int **gnutls_pkcs12_bag_get_friendly_name** (*gnutls_pkcs12_bag_t* **bag**, *unsigned* **indx**, *char* ** **name**)

The functions below are used to generate a PKCS #12 structure. An example of their usage is shown at subsection 6.4.4.

---

int **gnutls_pkcs12_set_bag** (*gnutls_pkcs12_t* **pkcs12**, *gnutls_pkcs12_bag_t* **bag**)

int **gnutls_pkcs12_bag_encrypt** (*gnutls_pkcs12_bag_t* **bag**, *const char* * **pass**, *unsigned int* **flags**)

int **gnutls_pkcs12_generate_mac** (*gnutls_pkcs12_t* **pkcs12**, *const char* * **pass**)

---

int **gnutls_pkcs12_bag_set_data** (*gnutls_pkcs12_bag_t* **bag**, *gnutls_pkcs12_bag_type_t* **type**, *const gnutls_datum_t* * **data**)

int **gnutls_pkcs12_bag_set_crl** (*gnutls_pkcs12_bag_t* **bag**, *gnutls_x509_crl_t* **crl**)

int **gnutls_pkcs12_bag_set_crt** (*gnutls_pkcs12_bag_t* **bag**, *gnutls_x509_crt_t* **crt**)

int **gnutls_pkcs12_bag_set_key_id** (*gnutls_pkcs12_bag_t* **bag**, *unsigned* **indx**, *const gnutls_datum_t* * **id**)

int **gnutls_pkcs12_bag_set_friendly_name** (*gnutls_pkcs12_bag_t* **bag**, *unsigned* **indx**, *const char* * **name**)

OpenSSL encrypted keys

Unfortunately the structures discussed in the previous sections are not the only structures that may hold an encrypted private key. For example the OpenSSL library offers a custom key encryption method. Those structures are also supported in GnuTLS with `gnutls_x509_privkey_import_openssl`.

3.2.6. Invoking certtool

Tool to parse and generate X.509 certificates, requests and private keys. It can be used interactively or non interactively by specifying the template command line option.

The tool accepts files or supported URIs via the –infile option. In case PIN is required for URI access you can provide it using the environment variables GNUTLS_PIN and GNUTLS_SO_PIN.

This section was generated by **AutoGen**, using the `agtexi-cmd` template and the option descriptions for the `certtool` program. This software is released under the GNU General Public License, version 3 or later.

int **gnutls_x509_privkey_import_openssl** (*gnutls_x509_privkey_t* **key**, *const gnutls_datum_t* * **data**, *const char* * **password**)

Description: This function will convert the given PEM encrypted to the native gnutls_-x509_privkey_t format. The output will be stored in key. The password should be in ASCII. If the password is not provided or wrong then **GNUTLS_E_DECRYPTION_FAILED** will be returned. If the Certificate is PEM encoded it should have a header of "PRIVATE KEY" and the "DEK-Info" header.

Returns: On success, **GNUTLS_E_SUCCESS** (0) is returned, otherwise a negative error value.

certtool help/usage ("--help")

This is the automatically generated usage text for certtool.

The text printed is the same whether selected with the **help** option ("--help") or the **more-help** option ("--more-help"). **more-help** will print the usage text by passing it through a pager program. **more-help** is disabled on platforms without a working **fork(2)** function. The **PAGER** environment variable is used to select the program, defaulting to "more". Both will exit with a status code of 0.

```
 1  certtool - GnuTLS certificate tool
 2  Usage:  certtool [ -<flag> [<val>] | --<name>[{=| }<val>] ]...
 3
 4    -d, --debug=num            Enable debugging
 5                                - it must be in the range:
 6                                  0 to 9999
 7    -V, --verbose              More verbose output
 8                                - may appear multiple times
 9        --infile=file          Input file
10                                - file must pre-exist
11        --outfile=str          Output file
12
13  Certificate related options:
14
15    -i, --certificate-info     Print information on the given certificate
16        --pubkey-info          Print information on a public key
17    -s, --generate-self-signed  Generate a self-signed certificate
18    -c, --generate-certificate  Generate a signed certificate
19        --generate-proxy       Generates a proxy certificate
20    -u, --update-certificate   Update a signed certificate
21        --fingerprint          Print the fingerprint of the given certificate
22        --key-id               Print the key ID of the given certificate
23        --v1                   Generate an X.509 version 1 certificate (with no extensions)
24        --sign-params=str      Sign a certificate with a specific signature algorithm
25
26  Certificate request related options:
27
28        --crq-info             Print information on the given certificate request
```

```
29   -q, --generate-request     Generate a PKCS #10 certificate request
30                                 - prohibits the option 'infile'
31       --no-crq-extensions    Do not use extensions in certificate requests
32
33  PKCS#12 file related options:
34
35       --p12-info             Print information on a PKCS #12 structure
36       --p12-name=str         The PKCS #12 friendly name to use
37       --to-p12               Generate a PKCS #12 structure
38
39  Private key related options:
40
41   -k, --key-info             Print information on a private key
42       --p8-info              Print information on a PKCS #8 structure
43       --to-rsa               Convert an RSA-PSS key to raw RSA format
44   -p, --generate-privkey     Generate a private key
45       --bits=num             Specify the number of bits for key generation
46       --curve=str            Specify the curve used for EC key generation
47       --sec-param=str        Specify the security level [low, legacy, medium, high, ultra]
48       --to-p8                Convert a given key to a PKCS #8 structure
49   -8, --pkcs8                Use PKCS #8 format for private keys
50       --provable             Generate a private key or parameters from a seed using a provable method
51       --verify-provable-privkey  Verify a private key generated from a seed using a provable method
52       --seed=str             When generating a private key use the given hex-encoded seed
53
54  CRL related options:
55
56   -l, --crl-info             Print information on the given CRL structure
57       --generate-crl         Generate a CRL
58       --verify-crl           Verify a Certificate Revocation List using a trusted list
59                                 - requires the option 'load-ca-certificate'
60
61  Certificate verification related options:
62
63   -e, --verify-chain         Verify a PEM encoded certificate chain
64       --verify               Verify a PEM encoded certificate (chain) against a trusted set
65       --verify-hostname=str  Specify a hostname to be used for certificate chain verification
66       --verify-email=str     Specify a email to be used for certificate chain verification
67                                 - prohibits the option 'verify-hostname'
68       --verify-purpose=str   Specify a purpose OID to be used for certificate chain verification
69       --verify-allow-broken  Allow broken algorithms, such as MD5 for verification
70
71  PKCS#7 structure options:
72
73       --p7-generate          Generate a PKCS #7 structure
74       --p7-sign              Signs using a PKCS #7 structure
75       --p7-detached-sign     Signs using a detached PKCS #7 structure
76       --p7-include-cert      The signer's certificate will be included in the cert list.
77                                 - disabled as '--no-p7-include-cert'
78                                 - enabled by default
79       --p7-time              Will include a timestamp in the PKCS #7 structure
80                                 - disabled as '--no-p7-time'
81       --p7-show-data         Will show the embedded data in the PKCS #7 structure
82                                 - disabled as '--no-p7-show-data'
83       --p7-info              Print information on a PKCS #7 structure
84       --p7-verify            Verify the provided PKCS #7 structure
85       --smime-to-p7          Convert S/MIME to PKCS #7 structure
86
```

```
 87 │ Other options:
 88 │
 89 │        --get-dh-params          List the included PKCS #3 encoded Diffie-Hellman parameters
 90 │        --dh-info                Print information PKCS #3 encoded Diffie-Hellman parameters
 91 │        --load-privkey=str       Loads a private key file
 92 │        --load-pubkey=str        Loads a public key file
 93 │        --load-request=str       Loads a certificate request file
 94 │        --load-certificate=str Loads a certificate file
 95 │        --load-ca-privkey=str  Loads the certificate authority's private key file
 96 │        --load-ca-certificate=str Loads the certificate authority's certificate file
 97 │        --load-crl=str           Loads the provided CRL
 98 │        --load-data=str          Loads auxiliary data
 99 │        --password=str           Password to use
100 │        --null-password          Enforce a NULL password
101 │        --empty-password         Enforce an empty password
102 │        --hex-numbers            Print big number in an easier format to parse
103 │        --cprint                 In certain operations it prints the information in C-friendly format
104 │        --key-type=str           Specify the key type to use on key generation
105 │        --hash=str               Hash algorithm to use for signing
106 │        --salt-size=num          Specify the RSA-PSS key default salt size
107 │        --inder                  Use DER format for input certificates, private keys, and DH parameters
108 │                                   - disabled as '--no-inder'
109 │        --inraw                  an alias for the 'inder' option
110 │        --outder                 Use DER format for output certificates, private keys, and DH parameters
111 │                                   - disabled as '--no-outder'
112 │        --outraw                 an alias for the 'outder' option
113 │        --template=str           Template file to use for non-interactive operation
114 │        --stdout-info            Print information to stdout instead of stderr
115 │        --ask-pass               Enable interaction for entering password when in batch mode.
116 │        --pkcs-cipher=str        Cipher to use for PKCS #8 and #12 operations
117 │        --provider=str           Specify the PKCS #11 provider library
118 │
119 │ Version, usage and configuration options:
120 │
121 │   -v, --version[=arg]           output version information and exit
122 │   -h, --help                    display extended usage information and exit
123 │   -!, --more-help               extended usage information passed thru pager
124 │
125 │ Options are specified by doubled hyphens and their name or by a single
126 │ hyphen and the flag character.
127 │
128 │ Tool to parse and generate X.509 certificates, requests and private keys.
129 │ It can be used interactively or non interactively by specifying the
130 │ template command line option.
131 │
132 │ The tool accepts files or supported URIs via the --infile option.  In case
133 │ PIN is required for URI access you can provide it using the environment
134 │ variables GNUTLS_PIN and GNUTLS_SO_PIN.
135 │
```

Base options

debug option (-d).

This is the "enable debugging" option. This option takes a number argument. Specifies the debug level.

cert-options options

Certificate related options.

pubkey-info option.

This is the "print information on a public key" option. The option combined with –load-request, –load-pubkey, –load-privkey and –load-certificate will extract the public key of the object in question.

fingerprint option.

This is the "print the fingerprint of the given certificate" option. This is a simple hash of the DER encoding of the certificate. It can be combined with the –hash parameter. However, it is recommended for identification to use the key-id which depends only on the certificate's key.

key-id option.

This is the "print the key id of the given certificate" option. This is a hash of the public key of the given certificate. It identifies the key uniquely, remains the same on a certificate renewal and depends only on signed fields of the certificate.

certificate-pubkey option.

This is the "print certificate's public key" option. This option is deprecated as a duplicate of –pubkey-info

NOTE: THIS OPTION IS DEPRECATED

sign-params option.

This is the "sign a certificate with a specific signature algorithm" option. This option takes a string argument. This option can be combined with –generate-certificate, to sign the certificate with a specific signature algorithm variant. The only option supported is 'RSA-PSS', and should be specified when the signer does not have a certificate which is marked for RSA-PSS use only.

crq-options options

Certificate request related options.

generate-request option (-q).

This is the "generate a pkcs #10 certificate request" option.

This option has some usage constraints. It:

- must not appear in combination with any of the following options: infile.

Will generate a PKCS #10 certificate request. To specify a private key use –load-privkey.

pkcs12-options options

PKCS#12 file related options.

p12-info option.

This is the "print information on a pkcs #12 structure" option. This option will dump the contents and print the metadata of the provided PKCS #12 structure.

p12-name option.

This is the "the pkcs #12 friendly name to use" option. This option takes a string argument. The name to be used for the primary certificate and private key in a PKCS #12 file.

to-p12 option.

This is the "generate a pkcs #12 structure" option. It requires a certificate, a private key and possibly a CA certificate to be specified.

key-options options

Private key related options.

p8-info option.

This is the "print information on a pkcs #8 structure" option. This option will print information about encrypted PKCS #8 structures. That option does not require the decryption of the structure.

to-rsa option.

This is the "convert an rsa-pss key to raw rsa format" option. It requires an RSA-PSS key as input and will output a raw RSA key. This command is necessary for compatibility with applications that cannot read RSA-PSS keys.

generate-privkey option (-p).

This is the "generate a private key" option. When generating RSA-PSS private keys, the –hash option will restrict the allowed hash for the key; in the same keys the –salt-size option is also acceptable.

curve option.

This is the "specify the curve used for ec key generation" option. This option takes a string argument. Supported values are secp192r1, secp224r1, secp256r1, secp384r1 and secp521r1.

sec-param option.

This is the "specify the security level [low, legacy, medium, high, ultra]" option. This option takes a string argument "`Security parameter`". This is alternative to the bits option.

to-p8 option.

This is the "convert a given key to a pkcs #8 structure" option. This needs to be combined with –load-privkey.

provable option.

This is the "generate a private key or parameters from a seed using a provable method" option. This will use the FIPS PUB186-4 algorithms (i.e., Shawe-Taylor) for provable key generation. When specified the private keys or parameters will be generated from a seed, and can be later validated with –verify-provable-privkey to be correctly generated from the seed. You may specify –seed or allow GnuTLS to generate one (recommended). This option can be combined with –generate-privkey or –generate-dh-params.

That option applies to RSA and DSA keys. On the DSA keys the PQG parameters are generated using the seed, and on RSA the two primes.

verify-provable-privkey option.

This is the "verify a private key generated from a seed using a provable method" option. This will use the FIPS-186-4 algorithms for provable key generation. You may specify –seed or use the seed stored in the private key structure.

seed option.

This is the "when generating a private key use the given hex-encoded seed" option. This option takes a string argument. The seed acts as a security parameter for the private key, and thus a seed size which corresponds to the security level of the private key should be provided (e.g., 256-bits seed).

crl-options options

CRL related options.

generate-crl option.

This is the "generate a crl" option. This option generates a Certificate Revocation List. When combined with –load-crl it would use the loaded CRL as base for the generated (i.e., all revoked certificates in the base will be copied to the new CRL).

verify-crl option.

This is the "verify a certificate revocation list using a trusted list" option.

This option has some usage constraints. It:

- must appear in combination with the following options: load-ca-certificate.

The trusted certificate list must be loaded with –load-ca-certificate.

cert-verify-options options

Certificate verification related options.

verify-chain option (-e).

This is the "verify a pem encoded certificate chain" option. Verifies the validity of a certificate chain. That is, an ordered set of certificates where each one is the issuer of the previous, and the first is the end-certificate to be validated. In a proper chain the last certificate is a self signed one. It can be combined with –verify-purpose or –verify-hostname.

verify option.

This is the "verify a pem encoded certificate (chain) against a trusted set" option. The trusted certificate list can be loaded with –load-ca-certificate. If no certificate list is provided, then the system's trusted certificate list is used. Note that during verification multiple paths may be explored. On a successful verification the successful path will be the last one. It can be combined with –verify-purpose or –verify-hostname.

verify-hostname option.

This is the "specify a hostname to be used for certificate chain verification" option. This option takes a string argument. This is to be combined with one of the verify certificate options.

verify-email option.

This is the "specify a email to be used for certificate chain verification" option. This option takes a string argument.

This option has some usage constraints. It:

- must not appear in combination with any of the following options: verify-hostname.

This is to be combined with one of the verify certificate options.

verify-purpose option.

This is the "specify a purpose oid to be used for certificate chain verification" option. This option takes a string argument. This object identifier restricts the purpose of the certificates to be verified. Example purposes are 1.3.6.1.5.5.7.3.1 (TLS WWW), 1.3.6.1.5.5.7.3.4 (EMAIL) etc. Note that a CA certificate without a purpose set (extended key usage) is valid for any purpose.

verify-allow-broken option.

This is the "allow broken algorithms, such as md5 for verification" option. This can be combined with –p7-verify, –verify or –verify-chain.

pkcs7-options options

PKCS#7 structure options.

p7-generate option.

This is the "generate a pkcs #7 structure" option. This option generates a PKCS #7 certificate container structure. To add certificates in the structure use –load-certificate and –load-crl.

p7-sign option.

This is the "signs using a pkcs #7 structure" option. This option generates a PKCS #7 structure containing a signature for the provided data from infile. The data are stored within the structure. The signer certificate has to be specified using –load-certificate and –load-privkey. The input to –load-certificate can be a list of certificates. In case of a list, the first certificate is used for signing and the other certificates are included in the structure.

p7-detached-sign option.

This is the "signs using a detached pkcs #7 structure" option. This option generates a PKCS #7 structure containing a signature for the provided data from infile. The signer certificate has to be specified using –load-certificate and –load-privkey. The input to –load-certificate can be a list of certificates. In case of a list, the first certificate is used for signing and the other certificates are included in the structure.

p7-include-cert option.

This is the "the signer's certificate will be included in the cert list." option.

This option has some usage constraints. It:

- can be disabled with –no-p7-include-cert.

- It is enabled by default.

This options works with –p7-sign or –p7-detached-sign and will include or exclude the signer's certificate into the generated signature.

p7-time option.

This is the "will include a timestamp in the pkcs #7 structure" option.

This option has some usage constraints. It:

- can be disabled with –no-p7-time.

This option will include a timestamp in the generated signature

p7-show-data option.

This is the "will show the embedded data in the pkcs #7 structure" option.

This option has some usage constraints. It:

- can be disabled with –no-p7-show-data.

This option can be combined with –p7-verify or –p7-info and will display the embedded signed data in the PKCS #7 structure.

p7-verify option.

This is the "verify the provided pkcs #7 structure" option. This option verifies the signed PKCS #7 structure. The certificate list to use for verification can be specified with –load-ca-certificate. When no certificate list is provided, then the system's certificate list is used. Alternatively a direct signer can be provided using –load-certificate. A key purpose can be enforced with the –verify-purpose option, and the –load-data option will utilize detached data.

other-options options

Other options.

generate-dh-params option.

This is the "generate pkcs #3 encoded diffie-hellman parameters" option. The will generate random parameters to be used with Diffie-Hellman key exchange. The output parameters will be in PKCS #3 format. Note that it is recommended to use the –get-dh-params option instead.

NOTE: THIS OPTION IS DEPRECATED

get-dh-params option.

This is the "list the included pkcs #3 encoded diffie-hellman parameters" option. Returns stored DH parameters in GnuTLS. Those parameters returned are defined in RFC7919, and can be considered standard parameters for a TLS key exchange. This option is provided for old applications which require DH parameters to be specified; modern GnuTLS applications should not require them.

load-privkey option.

This is the "loads a private key file" option. This option takes a string argument. This can be either a file or a PKCS #11 URL

load-pubkey option.

This is the "loads a public key file" option. This option takes a string argument. This can be either a file or a PKCS #11 URL

load-request option.

This is the "loads a certificate request file" option. This option takes a string argument. This option can be used with a file

load-certificate option.

This is the "loads a certificate file" option. This option takes a string argument. This option can be used with a file

load-ca-privkey option.

This is the "loads the certificate authority's private key file" option. This option takes a string argument. This can be either a file or a PKCS #11 URL

load-ca-certificate option.

This is the "loads the certificate authority's certificate file" option. This option takes a string argument. This can be either a file or a PKCS #11 URL

load-crl option.

This is the "loads the provided crl" option. This option takes a string argument. This option can be used with a file

load-data option.

This is the "loads auxiliary data" option. This option takes a string argument. This option can be used with a file

password option.

This is the "password to use" option. This option takes a string argument. You can use this option to specify the password in the command line instead of reading it from the tty. Note, that the command line arguments are available for view in others in the system. Specifying password as " is the same as specifying no password.

null-password option.

This is the "enforce a null password" option. This option enforces a NULL password. This is different than the empty or no password in schemas like PKCS #8.

empty-password option.

This is the "enforce an empty password" option. This option enforces an empty password. This is different than the NULL or no password in schemas like PKCS #8.

cprint option.

This is the "in certain operations it prints the information in c-friendly format" option. In certain operations it prints the information in C-friendly format, suitable for including into C programs.

rsa option.

This is the "generate rsa key" option. When combined with –generate-privkey generates an RSA private key.

NOTE: THIS OPTION IS DEPRECATED

dsa option.

This is the "generate dsa key" option. When combined with –generate-privkey generates a DSA private key.

NOTE: THIS OPTION IS DEPRECATED

ecc option.

This is the "generate ecc (ecdsa) key" option. When combined with –generate-privkey generates an elliptic curve private key to be used with ECDSA.

NOTE: THIS OPTION IS DEPRECATED

ecdsa option.

This is an alias for the `ecc` option, section 3.2.6.

key-type option.

This is the "specify the key type to use on key generation" option. This option takes a string argument. This option can be combined with –generate-privkey, to specify the key type to be generated. Valid options are, 'rsa', 'rsa-pss', 'dsa', 'ecdsa', and 'ed25519'.

hash option.

This is the "hash algorithm to use for signing" option. This option takes a string argument. Available hash functions are SHA1, RMD160, SHA256, SHA384, SHA512, SHA3-224, SHA3-256, SHA3-384, SHA3-512.

salt-size option.

This is the "specify the rsa-pss key default salt size" option. This option takes a number argument. Typical keys shouldn't set or restrict this option.

inder option.

This is the "use der format for input certificates, private keys, and dh parameters " option.

This option has some usage constraints. It:

- can be disabled with –no-inder.

The input files will be assumed to be in DER or RAW format. Unlike options that in PEM input would allow multiple input data (e.g. multiple certificates), when reading in DER format a single data structure is read.

inraw option.

This is an alias for the **inder** option, section 3.2.6.

outder option.

This is the "use der format for output certificates, private keys, and dh parameters" option.

This option has some usage constraints. It:

- can be disabled with –no-outder.

The output will be in DER or RAW format.

outraw option.

This is an alias for the **outder** option, section 3.2.6.

ask-pass option.

This is the "enable interaction for entering password when in batch mode." option. This option will enable interaction to enter password when in batch mode. That is useful when the template option has been specified.

pkcs-cipher option.

This is the "cipher to use for pkcs #8 and #12 operations" option. This option takes a string argument "**Cipher**". Cipher may be one of 3des, 3des-pkcs12, aes-128, aes-192, aes-256, rc2-40, arcfour.

provider option.

This is the "specify the pkcs #11 provider library" option. This option takes a string argument. This will override the default options in /etc/gnutls/pkcs11.conf

certtool exit status

One of the following exit values will be returned:

- 0 (EXIT_SUCCESS) Successful program execution.
- 1 (EXIT_FAILURE) The operation failed or the command syntax was not valid.

certtool See Also

p11tool (1)

certtool Examples

Generating private keys

To create an RSA private key, run:

```
$ certtool --generate-privkey --outfile key.pem --rsa
```

To create a DSA or elliptic curves (ECDSA) private key use the above command combined with 'dsa' or 'ecc' options.

Generating certificate requests

To create a certificate request (needed when the certificate is issued by another party), run:

```
1  certtool --generate-request --load-privkey key.pem \
2     --outfile request.pem
```

If the private key is stored in a smart card you can generate a request by specifying the private key object URL.

```
1  $ ./certtool --generate-request --load-privkey "pkcs11:..." \
2     --load-pubkey "pkcs11:..." --outfile request.pem
```

Generating a self-signed certificate

To create a self signed certificate, use the command:

```
1  $ certtool --generate-privkey --outfile ca-key.pem
2  $ certtool --generate-self-signed --load-privkey ca-key.pem \
3     --outfile ca-cert.pem
```

Note that a self-signed certificate usually belongs to a certificate authority, that signs other certificates.

Generating a certificate

To generate a certificate using the previous request, use the command:

```
1  $ certtool --generate-certificate --load-request request.pem \
2     --outfile cert.pem --load-ca-certificate ca-cert.pem \
3     --load-ca-privkey ca-key.pem
```

To generate a certificate using the private key only, use the command:

```
1  $ certtool --generate-certificate --load-privkey key.pem \
2     --outfile cert.pem --load-ca-certificate ca-cert.pem \
3     --load-ca-privkey ca-key.pem
```

Certificate information

To view the certificate information, use:

```
1  $ certtool --certificate-info --infile cert.pem
```

PKCS #12 structure generation

To generate a PKCS #12 structure using the previous key and certificate, use the command:

```
1  $ certtool --load-certificate cert.pem --load-privkey key.pem \
2     --to-p12 --outder --outfile key.p12
```

Some tools (reportedly web browsers) have problems with that file because it does not contain the CA certificate for the certificate. To work around that problem in the tool, you can use the –load-ca-certificate parameter as follows:

```
1  $ certtool --load-ca-certificate ca.pem \
2     --load-certificate cert.pem --load-privkey key.pem \
3     --to-p12 --outder --outfile key.p12
```

Obtaining Diffie-Hellman parameters

To obtain the RFC7919 parameters for Diffie-Hellman key exchange, use the command:

```
1  $ certtool --get-dh-params --outfile dh.pem --sec-param medium
```

Verifying a certificate

To verify a certificate in a file against the system's CA trust store use the following command:

```
1  $ certtool --verify --infile cert.pem
```

It is also possible to simulate hostname verification with the following options:

```
1  $ certtool --verify --verify-hostname www.example.com --infile cert.pem
```

Proxy certificate generation

Proxy certificate can be used to delegate your credential to a temporary, typically short-lived, certificate. To create one from the previously created certificate, first create a temporary key and then generate a proxy certificate for it, using the commands:

```
1  $ certtool --generate-privkey > proxy-key.pem
2  $ certtool --generate-proxy --load-ca-privkey key.pem \
3     --load-privkey proxy-key.pem --load-certificate cert.pem \
4     --outfile proxy-cert.pem
```

Certificate revocation list generation

To create an empty Certificate Revocation List (CRL) do:

```
1  $ certtool --generate-crl --load-ca-privkey x509-ca-key.pem \
2          --load-ca-certificate x509-ca.pem
```

To create a CRL that contains some revoked certificates, place the certificates in a file and use `--load-certificate` as follows:

```
1  $ certtool --generate-crl --load-ca-privkey x509-ca-key.pem \
2      --load-ca-certificate x509-ca.pem --load-certificate revoked-certs.pem
```

To verify a Certificate Revocation List (CRL) do:

```
1  $ certtool --verify-crl --load-ca-certificate x509-ca.pem < crl.pem
```

certtool Files

Certtool's template file format

A template file can be used to avoid the interactive questions of certtool. Initially create a file named 'cert.cfg' that contains the information about the certificate. The template can be used as below:

```
1  $ certtool --generate-certificate --load-privkey key.pem  \
2      --template cert.cfg --outfile cert.pem \
3      --load-ca-certificate ca-cert.pem --load-ca-privkey ca-key.pem
```

An example certtool template file that can be used to generate a certificate request or a self signed certificate follows.

```
1   # X.509 Certificate options
2   #
3   # DN options
4
5   # The organization of the subject.
6   organization = "Koko inc."
7
8   # The organizational unit of the subject.
9   unit = "sleeping dept."
10
11  # The locality of the subject.
12  # locality =
13
14  # The state of the certificate owner.
15  state = "Attiki"
16
17  # The country of the subject. Two letter code.
18  country = GR
19
20  # The common name of the certificate owner.
21  cn = "Cindy Lauper"
22
23  # A user id of the certificate owner.
24  #uid = "clauper"
```

```
25
26  # Set domain components
27  #dc = "name"
28  #dc = "domain"
29
30  # If the supported DN OIDs are not adequate you can set
31  # any OID here.
32  # For example set the X.520 Title and the X.520 Pseudonym
33  # by using OID and string pairs.
34  #dn_oid = "2.5.4.12 Dr."
35  #dn_oid = "2.5.4.65 jackal"
36
37  # This is deprecated and should not be used in new
38  # certificates.
39  # pkcs9_email = "none@none.org"
40
41  # An alternative way to set the certificate's distinguished name directly
42  # is with the "dn" option. The attribute names allowed are:
43  # C (country), street, O (organization), OU (unit), title, CN (common name),
44  # L (locality), ST (state), placeOfBirth, gender, countryOfCitizenship,
45  # countryOfResidence, serialNumber, telephoneNumber, surName, initials,
46  # generationQualifier, givenName, pseudonym, dnQualifier, postalCode, name,
47  # businessCategory, DC, UID, jurisdictionOfIncorporationLocalityName,
48  # jurisdictionOfIncorporationStateOrProvinceName,
49  # jurisdictionOfIncorporationCountryName, XmppAddr, and numeric OIDs.
50
51  #dn = "cn = Nikos,st = New\, Something,C=GR,surName=Mavrogiannopoulos,2.5.4.9=Arkadias"
52
53  # The serial number of the certificate
54  # Comment the field for a time-based serial number.
55  serial = 007
56
57  # In how many days, counting from today, this certificate will expire.
58  # Use -1 if there is no expiration date.
59  expiration_days = 700
60
61  # Alternatively you may set concrete dates and time. The GNU date string
62  # formats are accepted. See:
63  # http://www.gnu.org/software/tar/manual/html_node/Date-input-formats.html
64
65  #activation_date = "2004-02-29 16:21:42"
66  #expiration_date = "2025-02-29 16:24:41"
67
68  # X.509 v3 extensions
69
70  # A dnsname in case of a WWW server.
71  #dns_name = "www.none.org"
72  #dns_name = "www.morethanone.org"
73
74  # An othername defined by an OID and a hex encoded string
75  #other_name = "1.3.6.1.5.2.2 302ca00d1b0b56414e5245494e2e4f5247a11b3019a006020400000002a10f300d1b047269693
76  #other_name_utf8 = "1.2.4.5.6 A UTF8 string"
77  #other_name_octet = "1.2.4.5.6 A string that will be encoded as ASN.1 octet string"
78
79  # Allows writing an XmppAddr Identifier
80  #xmpp_name = juliet@im.example.com
81
82  # Names used in PKINIT
```

```
 83  #krb5_principal = user@REALM.COM
 84  #krb5_principal = HTTP/user@REALM.COM
 85
 86  # A subject alternative name URI
 87  #uri = "http://www.example.com"
 88
 89  # An IP address in case of a server.
 90  #ip_address = "192.168.1.1"
 91
 92  # An email in case of a person
 93  email = "none@none.org"
 94
 95  # TLS feature (rfc7633) extension. That can is used to indicate mandatory TLS
 96  # extension features to be provided by the server. In practice this is used
 97  # to require the Status Request (extid: 5) extension from the server. That is,
 98  # to require the server holding this certificate to provide a stapled OCSP response.
 99  # You can have multiple lines for multiple TLS features.
100
101  # To ask for OCSP status request use:
102  #tls_feature = 5
103
104  # Challenge password used in certificate requests
105  challenge_password = 123456
106
107  # Password when encrypting a private key
108  #password = secret
109
110  # An URL that has CRLs (certificate revocation lists)
111  # available. Needed in CA certificates.
112  #crl_dist_points = "http://www.getcrl.crl/getcrl/"
113
114  # Whether this is a CA certificate or not
115  #ca
116
117  # Subject Unique ID (in hex)
118  #subject_unique_id = 00153224
119
120  # Issuer Unique ID (in hex)
121  #issuer_unique_id = 00153225
122
123  #### Key usage
124
125  # The following key usage flags are used by CAs and end certificates
126
127  # Whether this certificate will be used to sign data (needed
128  # in TLS DHE ciphersuites). This is the digitalSignature flag
129  # in RFC5280 terminology.
130  signing_key
131
132  # Whether this certificate will be used to encrypt data (needed
133  # in TLS RSA ciphersuites). Note that it is preferred to use different
134  # keys for encryption and signing. This is the keyEncipherment flag
135  # in RFC5280 terminology.
136  encryption_key
137
138  # Whether this key will be used to sign other certificates. The
139  # keyCertSign flag in RFC5280 terminology.
140  #cert_signing_key
```

73

```
141
142  # Whether this key will be used to sign CRLs. The
143  # cRLSign flag in RFC5280 terminology.
144  #crl_signing_key
145
146  # The keyAgreement flag of RFC5280. It's purpose is loosely
147  # defined. Not use it unless required by a protocol.
148  #key_agreement
149
150  # The dataEncipherment flag of RFC5280. It's purpose is loosely
151  # defined. Not use it unless required by a protocol.
152  #data_encipherment
153
154  # The nonRepudiation flag of RFC5280. It's purpose is loosely
155  # defined. Not use it unless required by a protocol.
156  #non_repudiation
157
158  #### Extended key usage (key purposes)
159
160  # The following extensions are used in an end certificate
161  # to clarify its purpose. Some CAs also use it to indicate
162  # the types of certificates they are purposed to sign.
163
164
165  # Whether this certificate will be used for a TLS client;
166  # this sets the id-kp-serverAuth (1.3.6.1.5.5.7.3.1) of
167  # extended key usage.
168  #tls_www_client
169
170  # Whether this certificate will be used for a TLS server;
171  # This sets the id-kp-clientAuth (1.3.6.1.5.5.7.3.2) of
172  # extended key usage.
173  #tls_www_server
174
175  # Whether this key will be used to sign code. This sets the
176  # id-kp-codeSigning (1.3.6.1.5.5.7.3.3) of extended key usage
177  # extension.
178  #code_signing_key
179
180  # Whether this key will be used to sign OCSP data. This sets the
181  # id-kp-OCSPSigning (1.3.6.1.5.5.7.3.9) of extended key usage extension.
182  #ocsp_signing_key
183
184  # Whether this key will be used for time stamping. This sets the
185  # id-kp-timeStamping (1.3.6.1.5.5.7.3.8) of extended key usage extension.
186  #time_stamping_key
187
188  # Whether this key will be used for email protection. This sets the
189  # id-kp-emailProtection (1.3.6.1.5.5.7.3.4) of extended key usage extension.
190  #email_protection_key
191
192  # Whether this key will be used for IPsec IKE operations (1.3.6.1.5.5.7.3.17).
193  #ipsec_ike_key
194
195  ## adding custom key purpose OIDs
196
197  # for microsoft smart card logon
198  # key_purpose_oid = 1.3.6.1.4.1.311.20.2.2
```

```
199
200  # for email protection
201  # key_purpose_oid = 1.3.6.1.5.5.7.3.4
202
203  # for any purpose (must not be used in intermediate CA certificates)
204  # key_purpose_oid = 2.5.29.37.0
205
206  ### end of key purpose OIDs
207
208  ### Adding arbitrary extensions
209  # This requires to provide the extension OIDs, as well as the extension data in
210  # hex format. The following two options are available since GnuTLS 3.5.3.
211  #add_extension = "1.2.3.4 0x0AAB01ACFE"
212
213  # As above but encode the data as an octet string
214  #add_extension = "1.2.3.4 octet_string(0x0AAB01ACFE)"
215
216  # For portability critical extensions shouldn't be set to certificates.
217  #add_critical_extension = "5.6.7.8 0x1AAB01ACFE"
218
219  # When generating a certificate from a certificate
220  # request, then honor the extensions stored in the request
221  # and store them in the real certificate.
222  #honor_crq_extensions
223
224  # Alternatively only specific extensions can be copied.
225  #honor_crq_ext = 2.5.29.17
226  #honor_crq_ext = 2.5.29.15
227
228  # Path length contraint. Sets the maximum number of
229  # certificates that can be used to certify this certificate.
230  # (i.e. the certificate chain length)
231  #path_len = -1
232  #path_len = 2
233
234  # OCSP URI
235  # ocsp_uri = http://my.ocsp.server/ocsp
236
237  # CA issuers URI
238  # ca_issuers_uri = http://my.ca.issuer
239
240  # Certificate policies
241  #policy1 = 1.3.6.1.4.1.5484.1.10.99.1.0
242  #policy1_txt = "This is a long policy to summarize"
243  #policy1_url = http://www.example.com/a-policy-to-read
244
245  #policy2 = 1.3.6.1.4.1.5484.1.10.99.1.1
246  #policy2_txt = "This is a short policy"
247  #policy2_url = http://www.example.com/another-policy-to-read
248
249  # The number of additional certificates that may appear in a
250  # path before the anyPolicy is no longer acceptable.
251  #inhibit_anypolicy_skip_certs 1
252
253  # Name constraints
254
255  # DNS
256  #nc_permit_dns = example.com
```

```
257  #nc_exclude_dns = test.example.com
258
259  # EMAIL
260  #nc_permit_email = "nmav@ex.net"
261
262  # Exclude subdomains of example.com
263  #nc_exclude_email = .example.com
264
265  # Exclude all e-mail addresses of example.com
266  #nc_exclude_email = example.com
267
268  # IP
269  #nc_permit_ip = 192.168.0.0/16
270  #nc_exclude_ip = 192.168.5.0/24
271  #nc_permit_ip = fc0a:eef2:e7e7:a56e::/64
272
273
274  # Options for proxy certificates
275  #proxy_policy_language = 1.3.6.1.5.5.7.21.1
276
277
278  # Options for generating a CRL
279
280  # The number of days the next CRL update will be due.
281  # next CRL update will be in 43 days
282  #crl_next_update = 43
283
284  # this is the 5th CRL by this CA
285  # Comment the field for a time-based number.
286  #crl_number = 5
287
288  # Specify the update dates more precisely.
289  #crl_this_update_date = "2004-02-29 16:21:42"
290  #crl_next_update_date = "2025-02-29 16:24:41"
291
292  # The date that the certificates will be made seen as
293  # being revoked.
294  #crl_revocation_date = "2025-02-29 16:24:41"
295
```

3.2.7. Invoking ocsptool

On verification

Responses are typically signed/issued by designated certificates or certificate authorities and thus this tool requires on verification the certificate of the issuer or the full certificate chain in order to determine the appropriate signing authority. The specified certificate of the issuer is assumed trusted.

This section was generated by **AutoGen**, using the `agtexi-cmd` template and the option descriptions for the `ocsptool` program. This software is released under the GNU General Public License, version 3 or later.

ocsptool help/usage ("--help")

This is the automatically generated usage text for ocsptool.

The text printed is the same whether selected with the **help** option ("--help") or the **more-help** option ("--more-help"). **more-help** will print the usage text by passing it through a pager program. **more-help** is disabled on platforms without a working **fork(2)** function. The **PAGER** environment variable is used to select the program, defaulting to "**more**". Both will exit with a status code of 0.

```
 1  ocsptool - GnuTLS OCSP tool
 2  Usage:  ocsptool [ -<flag> [<val>] | --<name>[{=| }<val>] ]...
 3
 4    -d, --debug=num          Enable debugging
 5                                - it must be in the range:
 6                                  0 to 9999
 7    -V, --verbose            More verbose output
 8                                - may appear multiple times
 9        --infile=file        Input file
10                                - file must pre-exist
11        --outfile=str        Output file
12        --ask[=arg]          Ask an OCSP/HTTP server on a certificate validity
13    -e, --verify-response    Verify response
14    -i, --request-info       Print information on a OCSP request
15    -j, --response-info      Print information on a OCSP response
16    -q, --generate-request   Generates an OCSP request
17        --nonce              Use (or not) a nonce to OCSP request
18                                - disabled as '--no-nonce'
19        --load-chain=file    Reads a set of certificates forming a chain from file
20                                - file must pre-exist
21        --load-issuer=file   Reads issuer's certificate from file
22                                - file must pre-exist
23        --load-cert=file     Reads the certificate to check from file
24                                - file must pre-exist
25        --load-trust=file    Read OCSP trust anchors from file
26                                - prohibits the option 'load-signer'
27                                - file must pre-exist
28        --load-signer=file   Reads the OCSP response signer from file
29                                - prohibits the option 'load-trust'
30                                - file must pre-exist
31        --inder              Use DER format for input certificates and private keys
32                                - disabled as '--no-inder'
33    -Q, --load-request=file  Reads the DER encoded OCSP request from file
34                                - file must pre-exist
35    -S, --load-response=file Reads the DER encoded OCSP response from file
36                                - file must pre-exist
37        --ignore-errors      Ignore any verification errors
38        --verify-allow-broken Allow broken algorithms, such as MD5 for verification
39    -v, --version[=arg]      output version information and exit
40    -h, --help               display extended usage information and exit
41    -!, --more-help          extended usage information passed thru pager
42
43  Options are specified by doubled hyphens and their name or by a single
44  hyphen and the flag character.
45
46  ocsptool is a program that can parse and print information about OCSP
47  requests/responses, generate requests and verify responses.
```

debug option (-d)

This is the "enable debugging" option. This option takes a number argument. Specifies the debug level.

ask option

This is the "ask an ocsp/http server on a certificate validity" option. This option takes an optional string argument @fileserver name—url. Connects to the specified HTTP OCSP server and queries on the validity of the loaded certificate. Its argument can be a URL or a plain server name. It can be combined with –load-chain, where it checks all certificates in the provided chain, or with –load-cert and –load-issuer options. The latter checks the provided certificate against its specified issuer certificate.

verify-response option (-e)

This is the "verify response" option. Verifies the provided OCSP response against the system trust anchors (unless –load-trust is provided). It requires the –load-signer or –load-chain options to obtain the signer of the OCSP response.

request-info option (-i)

This is the "print information on a ocsp request" option. Display detailed information on the provided OCSP request.

response-info option (-j)

This is the "print information on a ocsp response" option. Display detailed information on the provided OCSP response.

load-trust option

This is the "read ocsp trust anchors from file" option. This option takes a file argument.

This option has some usage constraints. It:

- must not appear in combination with any of the following options: load-signer.

When verifying an OCSP response read the trust anchors from the provided file. When this is not provided, the system's trust anchors will be used.

verify-allow-broken option

This is the "allow broken algorithms, such as md5 for verification" option. This can be combined with –verify-response.

ocsptool exit status

One of the following exit values will be returned:

- 0 (EXIT_SUCCESS) Successful program execution.
- 1 (EXIT_FAILURE) The operation failed or the command syntax was not valid.

ocsptool See Also

certtool (1)

ocsptool Examples

Print information about an OCSP request

To parse an OCSP request and print information about the content, the **-i** or **--request-info** parameter may be used as follows. The **-Q** parameter specify the name of the file containing the OCSP request, and it should contain the OCSP request in binary DER format.

```
$ ocsptool -i -Q ocsp-request.der
```

The input file may also be sent to standard input like this:

```
$ cat ocsp-request.der | ocsptool --request-info
```

Print information about an OCSP response

Similar to parsing OCSP requests, OCSP responses can be parsed using the **-j** or **--response-info** as follows.

```
$ ocsptool -j -Q ocsp-response.der
$ cat ocsp-response.der | ocsptool --response-info
```

Generate an OCSP request

The **-q** or **--generate-request** parameters are used to generate an OCSP request. By default the OCSP request is written to standard output in binary DER format, but can be stored in a file using **--outfile**. To generate an OCSP request the issuer of the certificate to check needs to be specified with `--load-issuer` and the certificate to check with `--load-cert`. By default PEM format is used for these files, although `--inder` can be used to specify that the input files are in DER format.

```
1  $ ocsptool -q --load-issuer issuer.pem --load-cert client.pem \
2          --outfile ocsp-request.der
```

When generating OCSP requests, the tool will add an OCSP extension containing a nonce. This behaviour can be disabled by specifying `--no-nonce`.

Verify signature in OCSP response

To verify the signature in an OCSP response the `-e` or `--verify-response` parameter is used. The tool will read an OCSP response in DER format from standard input, or from the file specified by `--load-response`. The OCSP response is verified against a set of trust anchors, which are specified using `--load-trust`. The trust anchors are concatenated certificates in PEM format. The certificate that signed the OCSP response needs to be in the set of trust anchors, or the issuer of the signer certificate needs to be in the set of trust anchors and the OCSP Extended Key Usage bit has to be asserted in the signer certificate.

```
1  $ ocsptool -e --load-trust issuer.pem \
2          --load-response ocsp-response.der
```

The tool will print status of verification.

Verify signature in OCSP response against given certificate

It is possible to override the normal trust logic if you know that a certain certificate is supposed to have signed the OCSP response, and you want to use it to check the signature. This is achieved using `--load-signer` instead of `--load-trust`. This will load one certificate and it will be used to verify the signature in the OCSP response. It will not check the Extended Key Usage bit.

```
1  $ ocsptool -e --load-signer ocsp-signer.pem \
2          --load-response ocsp-response.der
```

This approach is normally only relevant in two situations. The first is when the OCSP response does not contain a copy of the signer certificate, so the `--load-trust` code would fail. The second is if you want to avoid the indirect mode where the OCSP response signer certificate is signed by a trust anchor.

Real-world example

Here is an example of how to generate an OCSP request for a certificate and to verify the response. For illustration we'll use the `blog.josefsson.org` host, which (as of writing) uses a certificate from CACert. First we'll use `gnutls-cli` to get a copy of the server certificate chain. The server is not required to send this information, but this particular one is configured to do so.

```
1  $ echo | gnutls-cli -p 443 blog.josefsson.org --save-cert chain.pem
```

The saved certificates normally contain a pointer to where the OCSP responder is located, in the Authority Information Access Information extension. For example, from `certtool -i <` `chain.pem` there is this information:

```
1  Authority Information Access Information (not critical):
2  Access Method: 1.3.6.1.5.5.7.48.1 (id-ad-ocsp)
3  Access Location URI: http://ocsp.CAcert.org/
```

This means that ocsptool can discover the servers to contact over HTTP. We can now request information on the chain certificates.

```
1  $ ocsptool --ask --load-chain chain.pem
```

The request is sent via HTTP to the OCSP server address found in the certificates. It is possible to override the address of the OCSP server as well as ask information on a particular certificate using –load-cert and –load-issuer.

```
1  $ ocsptool --ask http://ocsp.CAcert.org/ --load-chain chain.pem
```

3.2.8. Invoking danetool

Tool to generate and check DNS resource records for the DANE protocol.

This section was generated by **AutoGen**, using the **agtexi-cmd** template and the option descriptions for the **danetool** program. This software is released under the GNU General Public License, version 3 or later.

danetool help/usage ("--help")

This is the automatically generated usage text for danetool.

The text printed is the same whether selected with the **help** option ("--help") or the **more-help** option ("--more-help"). **more-help** will print the usage text by passing it through a pager program. **more-help** is disabled on platforms without a working **fork(2)** function. The **PAGER** environment variable is used to select the program, defaulting to "more". Both will exit with a status code of 0.

```
1  danetool - GnuTLS DANE tool
2  Usage:  danetool [ -<flag> [<val>] | --<name>[{=| }<val>] ]...
3
4    -d, --debug=num          Enable debugging
5                               - it must be in the range:
6                                 0 to 9999
7    -V, --verbose            More verbose output
8                               - may appear multiple times
```

```
 9        --infile=file          Input file
10                                 - file must pre-exist
11        --outfile=str          Output file
12        --load-pubkey=str      Loads a public key file
13        --load-certificate=str Loads a certificate file
14        --dlv=str              Sets a DLV file
15        --hash=str             Hash algorithm to use for signing
16        --check=str            Check a host's DANE TLSA entry
17        --check-ee             Check only the end-entity's certificate
18        --check-ca             Check only the CA's certificate
19        --tlsa-rr              Print the DANE RR data on a certificate or public key
20                                 - requires the option 'host'
21        --host=str             Specify the hostname to be used in the DANE RR
22        --proto=str            The protocol set for DANE data (tcp, udp etc.)
23        --port=str             The port or service to connect to, for DANE data
24        --app-proto=str        an alias for the 'starttls-proto' option
25        --starttls-proto=str   The application protocol to be used to obtain the server's certificate
26  (https, ftp, smtp, imap, ldap, xmpp, lmtp, pop3, nntp, sieve, postgres)
27        --ca                   Whether the provided certificate or public key is a Certificate
28  Authority
29        --x509                 Use the hash of the X.509 certificate, rather than the public key
30        --local                an alias for the 'domain' option
31                                 - enabled by default
32        --domain               The provided certificate or public key is issued by the local domain
33                                 - disabled as '--no-domain'
34                                 - enabled by default
35        --local-dns            Use the local DNS server for DNSSEC resolving
36                                 - disabled as '--no-local-dns'
37        --insecure             Do not verify any DNSSEC signature
38        --inder                Use DER format for input certificates and private keys
39                                 - disabled as '--no-inder'
40        --inraw                an alias for the 'inder' option
41        --print-raw            Print the received DANE data in raw format
42                                 - disabled as '--no-print-raw'
43        --quiet                Suppress several informational messages
44   -v, --version[=arg]         output version information and exit
45   -h, --help                  display extended usage information and exit
46   -!, --more-help             extended usage information passed thru pager
47
48  Options are specified by doubled hyphens and their name or by a single
49  hyphen and the flag character.
50
51  Tool to generate and check DNS resource records for the DANE protocol.
52
```

debug option (-d)

This is the "enable debugging" option. This option takes a number argument. Specifies the debug level.

load-pubkey option

This is the "loads a public key file" option. This option takes a string argument. This can be either a file or a PKCS #11 URL

load-certificate option

This is the "loads a certificate file" option. This option takes a string argument. This can be either a file or a PKCS #11 URL

dlv option

This is the "sets a dlv file" option. This option takes a string argument. This sets a DLV file to be used for DNSSEC verification.

hash option

This is the "hash algorithm to use for signing" option. This option takes a string argument. Available hash functions are SHA1, RMD160, SHA256, SHA384, SHA512.

check option

This is the "check a host's dane tlsa entry" option. This option takes a string argument. Obtains the DANE TLSA entry from the given hostname and prints information. Note that the actual certificate of the host can be provided using –load-certificate, otherwise danetool will connect to the server to obtain it. The exit code on verification success will be zero.

check-ee option

This is the "check only the end-entity's certificate" option. Checks the end-entity's certificate only. Trust anchors or CAs are not considered.

check-ca option

This is the "check only the ca's certificate" option. Checks the trust anchor's and CA's certificate only. End-entities are not considered.

tlsa-rr option

This is the "print the dane rr data on a certificate or public key" option.

This option has some usage constraints. It:

- must appear in combination with the following options: host.

This command prints the DANE RR data needed to enable DANE on a DNS server.

host option

This is the "specify the hostname to be used in the dane rr" option. This option takes a string argument "Hostname". This command sets the hostname for the DANE RR.

proto option

This is the "the protocol set for dane data (tcp, udp etc.)" option. This option takes a string argument "Protocol". This command specifies the protocol for the service set in the DANE data.

app-proto option

This is an alias for the `starttls-proto` option, section 3.2.8.

starttls-proto option

This is the "the application protocol to be used to obtain the server's certificate (https, ftp, smtp, imap, ldap, xmpp, lmtp, pop3, nntp, sieve, postgres)" option. This option takes a string argument. When the server's certificate isn't provided danetool will connect to the server to obtain the certificate. In that case it is required to know the protocol to talk with the server prior to initiating the TLS handshake.

ca option

This is the "whether the provided certificate or public key is a certificate authority" option. Marks the DANE RR as a CA certificate if specified.

x509 option

This is the "use the hash of the x.509 certificate, rather than the public key" option. This option forces the generated record to contain the hash of the full X.509 certificate. By default only the hash of the public key is used.

local option

This is an alias for the `domain` option, section 3.2.8.

domain option

This is the "the provided certificate or public key is issued by the local domain" option.

This option has some usage constraints. It:

- can be disabled with –no-domain.

- It is enabled by default.

DANE distinguishes certificates and public keys offered via the DNSSEC to trusted and local entities. This flag indicates that this is a domain-issued certificate, meaning that there could be no CA involved.

local-dns option

This is the "use the local dns server for dnssec resolving" option.

This option has some usage constraints. It:

- can be disabled with –no-local-dns.

This option will use the local DNS server for DNSSEC. This is disabled by default due to many servers not allowing DNSSEC.

insecure option

This is the "do not verify any dnssec signature" option. Ignores any DNSSEC signature verification results.

inder option

This is the "use der format for input certificates and private keys" option.

This option has some usage constraints. It:

- can be disabled with –no-inder.

The input files will be assumed to be in DER or RAW format. Unlike options that in PEM input would allow multiple input data (e.g. multiple certificates), when reading in DER format a single data structure is read.

inraw option

This is an alias for the `inder` option, section 3.2.8.

print-raw option

This is the "print the received dane data in raw format" option.

This option has some usage constraints. It:

- can be disabled with –no-print-raw.

This option will print the received DANE data.

quiet option

This is the "suppress several informational messages" option. In that case on the exit code can be used as an indication of verification success

danetool exit status

One of the following exit values will be returned:

- 0 (EXIT_SUCCESS) Successful program execution.
- 1 (EXIT_FAILURE) The operation failed or the command syntax was not valid.

danetool See Also

certtool (1)

danetool Examples

DANE TLSA RR generation

To create a DANE TLSA resource record for a certificate (or public key) that was issued localy and may or may not be signed by a CA use the following command.

```
$ danetool --tlsa-rr --host www.example.com --load-certificate cert.pem
```

To create a DANE TLSA resource record for a CA signed certificate, which will be marked as such use the following command.

```
$ danetool --tlsa-rr --host www.example.com --load-certificate cert.pem \
   --no-domain
```

The former is useful to add in your DNS entry even if your certificate is signed by a CA. That way even users who do not trust your CA will be able to verify your certificate using DANE.

In order to create a record for the CA signer of your certificate use the following.

```
$ danetool --tlsa-rr --host www.example.com --load-certificate cert.pem \
   --ca --no-domain
```

To read a server's DANE TLSA entry, use:

```
$ danetool --check www.example.com --proto tcp --port 443
```

To verify an HTTPS server's DANE TLSA entry, use:

```
$ danetool --check www.example.com --proto tcp --port 443 --load-certificate chain.pem
```

To verify an SMTP server's DANE TLSA entry, use:

```
$ danetool --check www.example.com --proto tcp --starttls-proto=smtp --load-certificate chain.pem
```

3.3. Shared-key and anonymous authentication

In addition to certificate authentication, the TLS protocol may be used with password, shared-key and anonymous authentication methods. The rest of this chapter discusses details of these methods.

3.3.1. SRP authentication

Authentication using SRP

GnuTLS supports authentication via the Secure Remote Password or SRP protocol (see [46, 45] for a description). The SRP key exchange is an extension to the TLS protocol, and it provides an authenticated with a password key exchange. The peers can be identified using a single password, or there can be combinations where the client is authenticated using SRP and the server using a certificate.

The advantage of SRP authentication, over other proposed secure password authentication schemes, is that SRP is not susceptible to off-line dictionary attacks. Moreover, SRP does not require the server to hold the user's password. This kind of protection is similar to the one used traditionally in the UNIX "/etc/passwd" file, where the contents of this file did not cause harm to the system security if they were revealed. The SRP needs instead of the plain password something called a verifier, which is calculated using the user's password, and if stolen cannot be used to impersonate the user.

Typical conventions in SRP are a password file, called "tpasswd" that holds the SRP verifiers (encoded passwords) and another file, "tpasswd.conf", which holds the allowed SRP parameters. The included in GnuTLS helper follow those conventions. The srptool program, discussed in the next section is a tool to manipulate the SRP parameters.

The implementation in GnuTLS is based on [41]. The supported key exchange methods are shown below.

- SRP: Authentication using the SRP protocol.

- SRP_DSS: Client authentication using the SRP protocol. Server is authenticated using a certificate with DSA parameters.

- SRP_RSA: Client authentication using the SRP protocol. Server is authenticated using a certificate with RSA parameters.

---

int **gnutls_srp_verifier** (*const char* * **username**, *const char* * **password**, *const gnutls_datum_t* * **salt**, *const gnutls_datum_t* * **generator**, *const gnutls_datum_t* * **prime**, *gnutls_datum_t* * **res**)

Description: This function will create an SRP verifier, as specified in RFC2945. The prime and generator should be one of the static parameters defined in gnutls/gnutls.h or may be generated. The verifier will be allocated with **gnutls_malloc()** and will be stored in res using binary format.

Returns: On success, **GNUTLS_E_SUCCESS** (0) is returned, or an error code.

---

int **gnutls_srp_base64_encode2** (*const gnutls_datum_t* * **data**, *gnutls_datum_t* * **result**)

int **gnutls_srp_base64_decode2** (*const gnutls_datum_t* * **b64_data**, *gnutls_datum_t* * **result**)

Invoking srptool

Simple program that emulates the programs in the Stanford SRP (Secure Remote Password) libraries using GnuTLS. It is intended for use in places where you don't expect SRP authentication to be the used for system users.

In brief, to use SRP you need to create two files. These are the password file that holds the users and the verifiers associated with them and the configuration file to hold the group parameters (called tpasswd.conf).

This section was generated by **AutoGen**, using the `agtexi-cmd` template and the option descriptions for the `srptool` program. This software is released under the GNU General Public License, version 3 or later.

srptool help/usage ("--help")

This is the automatically generated usage text for srptool.

The text printed is the same whether selected with the help option ("--help") or the more-help option ("--more-help"). more-help will print the usage text by passing it through a pager program. more-help is disabled on platforms without a working fork(2) function. The PAGER environment variable is used to select the program, defaulting to "more". Both will exit with a status code of 0.

```
1  srptool - GnuTLS SRP tool
2  Usage:  srptool [ -<flag> [<val>] | --<name>[{=| }<val>] ]...
3
4     -d, --debug=num          Enable debugging
5                                - it must be in the range:
6                                   0 to 9999
7     -i, --index=num          specify the index of the group parameters in tpasswd.conf to use
8     -u, --username=str       specify a username
9     -p, --passwd=str         specify a password file
10    -s, --salt=num           specify salt size
11        --verify             just verify the password.
12    -v, --passwd-conf=str    specify a password conf file.
13        --create-conf=str    Generate a password configuration file.
14    -v, --version[=arg]      output version information and exit
15    -h, --help               display extended usage information and exit
16    -!, --more-help          extended usage information passed thru pager
17
18  Options are specified by doubled hyphens and their name or by a single
19  hyphen and the flag character.
20
21  Simple program that emulates the programs in the Stanford SRP (Secure
22  Remote Password) libraries using GnuTLS.  It is intended for use in places
23  where you don't expect SRP authentication to be the used for system users.
24
25  In brief, to use SRP you need to create two files.  These are the password
26  file that holds the users and the verifiers associated with them and the
27  configuration file to hold the group parameters (called tpasswd.conf).
28
```

debug option (-d)

This is the "enable debugging" option. This option takes a number argument. Specifies the debug level.

verify option

This is the "just verify the password." option. Verifies the password provided against the password file.

passwd-conf option (-v)

This is the "specify a password conf file." option. This option takes a string argument. Specify a filename or a PKCS #11 URL to read the CAs from.

create-conf option

This is the "generate a password configuration file." option. This option takes a string argument. This generates a password configuration file (tpasswd.conf) containing the required for TLS parameters.

srptool exit status

One of the following exit values will be returned:

- 0 (EXIT_SUCCESS) Successful program execution.

- 1 (EXIT_FAILURE) The operation failed or the command syntax was not valid.

srptool See Also

gnutls-cli-debug (1), gnutls-serv (1), srptool (1), psktool (1), certtool (1)

srptool Examples

To create "`tpasswd.conf`" which holds the g and n values for SRP protocol (generator and a large prime), run:

```
1 $ srptool --create-conf /etc/tpasswd.conf
```

This command will create "`/etc/tpasswd`" and will add user 'test' (you will also be prompted for a password). Verifiers are stored by default in the way libsrp expects.

```
1 $ srptool --passwd /etc/tpasswd --passwd-conf /etc/tpasswd.conf -u test
```

This command will check against a password. If the password matches the one in "`/etc/tpasswd`" you will get an ok.

```
1 $ srptool --passwd /etc/tpasswd --passwd\-conf /etc/tpasswd.conf --verify -u test
```

3.3.2. PSK authentication

Authentication using PSK

Authentication using Pre-shared keys is a method to authenticate using usernames and binary keys. This protocol avoids making use of public key infrastructure and expensive calculations, thus it is suitable for constraint clients.

The implementation in GnuTLS is based on [11]. The supported PSK key exchange methods are:

- PSK: Authentication using the PSK protocol.

- DHE-PSK: Authentication using the PSK protocol and Diffie-Hellman key exchange. This method offers perfect forward secrecy.

- ECDHE-PSK: Authentication using the PSK protocol and Elliptic curve Diffie-Hellman key exchange. This method offers perfect forward secrecy.

- RSA-PSK: Authentication using the PSK protocol for the client and an RSA certificate for the server.

Helper functions to generate and maintain PSK keys are also included in GnuTLS.

---

int **gnutls_key_generate** (*gnutls_datum_t* * **key**, *unsigned int* **key_size**)

int **gnutls_hex_encode** (*const gnutls_datum_t* * **data**, *char* * **result**, *size_t* * **result_size**)

int **gnutls_hex_decode** (*const gnutls_datum_t* * **hex_data**, *void* * **result**, *size_t* * **result_size**)

Invoking psktool

Program that generates random keys for use with TLS-PSK. The keys are stored in hexadecimal format in a key file.

This section was generated by **AutoGen**, using the `agtexi-cmd` template and the option descriptions for the `psktool` program. This software is released under the GNU General Public License, version 3 or later.

psktool help/usage ("--help")

This is the automatically generated usage text for psktool.

The text printed is the same whether selected with the `help` option ("--help") or the `more-help` option ("--more-help"). `more-help` will print the usage text by passing it through a pager program. `more-help` is disabled on platforms without a working `fork(2)` function. The `PAGER` environment variable is used to select the program, defaulting to "`more`". Both will exit with a status code of 0.

```
 1  psktool - GnuTLS PSK tool
 2  Usage:  psktool [ -<flag> [<val>] | --<name>[{=| }<val>] ]...
 3
 4     -d, --debug=num            Enable debugging
 5                                - it must be in the range:
 6                                  0 to 9999
 7     -s, --keysize=num          Specify the key size in bytes (default is 32-bytes or 256-bits)
 8                                - it must be in the range:
 9                                  0 to 512
10     -u, --username=str         Specify the username to use
11     -p, --pskfile=str          Specify a pre-shared key file
12     -v, --version[=arg]        output version information and exit
13     -h, --help                 display extended usage information and exit
14     -!, --more-help            extended usage information passed thru pager
15
16  Options are specified by doubled hyphens and their name or by a single
17  hyphen and the flag character.
18
19  Program that generates random keys for use with TLS-PSK.  The keys are
20  stored in hexadecimal format in a key file.
21
```

debug option (-d)

This is the "enable debugging" option. This option takes a number argument. Specifies the debug level.

pskfile option (-p)

This is the "specify a pre-shared key file" option. This option takes a string argument. This option will specify the pre-shared key file to store the generated keys.

passwd option

This is an alias for the `pskfile` option, section 3.3.2.

psktool exit status

One of the following exit values will be returned:

- 0 (EXIT_SUCCESS) Successful program execution.

- 1 (EXIT_FAILURE) The operation failed or the command syntax was not valid.

psktool See Also

gnutls-cli-debug (1), gnutls-serv (1), srptool (1), certtool (1)

psktool Examples

To add a user 'psk_identity' in "`keys.psk`" for use with GnuTLS run:

```
$ ./psktool -u psk_identity -p keys.psk
Generating a random key for user 'psk_identity'
Key stored to keys.psk
$ cat keys.psk
psk_identity:88f3824b3e5659f52d00e959bacab954b6540344
$
```

This command will create "`keys.psk`" if it does not exist and will add user 'psk_identity'.

3.3.3. Anonymous authentication

The anonymous key exchange offers encryption without any indication of the peer's identity. This kind of authentication is vulnerable to a man in the middle attack, but can be used even if there is no prior communication or shared trusted parties with the peer. It is useful to establish a session over which certificate authentication will occur in order to hide the indentities of the participants from passive eavesdroppers.

Unless in the above case, it is not recommended to use anonymous authentication. In the cases where there is no prior communication with the peers, an alternative with better properties, such as key continuity, is trust on first use (see section 3.1.3).

The available key exchange algorithms for anonymous authentication are shown below, but note that few public servers support them, and they have to be explicitly enabled.

- ANON_DH: This algorithm exchanges Diffie-Hellman parameters.

- ANON_ECDH: This algorithm exchanges elliptic curve Diffie-Hellman parameters. It is more efficient than ANON_DH on equivalent security levels.

3.4. Selecting an appropriate authentication method

This section provides some guidance on how to use the available authentication methods in GnuTLS in various scenarios.

3.4.1. Two peers with an out-of-band channel

Let's consider two peers who need to communicate over an untrusted channel (the Internet), but have an out-of-band channel available. The latter channel is considered safe from eavesdropping and message modification and thus can be used for an initial bootstrapping of the protocol. The options available are:

- Pre-shared keys (see subsection 3.3.2). The server and a client communicate a shared randomly generated key over the trusted channel and use it to negotiate further sessions over the untrusted channel.

- Passwords (see subsection 3.3.1). The client communicates to the server its username and password of choice and uses it to negotiate further sessions over the untrusted channel.

- Public keys (see section 3.1). The client and the server exchange their public keys (or fingerprints of them) over the trusted channel. On future sessions over the untrusted channel they verify the key being the same (similar to section 3.1.3).

Provided that the out-of-band channel is trusted all of the above provide a similar level of protection. An out-of-band channel may be the initial bootstrapping of a user's PC in a corporate environment, in-person communication, communication over an alternative network (e.g. the phone network), etc.

3.4.2. Two peers without an out-of-band channel

When an out-of-band channel is not available a peer cannot be reliably authenticated. What can be done, however, is to allow some form of registration of users connecting for the first time and ensure that their keys remain the same after that initial connection. This is termed key continuity or trust on first use (TOFU).

The available option is to use public key authentication (see section 3.1). The client and the server store each other's public keys (or fingerprints of them) and associate them with their identity. On future sessions over the untrusted channel they verify the keys being the same (see section 3.1.3).

To mitigate the uncertainty of the information exchanged in the first connection other channels over the Internet may be used, e.g., DNSSEC (see section 3.1.3).

3.4.3. Two peers and a trusted third party

When a trusted third party is available (or a certificate authority) the most suitable option is to use certificate authentication (see section 3.1). The client and the server obtain certificates that associate their identity and public keys using a digital signature by the trusted party and use them to on the subsequent communications with each other. Each party verifies the peer's certificate using the trusted third party's signature. The parameters of the third party's signature are present in its certificate which must be available to all communicating parties.

While the above is the typical authentication method for servers in the Internet by using the commercial CAs, the users that act as clients in the protocol rarely possess such certificates. In that case a hybrid method can be used where the server is authenticated by the client using the commercial CAs and the client is authenticated based on some information the client provided over the initial server-authenticated channel. The available options are:

- Passwords (see subsection 3.3.1). The client communicates to the server its username and password of choice on the initial server-authenticated connection and uses it to negotiate further sessions. This is possible because the SRP protocol allows for the server to be authenticated using a certificate and the client using the password.

- Public keys (see section 3.1). The client sends its public key to the server (or a fingerprint of it) over the initial server-authenticated connection. On future sessions the client verifies the server using the third party certificate and the server verifies that the client's public key remained the same (see section 3.1.3).

enum **gnutls_certificate_status_t**:

GNUTLS_CERT_INVALID	The certificate is not signed by one of the known authorities or the signature is invalid (deprecated by the flags **GNUTLS_CERT_SIGNATURE_FAILURE** and **GNUTLS_CERT_SIGNER_NOT_FOUND**).
GNUTLS_CERT_REVOKED	Certificate is revoked by its authority. In X.509 this will be set only if CRLs are checked.
GNUTLS_CERT_SIGNER_NOT_FOUND	The certificate's issuer is not known. This is the case if the issuer is not included in the trusted certificate list.
GNUTLS_CERT_SIGNER_NOT_CA	The certificate's signer was not a CA. This may happen if this was a version 1 certificate, which is common with some CAs, or a version 3 certificate without the basic constrains extension.
GNUTLS_CERT_INSECURE_-ALGORITHM	The certificate was signed using an insecure algorithm such as MD2 or MD5. These algorithms have been broken and should not be trusted.
GNUTLS_CERT_NOT_ACTIVATED	The certificate is not yet activated.
GNUTLS_CERT_EXPIRED	The certificate has expired.
GNUTLS_CERT_SIGNATURE_FAILURE	The signature verification failed.
GNUTLS_CERT_REVOCATION_DATA_-SUPERSEDED	The revocation data are old and have been superseded.
GNUTLS_CERT_UNEXPECTED_-OWNER	The owner is not the expected one.
GNUTLS_CERT_REVOCATION_DATA_-ISSUED_IN_FUTURE	The revocation data have a future issue date.
GNUTLS_CERT_SIGNER_-CONSTRAINTS_FAILURE	The certificate's signer constraints were violated.
GNUTLS_CERT_MISMATCH	The certificate presented isn't the expected one (TOFU)
GNUTLS_CERT_PURPOSE_MISMATCH	The certificate or an intermediate does not match the intended purpose (extended key usage).
GNUTLS_CERT_MISSING_OCSP_-STATUS	The certificate requires the server to send the certificate status, but no status was received.
GNUTLS_CERT_INVALID_OCSP_-STATUS	The received OCSP status response is invalid.
GNUTLS_CERT_UNKNOWN_CRIT_-EXTENSIONS	The certificate has extensions marked as critical which are not supported.

Table 3.4.: The `gnutls_certificate_status_t` enumeration.

enum **gnutls_certificate_verify_flags**:

GNUTLS_VERIFY_DISABLE_CA_SIGN	If set a signer does not have to be a certificate authority. This flag should normally be disabled, unless you know what this means.
GNUTLS_VERIFY_DO_NOT_ALLOW_-IP_MATCHES	When verifying a hostname prevent textual IP addresses from matching IP addresses in the certificate. Treat the input only as a DNS name.
GNUTLS_VERIFY_DO_NOT_ALLOW_-SAME	If a certificate is not signed by anyone trusted but exists in the trusted CA list do not treat it as trusted.
GNUTLS_VERIFY_ALLOW_ANY_X509_-V1_CA_CRT	Allow CA certificates that have version 1 (both root and intermediate). This might be dangerous since those haven't the basicConstraints extension.
GNUTLS_VERIFY_ALLOW_SIGN_RSA_-MD2	Allow certificates to be signed using the broken MD2 algorithm.
GNUTLS_VERIFY_ALLOW_SIGN_RSA_-MD5	Allow certificates to be signed using the broken MD5 algorithm.
GNUTLS_VERIFY_DISABLE_TIME_-CHECKS	Disable checking of activation and expiration validity periods of certificate chains. Don't set this unless you understand the security implications.
GNUTLS_VERIFY_DISABLE_-TRUSTED_TIME_CHECKS	If set a signer in the trusted list is never checked for expiration or activation.
GNUTLS_VERIFY_DO_NOT_ALLOW_-X509_V1_CA_CRT	Do not allow trusted CA certificates that have version 1. This option is to be used to deprecate all certificates of version 1.
GNUTLS_VERIFY_DISABLE_CRL_-CHECKS	Disable checking for validity using certificate revocation lists or the available OCSP data.
GNUTLS_VERIFY_ALLOW_-UNSORTED_CHAIN	A certificate chain is tolerated if unsorted (the case with many TLS servers out there). This is the default since GnuTLS 3.1.4.
GNUTLS_VERIFY_DO_NOT_ALLOW_-UNSORTED_CHAIN	Do not tolerate an unsorted certificate chain.
GNUTLS_VERIFY_DO_NOT_ALLOW_-WILDCARDS	When including a hostname check in the verification, do not consider any wildcards.
GNUTLS_VERIFY_USE_TLS1_RSA	This indicates that a (raw) RSA signature is provided as in the TLS 1.0 protocol. Not all functions accept this flag.
GNUTLS_VERIFY_IGNORE_-UNKNOWN_CRIT_EXTENSIONS	This signals the verification process, not to fail on unknown critical extensions.
GNUTLS_VERIFY_ALLOW_SIGN_-WITH_SHA1	Allow certificates to be signed using the broken SHA1 hash algorithm.

Table 3.5.: The `gnutls_certificate_verify_flags` enumeration.

Purpose	OID	Description
GNUTLS_KP_TLS_WWW_SERVER	1.3.6.1.5.5.7.3.1	The certificate is to be used for TLS WWW authentication. When in a CA certificate, it indicates that the CA is allowed to sign certificates for TLS WWW authentication.
GNUTLS_KP_TLS_WWW_CLIENT	1.3.6.1.5.5.7.3.2	The certificate is to be used for TLS WWW client authentication. When in a CA certificate, it indicates that the CA is allowed to sign certificates for TLS WWW client authentication.
GNUTLS_KP_CODE_SIGNING	1.3.6.1.5.5.7.3.3	The certificate is to be used for code signing. When in a CA certificate, it indicates that the CA is allowed to sign certificates for code signing.
GNUTLS_KP_EMAIL_PROTECTION	1.3.6.1.5.5.7.3.4	The certificate is to be used for email protection. When in a CA certificate, it indicates that the CA is allowed to sign certificates for email users.
GNUTLS_KP_OCSP_SIGNING	1.3.6.1.5.5.7.3.9	The certificate is to be used for signing OCSP responses. When in a CA certificate, it indicates that the CA is allowed to sign certificates which sign OCSP reponses.
GNUTLS_KP_ANY	2.5.29.37.0	The certificate is to be used for any purpose. When in a CA certificate, it indicates that the CA is allowed to sign any kind of certificates.

Table 3.6.: Key purpose object identifiers.

Field	Description
version	The field that indicates the version of the CRL structure.
signature	A signature by the issuing authority.
issuer	Holds the issuer's distinguished name.
thisUpdate	The issuing time of the revocation list.
nextUpdate	The issuing time of the revocation list that will update that one.
revokedCertificates	List of revoked certificates serial numbers.
extensions	Optional CRL structure extensions.

Table 3.7.: Certificate revocation list fields.

Field	Description
version	The OCSP response version number (typically 1).
responder ID	An identifier of the responder (DN name or a hash of its key).
issue time	The time the response was generated.
thisUpdate	The issuing time of the revocation information.
nextUpdate	The issuing time of the revocation information that will update that one.
	Revoked certificates
certificate status	The status of the certificate.
certificate serial	The certificate's serial number.
revocationTime	The time the certificate was revoked.
revocationReason	The reason the certificate was revoked.

Table 3.8.: The most important OCSP response fields.

enum **gnutls_x509_crl_reason_t**:

GNUTLS_X509_CRLREASON_- **UNSPECIFIED**	Unspecified reason.
GNUTLS_X509_CRLREASON_- **KEYCOMPROMISE**	Private key compromised.
GNUTLS_X509_CRLREASON_- **CACOMPROMISE**	CA compromised.
GNUTLS_X509_CRLREASON_- **AFFILIATIONCHANGED**	Affiliation has changed.
GNUTLS_X509_CRLREASON_- **SUPERSEDED**	Certificate superseded.
GNUTLS_X509_CRLREASON_- **CESSATIONOFOPERATION**	Operation has ceased.
GNUTLS_X509_CRLREASON_- **CERTIFICATEHOLD**	Certificate is on hold.
GNUTLS_X509_CRLREASON_- **REMOVEFROMCRL**	Will be removed from delta CRL.
GNUTLS_X509_CRLREASON_- **PRIVILEGEWITHDRAWN**	Privilege withdrawn.
GNUTLS_X509_CRLREASON_- **AACOMPROMISE**	AA compromised.

Table 3.9.: The revocation reasons

enum **gnutls_pkcs_encrypt_flags_t**:	
GNUTLS_PKCS_PLAIN	Unencrypted private key.
GNUTLS_PKCS_PKCS12_3DES	PKCS-12 3DES.
GNUTLS_PKCS_PKCS12_ARCFOUR	PKCS-12 ARCFOUR.
GNUTLS_PKCS_PKCS12_RC2_40	PKCS-12 RC2-40.
GNUTLS_PKCS_PBES2_3DES	PBES2 3DES.
GNUTLS_PKCS_PBES2_AES_128	PBES2 AES-128.
GNUTLS_PKCS_PBES2_AES_192	PBES2 AES-192.
GNUTLS_PKCS_PBES2_AES_256	PBES2 AES-256.
GNUTLS_PKCS_NULL_PASSWORD	Some schemas distinguish between an empty and a NULL password.
GNUTLS_PKCS_PBES2_DES	PBES2 single DES.
GNUTLS_PKCS_PBES1_DES_MD5	-- undescribed --

Table 3.10.: Encryption flags

Abstract key types and Hardware security modules

In several cases storing the long term cryptographic keys in a hard disk or even in memory poses a significant risk. Once the system they are stored is compromised the keys must be replaced as the secrecy of future sessions is no longer guaranteed. Moreover, past sessions that were not protected by a perfect forward secrecy offering ciphersuite are also to be assumed compromised.

If such threats need to be addressed, then it may be wise storing the keys in a security module such as a smart card, an HSM or the TPM chip. Those modules ensure the protection of the cryptographic keys by only allowing operations on them and preventing their extraction. The purpose of the abstract key API is to provide an API that will allow the handle of keys in memory and files, as well as keys stored in such modules.

In GnuTLS the approach is to handle all keys transparently by the high level API, e.g., the API that loads a key or certificate from a file. The high-level API will accept URIs in addition to files that specify keys on an HSM or in TPM, and a callback function will be used to obtain any required keys. The URI format is defined in [30].

More information on the API is provided in the next sections. Examples of a URI of a certificate stored in an HSM, as well as a key stored in the TPM chip are shown below. To discover the URIs of the objects the p11tool (see subsection 4.3.8).

```
1  pkcs11:token=Nikos;serial=307521161601031;model=PKCS%2315; \
2  manufacturer=EnterSafe;object=test1;type=cert
3
```

4.1. Abstract key types

Since there are many forms of a public or private keys supported by GnuTLS such as X.509, PKCS #11 or TPM it is desirable to allow common operations on them. For these reasons the abstract gnutls_privkey_t and gnutls_pubkey_t were introduced in gnutls/abstract.h header. Those types are initialized using a specific type of key and then can be used to perform operations in an abstract way. For example in order to sign an X.509 certificate with a key that resides in a token the following steps can be used.

```
1   #inlude <gnutls/abstract.h>
2
3   void sign_cert( gnutls_x509_crt_t to_be_signed)
4   {
5   gnutls_x509_crt_t ca_cert;
6   gnutls_privkey_t abs_key;
7
8     /* initialize the abstract key */
9     gnutls_privkey_init(&abs_key);
10
11    /* keys stored in tokens are identified by URLs */
12    gnutls_privkey_import_url(abs_key, key_url);
13
14    gnutls_x509_crt_init(&ca_cert);
15    gnutls_x509_crt_import_url(&ca_cert, cert_url);
16
17    /* sign the certificate to be signed */
18    gnutls_x509_crt_privkey_sign(to_be_signed, ca_cert, abs_key,
19                          GNUTLS_DIG_SHA256, 0);
20  }
```

4.1.1. Public keys

An abstract **gnutls_pubkey_t** can be initialized using the functions below. It can be imported through an existing structure like **gnutls_x509_crt_t**, or through an ASN.1 encoding of the X.509 **SubjectPublicKeyInfo** sequence.

---

int **gnutls_pubkey_import_x509** (*gnutls_pubkey_t* **key**, *gnutls_x509_crt_t* **crt**, *unsigned int* **flags**)

int **gnutls_pubkey_import_pkcs11** (*gnutls_pubkey_t* **key**, *gnutls_pkcs11_obj_t* **obj**, *unsigned int* **flags**)

---

int **gnutls_pubkey_import_url** (*gnutls_pubkey_t* **key**, *const char ** **url**, *unsigned int* **flags**)

int **gnutls_pubkey_import_privkey** (*gnutls_pubkey_t* **key**, *gnutls_privkey_t* **pkey**, *unsigned int* **usage**, *unsigned int* **flags**)

int **gnutls_pubkey_import** (*gnutls_pubkey_t* **key**, *const gnutls_datum_t ** **data**, *gnutls_x509_crt_fmt_t* **format**)

int **gnutls_pubkey_export** (*gnutls_pubkey_t* **key**, *gnutls_x509_crt_fmt_t* **format**, *void ** **output_data**, *size_t ** **output_data_size**)

---

int **gnutls_pubkey_export2** (*gnutls_pubkey_t* **key**, *gnutls_x509_crt_fmt_t* **format**, *gnutls_datum_t* * **out**)

Description: This function will export the public key to DER or PEM format. The contents of the exported data is the SubjectPublicKeyInfo X.509 structure. The output buffer will be allocated using gnutls_malloc(). If the structure is PEM encoded, it will have a header of "BEGIN CERTIFICATE".

Returns: In case of failure a negative error code will be returned, and 0 on success.

Other helper functions that allow directly importing from raw X.509 structures are shown below.

---

int **gnutls_pubkey_import_x509_raw** (*gnutls_pubkey_t* **pkey**, *const gnutls_datum_t* * **data**, *gnutls_x509_crt_fmt_t* **format**, *unsigned int* **flags**)

An important function is `gnutls_pubkey_import_url` which will import public keys from URLs that identify objects stored in tokens (see section 4.3 and section 4.4). A function to check for a supported by GnuTLS URL is `gnutls_url_is_supported`.

---

unsigned **gnutls_url_is_supported** (*const char* * **url**)

Description: Check whether the provided **url** is supported. Depending on the system libraries GnuTLS may support pkcs11, tpmkey or other URLs.

Returns: return non-zero if the given URL is supported, and zero if it is not known.

Additional functions are available that will return information over a public key, such as a unique key ID, as well as a function that given a public key fingerprint would provide a memorable sketch.

Note that `gnutls_pubkey_get_key_id` calculates a SHA1 digest of the public key as a DER-formatted, subjectPublicKeyInfo object. Other implementations use different approaches, e.g., some use the "common method" described in section 4.2.1.2 of [8] which calculates a digest on a part of the subjectPublicKeyInfo object.

---

int **gnutls_pubkey_get_pk_algorithm** (*gnutls_pubkey_t* **key**, *unsigned int* * **bits**)

int **gnutls_pubkey_get_preferred_hash_algorithm** (*gnutls_pubkey_t* **key**, *gnutls_digest_algorithm_t* * **hash**, *unsigned int* * **mand**)

int **gnutls_pubkey_get_key_id** (*gnutls_pubkey_t* **key**, *unsigned int* **flags**, *unsigned char* * **output_data**, *size_t* * **output_data_size**)

int **gnutls_random_art** (*gnutls_random_art_t* **type**, *const char* * **key_type**, *unsigned int* **key_size**, *void* * **fpr**, *size_t* **fpr_size**, *gnutls_datum_t* * **art**)

To export the key-specific parameters, or obtain a unique key ID the following functions are provided.

---

int **gnutls_pubkey_export_rsa_raw2** (*gnutls_pubkey_t* **key**, *gnutls_datum_t* * **m**, *gnutls_datum_t* * **e**, *unsigned* **flags**)

int **gnutls_pubkey_export_dsa_raw2** (*gnutls_pubkey_t* **key**, *gnutls_datum_t* * **p**, *gnutls_datum_t* * **q**, *gnutls_datum_t* * **g**, *gnutls_datum_t* * **y**, *unsigned* **flags**)

int **gnutls_pubkey_export_ecc_raw2** (*gnutls_pubkey_t* **key**, *gnutls_ecc_curve_t* * **curve**, *gnutls_datum_t* * **x**, *gnutls_datum_t* * **y**, *unsigned int* **flags**)

int **gnutls_pubkey_export_ecc_x962** (*gnutls_pubkey_t* **key**, *gnutls_datum_t* * **parameters**, *gnutls_datum_t* * **ecpoint**)

4.1.2. Private keys

An abstract `gnutls_privkey_t` can be initialized using the functions below. It can be imported through an existing structure like `gnutls_x509_privkey_t`, but unlike public keys it cannot be exported. That is to allow abstraction over keys stored in hardware that makes available only operations.

---

int **gnutls_privkey_import_x509** (*gnutls_privkey_t* **pkey**, *gnutls_x509_privkey_t* **key**, *unsigned int* **flags**)

int **gnutls_privkey_import_pkcs11** (*gnutls_privkey_t* **pkey**, *gnutls_pkcs11_privkey_t* **key**, *unsigned int* **flags**)

Other helper functions that allow directly importing from raw X.509 structures are shown below. Again, as with public keys, private keys can be imported from a hardware module using URLs.

---

int **gnutls_privkey_import_url** (*gnutls_privkey_t* **key**, *const char ** **url**, *unsigned int* **flags**)

Description: This function will import a PKCS11 or TPM URL as a private key. The supported URL types can be checked using gnutls_url_is_supported().

Returns: On success, GNUTLS_E_SUCCESS (0) is returned, otherwise a negative error value.

---

int **gnutls_privkey_import_x509_raw** (*gnutls_privkey_t* **pkey**, *const gnutls_datum_t ** **data**, *gnutls_x509_crt_fmt_t* **format**, *const char ** **password**, *unsigned int* **flags**)

int **gnutls_privkey_get_pk_algorithm** (*gnutls_privkey_t* **key**, *unsigned int ** **bits**)

gnutls_privkey_type_t **gnutls_privkey_get_type** (*gnutls_privkey_t* **key**)

int **gnutls_privkey_status** (*gnutls_privkey_t* **key**)

In order to support cryptographic operations using an external API, the following function is provided. This allows for a simple extensibility API without resorting to PKCS #11.

On the private keys where exporting of parameters is possible (i.e., software keys), the following functions are also available.

---

int **gnutls_privkey_export_rsa_raw2** (*gnutls_privkey_t* **key**, *gnutls_datum_t* * **m**, *gnutls_datum_t* * **e**, *gnutls_datum_t* * **d**, *gnutls_datum_t* * **p**, *gnutls_datum_t* * **q**, *gnutls_datum_t ** **u**, *gnutls_datum_t ** **e1**, *gnutls_datum_t ** **e2**, *unsigned int* **flags**)

int **gnutls_privkey_export_dsa_raw2** (*gnutls_privkey_t* **key**, *gnutls_datum_t* * **p**, *gnutls_datum_t* * **q**, *gnutls_datum_t* * **g**, *gnutls_datum_t* * **y**, *gnutls_datum_t* * **x**, *unsigned int* **flags**)

int **gnutls_privkey_export_ecc_raw2** (*gnutls_privkey_t* **key**, *gnutls_ecc_curve_t* * **curve**, *gnutls_datum_t* * **x**, *gnutls_datum_t* * **y**, *gnutls_datum_t* * **k**, *unsigned int* **flags**)

---

int **gnutls_privkey_import_ext3** (*gnutls_privkey_t* **pkey**, *void*   * **userdata**, *gnutls_privkey_sign_func* **sign_fn**, *gnutls_privkey_decrypt_func* **decrypt_fn**, *gnutls_privkey_deinit_func* **deinit_fn**, *gnutls_privkey_info_func* **info_fn**, *unsigned*   *int* **flags**)

Description: This function will associate the given callbacks with the *gnutls_privkey_t* type. At least one of the two callbacks must be non-null. If a deinitialization function is provided then flags is assumed to contain **GNUTLS_PRIVKEY_IMPORT_AUTO_-RELEASE**. Note that the signing function is supposed to "raw" sign data, i.e., without any hashing or preprocessing. In case of RSA the DigestInfo will be provided, and the signing function is expected to do the PKCS #1 1.5 padding and the exponentiation. The info_fn must provide information on the algorithms supported by this private key, and should support the flags **GNUTLS_PRIVKEY_INFO_PK_ALGO** and **GNUTLS_PRIVKEY_-INFO_SIGN_ALGO**. It must return -1 on unknown flags.

Returns: On success, **GNUTLS_E_SUCCESS** (0) is returned, otherwise a negative error value.

4.1.3. Operations

The abstract key types can be used to access signing and signature verification operations with the underlying keys.

---

int **gnutls_pubkey_verify_data2** (*gnutls_pubkey_t* **pubkey**, *gnutls_sign_algorithm_t* **algo**, *unsigned*   *int* **flags**, *const*   *gnutls_datum_t*   * **data**, *const*   *gnutls_datum_t*   * **signature**)

Description: This function will verify the given signed data, using the parameters from the certificate.

Returns: In case of a verification failure **GNUTLS_E_PK_SIG_VERIFY_FAILED** is returned, and zero or positive code on success. For known to be insecure signatures this function will return **GNUTLS_E_INSUFFICIENT_SECURITY** unless the flag **GNUTLS_-VERIFY_ALLOW_BROKEN** is specified.

Signing existing structures, such as certificates, CRLs, or certificate requests, as well as associating public keys with structures is also possible using the key abstractions.

int **gnutls_pubkey_verify_hash2** (*gnutls_pubkey_t* **key**, *gnutls_sign_algorithm_t* **algo**, *unsigned int* **flags**, *const gnutls_datum_t* * **hash**, *const gnutls_datum_t* * **signature**)

Description: This function will verify the given signed digest, using the parameters from the public key. Note that unlike gnutls_privkey_sign_hash(), this function accepts a signature algorithm instead of a digest algorithm. You can use gnutls_pk_to_sign() to get the appropriate value.

Returns: In case of a verification failure **GNUTLS_E_PK_SIG_VERIFY_FAILED** is returned, and zero or positive code on success. For known to be insecure signatures this function will return **GNUTLS_E_INSUFFICIENT_SECURITY** unless the flag **GNUTLS_VERIFY_ALLOW_BROKEN** is specified.

---

int **gnutls_pubkey_encrypt_data** (*gnutls_pubkey_t* **key**, *unsigned int* **flags**, *const gnutls_datum_t* * **plaintext**, *gnutls_datum_t* * **ciphertext**)

Description: This function will encrypt the given data, using the public key. On success the **ciphertext** will be allocated using gnutls_malloc().

Returns: On success, **GNUTLS_E_SUCCESS** (0) is returned, otherwise a negative error value.

---

int **gnutls_privkey_sign_data** (*gnutls_privkey_t* **signer**, *gnutls_digest_algorithm_t* **hash**, *unsigned int* **flags**, *const gnutls_datum_t* * **data**, *gnutls_datum_t* * **signature**)

Description: This function will sign the given data using a signature algorithm supported by the private key. Signature algorithms are always used together with a hash functions. Different hash functions may be used for the RSA algorithm, but only the SHA family for the DSA keys. You may use gnutls_pubkey_get_preferred_hash_algorithm() to determine the hash algorithm.

Returns: On success, **GNUTLS_E_SUCCESS** (0) is returned, otherwise a negative error value.

---

int **gnutls_privkey_sign_hash** (*gnutls_privkey_t* **signer**, *gnutls_digest_algorithm_t* **hash_algo**, *unsigned int* **flags**, *const gnutls_datum_t* * **hash_data**, *gnutls_datum_t* * **signature**)

Description: This function will sign the given hashed data using a signature algorithm supported by the private key. Signature algorithms are always used together with a hash functions. Different hash functions may be used for the RSA algorithm, but only SHA-XXX for the DSA keys. You may use gnutls_pubkey_get_preferred_hash_algorithm() to determine the hash algorithm. The flags may be **GNUTLS_PRIVKEY_SIGN_FLAG_TLS1_RSA** or **GNUTLS_PRIVKEY_SIGN_FLAG_RSA_PSS**. In the former case this function will ignore hash_algo and perform a raw PKCS1 signature, and in the latter an RSA-PSS signature will be generated. Note that, not all algorithm support signing already hashed data. When signing with Ed25519, gnutls_privkey_sign_data() should be used.

Returns: On success, **GNUTLS_E_SUCCESS** (0) is returned, otherwise a negative error value.

---

int **gnutls_privkey_decrypt_data** (*gnutls_privkey_t* **key**, *unsigned int* **flags**, *const gnutls_datum_t* * **ciphertext**, *gnutls_datum_t* * **plaintext**)

Description: This function will decrypt the given data using the algorithm supported by the private key.

Returns: On success, **GNUTLS_E_SUCCESS** (0) is returned, otherwise a negative error value.

---

int **gnutls_x509_crq_set_pubkey** (*gnutls_x509_crq_t* **crq**, *gnutls_pubkey_t* **key**)

Description: This function will set the public parameters from the given public key to the request. The key can be deallocated after that.

Returns: On success, **GNUTLS_E_SUCCESS** (0) is returned, otherwise a negative error value.

---

int **gnutls_x509_crt_set_pubkey** (*gnutls_x509_crt_t* **crt**, *gnutls_pubkey_t* **key**)

Description: `This function will set the public parameters from the given public key to the certificate. The key can be deallocated after that.`

Returns: `On success, GNUTLS_E_SUCCESS (0) is returned, otherwise a negative error value.`

---

int **gnutls_x509_crt_privkey_sign** (*gnutls_x509_crt_t* **crt**, *gnutls_x509_crt_t* **issuer**, *gnutls_privkey_t* **issuer_key**, *gnutls_digest_algorithm_t* **dig**, *unsigned int* **flags**)

int **gnutls_x509_crl_privkey_sign** (*gnutls_x509_crl_t* **crl**, *gnutls_x509_crt_t* **issuer**, *gnutls_privkey_t* **issuer_key**, *gnutls_digest_algorithm_t* **dig**, *unsigned int* **flags**)

int **gnutls_x509_crq_privkey_sign** (*gnutls_x509_crq_t* **crq**, *gnutls_privkey_t* **key**, *gnutls_digest_algorithm_t* **dig**, *unsigned int* **flags**)

4.2. System and application-specific keys

4.2.1. System-specific keys

In several systems there are keystores which allow to read, store and use certificates and private keys. For these systems GnuTLS provides the system-key API in `gnutls/system-keys.h`. That API provides the ability to iterate through all stored keys, add and delete keys as well as use these keys using a URL which starts with "system:". The format of the URLs is system-specific. The `systemkey` tool is also provided to assist in listing keys and debugging.

The systems supported via this API are the following.

- Windows Cryptography API (CNG)

---

void **gnutls_system_key_iter_deinit** (*gnutls_system_key_iter_t* **iter**)

int **gnutls_system_key_add_x509** (*gnutls_x509_crt_t* **crt**, *gnutls_x509_privkey_t* **privkey**, *const char ** **label**, *char *** **cert_url**, *char *** **key_url**)

int **gnutls_system_key_delete** (*const char ** **cert_url**, *const char ** **key_url**)

---

int **gnutls_system_key_iter_get_info** (*gnutls_system_key_iter_t* * **iter**, *unsigned* **cert_type**, *char* ** **cert_url**, *char* ** **key_url**, *char* ** **label**, *gnutls_datum_t* * **der**, *unsigned int* **flags**)

Description: This function will return on each call a certificate and key pair URLs, as well as a label associated with them, and the DER-encoded certificate. When the iteration is complete it will return **GNUTLS_E_REQUESTED_DATA_NOT_AVAILABLE**. Typically cert_type should be **GNUTLS_CRT_X**509. All values set are allocated and must be cleared using gnutls_free(),

Returns: On success, **GNUTLS_E_SUCCESS** (0) is returned, otherwise a negative error value.

4.2.2. Application-specific keys

For systems where GnuTLS doesn't provide a system specific store, it may often be desirable to define a custom class of keys that are identified via URLs and available to GnuTLS calls such as **gnutls_certificate_set_x509_key_file2**. Such keys can be registered using the API in **gnutls/urls.h**. The function which registers such keys is **gnutls_register_custom_url**.

int **gnutls_register_custom_url** (*const gnutls_custom_url_st* * **st**)

Description: Register a custom URL. This will affect the following functions: gnutls_-url_is_supported(), gnutls_privkey_import_url(), gnutls_pubkey_import_url, gnutls_x509_crt_-import_url() and all functions that depend on them, e.g., gnutls_certificate_set_x509_-key_file2(). The provided structure and callback functions must be valid throughout the lifetime of the process. The registration of an existing URL type will fail with **GNUTLS_E_INVALID_REQUEST**. Since GnuTLS 3.5.0 this function can be used to override the builtin URLs. This function is not thread safe.

Returns: returns zero if the given structure was imported or a negative value otherwise.

The input to this function are three callback functions as well as the prefix of the URL, (e.g., "mypkcs11:") and the length of the prefix. The types of the callbacks are shown below, and are expected to use the exported gnutls functions to import the keys and certificates. E.g., a typical **import_key** callback should use **gnutls_privkey_import_ext3**.

```
typedef int (*gnutls_privkey_import_url_func)(gnutls_privkey_t pkey,
                                              const char *url,
                                              unsigned flags);

typedef int (*gnutls_x509_crt_import_url_func)(gnutls_x509_crt_t pkey,
```

```
 6                                               const char *url,
 7                                               unsigned flags);
 8
 9  /* The following callbacks are optional */
10
11  /* This is to enable gnutls_pubkey_import_url() */
12  typedef int (*gnutls_pubkey_import_url_func)(gnutls_pubkey_t pkey,
13                                           const char *url, unsigned flags);
14
15  /* This is to allow constructing a certificate chain. It will be provided
16   * the initial certificate URL and the certificate to find its issuer, and must
17   * return zero and the DER encoding of the issuer's certificate. If not available,
18   * it should return GNUTLS_E_REQUESTED_DATA_NOT_AVAILABLE. */
19  typedef int (*gnutls_get_raw_issuer_func)(const char *url, gnutls_x509_crt_t crt,
20                                      gnutls_datum_t *issuer_der, unsigned flags);
21
22  typedef struct custom_url_st {
23          const char *name;
24          unsigned name_size;
25          gnutls_privkey_import_url_func import_key;
26          gnutls_x509_crt_import_url_func import_crt;
27          gnutls_pubkey_import_url_func import_pubkey;
28          gnutls_get_raw_issuer_func get_issuer;
29  } gnutls_custom_url_st;
```

4.3. Smart cards and HSMs

In this section we present the smart-card and hardware security module (HSM) support in GnuTLS using PKCS #11 [2]. Hardware security modules and smart cards provide a way to store private keys and perform operations on them without exposing them. This decouples cryptographic keys from the applications that use them and provide an additional security layer against cryptographic key extraction. Since this can also be achieved in software components such as in Gnome keyring, we will use the term security module to describe any cryptographic key separation subsystem.

PKCS #11 is plugin API allowing applications to access cryptographic operations on a security module, as well as to objects residing on it. PKCS #11 modules exist for hardware tokens such as smart cards[1], cryptographic tokens, as well as for software modules like Gnome Keyring. The objects residing on a security module may be certificates, public keys, private keys or secret keys. Of those certificates and public/private key pairs can be used with GnuTLS. PKCS #11's main advantage is that it allows operations on private key objects such as decryption and signing without exposing the key. In GnuTLS the PKCS #11 functionality is available in `gnutls/pkcs11.h`.

---

[1]For example, OpenSC-supported cards.

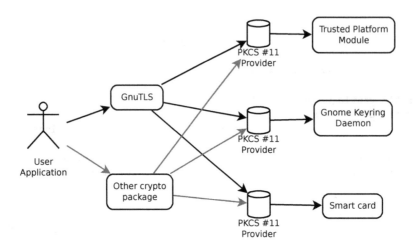

Figure 4.1.: PKCS #11 module usage.

4.3.1. Initialization

To allow all GnuTLS applications to transparently access smart cards and tokens, PKCS #11 is automatically initialized during the first call of a PKCS #11 related function, in a thread safe way. The default initialization process, utilizes p11-kit configuration, and loads any appropriate PKCS #11 modules. The p11-kit configuration files[2] are typically stored in `/etc/pkcs11/modules/`. For example a file that will instruct GnuTLS to load the OpenSC module, could be named `/etc/pkcs11/modules/opensc.module` and contain the following:

```
1  module: /usr/lib/opensc-pkcs11.so
```

If you use these configuration files, then there is no need for other initialization in GnuTLS, except for the PIN and token callbacks (see next section). In several cases, however, it is desirable to limit badly behaving modules (e.g., modules that add an unacceptable delay on initialization) to single applications. That can be done using the "enable-in:" option followed by the base name of applications that this module should be used.

It is also possible to manually initialize or even disable the PKCS #11 subsystem if the default settings are not desirable or not available (see subsection 4.3.2 for more information).

Note that, PKCS #11 modules behave in a peculiar way after a fork; they require a reinitialization of all the used PKCS #11 resources. While GnuTLS automates that process, there are corner cases where it is not possible to handle it correctly in an automated way[3]. For that, it is recommended not to mix fork() and PKCS #11 module usage. It is recommended to initialize and use any PKCS #11 resources in a single process.

Older versions of GnuTLS required to call **gnutls_pkcs11_reinit** after a fork() call; since 3.3.0 this is no longer required.

---

[2] http://p11-glue.freedesktop.org/

[3] For example when an open session is to be reinitialized, but the PIN is not available to GnuTLS (e.g., it was entered at a pinpad).

4.3.2. Manual initialization of user-specific modules

In systems where one cannot rely on a globally available p11-kit configuration to be available, it is still possible to utilize PKCS #11 objects. That can be done by loading directly the PKCS #11 shared module in the application using **gnutls_pkcs11_add_provider**, after having called **gnutls_pkcs11_init** specifying the GNUTLS_PKCS11_FLAG_MANUAL flag.

---

int **gnutls_pkcs11_add_provider** (*const char* * **name**, *const char* * **params**)

Description: This function will load and add a PKCS 11 module to the module list used in gnutls. After this function is called the module will be used for PKCS 11 operations. When loading a module to be used for certificate verification, use the string 'trusted' as params. Note that this function is not thread safe.

Returns: On success, **GNUTLS_E_SUCCESS** (0) is returned, otherwise a negative error value.

In that case, the application will only have access to the modules explictly loaded. If the GNUTLS_PKCS11_FLAG_MANUAL flag is specified and no calls to **gnutls_pkcs11_add_provider** are made, then the PKCS #11 functionality is effectively disabled.

---

int **gnutls_pkcs11_init** (*unsigned int* **flags**, *const char* * **deprecated_config_file**)

Description: This function will initialize the PKCS 11 subsystem in gnutls. It will read configuration files if **GNUTLS_PKCS11_FLAG_AUTO** is used or allow you to independently load PKCS 11 modules using gnutls_pkcs11_add_provider() if **GNUTLS_PKCS11_FLAG_MANUAL** is specified. You don't need to call this function since GnuTLS 3.3.0 because it is being called during the first request PKCS 11 operation. That call will assume the **GNUTLS_PKCS11_FLAG_AUTO** flag. If another flags are required then it must be called independently prior to any PKCS 11 operation.

Returns: On success, **GNUTLS_E_SUCCESS** (0) is returned, otherwise a negative error value.

4.3.3. Accessing objects that require a PIN

Objects stored in token such as a private keys are typically protected from access by a PIN or password. This PIN may be required to either read the object (if allowed) or to perform operations with it. To allow obtaining the PIN when accessing a protected object, as well as probe the user to insert the token the following functions allow to set a callback.

---

void **gnutls_pkcs11_set_token_function** (*gnutls_pkcs11_token_callback_t* **fn**, *void* * **userdata**)

void **gnutls_pkcs11_set_pin_function** (*gnutls_pin_callback_t* **fn**, *void* * **userdata**)

int **gnutls_pkcs11_add_provider** (*const char* * **name**, *const char* * **params**)

gnutls_pin_callback_t **gnutls_pkcs11_get_pin_function** (*void* ** **userdata**)

The callback is of type `gnutls_pin_callback_t` and will have as input the provided userdata, the PIN attempt number, a URL describing the token, a label describing the object and flags. The PIN must be at most of `pin_max` size and must be copied to pin variable. The function must return 0 on success or a negative error code otherwise.

```
typedef int (*gnutls_pin_callback_t) (void *userdata, int attempt,
                                      const char *token_url,
                                      const char *token_label,
                                      unsigned int flags,
                                      char *pin, size_t pin_max);
```

The flags are of `gnutls_pin_flag_t` type and are explained below.

---

enum gnutls_pin_flag_t :

GNUTLS_PIN_USER	The PIN for the user.
GNUTLS_PIN_SO	The PIN for the security officer (admin).
GNUTLS_PIN_FINAL_TRY	This is the final try before blocking.
GNUTLS_PIN_COUNT_LOW	Few tries remain before token blocks.
GNUTLS_PIN_CONTEXT_SPECIFIC	The PIN is for a specific action and key like signing.
GNUTLS_PIN_WRONG	Last given PIN was not correct.

Table 4.1.: The `gnutls_pin_flag_t` enumeration.

Note that due to limitations of PKCS #11 there are issues when multiple libraries are sharing a module. To avoid this problem GnuTLS uses p11-kit that provides a middleware to control access to resources over the multiple users.

To avoid conflicts with multiple registered callbacks for PIN functions, `gnutls_pkcs11_get_pin_function` may be used to check for any previously set functions. In addition context specific PIN functions are allowed, e.g., by using functions below.

---

void **gnutls_certificate_set_pin_function** (*gnutls_certificate_credentials_t* **cred**, *gnutls_pin_callback_t* **fn**, *void* * **userdata**)

void **gnutls_pubkey_set_pin_function** (*gnutls_pubkey_t* **key**, *gnutls_pin_callback_t* **fn**, *void* * **userdata**)

void **gnutls_privkey_set_pin_function** (*gnutls_privkey_t* **key**, *gnutls_pin_callback_t* **fn**, *void* * **userdata**)

void **gnutls_pkcs11_obj_set_pin_function** (*gnutls_pkcs11_obj_t* **obj**, *gnutls_pin_callback_t* **fn**, *void* * **userdata**)

void **gnutls_x509_crt_set_pin_function** (*gnutls_x509_crt_t* **crt**, *gnutls_pin_callback_t* **fn**, *void* * **userdata**)

4.3.4. Reading objects

All PKCS #11 objects are referenced by GnuTLS functions by URLs as described in [30]. This allows for a consistent naming of objects across systems and applications in the same system. For example a public key on a smart card may be referenced as:

```
1  pkcs11:token=Nikos;serial=307521161601031;model=PKCS%2315; \
2  manufacturer=EnterSafe;object=test1;type=public;\
3  id=32f153f3e37990b08624141077ca5dec2d15faed
```

while the smart card itself can be referenced as:

```
1  pkcs11:token=Nikos;serial=307521161601031;model=PKCS%2315;manufacturer=EnterSafe
```

Objects stored in a PKCS #11 token can typically be extracted if they are not marked as sensitive. Usually only private keys are marked as sensitive and cannot be extracted, while certificates and other data can be retrieved. The functions that can be used to enumerate and access objects are shown below.

---

int **gnutls_pkcs11_obj_list_import_url4** (*gnutls_pkcs11_obj_t* ** **p_list**, *unsigned int* * **n_list**, *const char* * **url**, *unsigned int* **flags**)

int **gnutls_pkcs11_obj_import_url** (*gnutls_pkcs11_obj_t* **obj**, *const char* * **url**, *unsigned int* **flags**)

int **gnutls_pkcs11_obj_export_url** (*gnutls_pkcs11_obj_t* **obj**, *gnutls_pkcs11_url_type_t* **detailed**, *char* ** **url**)

---

int **gnutls_pkcs11_obj_get_info** (*gnutls_pkcs11_obj_t* **obj,** *gnutls_pkcs11_obj_info_t*
itype, *void* * **output,** *size_t* * **output_size**)

Description: This function will return information about the PKCS11 certificate such as
the label, id as well as token information where the key is stored. When output is text
it returns null terminated string although output_size contains the size of the actual
data only. In versions previously to 3.6.0 this function included the null terminator to
output_size. After 3.6.0 the output size doesn't include the terminator character.

Returns: **GNUTLS_E_SUCCESS** (0) on success or a negative error code on error.

---

int **gnutls_x509_crt_import_pkcs11** (*gnutls_x509_crt_t* **crt,** *gnutls_pkcs11_obj_t*
pkcs11_crt)

int **gnutls_x509_crt_import_url** (*gnutls_x509_crt_t* **crt,** *const char* * **url,** *unsigned
int* **flags**)

int **gnutls_x509_crt_list_import_pkcs11** (*gnutls_x509_crt_t* * **certs,** *unsigned int*
cert_max, *gnutls_pkcs11_obj_t* * const **objs,** *unsigned int* **flags**)

Properties of the physical token can also be accessed and altered with GnuTLS. For example
data in a token can be erased (initialized), PIN can be altered, etc.

---

int **gnutls_pkcs11_token_init** (*const char* * **token_url,** *const char* * **so_pin,** *const
char* * **label**)

int **gnutls_pkcs11_token_get_url** (*unsigned int* **seq,** *gnutls_pkcs11_url_type_t* **detailed,** *char* ** **url**)

int **gnutls_pkcs11_token_get_info** (*const char* * **url,** *gnutls_pkcs11_token_info_t*
ttype, *void* * **output,** *size_t* * **output_size**)

int **gnutls_pkcs11_token_get_flags** (*const char* * **url,** *unsigned int* * **flags**)

int **gnutls_pkcs11_token_set_pin** (*const char* * **token_url,** *const char* * **oldpin,**
const char * **newpin,** *unsigned int* **flags**)

The following examples demonstrate the usage of the API. The first example will list all
available PKCS #11 tokens in a system and the latter will list all certificates in a token that
have a corresponding private key.

```
1   int i;
2   char* url;
3
4   gnutls_global_init();
5
6   for (i=0;;i++)
7     {
8       ret = gnutls_pkcs11_token_get_url(i, &url);
9       if (ret == GNUTLS_E_REQUESTED_DATA_NOT_AVAILABLE)
10        break;
11
12      if (ret < 0)
13        exit(1);
14
15      fprintf(stdout, "Token[%d]: URL: %s\n", i, url);
16      gnutls_free(url);
17    }
18  gnutls_global_deinit();
```

```
1   /* This example code is placed in the public domain. */
2
3   #include <config.h>
4   #include <gnutls/gnutls.h>
5   #include <gnutls/pkcs11.h>
6   #include <stdio.h>
7   #include <stdlib.h>
8
9   #define URL "pkcs11:URL"
10
11  int main(int argc, char **argv)
12  {
13          gnutls_pkcs11_obj_t *obj_list;
14          gnutls_x509_crt_t xcrt;
15          unsigned int obj_list_size = 0;
16          gnutls_datum_t cinfo;
17          int ret;
18          unsigned int i;
19
20          ret = gnutls_pkcs11_obj_list_import_url4(&obj_list, &obj_list_size, URL,
21                                  GNUTLS_PKCS11_OBJ_FLAG_CRT|
22                                  GNUTLS_PKCS11_OBJ_FLAG_WITH_PRIVKEY);
23          if (ret < 0)
24                  return -1;
25
26          /* now all certificates are in obj_list */
27          for (i = 0; i < obj_list_size; i++) {
28
29                  gnutls_x509_crt_init(&xcrt);
30
31                  gnutls_x509_crt_import_pkcs11(xcrt, obj_list[i]);
32
33                  gnutls_x509_crt_print(xcrt, GNUTLS_CRT_PRINT_FULL, &cinfo);
34
35                  fprintf(stdout, "cert[%d]:\n %s\n\n", i, cinfo.data);
36
37                  gnutls_free(cinfo.data);
```

```
38              gnutls_x509_crt_deinit(xcrt);
39         }
40
41         for (i = 0; i < obj_list_size; i++)
42              gnutls_pkcs11_obj_deinit(obj_list[i]);
43         gnutls_free(obj_list);
44
45         return 0;
46 }
```

4.3.5. Writing objects

With GnuTLS you can copy existing private keys and certificates to a token. Note that when copying private keys it is recommended to mark them as sensitive using the GNUTLS_-PKCS11_OBJ_FLAG_MARK_SENSITIVE to prevent its extraction. An object can be marked as private using the flag GNUTLS_PKCS11_OBJ_FLAG_MARK_PRIVATE, to require PIN to be entered before accessing the object (for operations or otherwise).

---

int **gnutls_pkcs11_copy_x509_privkey2** (*const* *char* * **token_url**, *gnutls_x509_privkey_t* **key**, *const char* * **label**, *const gnutls_datum_t* * **cid**, *unsigned int* **key_usage**, *unsigned int* **flags**)

Description: This function will copy a private key into a PKCS #11 token specified by a URL. It is highly recommended flags to contain **GNUTLS_PKCS**11_OBJ_FLAG_MARK_SENSITIVE unless there is a strong reason not to.

Returns: On success, **GNUTLS_E_SUCCESS** (0) is returned, otherwise a negative error value.

---

int **gnutls_pkcs11_copy_x509_crt2** (*const char* * **token_url**, *gnutls_x509_crt_t* **crt**, *const char* * **label**, *const gnutls_datum_t* * **cid**, *unsigned int* **flags**)

Description: This function will copy a certificate into a PKCS #11 token specified by a URL. Valid flags to mark the certificate: **GNUTLS_PKCS**11_OBJ_FLAG_MARK_TRUSTED, **GNUTLS_PKCS**11_OBJ_FLAG_MARK_SENSITIVE, **GNUTLS_PKCS**11_OBJ_FLAG_MARK_PRIVATE, **GNUTLS_PKCS**11_OBJ_FLAG_MARK_CA, **GNUTLS_PKCS**11_OBJ_FLAG_MARK_ALWAYS_AUTH.

Returns: On success, **GNUTLS_E_SUCCESS** (0) is returned, otherwise a negative error value.

---

int **gnutls_pkcs11_delete_url** (*const char* * **object_url,** *unsigned int* **flags**)

Description: `This function will delete objects matching the given URL. Note that not all tokens support the delete operation.`

Returns: `On success, the number of objects deleted is returned, otherwise a negative error value.`

4.3.6. Using a PKCS #11 token with TLS

It is possible to use a PKCS #11 token to a TLS session, as shown in subsection 6.1.8. In addition the following functions can be used to load PKCS #11 key and certificates by specifying a PKCS #11 URL instead of a filename.

---

int **gnutls_certificate_set_x509_trust_file** (*gnutls_certificate_credentials_t* **cred,** *const char* * **cafile,** *gnutls_x509_crt_fmt_t* **type**)

int **gnutls_certificate_set_x509_key_file2** (*gnutls_certificate_credentials_t* **res,** *const char* * **certfile,** *const char* * **keyfile,** *gnutls_x509_crt_fmt_t* **type,** *const char* * **pass,** *unsigned int* **flags**)

4.3.7. Verifying certificates over PKCS #11

The PKCS #11 API can be used to allow all applications in the same operating system to access shared cryptographic keys and certificates in a uniform way, as in Figure 4.1. That way applications could load their trusted certificate list, as well as user certificates from a common PKCS #11 module. Such a provider is the p11-kit trust storage module[4] and it provides access to the trusted Root CA certificates in a system. That provides a more dynamic list of Root CA certificates, as opposed to a static list in a file or directory.

That store, allows for blacklisting of CAs or certificates, as well as categorization of the Root CAs (Web verification, Code signing, etc.), in addition to restricting their purpose via stapled extensions[5]. GnuTLS will utilize the p11-kit trust module as the default trust store if configured to; i.e., if '–with-default-trust-store-pkcs11=pkcs11:' is given to the configure script.

4.3.8. Invoking p11tool

Program that allows operations on PKCS #11 smart cards and security modules.

---

[4]`http://p11-glue.freedesktop.org/trust-module.html`

[5]See the 'Restricting the scope of CA certificates' post at `http://nmav.gnutls.org/2016/06/restricting-scope-of-ca-certificates.html`

To use PKCS #11 tokens with GnuTLS the p11-kit configuration files need to be setup. That is create a .module file in /etc/pkcs11/modules with the contents 'module: /path/to/pkcs11.so'. Alternatively the configuration file /etc/gnutls/pkcs11.conf has to exist and contain a number of lines of the form 'load=/usr/lib/opensc-pkcs11.so'.

You can provide the PIN to be used for the PKCS #11 operations with the environment variables GNUTLS_PIN and GNUTLS_SO_PIN.

This section was generated by **AutoGen**, using the `agtexi-cmd` template and the option descriptions for the `p11tool` program. This software is released under the GNU General Public License, version 3 or later.

p11tool help/usage ("`--help`")

This is the automatically generated usage text for p11tool.

The text printed is the same whether selected with the `help` option ("`--help`") or the `more-help` option ("`--more-help`"). `more-help` will print the usage text by passing it through a pager program. `more-help` is disabled on platforms without a working `fork(2)` function. The `PAGER` environment variable is used to select the program, defaulting to "`more`". Both will exit with a status code of 0.

```
 1  p11tool - GnuTLS PKCS #11 tool
 2  Usage:  p11tool [ -<flag> [<val>] | --<name>[{=| }<val>] ]... [url]
 3
 4
 5  Tokens:
 6
 7          --list-tokens         List all available tokens
 8          --list-token-urls     List the URLs available tokens
 9          --list-mechanisms     List all available mechanisms in a token
10          --initialize          Initializes a PKCS #11 token
11          --initialize-pin      Initializes/Resets a PKCS #11 token user PIN
12          --initialize-so-pin   Initializes/Resets a PKCS #11 token security officer PIN
13          --set-pin=str         Specify the PIN to use on token operations
14          --set-so-pin=str      Specify the Security Officer's PIN to use on token initialization
15
16  Object listing:
17
18          --list-all            List all available objects in a token
19          --list-all-certs      List all available certificates in a token
20          --list-certs          List all certificates that have an associated private key
21          --list-all-privkeys   List all available private keys in a token
22          --list-privkeys       an alias for the 'list-all-privkeys' option
23          --list-keys           an alias for the 'list-all-privkeys' option
24          --list-all-trusted    List all available certificates marked as trusted
25          --export              Export the object specified by the URL
26                                   - prohibits these options:
27                                   export-stapled
28                                   export-chain
29                                   export-pubkey
30          --export-stapled      Export the certificate object specified by the URL
31                                   - prohibits these options:
32                                   export
```

```
33                                  export-chain
34                                  export-pubkey
35        --export-chain      Export the certificate specified by the URL and its chain of trust
36                                  - prohibits these options:
37                                  export-stapled
38                                  export
39                                  export-pubkey
40        --export-pubkey     Export the public key for a private key
41                                  - prohibits these options:
42                                  export-stapled
43                                  export
44                                  export-chain
45        --info              List information on an available object in a token
46        --trusted           an alias for the 'mark-trusted' option
47        --distrusted        an alias for the 'mark-distrusted' option
48
49  Key generation:
50
51        --generate-privkey=str Generate private-public key pair of given type
52        --bits=num          Specify the number of bits for the key generate
53        --curve=str         Specify the curve used for EC key generation
54        --sec-param=str     Specify the security level
55
56  Writing objects:
57
58        --set-id=str        Set the CKA_ID (in hex) for the specified by the URL object
59                                  - prohibits the option 'write'
60        --set-label=str     Set the CKA_LABEL for the specified by the URL object
61                                  - prohibits these options:
62                                  write
63                                  set-id
64        --write             Writes the loaded objects to a PKCS #11 token
65        --delete            Deletes the objects matching the given PKCS #11 URL
66        --label=str         Sets a label for the write operation
67        --id=str            Sets an ID for the write operation
68        --mark-wrap         Marks the generated key to be a wrapping key
69                                  - disabled as '--no-mark-wrap'
70        --mark-trusted      Marks the object to be written as trusted
71                                  - prohibits the option 'mark-distrusted'
72                                  - disabled as '--no-mark-trusted'
73        --mark-distrusted   When retrieving objects, it requires the objects to be distrusted
74  (blacklisted)
75                                  - prohibits the option 'mark-trusted'
76        --mark-decrypt      Marks the object to be written for decryption
77                                  - disabled as '--no-mark-decrypt'
78        --mark-sign         Marks the object to be written for signature generation
79                                  - disabled as '--no-mark-sign'
80        --mark-ca           Marks the object to be written as a CA
81                                  - disabled as '--no-mark-ca'
82        --mark-private      Marks the object to be written as private
83                                  - disabled as '--no-mark-private'
84        --ca                an alias for the 'mark-ca' option
85        --private           an alias for the 'mark-private' option
86        --secret-key=str    Provide a hex encoded secret key
87        --load-privkey=file Private key file to use
88                                  - file must pre-exist
89        --load-pubkey=file  Public key file to use
90                                  - file must pre-exist
```

```
91        --load-certificate=file Certificate file to use
92                             - file must pre-exist
93
94  Other options:
95
96     -d, --debug=num         Enable debugging
97                             - it must be in the range:
98                             0 to 9999
99        --outfile=str        Output file
100       --login              Force (user) login to token
101                            - disabled as '--no-login'
102       --so-login           Force security officer login to token
103                            - disabled as '--no-so-login'
104       --admin-login        an alias for the 'so-login' option
105       --test-sign          Tests the signature operation of the provided object
106       --sign-params=str    Sign with a specific signature algorithm
107       --hash=str           Hash algorithm to use for signing
108       --generate-random=num Generate random data
109    -8, --pkcs8             Use PKCS #8 format for private keys
110       --inder              Use DER/RAW format for input
111                            - disabled as '--no-inder'
112       --inraw              an alias for the 'inder' option
113       --outder             Use DER format for output certificates, private keys, and DH parameters
114                            - disabled as '--no-outder'
115       --outraw             an alias for the 'outder' option
116       --provider=file      Specify the PKCS #11 provider library
117       --detailed-url       Print detailed URLs
118                            - disabled as '--no-detailed-url'
119       --only-urls          Print a compact listing using only the URLs
120       --batch              Disable all interaction with the tool
121
122 Version, usage and configuration options:
123
124    -v, --version[=arg]      output version information and exit
125    -h, --help              display extended usage information and exit
126    -!, --more-help         extended usage information passed thru pager
127
128 Options are specified by doubled hyphens and their name or by a single
129 hyphen and the flag character.
130 Operands and options may be intermixed.  They will be reordered.
131
132 Program that allows operations on PKCS #11 smart cards and security
133 modules.
134
135 To use PKCS #11 tokens with GnuTLS the p11-kit configuration files need to
136 be setup.  That is create a .module file in /etc/pkcs11/modules with the
137 contents 'module: /path/to/pkcs11.so'.  Alternatively the configuration
138 file /etc/gnutls/pkcs11.conf has to exist and contain a number of lines of
139 the form 'load=/usr/lib/opensc-pkcs11.so'.
140
141 You can provide the PIN to be used for the PKCS #11 operations with the
142 environment variables GNUTLS_PIN and GNUTLS_SO_PIN.
143
```

token-related-options options

Tokens.

list-token-urls option.

This is the "list the urls available tokens" option. This is a more compact version of –list-tokens.

set-pin option.

This is the "specify the pin to use on token operations" option. This option takes a string argument. Alternatively the GNUTLS_PIN environment variable may be used.

set-so-pin option.

This is the "specify the security officer's pin to use on token initialization" option. This option takes a string argument. Alternatively the GNUTLS_SO_PIN environment variable may be used.

object-list-related-options options

Object listing.

list-all-privkeys option.

This is the "list all available private keys in a token" option. Lists all the private keys in a token that match the specified URL.

list-privkeys option.

This is an alias for the `list-all-privkeys` option, section 4.3.8.

list-keys option.

This is an alias for the `list-all-privkeys` option, section 4.3.8.

export-stapled option.

This is the "export the certificate object specified by the url" option.

This option has some usage constraints. It:

- must not appear in combination with any of the following options: export, export-chain, export-pubkey.

Exports the certificate specified by the URL while including any attached extensions to it. Since attached extensions are a p11-kit extension, this option is only available on p11-kit registered trust modules.

export-chain option.

This is the "export the certificate specified by the url and its chain of trust" option.

This option has some usage constraints. It:

- must not appear in combination with any of the following options: export-stapled, export, export-pubkey.

Exports the certificate specified by the URL and generates its chain of trust based on the stored certificates in the module.

export-pubkey option.

This is the "export the public key for a private key" option.

This option has some usage constraints. It:

- must not appear in combination with any of the following options: export-stapled, export, export-chain.

Exports the public key for the specified private key

trusted option.

This is an alias for the `mark-trusted` option, section 4.3.8.

distrusted option.

This is an alias for the `mark-distrusted` option, section 4.3.8.

keygen-related-options options

Key generation.

generate-privkey option.

This is the "generate private-public key pair of given type" option. This option takes a string argument. Generates a private-public key pair in the specified token. Acceptable types are RSA, ECDSA, and DSA. Should be combined with –sec-param or –bits.

generate-rsa option.

This is the "generate an rsa private-public key pair" option. Generates an RSA private-public key pair on the specified token. Should be combined with –sec-param or –bits.

NOTE: THIS OPTION IS DEPRECATED

generate-dsa option.

This is the "generate a dsa private-public key pair" option. Generates a DSA private-public key pair on the specified token. Should be combined with –sec-param or –bits.

NOTE: THIS OPTION IS DEPRECATED

generate-ecc option.

This is the "generate an ecdsa private-public key pair" option. Generates an ECDSA private-public key pair on the specified token. Should be combined with –curve, –sec-param or –bits.

NOTE: THIS OPTION IS DEPRECATED

bits option.

This is the "specify the number of bits for the key generate" option. This option takes a number argument. For applications which have no key-size restrictions the –sec-param option is recommended, as the sec-param levels will adapt to the acceptable security levels with the new versions of gnutls.

curve option.

This is the "specify the curve used for ec key generation" option. This option takes a string argument. Supported values are secp192r1, secp224r1, secp256r1, secp384r1 and secp521r1.

sec-param option.

This is the "specify the security level" option. This option takes a string argument "Security parameter". This is alternative to the bits option. Available options are [low, legacy, medium, high, ultra].

write-object-related-options options

Writing objects.

set-id option.

This is the "set the cka_id (in hex) for the specified by the url object" option. This option takes a string argument.

This option has some usage constraints. It:

- must not appear in combination with any of the following options: write.

Modifies or sets the CKA_ID in the specified by the URL object. The ID should be specified in hexadecimal format without a '0x' prefix.

set-label option.

This is the "set the cka_label for the specified by the url object" option. This option takes a string argument.

This option has some usage constraints. It:

- must not appear in combination with any of the following options: write, set-id.

Modifies or sets the CKA_LABEL in the specified by the URL object

write option.

This is the "writes the loaded objects to a pkcs #11 token" option. It can be used to write private, public keys, certificates or secret keys to a token. Must be combined with one of –load-privkey, –load-pubkey, –load-certificate option.

id option.

This is the "sets an id for the write operation" option. This option takes a string argument. Sets the CKA_ID to be set by the write operation. The ID should be specified in hexadecimal format without a '0x' prefix.

mark-wrap option.

This is the "marks the generated key to be a wrapping key" option.

This option has some usage constraints. It:

- can be disabled with –no-mark-wrap.

Marks the generated key with the CKA_WRAP flag.

mark-trusted option.

This is the "marks the object to be written as trusted" option.

This option has some usage constraints. It:

- can be disabled with –no-mark-trusted.

- must not appear in combination with any of the following options: mark-distrusted.

Marks the object to be generated/written with the CKA_TRUST flag.

mark-distrusted option.

This is the "when retrieving objects, it requires the objects to be distrusted (blacklisted)" option.

This option has some usage constraints. It:

- must not appear in combination with any of the following options: mark-trusted.

Ensures that the objects retrieved have the CKA_X_TRUST flag. This is p11-kit trust module extension, thus this flag is only valid with p11-kit registered trust modules.

mark-decrypt option.

This is the "marks the object to be written for decryption" option.

This option has some usage constraints. It:

- can be disabled with –no-mark-decrypt.

Marks the object to be generated/written with the CKA_DECRYPT flag set to true.

mark-sign option.

This is the "marks the object to be written for signature generation" option.

This option has some usage constraints. It:

- can be disabled with –no-mark-sign.

Marks the object to be generated/written with the CKA_SIGN flag set to true.

mark-ca option.

This is the "marks the object to be written as a ca" option.

This option has some usage constraints. It:

- can be disabled with –no-mark-ca.

Marks the object to be generated/written with the CKA_CERTIFICATE_CATEGORY as CA.

mark-private option.

This is the "marks the object to be written as private" option.

This option has some usage constraints. It:

- can be disabled with –no-mark-private.

Marks the object to be generated/written with the CKA_PRIVATE flag. The written object will require a PIN to be used.

ca option.

This is an alias for the `mark-ca` option, section 4.3.8.

private option.

This is an alias for the `mark-private` option, section 4.3.8.

secret-key option.

This is the "provide a hex encoded secret key" option. This option takes a string argument. This secret key will be written to the module if –write is specified.

other-options options

Other options.

debug option (-d).

This is the "enable debugging" option. This option takes a number argument. Specifies the debug level.

so-login option.

This is the "force security officer login to token" option.

This option has some usage constraints. It:

- can be disabled with –no-so-login.

Forces login to the token as security officer (admin).

admin-login option.

This is an alias for the **so-login** option, section 4.3.8.

test-sign option.

This is the "tests the signature operation of the provided object" option. It can be used to test the correct operation of the signature operation. If both a private and a public key are available this operation will sign and verify the signed data.

sign-params option.

This is the "sign with a specific signature algorithm" option. This option takes a string argument. This option can be combined with –test-sign, to sign with a specific signature algorithm variant. The only option supported is 'RSA-PSS', and should be specified in order to use RSA-PSS signature on RSA keys.

hash option.

This is the "hash algorithm to use for signing" option. This option takes a string argument. This option can be combined with test-sign. Available hash functions are SHA1, RMD160, SHA256, SHA384, SHA512, SHA3-224, SHA3-256, SHA3-384, SHA3-512.

generate-random option.

This is the "generate random data" option. This option takes a number argument. Asks the token to generate a number of bytes of random bytes.

inder option.

This is the "use der/raw format for input" option.

This option has some usage constraints. It:

- can be disabled with –no-inder.

Use DER/RAW format for input certificates and private keys.

inraw option.

This is an alias for the **inder** option, section 4.3.8.

outder option.

This is the "use der format for output certificates, private keys, and dh parameters" option.

This option has some usage constraints. It:

- can be disabled with –no-outder.

The output will be in DER or RAW format.

outraw option.

This is an alias for the **outder** option, section 4.3.8.

provider option.

This is the "specify the pkcs #11 provider library" option. This option takes a file argument. This will override the default options in /etc/gnutls/pkcs11.conf

provider-opts option.

This is the "specify parameters for the pkcs #11 provider library" option. This option takes a string argument. This is a PKCS#11 internal option used by few modules. Mainly for testing PKCS#11 modules.

NOTE: THIS OPTION IS DEPRECATED

batch option.

This is the "disable all interaction with the tool" option. In batch mode there will be no prompts, all parameters need to be specified on command line.

p11tool exit status

One of the following exit values will be returned:

- 0 (EXIT_SUCCESS) Successful program execution.

- 1 (EXIT_FAILURE) The operation failed or the command syntax was not valid.

p11tool See Also

certtool (1)

p11tool Examples

To view all tokens in your system use:

```
$ p11tool --list-tokens
```

To view all objects in a token use:

```
$ p11tool --login --list-all "pkcs11:TOKEN-URL"
```

To store a private key and a certificate in a token run:

```
$ p11tool --login --write "pkcs11:URL" --load-privkey key.pem \
        --label "Mykey"
$ p11tool --login --write "pkcs11:URL" --load-certificate cert.pem \
        --label "Mykey"
```

Note that some tokens require the same label to be used for the certificate and its corresponding private key.

To generate an RSA private key inside the token use:

```
$ p11tool --login --generate-privkey rsa --bits 1024 --label "MyNewKey" \
        --outfile MyNewKey.pub "pkcs11:TOKEN-URL"
```

The bits parameter in the above example is explicitly set because some tokens only support limited choices in the bit length. The output file is the corresponding public key. This key can be used to general a certificate request with certtool.

```
certtool --generate-request --load-privkey "pkcs11:KEY-URL" \
    --load-pubkey MyNewKey.pub --outfile request.pem
```

4.4. Trusted Platform Module (TPM)

In this section we present the Trusted Platform Module (TPM) support in GnuTLS. Note that we recommend against using TPM with this API because it is restricted to TPM 1.2. We recommend instead to use PKCS#11 wrappers for TPM such as CHAPS[6] or opencryptoki[7]. These will allow using the standard smart card and HSM functionality (see section 4.3) for TPM keys.

There was a big hype when the TPM chip was introduced into computers. Briefly it is a co-processor in your PC that allows it to perform calculations independently of the main processor. This has good and bad side-effects. In this section we focus on the good ones; these are the fact that you can use the TPM chip to perform cryptographic operations on keys stored in it, without accessing them. That is very similar to the operation of a PKCS #11 smart card. The chip allows for storage and usage of RSA keys, but has quite some operational differences from PKCS #11 module, and thus require different handling. The basic TPM operations supported and used by GnuTLS, are key generation and signing. That support is currently limited to TPM 1.2.

The next sections assume that the TPM chip in the system is already initialized and in a operational state. If not, ensure that the TPM chip is enabled by your BIOS, that the `tcsd` daemon is running, and that TPM ownership is set (by running `tpm_takeownership`).

In GnuTLS the TPM functionality is available in `gnutls/tpm.h`.

4.4.1. Keys in TPM

The RSA keys in the TPM module may either be stored in a flash memory within TPM or stored in a file in disk. In the former case the key can provide operations as with PKCS #11 and is identified by a URL. The URL is described in [23] and is of the following form.

`tpmkey:uuid=42309df8-d101-11e1-a89a-97bb33c23ad1;storage=user`

It consists from a unique identifier of the key as well as the part of the flash memory the key is stored at. The two options for the storage field are 'user' and 'system'. The user keys are typically only available to the generating user and the system keys to all users. The stored in TPM keys are called registered keys.

The keys that are stored in the disk are exported from the TPM but in an encrypted form. To access them two passwords are required. The first is the TPM Storage Root Key (SRK), and the other is a key-specific password. Also those keys are identified by a URL of the form:

`tpmkey:file=/path/to/file`

When objects require a PIN to be accessed the same callbacks as with PKCS #11 objects are expected (see subsection 4.3.3). Note that the PIN function may be called multiple times to unlock the SRK and the specific key in use. The label in the key function will then be set to 'SRK' when unlocking the SRK key, or to 'TPM' when unlocking any other key.

---

[6]https://github.com/google/chaps-linux
[7]https://sourceforge.net/projects/opencryptoki/

4.4.2. Key generation

All keys used by the TPM must be generated by the TPM. This can be done using `gnutls_tpm_privkey_generate`.

---

int **gnutls_tpm_privkey_generate** (*gnutls_pk_algorithm_t* **pk**, *unsigned int* **bits**, *const char * **srk_password**, *const char * **key_password**, *gnutls_tpmkey_fmt_t* **format**, *gnutls_x509_crt_fmt_t* **pub_format**, *gnutls_datum_t * **privkey**, *gnutls_datum_t * **pubkey**, *unsigned int* **flags**)

Description: This function will generate a private key in the TPM chip. The private key will be generated within the chip and will be exported in a wrapped with TPM's master key form. Furthermore the wrapped key can be protected with the provided password. Note that bits in TPM is quantized value. If the input value is not one of the allowed values, then it will be quantized to one of 512, 1024, 2048, 4096, 8192 and 16384. Allowed flags are:

Returns: On success, **GNUTLS_E_SUCCESS** (0) is returned, otherwise a negative error value.

---

int **gnutls_tpm_get_registered** (*gnutls_tpm_key_list_t * **list**)

void **gnutls_tpm_key_list_deinit** (*gnutls_tpm_key_list_t* **list**)

int **gnutls_tpm_key_list_get_url** (*gnutls_tpm_key_list_t* **list**, *unsigned int* **idx**, *char ** **url**, *unsigned int* **flags**)

---

int **gnutls_tpm_privkey_delete** (*const char * **url**, *const char * **srk_password**)

Description: This function will unregister the private key from the TPM chip.

Returns: On success, **GNUTLS_E_SUCCESS** (0) is returned, otherwise a negative error value.

133

4.4.3. Using keys

Importing keys

The TPM keys can be used directly by the abstract key types and do not require any special structures. Moreover functions like `gnutls_certificate_set_x509_key_file2` can access TPM URLs.

---

int **gnutls_privkey_import_tpm_raw** (*gnutls_privkey_t* **pkey**, *const gnutls_datum_t* * **fdata**, *gnutls_tpmkey_fmt_t* **format**, *const char* * **srk_password**, *const char* * **key_password**, *unsigned int* **flags**)

int **gnutls_pubkey_import_tpm_raw** (*gnutls_pubkey_t* **pkey**, *const gnutls_datum_t* * **fdata**, *gnutls_tpmkey_fmt_t* **format**, *const char* * **srk_password**, *unsigned int* **flags**)

---

int **gnutls_privkey_import_tpm_url** (*gnutls_privkey_t* **pkey**, *const char* * **url**, *const char* * **srk_password**, *const char* * **key_password**, *unsigned int* **flags**)

Description: This function will import the given private key to the abstract *gnutls_privkey_t* type. Note that unless **GNUTLS_PRIVKEY_DISABLE_CALLBACKS** is specified, if incorrect (or NULL) passwords are given the PKCS11 callback functions will be used to obtain the correct passwords. Otherwise if the SRK password is wrong **GNUTLS_E_TPM_SRK_PASSWORD_ERROR** is returned and if the key password is wrong or not provided then **GNUTLS_E_TPM_KEY_PASSWORD_ERROR** is returned.

Returns: On success, **GNUTLS_E_SUCCESS** (0) is returned, otherwise a negative error value.

---

int **gnutls_pubkey_import_tpm_url** (*gnutls_pubkey_t* **pkey**, *const char* * **url**, *const char* * **srk_password**, *unsigned int* **flags**)

Description: This function will import the given private key to the abstract *gnutls_privkey_t* type. Note that unless **GNUTLS_PUBKEY_DISABLE_CALLBACKS** is specified, if incorrect (or NULL) passwords are given the PKCS11 callback functions will be used to obtain the correct passwords. Otherwise if the SRK password is wrong **GNUTLS_E_TPM_SRK_PASSWORD_ERROR** is returned.

Returns: On success, **GNUTLS_E_SUCCESS** (0) is returned, otherwise a negative error value.

Listing and deleting keys

The registered keys (that are stored in the TPM) can be listed using one of the following functions. Those keys are unfortunately only identified by their UUID and have no label or other human friendly identifier. Keys can be deleted from permament storage using `gnutls_tpm_privkey_delete`.

---

int **gnutls_tpm_get_registered** (*gnutls_tpm_key_list_t* * **list**)

void **gnutls_tpm_key_list_deinit** (*gnutls_tpm_key_list_t* **list**)

int **gnutls_tpm_key_list_get_url** (*gnutls_tpm_key_list_t* **list**, *unsigned int* **idx**, *char* ** **url**, *unsigned int* **flags**)

---

int **gnutls_tpm_privkey_delete** (*const char* * **url**, *const char* * **srk_password**)

Description: `This function will unregister the private key from the TPM chip.`

Returns: `On success,` **GNUTLS_E_SUCCESS** `(0) is returned, otherwise a negative error value.`

4.4.4. Invoking tpmtool

Program that allows handling cryptographic data from the TPM chip.

This section was generated by **AutoGen**, using the `agtexi-cmd` template and the option descriptions for the `tpmtool` program. This software is released under the GNU General Public License, version 3 or later.

tpmtool help/usage ("`--help`")

This is the automatically generated usage text for tpmtool.

The text printed is the same whether selected with the `help` option ("`--help`") or the `more-help` option ("`--more-help`"). `more-help` will print the usage text by passing it through a pager program. `more-help` is disabled on platforms without a working `fork(2)` function. The `PAGER` environment variable is used to select the program, defaulting to "`more`". Both will exit with a status code of 0.

```
 1  tpmtool - GnuTLS TPM tool
 2  Usage:  tpmtool [ -<flag> [<val>] | --<name>[{=| }<val>] ]...
 3
 4     -d, --debug=num            Enable debugging
 5                                   - it must be in the range:
 6                                     0 to 9999
 7        --infile=file           Input file
 8                                   - file must pre-exist
 9        --outfile=str           Output file
10        --generate-rsa          Generate an RSA private-public key pair
11        --register              Any generated key will be registered in the TPM
12                                   - requires the option 'generate-rsa'
13        --signing               Any generated key will be a signing key
14                                   - requires the option 'generate-rsa'
15                                   -- and prohibits the option 'legacy'
16        --legacy                Any generated key will be a legacy key
17                                   - requires the option 'generate-rsa'
18                                   -- and prohibits the option 'signing'
19        --user                  Any registered key will be a user key
20                                   - requires the option 'register'
21                                   -- and prohibits the option 'system'
22        --system                Any registered key will be a system key
23                                   - requires the option 'register'
24                                   -- and prohibits the option 'user'
25        --pubkey=str            Prints the public key of the provided key
26        --list                  Lists all stored keys in the TPM
27        --delete=str            Delete the key identified by the given URL (UUID).
28        --test-sign=str         Tests the signature operation of the provided object
29        --sec-param=str         Specify the security level [low, legacy, medium, high, ultra].
30        --bits=num              Specify the number of bits for key generate
31        --inder                 Use the DER format for keys.
32                                   - disabled as '--no-inder'
33        --outder                Use DER format for output keys
34                                   - disabled as '--no-outder'
35     -v, --version[=arg]        output version information and exit
36     -h, --help                 display extended usage information and exit
37     -!, --more-help            extended usage information passed thru pager
38
39  Options are specified by doubled hyphens and their name or by a single
40  hyphen and the flag character.
41
42  Program that allows handling cryptographic data from the TPM chip.
43
```

debug option (-d)

This is the "enable debugging" option. This option takes a number argument. Specifies the debug level.

generate-rsa option

This is the "generate an rsa private-public key pair" option. Generates an RSA private-public key pair in the TPM chip. The key may be stored in file system and protected by a PIN, or stored (registered) in the TPM chip flash.

user option

This is the "any registered key will be a user key" option.

This option has some usage constraints. It:

- must appear in combination with the following options: register.

- must not appear in combination with any of the following options: system.

The generated key will be stored in a user specific persistent storage.

system option

This is the "any registered key will be a system key" option.

This option has some usage constraints. It:

- must appear in combination with the following options: register.

- must not appear in combination with any of the following options: user.

The generated key will be stored in system persistent storage.

test-sign option

This is the "tests the signature operation of the provided object" option. This option takes a string argument "url". It can be used to test the correct operation of the signature operation. This operation will sign and verify the signed data.

sec-param option

This is the "specify the security level [low, legacy, medium, high, ultra]." option. This option takes a string argument "Security parameter". This is alternative to the bits option. Note however that the values allowed by the TPM chip are quantized and given values may be rounded up.

inder option

This is the "use the der format for keys." option.

This option has some usage constraints. It:

- can be disabled with –no-inder.

The input files will be assumed to be in the portable DER format of TPM. The default format is a custom format used by various TPM tools

outder option

This is the "use der format for output keys" option.

This option has some usage constraints. It:

- can be disabled with –no-outder.

The output will be in the TPM portable DER format.

tpmtool exit status

One of the following exit values will be returned:

- 0 (EXIT_SUCCESS) Successful program execution.
- 1 (EXIT_FAILURE) The operation failed or the command syntax was not valid.

tpmtool See Also

p11tool (1), certtool (1)

tpmtool Examples

To generate a key that is to be stored in file system use:

```
1  $ tpmtool --generate-rsa --bits 2048 --outfile tpmkey.pem
```

To generate a key that is to be stored in TPM's flash use:

```
1  $ tpmtool --generate-rsa --bits 2048 --register --user
```

To get the public key of a TPM key use:

```
1  $ tpmtool --pubkey tpmkey:uuid=58ad734b-bde6-45c7-89d8-756a55ad1891;storage=user \
2          --outfile pubkey.pem
```

or if the key is stored in the file system:

```
$ tpmtool --pubkey tpmkey:file=tmpkey.pem --outfile pubkey.pem
```

To list all keys stored in TPM use:

```
$ tpmtool --list
```

5

How to use GnuTLS in applications

5.1. Introduction

This chapter tries to explain the basic functionality of the current GnuTLS library. Note that there may be additional functionality not discussed here but included in the library. Checking the header files in "`/usr/include/gnutls/`" and the manpages is recommended.

5.1.1. General idea

A brief description of how GnuTLS sessions operate is shown at Figure 5.1. This section will become more clear when it is completely read. As shown in the figure, there is a read-only global state that is initialized once by the global initialization function. This global structure, among others, contains the memory allocation functions used, structures needed for the ASN.1 parser and depending on the system's CPU, pointers to hardware accelerated encryption functions. This structure is never modified by any GnuTLS function, except for the deinitialization function which frees all allocated memory and must be called after the program has permanently finished using GnuTLS.

The credentials structures are used by the authentication methods, such as certificate authentication. They store certificates, privates keys, and other information that is needed to prove the identity to the peer, and/or verify the identity of the peer. The information stored in the credentials structures is initialized once and then can be shared by many TLS sessions.

A GnuTLS session contains all the required state and information to handle one secure connection. The session communicates with the peers using the provided functions of the transport layer. Every session has a unique session ID shared with the peer.

Since TLS sessions can be resumed, servers need a database back-end to hold the session's parameters. Every GnuTLS session after a successful handshake calls the appropriate back-end function (see subsection 2.5.4) to store the newly negotiated session. The session database is examined by the server just after having received the client hello[1], and if the session ID sent by the client, matches a stored session, the stored session will be retrieved, and the new session will be a resumed one, and will share the same session ID with the previous one.

---

[1]The first message in a TLS handshake

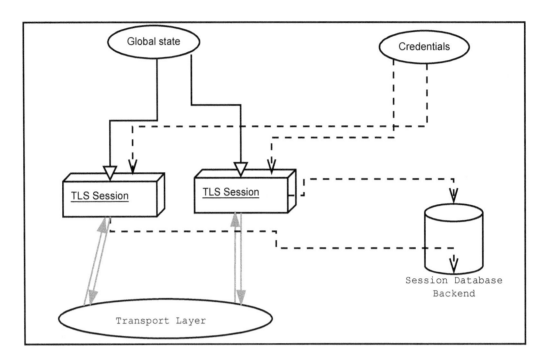

Figure 5.1.: High level design of GnuTLS.

5.1.2. Error handling

There two types of GnuTLS functions. The first type returns a boolean value, true (non-zero) or false (zero) value; these functions are defined to return an unsigned integer type. The other type returns a signed integer type with zero (or a positive number) indicating success and a negative value indicating failure. For the latter type it is recommended to check for errors as following.

```
1    ret = gnutls_function();
2    if (ret < 0) {
3        return -1;
4    }
```

The above example checks for a failure condition rather than for explicit success (e.g., equality to zero). That has the advantage that future extensions of the API can be extended to provide additional information via positive returned values (see for example **gnutls_certificate_set_x509_key_file**).

For certain operations such as TLS handshake and TLS packet receive there is the notion of fatal and non-fatal error codes. Fatal errors terminate the TLS session immediately and further sends and receives will be disallowed. Such an example is GNUTLS_E_DECRYPTION_FAILED. Non-fatal errors may warn about something, i.e., a warning alert was received, or indicate the some action has to be taken. This is the case with the error code GNUTLS_E_REHANDSHAKE returned by **gnutls_record_recv**. This error code indicates that the server requests a re-handshake. The client may ignore this request, or may reply with an alert. You can test if an error code is a fatal one by using the **gnutls_error_is_fatal**. All errors can be converted to a descriptive string using `gnutls_strerror`.

If any non fatal errors, that require an action, are to be returned by a function, these error codes will be documented in the function's reference. For example the error codes `GNUTLS_-E_WARNING_ALERT_RECEIVED` and `GNUTLS_E_FATAL_ALERT_RECEIVED` that may returned when receiving data, should be handled by notifying the user of the alert (as explained in section 5.9). See Appendix D, for a description of the available error codes.

5.1.3. Common types

All strings that are to provided as input to GnuTLS functions should be in UTF-8 unless otherwise specified. Output strings are also in UTF-8 format unless otherwise specified. When functions take as input passwords, they will normalize them using [37] rules (since GnuTLS 3.5.7).

When data of a fixed size are provided to GnuTLS functions then the helper structure `gnutls_datum_t` is often used. Its definition is shown below.

```
typedef struct
{
  unsigned char *data;
  unsigned int size;
} gnutls_datum_t;
```

In functions where this structure is a returned type, if the function succeeds, it is expected from the caller to use `gnutls_free()` to deinitialize the data element after use, unless otherwise specified. If the function fails, the contents of the `gnutls_datum_t` should be considered undefined and must not be deinitialized.

Other functions that require data for scattered read use a structure similar to `struct iovec` typically used by `readv`. It is shown below.

```
typedef struct
{
  void *iov_base;            /* Starting address */
  size_t iov_len;            /* Number of bytes to transfer */
} giovec_t;
```

5.1.4. Debugging and auditing

In many cases things may not go as expected and further information, to assist debugging, from GnuTLS is desired. Those are the cases where the `gnutls_global_set_log_level` and `gnutls_global_set_log_function` are to be used. Those will print verbose information on the GnuTLS functions internal flow.

void **gnutls_global_set_log_level** (*int* **level**)

void **gnutls_global_set_log_function** (*gnutls_log_func* **log_func**)

Alternatively the environment variable GNUTLS_DEBUG_LEVEL can be set to a logging level and GnuTLS will output debugging output to standard error. Other available environment variables are shown in Table 5.1.

Variable	Purpose
GNUTLS_DEBUG_LEVEL	When set to a numeric value, it sets the default debugging level for GnuTLS applications.
SSLKEYLOGFILE	When set to a filename, GnuTLS will append to it the session keys in the NSS Key Log format. That format can be read by wireshark and will allow decryption of the session for debugging.
GNUTLS_CPUID_OVERRIDE	That environment variable can be used to explicitly enable/disable the use of certain CPU capabilities. Note that CPU detection cannot be overridden, i.e., VIA options cannot be enabled on an Intel CPU. The currently available options are: @itemize
0x1: Disable all run-time detected optimizations	
0x2: Enable AES-NI	
0x4: Enable SSSE3	
0x8: Enable PCLMUL	
0x10: Enable AVX	
0x100000: Enable VIA padlock	
0x200000: Enable VIA PHE	
0x400000: Enable VIA PHE SHA512 @end itemize	
GNUTLS_FORCE_FIPS_MODE	In setups where GnuTLS is compiled with support for FIPS140-2 (see section 8.7).

Table 5.1.: Environment variables used by the library.

When debugging is not required, important issues, such as detected attacks on the protocol still need to be logged. This is provided by the logging function set by **gnutls_global_set_audit_log_function**. The provided function will receive an message and the corresponding TLS session. The session information might be used to derive IP addresses or other information about the peer involved.

---

void **gnutls_global_set_audit_log_function** (*gnutls_audit_log_func* **log_func**)

Description: `This is the function to set the audit logging function. This is a function to report important issues, such as possible attacks in the protocol. This is different from gnutls_global_set_log_function() because it will report also session-specific events. The session parameter will be null if there is no corresponding TLS session. gnutls_audit_log_func is of the form, void (*gnutls_audit_log_func)(gnutls_session_t, const char*);`

5.1.5. Thread safety

The GnuTLS library is thread safe by design, meaning that objects of the library such as TLS sessions, can be safely divided across threads as long as a single thread accesses a single object. This is sufficient to support a server which handles several sessions per thread. If, however, an object needs to be shared across threads then access must be protected with a mutex. Read-only access to objects, for example the credentials holding structures, is also thread-safe.

A `gnutls_session_t` object can be shared by two threads, one sending, the other receiving. In that case rehandshakes, if required, must only be handled by a single thread being active. The termination of a session should be handled, either by a single thread being active, or by the sender thread using `gnutls_bye` with `GNUTLS_SHUT_WR` and the receiving thread waiting for a return value of zero.

The random generator of the cryptographic back-end, utilizes mutex locks (e.g., pthreads on GNU/Linux and CriticalSection on Windows) which are setup by GnuTLS on library initialization. Prior to version 3.3.0 they were setup by calling `gnutls_global_init`.[2] Note that, on Glibc systems the GnuTLS library does not link with the libpthread library by default, it utilizes the Glibc mutex stubs, which allows Glibc to use the non-multithreaded (and optimized) variants of its algorithms. That, however, for applications using GnuTLS that may potentially utilize mutexes, requires them to explicitly link with libpthread.

5.1.6. Running in a sandbox

Given that TLS protocol handling as well as X.509 certificate parsing are complicated processes involving several thousands lines of code, it is often desirable (and recommended) to run the TLS session handling in a sandbox like seccomp. That has to be allowed by the overall software design, but if available, it adds an additional layer of protection by preventing parsing errors from becoming vessels for further security issues such as code execution.

GnuTLS requires the following system calls to be available for its proper operation.

- nanosleep
- time

---

[2] On special systems you could manually specify the locking system using the function `gnutls_global_set_mutex` before calling any other GnuTLS function. Setting mutexes manually is not recommended.

- gettimeofday

- clock_gettime

- getrusage

- getpid

- send

- recv

- sendmsg

- read (to read from /dev/urandom)

- getrandom (this is Linux-kernel specific)

- poll

As well as any calls needed for memory allocation to work. Note however, that GnuTLS depends on libc for the system calls, and there is no guarantee that libc will call the expected system call. For that it is recommended to test your program in all the targetted platforms when filters like seccomp are in place.

An example with a seccomp filter from GnuTLS' test suite is at: `http://gitlab.com/gnutls/gnutls/blob/master/tests/seccomp.c`.

5.1.7. Sessions and fork

A `gnutls_session_t` object can be shared by two processes after a fork, one sending, the other receiving. In that case rehandshakes, cannot and must not be performed. As with threads, the termination of a session should be handled by the sender process using `gnutls_bye` with `GNUTLS_SHUT_WR` and the receiving process waiting for a return value of zero.

5.1.8. Callback functions

There are several cases where GnuTLS may need out of band input from your program. This is now implemented using some callback functions, which your program is expected to register.

An example of this type of functions are the push and pull callbacks which are used to specify the functions that will retrieve and send data to the transport layer.

---

void **gnutls_transport_set_push_function** (*gnutls_session_t* **session,** *gnutls_push_func* **push_func)**

void **gnutls_transport_set_pull_function** (*gnutls_session_t* **session,** *gnutls_pull_func* **pull_func)**

Other callback functions may require more complicated input and data to be allocated. Such an example is `gnutls_srp_set_server_credentials_function`. All callbacks should allocate and free memory using `gnutls_malloc` and `gnutls_free`.

5.2. Preparation

To use GnuTLS, you have to perform some changes to your sources and your build system. The necessary changes are explained in the following subsections.

5.2.1. Headers

All the data types and functions of the GnuTLS library are defined in the header file "`gnutls/gnutls.h`". This must be included in all programs that make use of the GnuTLS library.

5.2.2. Initialization

The GnuTLS library is initialized on load; prior to 3.3.0 was initialized by calling `gnutls_global_init`[3]. The initialization typically enables CPU-specific acceleration, performs any required precalculations needed, opens any required system devices (e.g., /dev/urandom on Linux) and initializes subsystems that could be used later.

The resources allocated by the initialization process will be released on library deinitialization.

Note that on certain systems file descriptors may be kept open by GnuTLS (e.g. /dev/urandom) on library load. Applications closing all unknown file descriptors must immediately call `gnutls_global_init`, after that, to ensure they don't disrupt GnuTLS' operation.

5.2.3. Version check

It is often desirable to check that the version of 'gnutls' used is indeed one which fits all requirements. Even with binary compatibility new features may have been introduced but due to problem with the dynamic linker an old version is actually used. So you may want to check that the version is okay right after program start-up. See the function `gnutls_check_version`.

On the other hand, it is often desirable to support more than one versions of the library. In that case you could utilize compile-time feature checks using the `GNUTLS_VERSION_NUMBER` macro. For example, to conditionally add code for GnuTLS 3.2.1 or later, you may use:

---

[3] The original behavior of requiring explicit initialization can obtained by setting the GNUTLS_NO_EXPLICIT_INIT environment variable to 1, or by using the macro GNUTLS_SKIP_GLOBAL_INIT in a global section of your program –the latter works in systems with support for weak symbols only.

```
1  #if GNUTLS_VERSION_NUMBER >= 0x030201
2    ...
3  #endif
```

5.2.4. Building the source

If you want to compile a source file including the "**gnutls/gnutls.h**" header file, you must make sure that the compiler can find it in the directory hierarchy. This is accomplished by adding the path to the directory in which the header file is located to the compilers include file search path (via the "**-I**" option).

However, the path to the include file is determined at the time the source is configured. To solve this problem, the library uses the external package "**pkg-config**" that knows the path to the include file and other configuration options. The options that need to be added to the compiler invocation at compile time are output by the "**--cflags**" option to "**pkg-config gnutls**". The following example shows how it can be used at the command line:

```
1  gcc -c foo.c `pkg-config gnutls --cflags`
```

Adding the output of pkg-config gnutls –cflags to the compilers command line will ensure that the compiler can find the "**gnutls/gnutls.h**" header file.

A similar problem occurs when linking the program with the library. Again, the compiler has to find the library files. For this to work, the path to the library files has to be added to the library search path (via the "**-L**" option). For this, the option "**--libs**" to "**pkg-config gnutls**" can be used. For convenience, this option also outputs all other options that are required to link the program with the library (for instance, the -ltasn1 option). The example shows how to link "**foo.o**" with the library to a program "**foo**".

```
1  gcc -o foo foo.o `pkg-config gnutls --libs`
```

Of course you can also combine both examples to a single command by specifying both options to "**pkg-config**":

```
1  gcc -o foo foo.c `pkg-config gnutls --cflags --libs`
```

When a program uses the GNU autoconf system, then the following line or similar can be used to detect the presence of GnuTLS.

```
1  PKG_CHECK_MODULES([LIBGNUTLS], [gnutls >= 3.3.0])
2
3  AC_SUBST([LIBGNUTLS_CFLAGS])
4  AC_SUBST([LIBGNUTLS_LIBS])
```

5.3. Session initialization

In the previous sections we have discussed the global initialization required for GnuTLS as well as the initialization required for each authentication method's credentials (see subsection 2.5.2). In this section we elaborate on the TLS or DTLS session initiation. Each session is initialized using **gnutls_init** which among others is used to specify the type of the connection (server or client), and the underlying protocol type, i.e., datagram (UDP) or reliable (TCP).

---

int **gnutls_init** (*gnutls_session_t* * **session,** *unsigned int* **flags**)

Description: This function initializes the provided session. Every session must be initialized before use, and must be deinitialized after used by calling gnutls_deinit(). flags can be any combination of flags from **gnutls_init_flags_t**. Note that since version 3.1.2 this function enables some common TLS extensions such as session tickets and OCSP certificate status request in client side by default. To prevent that use the **GNUTLS_-NO_EXTENSIONS** flag.

Returns: GNUTLS_E_SUCCESS on success, or an error code.

After the session initialization details on the allowed ciphersuites and protocol versions should be set using the priority functions such as **gnutls_priority_set** and **gnutls_priority_set_-direct**. We elaborate on them in section 5.10. The credentials used for the key exchange method, such as certificates or usernames and passwords should also be associated with the session current session using **gnutls_credentials_set**.

---

int **gnutls_credentials_set** (*gnutls_session_t* **session,** *gnutls_credentials_type_t* **type,** *void* * **cred**)

Description: Sets the needed credentials for the specified type. E.g. username, password - or public and private keys etc. The cred parameter is a structure that depends on the specified type and on the current session (client or server). In order to minimize memory usage, and share credentials between several threads gnutls keeps a pointer to cred, and not the whole cred structure. Thus you will have to keep the structure allocated until you call gnutls_deinit(). For **GNUTLS_CRD_ANON**, cred should be *gnutls_anon_-client_credentials_t* in case of a client. In case of a server it should be *gnutls_anon_server_-credentials_t*. For **GNUTLS_CRD_SRP**, cred should be *gnutls_srp_client_credentials_t* in case of a client, and *gnutls_srp_server_credentials_t*, in case of a server. For **GNUTLS_CRD_-CERTIFICATE**, cred should be *gnutls_certificate_credentials_t*.

Returns: On success, **GNUTLS_E_SUCCESS** (0) is returned, otherwise a negative error code is returned.

5.4. Associating the credentials

Each authentication method is associated with a key exchange method, and a credentials type. The contents of the credentials is method-dependent, e.g. certificates for certificate authentication and should be initialized and associated with a session (see `gnutls_credentials_set`). A mapping of the key exchange methods with the credential types is shown in Table 5.3.

5.4.1. Certificates

Server certificate authentication

When using certificates the server is required to have at least one certificate and private key pair. Clients may not hold such a pair, but a server could require it. In this section we discuss general issues applying to both client and server certificates. The next section will elaborate on issues arising from client authentication only.

---

int **gnutls_certificate_allocate_credentials** (*gnutls_certificate_credentials_t* * **res**)

void **gnutls_certificate_free_credentials** (*gnutls_certificate_credentials_t* **sc**)

After the credentials structures are initialized, the certificate and key pair must be loaded. This occurs before any TLS session is initialized, and the same structures are reused for multiple sessions. Depending on the certificate type different loading functions are available, as shown below. For X.509 certificates, the functions will accept and use a certificate chain that leads to a trusted authority. The certificate chain must be ordered in such way that every certificate certifies the one before it. The trusted authority's certificate need not to be included since the peer should possess it already.

---

int **gnutls_certificate_set_x509_key_file2** (*gnutls_certificate_credentials_t* **res**, *const char* * **certfile**, *const char* * **keyfile**, *gnutls_x509_crt_fmt_t* **type**, *const char* * **pass**, *unsigned int* **flags**)

int **gnutls_certificate_set_x509_key_mem2** (*gnutls_certificate_credentials_t* **res**, *const gnutls_datum_t* * **cert**, *const gnutls_datum_t* * **key**, *gnutls_x509_crt_fmt_t* **type**, *const char* * **pass**, *unsigned int* **flags**)

int **gnutls_certificate_set_x509_key** (*gnutls_certificate_credentials_t* **res**, *gnutls_x509_crt_t* * **cert_list**, *int* **cert_list_size**, *gnutls_x509_privkey_t* **key**)

It is recommended to use the higher level functions such as `gnutls_certificate_set_x509_-`

`key_file2` which accept not only file names but URLs that specify objects stored in token, or system certificates and keys (see section 4.2). For these cases, another important function is `gnutls_certificate_set_pin_function`, that allows setting a callback function to retrieve a PIN if the input keys are protected by PIN.

---

void **gnutls_certificate_set_pin_function** (*gnutls_certificate_credentials_t*   **cred**, *gnutls_pin_callback_t* **fn**, *void* * **userdata**)

Description: `This function will set a callback function to be used when required to access a protected object. This function overrides any other global PIN functions. Note that this function must be called right after initialization to have effect.`

If the imported keys and certificates need to be accessed before any TLS session is established, it is convenient to use `gnutls_certificate_set_key` in combination with `gnutls_pcert_import_x509_raw` and `gnutls_privkey_import_x509_raw`.

---

int **gnutls_certificate_set_key** (*gnutls_certificate_credentials_t* **res**, *const*   *char* ** **names**, *int* **names_size**, *gnutls_pcert_st*   * **pcert_list**, *int* **pcert_list_size**, *gnutls_privkey_t* **key**)

Description: `This function sets a certificate/private key pair in the gnutls_certificate_credentials_t type. This function may be called more than once, in case multiple keys/certificates exist for the server. For clients that want to send more than their own end- entity certificate (e.g., also an intermediate CA cert), the full certificate chain must be provided in pcert_list. Note that the key and the elements of pcert_list will become part of the credentials structure and must not be deallocated. They will be automatically deallocated when the res structure is deinitialized. If that function fails to load the res structure is at an undefined state, it must not be reused to load other keys or certificates. Note that, this function by default returns zero on success and a negative value on error. Since 3.5.6, when the flag` **GNUTLS_CERTIFICATE_API_V2** `is set using gnutls_certificate_set_flags() it returns an index (greater or equal to zero). That index can be used to other functions to refer to the added key-pair.`

Returns: `On success this functions returns zero, and otherwise a negative value on error (see above for modifying that behavior).`

If multiple certificates are used with the functions above each client's request will be served with the certificate that matches the requested name (see subsection 2.6.2).

As an alternative to loading from files or buffers, a callback may be used for the server or the client to specify the certificate and the key at the handshake time. In that case a certificate should be selected according the peer's signature algorithm preferences. To get those preferences use **gnutls_sign_algorithm_get_requested**. Both functions are shown below.

151

> *void* **gnutls_certificate_set_retrieve_function** (*gnutls_certificate_credentials_t* **cred**, *gnutls_certificate_retrieve_function* * **func**)
>
> *void* **gnutls_certificate_set_retrieve_function2** (*gnutls_certificate_credentials_t* **cred**, *gnutls_certificate_retrieve_function2* * **func**)
>
> *int* **gnutls_sign_algorithm_get_requested** (*gnutls_session_t* **session**, *size_t* **indx**, *gnutls_sign_algorithm_t* * **algo**)

The functions above do not handle the requested server name automatically. A server would need to check the name requested by the client using `gnutls_server_name_get`, and serve the appropriate certificate. Note that some of these functions require the `gnutls_pcert_st` structure to be filled in. Helper functions to fill in the structure are listed below.

```
typedef struct gnutls_pcert_st
{
  gnutls_pubkey_t pubkey;
  gnutls_datum_t cert;
  gnutls_certificate_type_t type;
} gnutls_pcert_st;
```

> *int* **gnutls_pcert_import_x509** (*gnutls_pcert_st* * **pcert**, *gnutls_x509_crt_t* **crt**, *unsigned int* **flags**)
>
> *int* **gnutls_pcert_import_x509_raw** (*gnutls_pcert_st* * **pcert**, *const gnutls_datum_t* * **cert**, *gnutls_x509_crt_fmt_t* **format**, *unsigned int* **flags**)
>
> *void* **gnutls_pcert_deinit** (*gnutls_pcert_st* * **pcert**)

In a handshake, the negotiated cipher suite depends on the certificate's parameters, so some key exchange methods might not be available with all certificates. GnuTLS will disable ciphersuites that are not compatible with the key, or the enabled authentication methods. For example keys marked as sign-only, will not be able to access the plain RSA ciphersuites, that require decryption. It is not recommended to use RSA keys for both signing and encryption. If possible use a different key for the `DHE-RSA` which uses signing and `RSA` that requires decryption. All the key exchange methods shown in Table 3.1 are available in certificate authentication.

Client certificate authentication

If a certificate is to be requested from the client during the handshake, the server will send a certificate request message. This behavior is controlled `gnutls_certificate_server_set_-request`. The request contains a list of the acceptable by the server certificate signers. This list is constructed using the trusted certificate authorities of the server. In cases where the server supports a large number of certificate authorities it makes sense not to advertise all of the names to save bandwidth. That can be controlled using the function gnutls_certificate_-send_x509_rdn_sequence. This however will have the side-effect of not restricting the client to certificates signed by server's acceptable signers.

---

void **gnutls_certificate_server_set_request** (*gnutls_session_t* **session**, *gnutls_certificate_request_t* **req**)

Description: This function specifies if we (in case of a server) are going to send a certificate request message to the client. If req is GNUTLS_CERT_REQUIRE then the server will return an error if the peer does not provide a certificate. If you do not call this function then the client will not be asked to send a certificate.

---

void **gnutls_certificate_send_x509_rdn_sequence** (*gnutls_session_t* **session**, *int* **status**)

Description: If status is non zero, this function will order gnutls not to send the rdnSequence in the certificate request message. That is the server will not advertise its trusted CAs to the peer. If status is zero then the default behaviour will take effect, which is to advertise the server's trusted CAs. This function has no effect in clients, and in authentication methods other than certificate with X.509 certificates.

On the client side, it needs to set its certificates on the credentials structure, similarly to server side from a file, or via a callback. Once the certificates are available in the credentials structure, the client will send them if during the handshake the server requests a certificate signed by the issuer of its CA.

In the case a single certificate is available and the server does not specify a signer's list, then that certificate is always sent. It is, however possible, to send a certificate even when the advertised CA list by the server contains CAs other than its signer. That can be achieved using the GNUTLS_FORCE_CLIENT_CERT flag in gnutls_init.

---

int **gnutls_certificate_set_x509_key_file** (*gnutls_certificate_credentials_t* **res**, *const char ** **certfile**, *const char ** **keyfile**, *gnutls_x509_crt_fmt_t* **type**)

int **gnutls_certificate_set_x509_simple_pkcs12_file** (*gnutls_certificate_credentials_t* **res**, *const char ** **pkcs12file**, *gnutls_x509_crt_fmt_t* **type**, *const char ** **password**)

void **gnutls_certificate_set_retrieve_function2** (*gnutls_certificate_credentials_t* **cred**, *gnutls_certificate_retrieve_function2 ** **func**)

Client or server certificate verification

Certificate verification is possible by loading the trusted authorities into the credentials structure by using the following functions, applicable to X.509 certificates. In modern systems it is recommended to utilize `gnutls_certificate_set_x509_system_trust` which will load the trusted authorities from the system store.

---

int **gnutls_certificate_set_x509_system_trust** (*gnutls_certificate_credentials_t* **cred**)

Description: `This function adds the system's default trusted CAs in order to verify client or server certificates. In the case the system is currently unsupported` **GNUTLS_-E_UNIMPLEMENTED_FEATURE** `is returned.`

Returns: `the number of certificates processed or a negative error code on error.`

---

int **gnutls_certificate_set_x509_trust_file** (*gnutls_certificate_credentials_t* **cred,** *const char* * **cafile,** *gnutls_x509_crt_fmt_t* **type**)

int **gnutls_certificate_set_x509_trust_dir** (*gnutls_certificate_credentials_t* **cred,** *const char* * **ca_dir,** *gnutls_x509_crt_fmt_t* **type**)

The peer's certificate will be automatically verified if `gnutls_session_set_verify_cert` is called prior to handshake.

Alternatively, one must set a callback function during the handshake using `gnutls_certificate_set_verify_function`, which will verify the peer's certificate once received. The verification should happen using `gnutls_certificate_verify_peers3` within the callback. It will verify the certificate's signature and the owner of the certificate. That will provide a brief verification output. If a detailed output is required one should call `gnutls_certificate_get_peers` to obtain the raw certificate of the peer and verify it using the functions discussed in subsection 3.1.1.

In both the automatic and the manual cases, the verification status returned can be printed using `gnutls_certificate_verification_status_print`.

---

int **gnutls_certificate_verify_peers3** (*gnutls_session_t* **session,** *const char* * **hostname,** *unsigned int* * **status**)

void **gnutls_certificate_set_verify_function** (*gnutls_certificate_credentials_t* **cred,** *gnutls_certificate_verify_function* * **func**)

---

void **gnutls_session_set_verify_cert** (*gnutls_session_t* **session,** *const char* * **host-name,** *unsigned* **flags**)

Description: This function instructs GnuTLS to verify the peer's certificate using the provided hostname. If the verification fails the handshake will also fail with **GNUTLS-E_CERTIFICATE_VERIFICATION_ERROR**. In that case the verification result can be obtained using gnutls_session_get_verify_cert_status(). The **hostname** pointer provided must remain valid for the lifetime of the session. More precisely it should be available during any subsequent handshakes. If no hostname is provided, no hostname verification will be performed. For a more advanced verification function check gnutls_session_set_verify_cert2(). If **flags** is provided which contain a profile, this function should be called after any session priority setting functions. The gnutls_session_set_verify_cert() function is intended to be used by TLS clients to verify the server's certificate.

5.4.2. SRP

The initialization functions in SRP credentials differ between client and server. Clients supporting SRP should set the username and password prior to connection, to the credentials structure. Alternatively **gnutls_srp_set_client_credentials_function** may be used instead, to specify a callback function that should return the SRP username and password. The callback is called once during the TLS handshake.

---

int **gnutls_srp_allocate_server_credentials** (*gnutls_srp_server_credentials_t* * **sc**)

int **gnutls_srp_allocate_client_credentials** (*gnutls_srp_client_credentials_t* * **sc**)

void **gnutls_srp_free_server_credentials** (*gnutls_srp_server_credentials_t* **sc**)

void **gnutls_srp_free_client_credentials** (*gnutls_srp_client_credentials_t* **sc**)

int **gnutls_srp_set_client_credentials** (*gnutls_srp_client_credentials_t* **res,** *const char* * **username,** *const char* * **password**)

In server side the default behavior of GnuTLS is to read the usernames and SRP verifiers from password files. These password file format is compatible the with the *Stanford srp libraries* format. If a different password file format is to be used, then **gnutls_srp_set_server_credentials_function** should be called, to set an appropriate callback.

---

void **gnutls_srp_set_client_credentials_function** (*gnutls_srp_client_credentials_t* cred, *gnutls_srp_client_credentials_function* * **func**)

Description: This function can be used to set a callback to retrieve the username and password for client SRP authentication. The callback's function form is: int (*callback)(gnutls_session_t, char** username, char**password); The **username** and **password** must be allocated using gnutls_malloc(). **username** and **password** should be ASCII strings or UTF-8 strings prepared using the "SASLprep" profile of "stringprep". The callback function will called once per handshake before the initial hello message is sent. The callback should not return a negative error code the second time called, since the handshake procedure will be aborted. The callback function should return 0 on success. -1 indicates an error.

---

int **gnutls_srp_set_server_credentials_file** (*gnutls_srp_server_credentials_t* **res**, *const char* * **password_file**, *const char* * **password_conf_file**)

Description: This function sets the password files, in a *gnutls_srp_server_credentials_t* type. Those password files hold usernames and verifiers and will be used for SRP authentication.

Returns: On success, **GNUTLS_E_SUCCESS** (0) is returned, or an error code.

---

void **gnutls_srp_set_server_credentials_function** (*gnutls_srp_server_credentials_t* cred, *gnutls_srp_server_credentials_function* * **func**)

Description: This function can be used to set a callback to retrieve the user's SRP credentials. The callback's function form is: int (*callback)(gnutls_session_t, const char* username, gnutls_datum_t *salt, gnutls_datum_t *verifier, gnutls_datum_t *generator, gnutls_datum_t *prime); **username** contains the actual username. The **salt**, **verifier**, **generator** and **prime** must be filled in using the gnutls_malloc(). For convenience **prime** and **generator** may also be one of the static parameters defined in gnutls.h. Initially, the data field is NULL in every *gnutls_datum_t* structure that the callback has to fill in. When the callback is done GnuTLS deallocates all of those buffers which are non-NULL, regardless of the return value. In order to prevent attackers from guessing valid usernames, if a user does not exist, g and n values should be filled in using a random user's parameters. In that case the callback must return the special value (1). See *gnutls_srp_set_server_fake_salt_seed* too. If this is not required for your application, return a negative number from the callback to abort the handshake. The callback function will only be called once per handshake. The callback function should return 0 on success, while -1 indicates an error.

5.4.3. PSK

The initialization functions in PSK credentials differ between client and server.

---

int **gnutls_psk_allocate_server_credentials** (*gnutls_psk_server_credentials_t* * **sc**)

int **gnutls_psk_allocate_client_credentials** (*gnutls_psk_client_credentials_t* * **sc**)

void **gnutls_psk_free_server_credentials** (*gnutls_psk_server_credentials_t* **sc**)

void **gnutls_psk_free_client_credentials** (*gnutls_psk_client_credentials_t* **sc**)

Clients supporting PSK should supply the username and key before a TLS session is established. Alternatively `gnutls_psk_set_client_credentials_function` can be used to specify a callback function. This has the advantage that the callback will be called only if PSK has been negotiated.

---

int **gnutls_psk_set_client_credentials** (*gnutls_psk_client_credentials_t* **res**, *const char* * **username**, *const gnutls_datum_t* * **key**, *gnutls_psk_key_flags* **flags**)

---

void **gnutls_psk_set_client_credentials_function** (*gnutls_psk_client_credentials_t* **cred**, *gnutls_psk_client_credentials_function* * **func**)

Description: `This function can be used to set a callback to retrieve the username and password for client PSK authentication. The callback's function form is: int (*callback)(gnutls_session_t, char** username, gnutls_datum_t* key); The username and key→data must be allocated using gnutls_malloc(). username should be ASCII strings or UTF-8 strings prepared using the "SASLprep" profile of "stringprep". The callback function will be called once per handshake. The callback function should return 0 on success. -1 indicates an error.`

In server side the default behavior of GnuTLS is to read the usernames and PSK keys from a password file. The password file should contain usernames and keys in hexadecimal format. The name of the password file can be stored to the credentials structure by calling `gnutls_psk_set_server_credentials_file`. If a different password file format is to be used, then a callback should be set instead by `gnutls_psk_set_server_credentials_function`.

The server can help the client chose a suitable username and password, by sending a hint. Note that there is no common profile for the PSK hint and applications are discouraged to use it. A server, may specify the hint by calling **gnutls_psk_set_server_credentials_hint**. The client can retrieve the hint, for example in the callback function, using **gnutls_psk_client_get_hint**.

---

int **gnutls_psk_set_server_credentials_file** (*gnutls_psk_server_credentials_t* **res**, *const char* * **password_file**)

Description: This function sets the password file, in a *gnutls_psk_server_credentials_t* type. This password file holds usernames and keys and will be used for PSK authentication.

Returns: On success, **GNUTLS_E_SUCCESS** (0) is returned, otherwise an error code is returned.

---

void **gnutls_psk_set_server_credentials_function** (*gnutls_psk_server_credentials_t* **cred**, *gnutls_psk_server_credentials_function* * **func**)

int **gnutls_psk_set_server_credentials_hint** (*gnutls_psk_server_credentials_t* **res**, *const char* * **hint**)

const char * **gnutls_psk_client_get_hint** (*gnutls_session_t* **session**)

5.4.4. Anonymous

The key exchange methods for anonymous authentication since GnuTLS 3.6.0 will utilize the RFC7919 parameters, unless explicit parameters have been provided and associated with an anonymous credentials structure. Check subsection 5.12.4 for more information. The initialization functions for the credentials are shown below.

---

int **gnutls_anon_allocate_server_credentials** (*gnutls_anon_server_credentials_t* * **sc**)

int **gnutls_anon_allocate_client_credentials** (*gnutls_anon_client_credentials_t* * **sc**)

void **gnutls_anon_free_server_credentials** (*gnutls_anon_server_credentials_t* **sc**)

void **gnutls_anon_free_client_credentials** (*gnutls_anon_client_credentials_t* **sc**)

5.5. Setting up the transport layer

The next step is to setup the underlying transport layer details. The Berkeley sockets are implicitly used by GnuTLS, thus a call to **gnutls_transport_set_int** would be sufficient to specify the socket descriptor.

---

void **gnutls_transport_set_int** (*gnutls_session_t* **session,** *int* **fd**)

void **gnutls_transport_set_int2** (*gnutls_session_t* **session,** *int* **recv_fd,** *int* **send_fd**)

If however another transport layer than TCP is selected, then a pointer should be used instead to express the parameter to be passed to custom functions. In that case the following functions should be used instead.

---

void **gnutls_transport_set_ptr** (*gnutls_session_t* **session,** *gnutls_transport_ptr_t* **ptr**)

void **gnutls_transport_set_ptr2** (*gnutls_session_t* **session,** *gnutls_transport_ptr_t* **recv_ptr,** *gnutls_transport_ptr_t* **send_ptr**)

Moreover all of the following push and pull callbacks should be set.

---

void **gnutls_transport_set_push_function** (*gnutls_session_t* **session,** *gnutls_push_func* **push_func**)

Description: This is the function where you set a push function for gnutls to use in order to send data. If you are going to use berkeley style sockets, you do not need to use this function since the default send(2) will probably be ok. Otherwise you should specify this function for gnutls to be able to send data. The callback should return a positive number indicating the bytes sent, and -1 on error. push_func is of the form, ssize_t (*gnutls_push_func)(gnutls_transport_ptr_t, const void*, size_t);

The functions above accept a callback function which should return the number of bytes written, or -1 on error and should set **errno** appropriately. In some environments, setting **errno** is unreliable. For example Windows have several errno variables in different CRTs, or in other systems it may be a non thread-local variable. If this is a concern to you, call **gnutls_-transport_set_errno** with the intended errno value instead of setting **errno** directly.

GnuTLS currently only interprets the EINTR, EAGAIN and EMSGSIZE errno values and returns the corresponding GnuTLS error codes:

void **gnutls_transport_set_vec_push_function** (*gnutls_session_t* **session**, *gnutls_vec_push_func* **vec_func**)

Description: Using this function you can override the default writev(2) function for gnutls to send data. Setting this callback instead of gnutls_transport_set_push_function() is recommended since it introduces less overhead in the TLS handshake process. vec_func is of the form, ssize_t (*gnutls_vec_push_func) (gnutls_transport_ptr_t, const giovec_t * iov, int iovcnt);

void **gnutls_transport_set_pull_function** (*gnutls_session_t* **session**, *gnutls_pull_func* **pull_func**)

Description: This is the function where you set a function for gnutls to receive data. Normally, if you use berkeley style sockets, do not need to use this function since the default recv(2) will probably be ok. The callback should return 0 on connection termination, a positive number indicating the number of bytes received, and -1 on error. gnutls_pull_func is of the form, ssize_t (*gnutls_pull_func)(gnutls_transport_ptr_t, void*, size_t);

void **gnutls_transport_set_pull_timeout_function** (*gnutls_session_t* **session**, *gnutls_pull_timeout_func* **func**)

Description: This is the function where you set a function for gnutls to know whether data are ready to be received. It should wait for data a given time frame in milliseconds. The callback should return 0 on timeout, a positive number if data can be received, and -1 on error. You'll need to override this function if select() is not suitable for the provided transport calls. As with select(), if the timeout value is zero the callback should return zero if no data are immediately available. The special value **GNUTLS_INDEFINITE_TIMEOUT** indicates that the callback should wait indefinitely for data. gnutls_pull_timeout_func is of the form, int (*gnutls_pull_timeout_func)(gnutls_transport_ptr_t, unsigned int ms); This callback is necessary when gnutls_handshake_set_timeout() or gnutls_record_set_timeout() are set, and for calculating the DTLS mode timeouts. In short, this callback should be set when a custom pull function is registered. The callback will not be used when the session is in TLS mode with non-blocking sockets. That is, when **GNUTLS_NONBLOCK** is specified for a TLS session in gnutls_init(). For compatibility with future GnuTLS versions it is recommended to always set this function when a custom pull function is registered. The helper function gnutls_system_recv_timeout() is provided to simplify writing callbacks.

---

void **gnutls_transport_set_errno** (*gnutls_session_t* **session**, *int* **err**)

Description: `Store err in the session-specific errno variable. Useful values for err are EINTR, EAGAIN and EMSGSIZE, other values are treated will be treated as real errors in the push/pull function. This function is useful in replacement push and pull functions set by gnutls_transport_set_push_function() and gnutls_transport_set_pull_function() under Windows, where the replacements may not have access to the same errno variable that is used by GnuTLS (e.g., the application is linked to msvcr71.dll and gnutls is linked to msvcrt.dll).`

- `GNUTLS_E_INTERRUPTED`

- `GNUTLS_E_AGAIN`

- `GNUTLS_E_LARGE_PACKET`

The EINTR and EAGAIN values are returned by interrupted system calls, or when non blocking IO is used. All GnuTLS functions can be resumed (called again), if any of the above error codes is returned. The EMSGSIZE value is returned when attempting to send a large datagram.

In the case of DTLS it is also desirable to override the generic transport functions with functions that emulate the operation of **recvfrom** and **sendto**. In addition DTLS requires timers during the receive of a handshake message, set using the **gnutls_transport_set_pull_timeout_-function** function. To check the retransmission timers the function **gnutls_dtls_get_timeout** is provided, which returns the time remaining until the next retransmission, or better the time until **gnutls_handshake** should be called again.

5.5.1. Asynchronous operation

GnuTLS can be used with asynchronous socket or event-driven programming. The approach is similar to using Berkeley sockets under such an environment. The blocking, due to network interaction, calls such as **gnutls_handshake**, **gnutls_record_recv**, can be set to non-blocking by setting the underlying sockets to non-blocking. If other push and pull functions are setup, then they should behave the same way as **recv** and **send** when used in a non-blocking way, i.e., return -1 and set errno to **EAGAIN**. Since, during a TLS protocol session GnuTLS does not block except for network interaction, the non blocking **EAGAIN** errno will be propagated and GnuTLS functions will return the **GNUTLS_E_AGAIN** error code. Such calls can be resumed the same way as a system call would. The only exception is **gnutls_record_send**, which if interrupted subsequent calls need not to include the data to be sent (can be called with NULL argument).

When using the **poll** or **select** system calls though, one should remember that they only apply to the kernel sockets API. To check for any available buffered data in a GnuTLS session, utilize **gnutls_record_check_pending**, either before the **poll** system call, or after a call to **gnutls_-**

void **gnutls_transport_set_pull_timeout_function** (*gnutls_session_t* **session**, *gnutls_pull_timeout_func* **func**)

Description: This is the function where you set a function for gnutls to know whether data are ready to be received. It should wait for data a given time frame in milliseconds. The callback should return 0 on timeout, a positive number if data can be received, and -1 on error. You'll need to override this function if select() is not suitable for the provided transport calls. As with select(), if the timeout value is zero the callback should return zero if no data are immediately available. The special value **GNUTLS_INDEFINITE_TIMEOUT** indicates that the callback should wait indefinitely for data. gnutls_pull_timeout_func is of the form, int (*gnutls_pull_timeout_func)(gnutls_transport_ptr_t, unsigned int ms); This callback is necessary when gnutls_handshake_set_timeout() or gnutls_record_set_timeout() are set, and for calculating the DTLS mode timeouts. In short, this callback should be set when a custom pull function is registered. The callback will not be used when the session is in TLS mode with non-blocking sockets. That is, when **GNUTLS_NONBLOCK** is specified for a TLS session in gnutls_init(). For compatibility with future GnuTLS versions it is recommended to always set this function when a custom pull function is registered. The helper function gnutls_system_recv_timeout() is provided to simplify writing callbacks.

unsigned int **gnutls_dtls_get_timeout** (*gnutls_session_t* **session**)

Description: This function will return the milliseconds remaining for a retransmission of the previously sent handshake message. This function is useful when DTLS is used in non-blocking mode, to estimate when to call gnutls_handshake() if no packets have been received.

Returns: the remaining time in milliseconds.

record_recv. Data queued by **gnutls_record_send** (when interrupted) can be discarded using gnutls_record_discard_queued.

An example of GnuTLS' usage with asynchronous operation can be found in **doc/examples/tlsproxy**.

The following paragraphs describe the detailed requirements for non-blocking operation when using the TLS or DTLS protocols.

TLS protocol

There are no special requirements for the TLS protocol operation in non-blocking mode if a non-blocking socket is used.

It is recommended, however, for future compatibility, when in non-blocking mode, to call the gnutls_init function with the GNUTLS_NONBLOCK flag set (see section 5.3).

Datagram TLS protocol

When in non-blocking mode the function, the gnutls_init function must be called with the GNUTLS_NONBLOCK flag set (see section 5.3).

In contrast with the TLS protocol, the pull timeout function is required, but will only be called with a timeout of zero. In that case it should indicate whether there are data to be received or not. When not using the default pull function, then gnutls_transport_set_pull_timeout_-function should be called.

Although in the TLS protocol implementation each call to receive or send function implies to restoring the same function that was interrupted, in the DTLS protocol this requirement isn't true. There are cases where a retransmission is required, which are indicated by a received message and thus gnutls_record_get_direction must be called to decide which direction to check prior to restoring a function call.

---

int **gnutls_record_get_direction** (*gnutls_session_t* **session**)

Description: This function provides information about the internals of the record protocol and is only useful if a prior gnutls function call, e.g. gnutls_handshake(), was interrupted for some reason. That is, if a function returned **GNUTLS_E_-INTERRUPTED** or **GNUTLS_E_AGAIN**. In such a case, you might want to call select() or poll() before restoring the interrupted gnutls function. This function's output is unreliable if you are using the same **session** in different threads, for sending and receiving.

Returns: 0 if interrupted while trying to read data, or 1 while trying to write data.

When calling gnutls_handshake through a multi-plexer, to be able to handle properly the DTLS handshake retransmission timers, the function gnutls_dtls_get_timeout should be used to estimate when to call gnutls_handshake if no data have been received.

5.5.2. Reducing round-trips

The full TLS 1.2 handshake requires 2 round-trips to complete, and when combined with TCP's SYN and SYN-ACK negotiation it extends to 3 full round-trips. While, the abbreviated (resumed) TLS handshake drops that to 2.5 round-trips, it still adds considerable latency, reducing its applicability to certain applications.

In client side, it is possible to take advantage of the TCP fast open [7] mechanism on operating systems that support it. That can be done either by manually crafting the push and pull callbacks, or by utilizing `gnutls_transport_set_fastopen`. In that case the initial TCP handshake is eliminated, reducing the TLS handshake round-trip to 2. Note, that in that case any connection failures will be reported during the `gnutls_handshake` function call with error code `GNUTLS_E_PUSH_ERROR`.

---

void **gnutls_transport_set_fastopen** (*gnutls_session_t* **session**, *int* **fd**, *struct sockaddr * * **connect_addr**, *socklen_t* **connect_addrlen**, *unsigned int* **flags**)

Description: `Enables TCP Fast Open (TFO) for the specified TLS client session. That means that TCP connection establishment and the transmission of the first TLS client hello packet are combined. The peer's address must be specified in` **connect_addr** `and` **connect_addrlen**`, and the socket specified by` **fd** `should not be connected. TFO only works for TCP sockets of type AF_INET and AF_INET6. If the OS doesn't support TCP fast open this function will result to gnutls using connect() transparently during the first write.`

Note: *This function overrides all the transport callback functions. If this is undesirable, TCP Fast Open must be implemented on the user callback functions without calling this function. When using this function, transport callbacks must not be set, and gnutls_transport_set_ptr() or gnutls_transport_set_int() must not be called. On GNU/Linux TFO has to be enabled at the system layer, that is in /proc/sys/net/ipv4/tcp_fastopen, bit 0 has to be set. This function has no effect on server sessions.*

In non-resumed sessions it is possible to further reduce the round-trips to a single one by taking advantage of the subsection 2.6.8 TLS extension. This can be enabled by setting the GNUTLS_ENABLE_FALSE_START flag on `gnutls_init`.

5.5.3. DTLS sessions

Because datagram TLS can operate over connections where the client cannot be reliably verified, functionality in the form of cookies, is available to prevent denial of service attacks to servers. GnuTLS requires a server to generate a secret key that is used to sign a cookie[4]. That cookie is sent to the client using `gnutls_dtls_cookie_send`, and the client must reply using the correct cookie. The server side should verify the initial message sent by client using `gnutls_dtls_cookie_verify`. If successful the session should be initialized and associated with the cookie using `gnutls_dtls_prestate_set`, before proceeding to the handshake.

---

[4]A key of 128 bits or 16 bytes should be sufficient for this purpose.

---

int **gnutls_key_generate** (*gnutls_datum_t* * **key**, *unsigned int* **key_size**)

int **gnutls_dtls_cookie_send** (*gnutls_datum_t* * **key**, *void* * **client_data**, *size_t* **client_data_size**, *gnutls_dtls_prestate_st* * **prestate**, *gnutls_transport_ptr_t* **ptr**, *gnutls_push_func* **push_func**)

int **gnutls_dtls_cookie_verify** (*gnutls_datum_t* * **key**, *void* * **client_data**, *size_t* **client_data_size**, *void* * **_msg**, *size_t* **msg_size**, *gnutls_dtls_prestate_st* * **prestate**)

void **gnutls_dtls_prestate_set** (*gnutls_session_t* **session**, *gnutls_dtls_prestate_st* * **prestate**)

Note that the above apply to server side only and they are not mandatory to be used. Not using them, however, allows denial of service attacks. The client side cookie handling is part of `gnutls_handshake`.

Datagrams are typically restricted by a maximum transfer unit (MTU). For that both client and server side should set the correct maximum transfer unit for the layer underneath GnuTLS. This will allow proper fragmentation of DTLS messages and prevent messages from being silently discarded by the transport layer. The "correct" maximum transfer unit can be obtained through a path MTU discovery mechanism [25].

---

void **gnutls_dtls_set_mtu** (*gnutls_session_t* **session**, *unsigned int* **mtu**)

unsigned int **gnutls_dtls_get_mtu** (*gnutls_session_t* **session**)

unsigned int **gnutls_dtls_get_data_mtu** (*gnutls_session_t* **session**)

5.5.4. DTLS and SCTP

Although DTLS can run under any reliable or unreliable layer, there are special requirements for SCTP according to [43]. We summarize the most important below, however for a full treatment we refer to [43].

- The MTU set via `gnutls_dtls_set_mtu` must be 2 textasciicircum14.

- Replay detection must be disabled; use the flag `GNUTLS_NO_REPLAY_PROTECTION` with `gnutls_init`.

- Retransmission of messages must be disabled; use `gnutls_dtls_set_timeouts` with a retransmission timeout larger than the total.

- Handshake, Alert and ChangeCipherSpec messages must be sent over stream 0 with unlimited reliability and with the ordered delivery feature.

- During a rehandshake, the caching of messages with unknown epoch is not handled by GnuTLS; this must be implemented in a special pull function.

5.6. TLS handshake

Once a session has been initialized and a network connection has been set up, TLS and DTLS protocols perform a handshake. The handshake is the actual key exchange.

---

int **gnutls_handshake** (*gnutls_session_t* **session**)

Description: This function does the handshake of the TLS/SSL protocol, and initializes the TLS connection. This function will fail if any problem is encountered, and will return a negative error code. In case of a client, if the client has asked to resume a session, but the server couldn't, then a full handshake will be performed. The non-fatal errors expected by this function are: **GNUTLS_E_INTERRUPTED, GNUTLS_E_AGAIN, GNUTLS_E_WARNING_ALERT_RECEIVED**, and **GNUTLS_E_GOT_APPLICATION_DATA**, the latter only in a case of rehandshake. The former two interrupt the handshake procedure due to the lower layer being interrupted, and the latter because of an alert that may be sent by a server (it is always a good idea to check any received alerts). On these errors call this function again, until it returns 0; cf. gnutls_record_get_direction() and gnutls_error_is_fatal(). In DTLS sessions the non-fatal error **GNUTLS_E_LARGE_PACKET** is also possible, and indicates that the MTU should be adjusted. If this function is called by a server after a rehandshake request then **GNUTLS_E_GOT_APPLICATION_DATA** or **GNUTLS_E_WARNING_ALERT_RECEIVED** may be returned. Note that these are non fatal errors, only in the specific case of a rehandshake. Their meaning is that the client rejected the rehandshake request or in the case of **GNUTLS_E_GOT_APPLICATION_DATA** it could also mean that some data were pending. A client may receive that error code if it initiates the handshake and the server doesn't agreed.

Returns: GNUTLS_E_SUCCESS on success, otherwise a negative error code.

---

void **gnutls_handshake_set_timeout** (*gnutls_session_t* **session**, *unsigned int* **ms**)

Description: This function sets the timeout for the TLS handshake process to the provided value. Use an ms value of zero to disable timeout, or **GNUTLS_DEFAULT_HANDSHAKE_TIMEOUT** for a reasonable default value. For the DTLS protocol, the more detailed gnutls_dtls_set_timeouts() is provided. This function requires to set a pull timeout callback. See gnutls_transport_set_pull_timeout_function().

In GnuTLS 3.5.0 and later it is recommended to use `gnutls_session_set_verify_cert` for the handshake process to ensure the verification of the peer's identity.

In older GnuTLS versions it is required to manually verify the peer's certificate during the handshake by using `gnutls_certificate_set_verify_function`, and `gnutls_certificate_verify_peers2`. See section 3.1 for more information.

---

void **gnutls_session_set_verify_cert** (*gnutls_session_t* **session,** *const char* * **hostname,** *unsigned* **flags)**

int **gnutls_certificate_verify_peers2** (*gnutls_session_t* **session,** *unsigned int* * **status)**

5.7. Data transfer and termination

Once the handshake is complete and peer's identity has been verified data can be exchanged. The available functions resemble the POSIX `recv` and `send` functions. It is suggested to use `gnutls_error_is_fatal` to check whether the error codes returned by these functions are fatal for the protocol or can be ignored.

---

ssize_t **gnutls_record_send** (*gnutls_session_t* **session,** *const void* * **data,** *size_t* **data_size)**

Description: This function has the similar semantics with send(). The only difference is that it accepts a GnuTLS session, and uses different error codes. Note that if the send buffer is full, send() will block this function. See the send() documentation for more information. You can replace the default push function which is send(), by using gnutls_-transport_set_push_function(). If the EINTR is returned by the internal push function then **GNUTLS_E_INTERRUPTED** will be returned. If **GNUTLS_E_INTERRUPTED** or **GNUTLS_E_AGAIN** is returned, you must call this function again, with the exact same parameters; alternatively you could provide a **NULL** pointer for data, and 0 for size. cf. gnutls_record_get_direction(). Note that in DTLS this function will return the **GNUTLS_-E_LARGE_PACKET** error code if the send data exceed the data MTU value – as returned by gnutls_dtls_get_data_mtu(). The errno value EMSGSIZE also maps to **GNUTLS_E_LARGE_-PACKET**. Note that since 3.2.13 this function can be called under cork in DTLS mode, and will refuse to send data over the MTU size by returning **GNUTLS_E_LARGE_PACKET**.

Returns: The number of bytes sent, or a negative error code. The number of bytes sent might be less than **data_size**. The maximum number of bytes this function can send in a single call depends on the negotiated maximum record size.

---

ssize_t **gnutls_record_recv** (*gnutls_session_t* **session,** *void*   * **data,** *size_t* **data_size)**

Description: This function has the similar semantics with recv(). The only difference is that it accepts a GnuTLS session, and uses different error codes. In the special case that the peer requests a renegotiation, the caller will receive an error code of **GNUTLS_E_REHANDSHAKE**. In case of a client, this message may be simply ignored, replied with an alert **GNUTLS_A_NO_RENEGOTIATION**, or replied with a new handshake, depending on the client's will. A server receiving this error code can only initiate a new handshake or terminate the session. If **EINTR** is returned by the internal pull function (the default is recv()) then **GNUTLS_E_INTERRUPTED** will be returned. If **GNUTLS_E_INTERRUPTED** or **GNUTLS_E_AGAIN** is returned, you must call this function again to get the data. See also gnutls_record_get_direction().

Returns: The number of bytes received and zero on EOF (for stream connections). A negative error code is returned in case of an error. The number of bytes received might be less than the requested **data_size**.

Although, in the TLS protocol the receive function can be called at any time, when DTLS is used the GnuTLS receive functions must be called once a message is available for reading, even if no data are expected. This is because in DTLS various (internal) actions may be required due to retransmission timers. Moreover, an extended receive function is shown below, which allows the extraction of the message's sequence number. Due to the unreliable nature of the protocol, this field allows distinguishing out-of-order messages.

The `gnutls_record_check_pending` helper function is available to allow checking whether data are available to be read in a GnuTLS session buffers. Note that this function complements but does not replace `poll`, i.e., `gnutls_record_check_pending` reports no data to be read, `poll` should be called to check for data in the network buffers.

---

int **gnutls_error_is_fatal** (*int* **error)**

Description: If a GnuTLS function returns a negative error code you may feed that value to this function to see if the error condition is fatal to a TLS session (i.e., must be terminated). Note that you may also want to check the error code manually, since some non-fatal errors to the protocol (such as a warning alert or a rehandshake request) may be fatal for your program. This function is only useful if you are dealing with errors from functions that relate to a TLS session (e.g., record layer or handshake layer handling functions).

Returns: Non-zero value on fatal errors or zero on non-fatal.

---

ssize_t **gnutls_record_recv_seq** (*gnutls_session_t* **session,** *void*   * **data,** *size_t* **data_size,** *unsigned char* * **seq)**

Description: This function is the same as gnutls_record_recv(), except that it returns in addition to data, the sequence number of the data. This is useful in DTLS where record packets might be received out-of-order. The returned 8-byte sequence number is an integer in big-endian format and should be treated as a unique message identification.

Returns: The number of bytes received and zero on EOF. A negative error code is returned in case of an error. The number of bytes received might be less than **data_size.**

---

size_t **gnutls_record_check_pending** (*gnutls_session_t* **session)**

Description: This function checks if there are unread data in the gnutls buffers. If the return value is non-zero the next call to gnutls_record_recv() is guaranteed not to block.

Returns: Returns the size of the data or zero.

---

int **gnutls_record_get_direction** (*gnutls_session_t* **session)**

Once a TLS or DTLS session is no longer needed, it is recommended to use **gnutls_bye** to terminate the session. That way the peer is notified securely about the intention of termination, which allows distinguishing it from a malicious connection termination. A session can be deinitialized with the **gnutls_deinit** function.

5.8. Buffered data transfer

Although **gnutls_record_send** is sufficient to transmit data to the peer, when many small chunks of data are to be transmitted it is inefficient and wastes bandwidth due to the TLS record overhead. In that case it is preferrable to combine the small chunks before transmission. The following functions provide that functionality.

169

int **gnutls_bye** (*gnutls_session_t* **session,** *gnutls_close_request_t* **how**)

Description: Terminates the current TLS/SSL connection. The connection should have been initiated using gnutls_handshake(). how should be one of **GNUTLS_SHUT_RDWR, GNUTLS_SHUT_WR.** In case of **GNUTLS_SHUT_RDWR** the TLS session gets terminated and further receives and sends will be disallowed. If the return value is zero you may continue using the underlying transport layer. **GNUTLS_SHUT_RDWR** sends an alert containing a close request and waits for the peer to reply with the same message. In case of **GNUTLS_SHUT_WR** the TLS session gets terminated and further sends will be disallowed. In order to reuse the connection you should wait for an EOF from the peer. **GNUTLS_SHUT_WR** sends an alert containing a close request. Note that not all implementations will properly terminate a TLS connection. Some of them, usually for performance reasons, will terminate only the underlying transport layer, and thus not distinguishing between a malicious party prematurely terminating the connection and normal termination. This function may also return **GNUTLS_E_AGAIN** or **GNUTLS_E_INTERRUPTED**; cf. gnutls_record_get_direction().

Returns: **GNUTLS_E_SUCCESS** on success, or an error code, see function documentation for entire semantics.

---

void **gnutls_deinit** (*gnutls_session_t* **session**)

Description: This function clears all buffers associated with the session. This function will also remove session data from the session database if the session was terminated abnormally.

5.9. Handling alerts

During a TLS connection alert messages may be exchanged by the two peers. Those messages may be fatal, meaning the connection must be terminated afterwards, or warning when something needs to be reported to the peer, but without interrupting the session. The error codes GNUTLS_E_WARNING_ALERT_RECEIVED or GNUTLS_E_FATAL_ALERT_RECEIVED signal those alerts when received, and may be returned by all GnuTLS functions that receive data from the

---

void **gnutls_record_cork** (*gnutls_session_t* **session**)

Description: If called, gnutls_record_send() will no longer send any records. Any sent records will be cached until gnutls_record_uncork() is called. This function is safe to use with DTLS after GnuTLS 3.3.0.

---

int **gnutls_record_uncork** (*gnutls_session_t* **session**, *unsigned int* **flags**)

Description: This resets the effect of gnutls_record_cork(), and flushes any pending data. If the **GNUTLS_RECORD_WAIT** flag is specified then this function will block until the data is sent or a fatal error occurs (i.e., the function will retry on **GNUTLS_E_AGAIN** and **GNUTLS_E_INTERRUPTED**). If the flag **GNUTLS_-RECORD_WAIT** is not specified and the function is interrupted then the **GNUTLS_-E_AGAIN** or **GNUTLS_E_INTERRUPTED** errors will be returned. To obtain the data left in the corked buffer use gnutls_record_check_corked().

Returns: On success the number of transmitted data is returned, or otherwise a negative error code.

---

peer, being **gnutls_handshake** and **gnutls_record_recv**.

If those error codes are received the alert and its level should be logged or reported to the peer using the functions below.

---

gnutls_alert_description_t **gnutls_alert_get** (*gnutls_session_t* **session**)

Description: This function will return the last alert number received. This function should be called when **GNUTLS_E_WARNING_ALERT_RECEIVED** or **GNUTLS_E_-FATAL_ALERT_RECEIVED** errors are returned by a gnutls function. The peer may send alerts if he encounters an error. If no alert has been received the returned value is undefined.

Returns: the last alert received, a *gnutls_alert_description_t* value.

---

*const char ** **gnutls_alert_get_name** (*gnutls_alert_description_t* **alert**)

Description: This function will return a string that describes the given alert number, or **NULL**. See gnutls_alert_get().

Returns: string corresponding to *gnutls_alert_description_t* value.

The peer may also be warned or notified of a fatal issue by using one of the functions below. All the available alerts are listed in section 2.4.

---

int **gnutls_alert_send** (*gnutls_session_t* **session**, *gnutls_alert_level_t* **level**, *gnutls_alert_description_t* **desc**)

Description: This function will send an alert to the peer in order to inform him of something important (eg. his Certificate could not be verified). If the alert level is Fatal then the peer is expected to close the connection, otherwise he may ignore the alert and continue. The error code of the underlying record send function will be returned, so you may also receive **GNUTLS_E_INTERRUPTED** or **GNUTLS_E_AGAIN** as well.

Returns: On success, **GNUTLS_E_SUCCESS** (0) is returned, otherwise an error code is returned.

---

int **gnutls_error_to_alert** (*int* **err**, *int ** **level**)

Description: Get an alert depending on the error code returned by a gnutls function. All alerts sent by this function should be considered fatal. The only exception is when err is **GNUTLS_E_REHANDSHAKE**, where a warning alert should be sent to the peer indicating that no renegotiation will be performed. If there is no mapping to a valid alert the alert to indicate internal error is returned.

Returns: the alert code to use for a particular error code.

5.10. Priority strings

How to use Priority Strings

The GnuTLS priority strings specify the TLS session's handshake algorithms and options in a compact, easy-to-use format. These strings are intended as a user-specified override of the library defaults.

That is, we recommend applications using the default settings (c.f. `gnutls_set_default_priority`), and provide the user with access to priority strings for overriding the default behavior, on configuration files, or other UI. Following such a principle, makes the GnuTLS library as the default settings provider. That is necessary and a good practice, because TLS protocol hardening and phasing out of legacy algorithms, is easier to co-ordinate when happens in a single library.

> *int* **gnutls_set_default_priority** (*gnutls_session_t* **session**)
>
> *int* **gnutls_priority_set_direct** (*gnutls_session_t* **session**, *const char* * **priorities**, *const char* ** **err_pos**)

The priority string translation to the internal GnuTLS form requires processing and the generated internal form also occupies some memory. For that, it is recommended to do that processing once in server side, and share the generated data across sessions. The following functions allow the generation of a "priority cache" and the sharing of it across sessions.

> *int* **gnutls_priority_init** (*gnutls_priority_t* * **priority_cache**, *const char* * **priorities**, *const char* ** **err_pos**)
>
> *int* **gnutls_priority_set** (*gnutls_session_t* **session**, *gnutls_priority_t* **priority**)
>
> *void* **gnutls_priority_deinit** (*gnutls_priority_t* **priority_cache**)

Using Priority Strings

A priority string string may contain a single initial keyword such as in Table 5.4 and may be followed by additional algorithm or special keywords. Note that their description is intentionally avoiding specific algorithm details, as the priority strings are not constant between gnutls versions (they are periodically updated to account for cryptographic advances while providing compatibility with old clients and servers).

Unless the initial keyword is "NONE" the defaults (in preference order) are for TLS protocols TLS 1.2, TLS1.1, TLS1.0; for certificate types X.509. In key exchange algorithms when in NORMAL or SECURE levels the perfect forward secrecy algorithms take precedence of the other protocols. In all cases all the supported key exchange algorithms are enabled.

Note that the SECURE levels distinguish between overall security level and message authenticity security level. That is because the message authenticity security level requires the adversary to break the algorithms at real-time during the protocol run, whilst the overall security level refers to off-line adversaries (e.g. adversaries breaking the ciphertext years after it was captured).

The NONE keyword, if used, must followed by keywords specifying the algorithms and protocols to be enabled. The other initial keywords do not require, but may be followed by such keywords. All level keywords can be combined, and for example a level of "SECURE256:+SECURE128" is allowed.

The order with which every algorithm or protocol is specified is significant. Algorithms specified before others will take precedence. The supported in the GnuTLS version corresponding to this document algorithms and protocols are shown in Table 5.5; to list the supported algorithms in your currently using version use **gnutls-cli -l**.

To avoid collisions in order to specify a protocol version with "VERS-", signature algorithms with "SIGN-" and certificate types with "CTYPE-". All other algorithms don't need a prefix. Each specified keyword (except for *special keywords*) can be prefixed with any of the following characters.

- '!' or '-' appended with an algorithm will remove this algorithm.

- "+" appended with an algorithm will add this algorithm.

Note that the DHE key exchange methods are generally slower[6] than their elliptic curves counterpart (ECDHE).

The available special keywords are shown in Table 5.6 and Table 5.7.

Finally the ciphersuites enabled by any priority string can be listed using the **gnutls-cli** application (see section 7.1), or by using the priority functions as in subsection 6.4.3.

Example priority strings are:

```
 1  The system imposed security level:
 2      "SYSTEM"
 3
 4  The default priority without the HMAC-MD5:
 5      "NORMAL:-MD5"
 6
 7  Specifying RSA with AES-128-CBC:
 8      "NONE:+VERS-TLS-ALL:+MAC-ALL:+RSA:+AES-128-CBC:+SIGN-ALL:+COMP-NULL"
 9
10  Specifying the defaults plus ARCFOUR-128:
11      "NORMAL:+ARCFOUR-128"
12
13  Enabling the 128-bit secure ciphers, while disabling TLS 1.0:
14      "SECURE128:-VERS-TLS1.0"
15
16  Enabling the 128-bit and 192-bit secure ciphers, while disabling all TLS versions
17  except TLS 1.2:
18      "SECURE128:+SECURE192:-VERS-ALL:+VERS-TLS1.2"
```

5.11. Selecting cryptographic key sizes

Because many algorithms are involved in TLS, it is not easy to set a consistent security level. For this reason in Table 5.8 we present some correspondence between key sizes of symmetric algorithms and public key algorithms based on [3]. Those can be used to generate certificates

---

[6]It depends on the group in use. Groups with less bits are always faster, but the number of bits ties with the security parameter. See section 5.11 for the acceptable security levels.

with appropriate key sizes as well as select parameters for Diffie-Hellman and SRP authentication.

The first column provides a security parameter in a number of bits. This gives an indication of the number of combinations to be tried by an adversary to brute force a key. For example to test all possible keys in a 112 bit security parameter 2 *textasciicircum*112 combinations have to be tried. For today's technology this is infeasible. The next two columns correlate the security parameter with actual bit sizes of parameters for DH, RSA, SRP and ECC algorithms. A mapping to `gnutls_sec_param_t` value is given for each security parameter, on the next column, and finally a brief description of the level.

Note, however, that the values suggested here are nothing more than an educated guess that is valid today. There are no guarantees that an algorithm will remain unbreakable or that these values will remain constant in time. There could be scientific breakthroughs that cannot be predicted or total failure of the current public key systems by quantum computers. On the other hand though the cryptosystems used in TLS are selected in a conservative way and such catastrophic breakthroughs or failures are believed to be unlikely. The NIST publication SP 800-57 [1] contains a similar table.

When using GnuTLS and a decision on bit sizes for a public key algorithm is required, use of the following functions is recommended:

---

unsigned   *int* **gnutls_sec_param_to_pk_bits** (*gnutls_pk_algorithm_t* **algo**, *gnutls_sec_param_t* **param**)

Description: `When generating private and public key pairs a difficult question is which size of "bits" the modulus will be in RSA and the group size in DSA. The easy answer is 1024, which is also wrong. This function will convert a human understandable security parameter to an appropriate size for the specific algorithm.`

Returns: `The number of bits, or (0).`

---

gnutls_sec_param_t **gnutls_pk_bits_to_sec_param** (*gnutls_pk_algorithm_t* **algo**, *unsigned int* **bits**)

Description: `This is the inverse of gnutls_sec_param_to_pk_bits(). Given an algorithm and the number of bits, it will return the security parameter. This is a rough indication.`

Returns: `The security parameter.`

Those functions will convert a human understandable security parameter of `gnutls_sec_param_t` type, to a number of bits suitable for a public key algorithm.

const char * **gnutls_sec_param_get_name** (*gnutls_sec_param_t* **param**)

The following functions will set the minimum acceptable group size for Diffie-Hellman and SRP authentication.

void **gnutls_dh_set_prime_bits** (*gnutls_session_t* **session**, *unsigned int* **bits**)

void **gnutls_srp_set_prime_bits** (*gnutls_session_t* **session**, *unsigned int* **bits**)

5.12. Advanced topics

5.12.1. Session resumption

Client side

To reduce time and roundtrips spent in a handshake the client can request session resumption from a server that previously shared a session with the client. For that the client has to retrieve and store the session parameters. Before establishing a new session to the same server the parameters must be re-associated with the GnuTLS session using `gnutls_session_set_data`.

int **gnutls_session_get_data2** (*gnutls_session_t* **session**, *gnutls_datum_t* * **data**)

int **gnutls_session_get_id2** (*gnutls_session_t* **session**, *gnutls_datum_t* * **session_id**)

int **gnutls_session_set_data** (*gnutls_session_t* **session**, *const void* * **session_data**, *size_t* **session_data_size**)

Keep in mind that sessions will be expired after some time, depending on the server, and a server may choose not to resume a session even when requested to. The expiration is to prevent temporal session keys from becoming long-term keys. Also note that as a client you must enable, using the priority functions, at least the algorithms used in the last session.

---

int **gnutls_session_is_resumed** (*gnutls_session_t* **session**)

Description: `Check whether session is resumed or not.`

Returns: `non zero if this session is resumed, or a zero if this is a new session.`

Server side

In order to support resumption a server can store the session security parameters in a local database or by using session tickets (see subsection 2.6.3) to delegate storage to the client. Because session tickets might not be supported by all clients, servers could combine the two methods.

A storing server needs to specify callback functions to store, retrieve and delete session data. These can be registered with the functions below. The stored sessions in the database can be checked using `gnutls_db_check_entry` for expiration.

---

void **gnutls_db_set_retrieve_function** (*gnutls_session_t* **session**, *gnutls_db_retr_func* **retr_func**)

void **gnutls_db_set_store_function** (*gnutls_session_t* **session**, *gnutls_db_store_func* **store_func**)

void **gnutls_db_set_ptr** (*gnutls_session_t* **session**, *void* * **ptr**)

void **gnutls_db_set_remove_function** (*gnutls_session_t* **session**, *gnutls_db_remove_func* **rem_func**)

---

int **gnutls_db_check_entry** (*gnutls_session_t* **session**, *gnutls_datum_t* **session_entry**)

A server utilizing tickets should generate ticket encryption and authentication keys using `gnutls_session_ticket_key_generate`. Those keys should be associated with the GnuTLS session using `gnutls_session_ticket_enable_server`, and should be rotated regularly (e.g., every few hours), to prevent them from becoming long-term keys which if revealed could be used to decrypt all previous sessions.

A server enabling both session tickets and a storage for session data would use session tickets when clients support it and the storage otherwise.

---

int **gnutls_session_ticket_enable_server** (*gnutls_session_t* **session,** *const* *gnutls_datum_t* * **key**)

Description: Request that the server should attempt session resumption using SessionTicket. key must be initialized with gnutls_session_ticket_key_generate(), and should be overwritten using gnutls_memset() before being released.

Returns: On success, **GNUTLS_E_SUCCESS** (0) is returned, or an error code.

---

int **gnutls_session_ticket_key_generate** (*gnutls_datum_t* * **key**)

Description: Generate a random key to encrypt security parameters within SessionTicket.

Returns: On success, **GNUTLS_E_SUCCESS** (0) is returned, or an error code.

5.12.2. Certificate verification

In this section the functionality for additional certificate verification methods is listed. These methods are intended to be used in addition to normal PKI verification, in order to reduce the risk of a compromised CA being undetected.

Trust on first use

The GnuTLS library includes functionality to use an SSH-like trust on first use authentication. The available functions to store and verify public keys are listed below.

In addition to the above the `gnutls_store_commitment` can be used to implement a key-pinning architecture as in [12]. This provides a way for web server to commit on a public key that is not yet active.

The storage and verification functions may be used with the default text file based back-end,

---

int **gnutls_session_resumption_requested** (*gnutls_session_t* **session**)

Description: Check whether the client has asked for session resumption. This function is valid only on server side.

Returns: non zero if session resumption was asked, or a zero if not.

---

int **gnutls_verify_stored_pubkey** (*const char* * **db_name**, *gnutls_tdb_t* **tdb**, *const char* * **host**, *const char* * **service**, *gnutls_certificate_type_t* **cert_type**, *const gnutls_datum_t* * **cert**, *unsigned int* **flags**)

Description: This function will try to verify the provided (raw or DER-encoded) certificate using a list of stored public keys. The service field if non-NULL should be a port number. The retrieve variable if non-null specifies a custom backend for the retrieval of entries. If it is NULL then the default file backend will be used. In POSIX-like systems the file backend uses the $HOME/.gnutls/known_hosts file. Note that if the custom storage backend is provided the retrieval function should return **GNUTLS_E_CERTIFICATE_KEY_MISMATCH** if the host/service pair is found but key doesn't match, **GNUTLS_E_NO_CERTIFICATE_FOUND** if no such host/service with the given key is found, and 0 if it was found. The storage function should return 0 on success.

Returns: If no associated public key is found then **GNUTLS_E_NO_CERTIFICATE_FOUND** will be returned. If a key is found but does not match **GNUTLS_E_CERTIFICATE_KEY_MISMATCH** is returned. On success, **GNUTLS_E_SUCCESS** (0) is returned, or a negative error value on other errors.

int **gnutls_store_pubkey** (*const char* * **db_name**, *gnutls_tdb_t* **tdb**, *const char* * **host**, *const char* * **service**, *gnutls_certificate_type_t* **cert_type**, *const gnutls_datum_t* * **cert**, *time_t* **expiration**, *unsigned int* **flags**)

Description: This function will store the provided (raw or DER-encoded) certificate to the list of stored public keys. The key will be considered valid until the provided expiration time. The store variable if non-null specifies a custom backend for the storage of entries. If it is NULL then the default file backend will be used. Unless an alternative **tdb** is provided, the storage format is a textual format consisting of a line for each host with fields separated by '|'. The contents of the fields are a format-identifier which is set to 'g0', the hostname that the rest of the data applies to, the numeric port or host name, the expiration time in seconds since the epoch (0 for no expiration), and a base64 encoding of the raw (DER) public key information (SPKI) of the peer.

Returns: On success, **GNUTLS_E_SUCCESS** (0) is returned, otherwise a negative error value.

---

int **gnutls_store_commitment** (*const char* * **db_name**, *gnutls_tdb_t* **tdb**, *const char* * **host**, *const char* * **service**, *gnutls_digest_algorithm_t* **hash_algo**, *const gnutls_datum_t* * **hash**, *time_t* **expiration**, *unsigned int* **flags**)

Description: This function will store the provided hash commitment to the list of stored public keys. The key with the given hash will be considered valid until the provided expiration time. The store variable if non-null specifies a custom backend for the storage of entries. If it is NULL then the default file backend will be used. Note that this function is not thread safe with the default backend.

Returns: On success, **GNUTLS_E_SUCCESS** (0) is returned, otherwise a negative error value.

---

or another back-end may be specified. That should contain storage and retrieval functions and specified as below.

---

int **gnutls_tdb_init** (*gnutls_tdb_t* * **tdb**)

void **gnutls_tdb_deinit** (*gnutls_tdb_t* **tdb**)

void **gnutls_tdb_set_verify_func** (*gnutls_tdb_t* **tdb**, *gnutls_tdb_verify_func* **verify**)

void **gnutls_tdb_set_store_func** (*gnutls_tdb_t* **tdb**, *gnutls_tdb_store_func* **store**)

void **gnutls_tdb_set_store_commitment_func** (*gnutls_tdb_t* **tdb**, *gnutls_tdb_store_commitment_func* **cstore**)

DANE verification

Since the DANE library is not included in GnuTLS it requires programs to be linked against it. This can be achieved with the following commands.

```
gcc -o foo foo.c `pkg-config gnutls-dane --cflags --libs`
```

When a program uses the GNU autoconf system, then the following line or similar can be used to detect the presence of the library.

```
PKG_CHECK_MODULES([LIBDANE], [gnutls-dane >= 3.0.0])
```

```
3 AC_SUBST([LIBDANE_CFLAGS])
4 AC_SUBST([LIBDANE_LIBS])
```

The high level functionality provided by the DANE library is shown below.

---

int **dane_verify_crt** (*dane_state_t* **s**, *const*   *gnutls_datum_t*   * **chain**, *unsigned* **chain_size**, *gnutls_certificate_type_t* **chain_type**, *const*   *char*   * **hostname**, *const* *char* * **proto**, *unsigned int* **port**, *unsigned int* **sflags**, *unsigned int* **vflags**, *unsigned int* * **verify**)

Description: This function will verify the given certificate chain against the CA constrains and/or the certificate available via DANE. If no information via DANE can be obtained the flag **DANE_VERIFY_NO_DANE_INFO** is set. If a DNSSEC signature is not available for the DANE record then the verify flag **DANE_VERIFY_NO_DNSSEC_-DATA** is set. Due to the many possible options of DANE, there is no single threat model countered. When notifying the user about DANE verification results it may be better to mention: DANE verification did not reject the certificate, rather than mentioning a successful DANE verication. Note that this function is designed to be run in addition to PKIX - certificate chain - verification. To be run independently the **DANE_VFLAG_-ONLY_CHECK_EE_USAGE** flag should be specified; then the function will check whether the key of the peer matches the key advertized in the DANE entry.

Returns: a negative error code on error and **DANE_E_SUCCESS** (0) when the DANE entries were successfully parsed, irrespective of whether they were verified (see **verify** for that information). If no usable entries were encountered **DANE_E_REQUESTED_DATA_-NOT_AVAILABLE** will be returned.

---

int **dane_verify_session_crt** (*dane_state_t* **s**, *gnutls_session_t* **session**, *const char* * **hostname**, *const char* * **proto**, *unsigned int* **port**, *unsigned int* **sflags**, *unsigned int* **vflags**, *unsigned int* * **verify**)

const char * **dane_strerror** (*int* **error**)

Note that the **dane_state_t** structure that is accepted by both verification functions is optional. It is required when many queries are performed to optimize against multiple re-initializations of the resolving back-end and loading of DNSSEC keys.

The following flags are returned by the verify functions to indicate the status of the verification.

In order to generate a DANE TLSA entry to use in a DNS server you may use danetool (see subsection 3.2.8).

5.12.3. Re-authentication

In TLS there is no distinction between rekey, re-authentication, and re-negotiation. All of these use cases are handled by the TLS' rehandshake process. For that reason in GnuTLS rehandshake is not transparent to the application, and the application must explicitly take control of that process. In addition GnuTLS since version 3.5.0 will not allow the peer to switch identities during a rehandshake. The threat addressed by that behavior depends on the application protocol, but primarily it protects applications from being misled by a rehandshake which switches the peer's identity. Applications can disable this protection by using the GNUTLS_ALLOW_ID_CHANGE flag in gnutls_init.

The following paragraphs explain how to safely use the rehandshake process.

Client side

According to the TLS specification a client may initiate a rehandshake at any time. That can be achieved by calling **gnutls_handshake** and rely on its return value for the outcome of the handshake (the server may deny a rehandshake). If a server requests a re-handshake, then a call to **gnutls_record_recv** will return GNUTLS_E_REHANDSHAKE in the client, instructing it to call **gnutls_handshake**. To deny a rehandshake request by the server it is recommended to send a warning alert of type GNUTLS_A_NO_RENEGOTIATION.

Due to limitations of early protocol versions, it is required to check whether safe renegotiation is in place, i.e., using **gnutls_safe_renegotiation_status**, which ensures that the server remains the same as the initial.

---

unsigned **gnutls_safe_renegotiation_status** (*gnutls_session_t* **session**)

Description: `Can be used to check whether safe renegotiation is being used in the current session.`

Returns: `0 when safe renegotiation is not used and non (0) when safe renegotiation is used.`

Server side

A server which wants to instruct the client to re-authenticate, should call **gnutls_rehandshake** and wait for the client to re-authenticate. It is recommended to only request re-handshake when safe renegotiation is enabled for that session (see **gnutls_safe_renegotiation_status** and the discussion in subsection 2.6.5).

---

int **gnutls_rehandshake** (*gnutls_session_t* **session**)

Description: This function will renegotiate security parameters with the client. This should only be called in case of a server. This message informs the peer that we want to renegotiate parameters (perform a handshake). If this function succeeds (returns 0), you must call the gnutls_handshake() function in order to negotiate the new parameters. Since TLS is full duplex some application data might have been sent during peer's processing of this message. In that case one should call gnutls_record_recv() until GNUTLS_E_REHANDSHAKE is returned to clear any pending data. Care must be taken, if rehandshake is mandatory, to terminate if it does not start after some threshold. If the client does not wish to renegotiate parameters he should reply with an alert message, thus the return code will be **GNUTLS_E_WARNING_ALERT_RECEIVED** and the alert will be **GNUTLS_A_NO_-RENEGOTIATION**. A client may also choose to ignore this message.

Returns: **GNUTLS_E_SUCCESS** on success, otherwise a negative error code.

5.12.4. Parameter generation

Prior to GnuTLS 3.6.0 for the ephemeral or anonymous Diffie-Hellman (DH) TLS ciphersuites the application was required to generate or provide DH parameters. That is no longer necessary as GnuTLS utilizes DH parameters and negotiation from [14].

Applications can tune the used parameters by explicitly specifying them in the priority string. In server side applications can set the minimum acceptable level of DH parameters by calling `gnutls_certificate_set_known_dh_params`, `gnutls_anon_set_server_known_dh_params`, or `gnutls_psk_set_server_known_dh_params`, depending on the type of the credentials, to set the lower acceptable parameter limits. Typical applications should rely on the default settings.

---

int **gnutls_certificate_set_known_dh_params** (*gnutls_certificate_credentials_t* **res**, *gnutls_sec_param_t* **sec_param**)

Deprecated: This function is unnecessary and discouraged on GnuTLS 3.6.0 or later. Since 3.6.0, DH parameters are negotiated following RFC7919.

int **gnutls_anon_set_server_known_dh_params** (*gnutls_anon_server_credentials_t* **res**, *gnutls_sec_param_t* **sec_param**)

Deprecated: This function is unnecessary and discouraged on GnuTLS 3.6.0 or later. Since 3.6.0, DH parameters are negotiated following RFC7919.

int **gnutls_psk_set_server_known_dh_params** (*gnutls_psk_server_credentials_t* **res**, *gnutls_sec_param_t* **sec_param**)

Deprecated: This function is unnecessary and discouraged on GnuTLS 3.6.0 or later. Since 3.6.0, DH parameters are negotiated following RFC7919.

Legacy parameter generation

Note that older than 3.5.6 versions of GnuTLS provided functions to generate or import arbitrary DH parameters from a file. This practice is still supported but discouraged in current versions. There is no known advantage from using random parameters, while there have been several occasions where applications were utilizing incorrect, weak or insecure parameters. This is the main reason GnuTLS includes the well-known parameters of [14] and recommends applications utilizing them.

In older applications which require to specify explicit DH parameters, we recommend using `certtool` (of GnuTLS 3.5.6 or later) with the `--get-dh-params` option to obtain the FFDHE parameters discussed above. The output parameters of the tool are in PKCS#3 format and can be imported by most existing applications.

The following functions are still supported but considered obsolete.

---

int **gnutls_dh_params_generate2** (*gnutls_dh_params_t* **dparams**, *unsigned int* **bits**)

int **gnutls_dh_params_import_pkcs3** (*gnutls_dh_params_t* **params**, *const gnutls_datum_t* * **pkcs3_params**, *gnutls_x509_crt_fmt_t* **format**)

void **gnutls_certificate_set_dh_params** (*gnutls_certificate_credentials_t* **res**, *gnutls_dh_params_t* **dh_params**)

Deprecated: This function is unnecessary and discouraged on GnuTLS 3.6.0 or later. Since 3.6.0, DH parameters are negotiated following RFC7919.

5.12.5. Deriving keys for other applications/protocols

In several cases, after a TLS connection is established, it is desirable to derive keys to be used in another application or protocol (e.g., in an other TLS session using pre-shared keys). The following describe GnuTLS' implementation of RFC5705 to extract keys based on a session's master secret.

The API to use is `gnutls_prf_rfc5705`. The function needs to be provided with a label, and additional context data to mix in the `context` parameter.

---

int **gnutls_prf_rfc5705** (*gnutls_session_t* **session**, *size_t* **label_size**, *const char* * **label**, *size_t* **context_size**, *const char* * **context**, *size_t* **outsize**, *char* * **out**)

Description: Applies the TLS Pseudo-Random-Function (PRF) on the master secret and the provided data, seeded with the client and server random fields, as specified in RFC5705. The label variable usually contains a string denoting the purpose for the generated data. The server_random_first indicates whether the client random field or the server random field should be first in the seed. Non-zero indicates that the server random field is first, 0 that the client random field is first. The context variable can be used to add more data to the seed, after the random variables. It can be used to make sure the generated output is strongly connected to some additional data (e.g., a string used in user authentication). The output is placed in out, which must be pre-allocated. Note that, to provide the RFC5705 context, the context variable must be non-null.

Returns: GNUTLS_E_SUCCESS on success, or an error code.

For example, after establishing a TLS session using **gnutls_handshake**, you can obtain 32-bytes to be used as key, using this call:

```
1  #define MYLABEL "EXPORTER-My-protocol-name"
2  #define MYCONTEXT "my-protocol's-1st-session"
3
```

```
4  char out[32];
5  rc = gnutls_prf_rfc5705 (session, sizeof(MYLABEL)-1, MYLABEL,
6                           sizeof(MYCONTEXT)-1, MYCONTEXT, 32, out);
```

The output key depends on TLS' master secret, and is the same on both client and server.

For legacy applications which need to use a more flexible API, there is **gnutls_prf**, which in addition, allows to switch the mix of the client and server random nonces, using the **server_random_first** parameter. For additional flexibility and low-level access to the TLS1.2 PRF, there is a low-level TLS PRF interface called **gnutls_prf_raw**. That however is not functional under newer protocol versions.

5.12.6. Channel bindings

In user authentication protocols (e.g., EAP or SASL mechanisms) it is useful to have a unique string that identifies the secure channel that is used, to bind together the user authentication with the secure channel. This can protect against man-in-the-middle attacks in some situations. That unique string is called a "channel binding". For background and discussion see [44].

In GnuTLS you can extract a channel binding using the **gnutls_session_channel_binding** function. Currently only the type **GNUTLS_CB_TLS_UNIQUE** is supported, which corresponds to the **tls-unique** channel binding for TLS defined in [4].

The following example describes how to print the channel binding data. Note that it must be run after a successful TLS handshake.

```
1  {
2    gnutls_datum_t cb;
3    int rc;
4
5    rc = gnutls_session_channel_binding (session,
6                                         GNUTLS_CB_TLS_UNIQUE,
7                                         &cb);
8    if (rc)
9      fprintf (stderr, "Channel binding error: %s\n",
10              gnutls_strerror (rc));
11   else
12     {
13       size_t i;
14       printf ("- Channel binding 'tls-unique': ");
15       for (i = 0; i < cb.size; i++)
16         printf ("%02x", cb.data[i]);
17       printf ("\n");
18     }
19 }
```

5.12.7. Interoperability

The TLS protocols support many ciphersuites, extensions and version numbers. As a result, few implementations are not able to properly interoperate once faced with extensions or version protocols they do not support and understand. The TLS protocol allows for a graceful downgrade to the commonly supported options, but practice shows it is not always implemented correctly.

Because there is no way to achieve maximum interoperability with broken peers without sacrificing security, GnuTLS ignores such peers by default. This might not be acceptable in cases where maximum compatibility is required. Thus we allow enabling compatibility with broken peers using priority strings (see section 5.10). A conservative priority string that would disable certain TLS protocol options that are known to cause compatibility problems, is shown below.

```
NORMAL:%COMPAT
```

For very old broken peers that do not tolerate TLS version numbers over TLS 1.0 another priority string is:

```
NORMAL:-VERS-ALL:+VERS-TLS1.0:+VERS-SSL3.0:%COMPAT
```

This priority string will in addition to above, only enable SSL 3.0 and TLS 1.0 as protocols.

5.12.8. Compatibility with the OpenSSL library

To ease GnuTLS' integration with existing applications, a compatibility layer with the OpenSSL library is included in the **gnutls-openssl** library. This compatibility layer is not complete and it is not intended to completely re-implement the OpenSSL API with GnuTLS. It only provides limited source-level compatibility.

The prototypes for the compatibility functions are in the "**gnutls/openssl.h**" header file. The limitations imposed by the compatibility layer include:

- Error handling is not thread safe.

enum **gnutls_init_flags_t**:

GNUTLS_SERVER	Connection end is a server.
GNUTLS_CLIENT	Connection end is a client.
GNUTLS_DATAGRAM	Connection is datagram oriented (DTLS). Since 3.0.0.
GNUTLS_NONBLOCK	Connection should not block. Since 3.0.0.
GNUTLS_NO_EXTENSIONS	Do not enable any TLS extensions by default (since 3.1.2).
GNUTLS_NO_REPLAY_PROTECTION	Disable any replay protection in DTLS. This must only be used if replay protection is achieved using other means. Since 3.2.2.
GNUTLS_NO_SIGNAL	In systems where SIGPIPE is delivered on send, it will be disabled. That flag has effect in systems which support the MSG_NOSIGNAL sockets flag (since 3.4.2).
GNUTLS_ALLOW_ID_CHANGE	Allow the peer to replace its certificate, or change its ID during a rehandshake. This change is often used in attacks and thus prohibited by default. Since 3.5.0.
GNUTLS_ENABLE_FALSE_START	Enable the TLS false start on client side if the negotiated ciphersuites allow it. This will enable sending data prior to the handshake being complete, and may introduce a risk of crypto failure when combined with certain key exchanged; for that GnuTLS may not enable that option in ciphersuites that are known to be not safe for false start. Since 3.5.0.
GNUTLS_FORCE_CLIENT_CERT	When in client side and only a single cert is specified, send that certificate irrespective of the issuers expected by the server. Since 3.5.0.
GNUTLS_NO_TICKETS	Flag to indicate that the session should not use resumption with session tickets.

Table 5.2.: The `gnutls_init_flags_t` enumeration.

Authentication method	Key exchange	Client credentials	Server credentials
Certificate	KX_RSA, KX_DHE_RSA, KX_DHE_DSS, KX_ECDHE_RSA, KX_ECDHE_ECDSA	CRD_CERTIFICATE	CRD_CERTIFICATE
Password and certificate	KX_SRP_RSA, KX_SRP_DSS	CRD_SRP	CRD_CERTIFICATE, CRD_SRP
Password	KX_SRP	CRD_SRP	CRD_SRP
Anonymous	KX_ANON_DH, KX_ANON_ECDH	CRD_ANON	CRD_ANON
Pre-shared key	KX_PSK, KX_DHE_PSK, KX_ECDHE_PSK	CRD_PSK	CRD_PSK

Table 5.3.: Key exchange algorithms and the corresponding credential types.

Keyword	Description
@KEYWORD	Means that a compile-time specified system configuration file[5] will be used to expand the provided keyword. That is used to impose system-specific policies. It may be followed by additional options that will be appended to the system string (e.g., "@SYSTEM:+SRP"). The system file should have the format 'KEYWORD=VALUE', e.g., 'SYSTEM=NORMAL:+ARCFOUR-128'. Since version 3.5.1 it is allowed to specify fallback keywords such as @KEYWORD1,@KEYWORD2, and the first valid keyword will be used.
PERFORMANCE	All the known to be secure ciphersuites are enabled, limited to 128 bit ciphers and sorted by terms of speed performance. The message authenticity security level is of 64 bits or more, and the certificate verification profile is set to GNUTLS_PROFILE_LOW (80-bits).
NORMAL	Means all the known to be secure ciphersuites. The ciphers are sorted by security margin, although the 256-bit ciphers are included as a fallback only. The message authenticity security level is of 64 bits or more, and the certificate verification profile is set to GNUTLS_PROFILE_LOW (80-bits). This priority string implicitly enables ECDHE and DHE. The ECDHE ciphersuites are placed first in the priority order, but due to compatibility issues with the DHE ciphersuites they are placed last in the priority order, after the plain RSA ciphersuites.
LEGACY	This sets the NORMAL settings that were used for GnuTLS 3.2.x or earlier. There is no verification profile set, and the allowed DH primes are considered weak today (but are often used by misconfigured servers).
PFS	Means all the known to be secure ciphersuites that support perfect forward secrecy (ECDHE and DHE). The ciphers are sorted by security margin, although the 256-bit ciphers are included as a fallback only. The message authenticity security level is of 80 bits or more, and the certificate verification profile is set to GNUTLS_PROFILE_LOW (80-bits). This option is available since 3.2.4 or later.
SECURE128	Means all known to be secure ciphersuites that offer a security level 128-bit or more. The message authenticity security level is of 80 bits or more, and the certificate verification profile is set to GNUTLS_PROFILE_LOW (80-bits).
SECURE192	Means all the known to be secure ciphersuites that offer a security level 192-bit or more. The message authenticity security level is of 128 bits or more, and the certificate verification profile is set to GNUTLS_PROFILE_HIGH (128-bits).
SECURE256	Currently alias for SECURE192. This option, will enable ciphers which use a 256-bit key but, due to limitations of the TLS protocol, the overall security level will be 192-bits (the security level depends on more factors than cipher key size).
SUITEB128	Means all the NSA Suite B cryptography (RFC5430) ciphersuites with an 128 bit security level, as well as the enabling of the corresponding verification profile.
SUITEB192	Means all the NSA Suite B cryptography (RFC5430) ciphersuites with an 192 bit security level, as well as the enabling of the corre-

Type	Keywords
Ciphers	Examples are AES-128-GCM, AES-256-GCM, AES-256-CBC; see also Table 2.1 for more options. Catch all name is CIPHER-ALL which will add all the algorithms from NORMAL priority.
Key exchange	RSA, DHE-RSA, DHE-DSS, SRP, SRP-RSA, SRP-DSS, PSK, DHE-PSK, ECDHE-RSA, ECDHE-ECDSA, ECDHE-PSK, ANON-ECDH, ANON-DH. The Catch all name is KX-ALL which will add all the algorithms from NORMAL priority. Add `!DHE-RSA:!DHE-DSS` to the priority string to disable DHE.
MAC	MD5, SHA1, SHA256, SHA384, AEAD (used with GCM ciphers only). All algorithms from NORMAL priority can be accessed with MAC-ALL.
Compression algorithms	COMP-NULL, COMP-DEFLATE. Catch all is COMP-ALL.
TLS versions	VERS-TLS1.0, VERS-TLS1.1, VERS-TLS1.2, VERS-DTLS1.0, VERS-DTLS1.2. Catch all are VERS-ALL, VERS-TLS-ALL and VERS-DTLS-ALL, and will enable all protocols from NORMAL priority.
Signature algorithms	SIGN-RSA-SHA1, SIGN-RSA-SHA224, SIGN-RSA-SHA256, SIGN-RSA-SHA384, SIGN-RSA-SHA512, SIGN-DSA-SHA1, SIGN-DSA-SHA224, SIGN-DSA-SHA256, SIGN-RSA-MD5, SIGN-ECDSA-SHA1, SIGN-ECDSA-SHA224, SIGN-ECDSA-SHA256, SIGN-ECDSA-SHA384, SIGN-ECDSA-SHA512, SIGN-RSA-PSS-SHA256, SIGN-RSA-PSS-SHA384, SIGN-RSA-PSS-SHA512. Catch all which enables all algorithms from NORMAL priority is SIGN-ALL. This option is only considered for TLS 1.2 and later.
Elliptic curves	CURVE-SECP192R1, CURVE-SECP224R1, CURVE-SECP256R1, CURVE-SECP384R1, CURVE-SECP521R1, and CURVE-X25519. Catch all which enables all curves from NORMAL priority is CURVE-ALL. Note that the CURVE keyword is kept for backwards compatibility only, for new applications see the GROUP keyword below.
Groups	GROUP-SECP256R1, GROUP-SECP384R1, GROUP-SECP521R1, GROUP-X25519, GROUP-FFDHE2048, GROUP-FFDHE3072, GROUP-FFDHE4096 and GROUP-FFDHE8192. Groups include both elliptic curve groups, e.g., SECP256R1, as well as finite field groups such as FFDHE2048. Catch all which enables all groups from NORMAL priority is GROUP-ALL.
Certificate type	The only option currently is CTYPE-X509. Catch all is CTYPE-ALL.

Table 5.5.: The supported algorithm keywords in priority strings.

Keyword	Description
%COMPAT	will enable compatibility mode. It might mean that violations of the protocols are allowed as long as maximum compatibility with problematic clients and servers is achieved. More specifically this string would disable TLS record random padding, tolerate packets over the maximum allowed TLS record, and add a padding to TLS Client Hello packet to prevent it being in the 256-512 range which is known to be causing issues with a commonly used firewall (see the %DUMBFW option).
%DUMBFW	will add a private extension with bogus data that make the client hello exceed 512 bytes. This avoids a black hole behavior in some firewalls. This is the [21] client hello padding extension, also enabled with %COMPAT.
%NO_EXTENSIONS	will prevent the sending of any TLS extensions in client side. Note that TLS 1.2 requires extensions to be used, as well as safe renegotiation thus this option must be used with care.
%NO_TICKETS	will prevent the advertizing of the TLS session ticket extension. This is implied by the PFS keyword.
%NO_SESSION_HASH	will prevent the advertizing the TLS extended master secret (session hash) extension.
%SERVER_PRECEDENCE	The ciphersuite will be selected according to server priorities and not the client's.
%SSL3_RECORD_VERSION	will use SSL3.0 record version in client hello. By default GnuTLS will set the minimum supported version as the client hello record version (do not confuse that version with the proposed handshake version at the client hello).
%LATEST_RECORD_VERSION	will use the latest TLS version record version in client hello.

Table 5.6.: Special priority string keywords.

Keyword	Description
%STATELESS_COMPRESSION	ignored; no longer used.
%DISABLE_WILDCARDS	will disable matching wildcards when comparing hostnames in certificates.
%NO_ETM	will disable the encrypt-then-mac TLS extension (RFC7366). This is implied by the %COMPAT keyword.
%DISABLE_SAFE_RENEGOTIATION	will completely disable safe renegotiation completely. Do not use unless you know what you are doing.
%UNSAFE_RENEGOTIATION	will allow handshakes and re-handshakes without the safe renegotiation extension. Note that for clients this mode is insecure (you may be under attack), and for servers it will allow insecure clients to connect (which could be fooled by an attacker). Do not use unless you know what you are doing and want maximum compatibility.
%PARTIAL_RENEGOTIATION	will allow initial handshakes to proceed, but not re-handshakes. This leaves the client vulnerable to attack, and servers will be compatible with non-upgraded clients for initial handshakes. This is currently the default for clients and servers, for compatibility reasons.
%SAFE_RENEGOTIATION	will enforce safe renegotiation. Clients and servers will refuse to talk to an insecure peer. Currently this causes interoperability problems, but is required for full protection.
%FALLBACK_SCSV	will enable the use of the fallback signaling cipher suite value in the client hello. Note that this should be set only by applications that try to reconnect with a downgraded protocol version. See RFC7507 for details.
%VERIFY_ALLOW_BROKEN	will allow signatures with known to be broken algorithms (such as MD5 or SHA1) in certificate chains.
%VERIFY_ALLOW_SIGN_RSA_MD5	will allow RSA-MD5 signatures in certificate chains.
%VERIFY_ALLOW_SIGN_WITH_SHA1	will allow signatures with SHA1 hash algorithm in certificate chains.
%VERIFY_DISABLE_CRL_CHECKS	will disable CRL or OCSP checks in the verification of the certificate chain.
%VERIFY_ALLOW_X509_V1_CA_CRT	will allow V1 CAs in chains.
%PROFILE_(LOW—LEGACY—MEDIUM—HIGH—ULTRA)	require a certificate verification profile the corresponds to the specified security level, see Table 5.8 for the mappings to values.
%PROFILE_(SUITEB128—SUITEB192)	require a certificate verification profile the corresponds to SUITEB. Note that an initial keyword that enables SUITEB automatically sets the profile.

Security bits	RSA, DH and SRP parameter size	ECC key size	Security parameter (profile)	Description
<64	<768	<128	INSECURE	Considered to be insecure
64	768	128	VERY WEAK	Short term protection against individuals
72	1008	160	WEAK	Short term protection against small organizations
80	1024	160	LOW	Very short term protection against agencies (corresponds to ENISA legacy level)
96	1776	192	LEGACY	Legacy standard level
112	2048	224	MEDIUM	Medium-term protection
128	3072	256	HIGH	Long term protection (corresponds to ENISA future level)
192	8192	384	ULTRA	Even longer term protection
256	15424	512	FUTURE	Foreseeable future

Table 5.8.: Key sizes and security parameters.

```
enum dane_verify_status_t:
    DANE_VERIFY_CA_CONSTRAINTS_-      The CA constraints were violated.
    VIOLATED
    DANE_VERIFY_CERT_DIFFERS          The certificate obtained via DNS differs.
    DANE_VERIFY_UNKNOWN_DANE_-        No known DANE data was found in the DNS record.
    INFO
```

Table 5.9.: The DANE verification status flags.

6

GnuTLS application examples

In this chapter several examples of real-world use cases are listed. The examples are simplified to promote readability and contain little or no error checking.

6.1. Client examples

This section contains examples of TLS and SSL clients, using GnuTLS. Note that some of the examples require functions implemented by another example.

6.1.1. Simple client example with X.509 certificate support

Let's assume now that we want to create a TCP client which communicates with servers that use X.509 certificate authentication. The following client is a very simple TLS client, which uses the high level verification functions for certificates, but does not support session resumption.

Note that this client utilizes functionality present in the latest GnuTLS version. For a reasonably portable version see subsection 6.1.11.

```
1  /* This example code is placed in the public domain. */
2
3  #ifdef HAVE_CONFIG_H
4  #include <config.h>
5  #endif
6
7  #include <stdio.h>
8  #include <stdlib.h>
9  #include <string.h>
10 #include <assert.h>
11 #include <gnutls/gnutls.h>
12 #include <gnutls/x509.h>
13 #include "examples.h"
14
15 /* A very basic TLS client, with X.509 authentication and server certificate
16  * verification. Note that error recovery is minimal for simplicity.
17  */
18
19 #define CHECK(x) assert((x)>=0)
20
```

```
21  #define MAX_BUF 1024
22  #define MSG "GET / HTTP/1.0\r\n\r\n"
23
24  extern int tcp_connect(void);
25  extern void tcp_close(int sd);
26
27  int main(void)
28  {
29          int ret, sd, ii;
30          gnutls_session_t session;
31          char buffer[MAX_BUF + 1], *desc;
32          gnutls_datum_t out;
33          int type;
34          unsigned status;
35          gnutls_certificate_credentials_t xcred;
36
37          if (gnutls_check_version("3.4.6") == NULL) {
38                  fprintf(stderr, "GnuTLS 3.4.6 or later is required for this example\n");
39                  exit(1);
40          }
41
42          /* for backwards compatibility with gnutls < 3.3.0 */
43          CHECK(gnutls_global_init());
44
45          /* X509 stuff */
46          CHECK(gnutls_certificate_allocate_credentials(&xcred));
47
48          /* sets the system trusted CAs for Internet PKI */
49          CHECK(gnutls_certificate_set_x509_system_trust(xcred));
50
51          /* If client holds a certificate it can be set using the following:
52           *
53           gnutls_certificate_set_x509_key_file (xcred, "cert.pem", "key.pem",
54           GNUTLS_X509_FMT_PEM);
55           */
56
57          /* Initialize TLS session */
58          CHECK(gnutls_init(&session, GNUTLS_CLIENT));
59
60          CHECK(gnutls_server_name_set(session, GNUTLS_NAME_DNS, "my_host_name",
61                                       strlen("my_host_name")));
62
63          /* It is recommended to use the default priorities */
64          CHECK(gnutls_set_default_priority(session));
65
66          /* put the x509 credentials to the current session
67           */
68          CHECK(gnutls_credentials_set(session, GNUTLS_CRD_CERTIFICATE, xcred));
69          gnutls_session_set_verify_cert(session, "my_host_name", 0);
70
71          /* connect to the peer
72           */
73          sd = tcp_connect();
74
75          gnutls_transport_set_int(session, sd);
76          gnutls_handshake_set_timeout(session,
77                                       GNUTLS_DEFAULT_HANDSHAKE_TIMEOUT);
78
```

```
79      /* Perform the TLS handshake
80       */
81      do {
82              ret = gnutls_handshake(session);
83      }
84      while (ret < 0 && gnutls_error_is_fatal(ret) == 0);
85      if (ret < 0) {
86              if (ret == GNUTLS_E_CERTIFICATE_VERIFICATION_ERROR) {
87                      /* check certificate verification status */
88                      type = gnutls_certificate_type_get(session);
89                      status = gnutls_session_get_verify_cert_status(session);
90                      CHECK(gnutls_certificate_verification_status_print(status,
91                              type, &out, 0));
92                      printf("cert verify output: %s\n", out.data);
93                      gnutls_free(out.data);
94              }
95              fprintf(stderr, "*** Handshake failed: %s\n", gnutls_strerror(ret));
96              goto end;
97      } else {
98              desc = gnutls_session_get_desc(session);
99              printf("- Session info: %s\n", desc);
100             gnutls_free(desc);
101     }
102
103     /* send data */
104     CHECK(gnutls_record_send(session, MSG, strlen(MSG)));
105
106     ret = gnutls_record_recv(session, buffer, MAX_BUF);
107     if (ret == 0) {
108             printf("- Peer has closed the TLS connection\n");
109             goto end;
110     } else if (ret < 0 && gnutls_error_is_fatal(ret) == 0) {
111             fprintf(stderr, "*** Warning: %s\n", gnutls_strerror(ret));
112     } else if (ret < 0) {
113             fprintf(stderr, "*** Error: %s\n", gnutls_strerror(ret));
114             goto end;
115     }
116
117     if (ret > 0) {
118             printf("- Received %d bytes: ", ret);
119             for (ii = 0; ii < ret; ii++) {
120                     fputc(buffer[ii], stdout);
121             }
122             fputs("\n", stdout);
123     }
124
125     CHECK(gnutls_bye(session, GNUTLS_SHUT_RDWR));
126
127 end:
128
129     tcp_close(sd);
130
131     gnutls_deinit(session);
132
133     gnutls_certificate_free_credentials(xcred);
134
135     gnutls_global_deinit();
136
```

197

```
137          return 0;
138  }
```

6.1.2. Simple client example with SSH-style certificate verification

This is an alternative verification function that will use the X.509 certificate authorities for verification, but also assume an trust on first use (SSH-like) authentication system. That is the user is prompted on unknown public keys and known public keys are considered trusted.

```
1   /* This example code is placed in the public domain. */
2
3   #ifdef HAVE_CONFIG_H
4   #include <config.h>
5   #endif
6
7   #include <stdio.h>
8   #include <stdlib.h>
9   #include <string.h>
10  #include <gnutls/gnutls.h>
11  #include <gnutls/x509.h>
12  #include <assert.h>
13  #include "examples.h"
14
15  #define CHECK(x) assert((x)>=0)
16
17  /* This function will verify the peer's certificate, check
18   * if the hostname matches. In addition it will perform an
19   * SSH-style authentication, where ultimately trusted keys
20   * are only the keys that have been seen before.
21   */
22  int _ssh_verify_certificate_callback(gnutls_session_t session)
23  {
24          unsigned int status;
25          const gnutls_datum_t *cert_list;
26          unsigned int cert_list_size;
27          int ret, type;
28          gnutls_datum_t out;
29          const char *hostname;
30
31          /* read hostname */
32          hostname = gnutls_session_get_ptr(session);
33
34          /* This verification function uses the trusted CAs in the credentials
35           * structure. So you must have installed one or more CA certificates.
36           */
37          CHECK(gnutls_certificate_verify_peers3(session, hostname, &status));
38
39          type = gnutls_certificate_type_get(session);
40
41          CHECK(gnutls_certificate_verification_status_print(status,
42                                                      type, &out, 0));
43          printf("%s", out.data);
44
45          gnutls_free(out.data);
46
```

```
47        if (status != 0)        /* Certificate is not trusted */
48                return GNUTLS_E_CERTIFICATE_ERROR;
49
50        /* Do SSH verification */
51        cert_list = gnutls_certificate_get_peers(session, &cert_list_size);
52        if (cert_list == NULL) {
53                printf("No certificate was found!\n");
54                return GNUTLS_E_CERTIFICATE_ERROR;
55        }
56
57        /* service may be obtained alternatively using getservbyport() */
58        ret = gnutls_verify_stored_pubkey(NULL, NULL, hostname, "https",
59                                        type, &cert_list[0], 0);
60        if (ret == GNUTLS_E_NO_CERTIFICATE_FOUND) {
61                printf("Host %s is not known.", hostname);
62                if (status == 0)
63                        printf("Its certificate is valid for %s.\n",
64                                hostname);
65
66                /* the certificate must be printed and user must be asked on
67                 * whether it is trustworthy. --see gnutls_x509_crt_print() */
68
69                /* if not trusted */
70                return GNUTLS_E_CERTIFICATE_ERROR;
71        } else if (ret == GNUTLS_E_CERTIFICATE_KEY_MISMATCH) {
72                printf
73                    ("Warning: host %s is known but has another key associated.",
74                     hostname);
75                printf
76                    ("It might be that the server has multiple keys, or you are under attack\n");
77                if (status == 0)
78                        printf("Its certificate is valid for %s.\n",
79                                hostname);
80
81                /* the certificate must be printed and user must be asked on
82                 * whether it is trustworthy. --see gnutls_x509_crt_print() */
83
84                /* if not trusted */
85                return GNUTLS_E_CERTIFICATE_ERROR;
86        } else if (ret < 0) {
87                printf("gnutls_verify_stored_pubkey: %s\n",
88                        gnutls_strerror(ret));
89                return ret;
90        }
91
92        /* user trusts the key -> store it */
93        if (ret != 0) {
94                CHECK(gnutls_store_pubkey(NULL, NULL, hostname, "https",
95                                        type, &cert_list[0], 0, 0));
96        }
97
98        /* notify gnutls to continue handshake normally */
99        return 0;
100 }
```

199

6.1.3. Simple client example with anonymous authentication

The simplest client using TLS is the one that doesn't do any authentication. This means no external certificates or passwords are needed to set up the connection. As could be expected, the connection is vulnerable to man-in-the-middle (active or redirection) attacks. However, the data are integrity protected and encrypted from passive eavesdroppers.

Note that due to the vulnerable nature of this method very few public servers support it.

```
1  /* This example code is placed in the public domain. */
2
3  #ifdef HAVE_CONFIG_H
4  #include <config.h>
5  #endif
6
7  #include <stdio.h>
8  #include <stdlib.h>
9  #include <string.h>
10 #include <sys/types.h>
11 #include <sys/socket.h>
12 #include <arpa/inet.h>
13 #include <unistd.h>
14 #include <gnutls/gnutls.h>
15
16 /* A very basic TLS client, with anonymous authentication.
17  */
18
19 #define MAX_BUF 1024
20 #define MSG "GET / HTTP/1.0\r\n\r\n"
21
22 extern int tcp_connect(void);
23 extern void tcp_close(int sd);
24
25 int main(void)
26 {
27         int ret, sd, ii;
28         gnutls_session_t session;
29         char buffer[MAX_BUF + 1];
30         gnutls_anon_client_credentials_t anoncred;
31         /* Need to enable anonymous KX specifically. */
32
33         gnutls_global_init();
34
35         gnutls_anon_allocate_client_credentials(&anoncred);
36
37         /* Initialize TLS session
38          */
39         gnutls_init(&session, GNUTLS_CLIENT);
40
41         /* Use default priorities */
42         gnutls_priority_set_direct(session,
43                                    "PERFORMANCE:+ANON-ECDH:+ANON-DH",
44                                    NULL);
45
46         /* put the anonymous credentials to the current session
47          */
48         gnutls_credentials_set(session, GNUTLS_CRD_ANON, anoncred);
```

```
49
50          /* connect to the peer
51           */
52          sd = tcp_connect();
53
54          gnutls_transport_set_int(session, sd);
55          gnutls_handshake_set_timeout(session,
56                                   GNUTLS_DEFAULT_HANDSHAKE_TIMEOUT);
57
58          /* Perform the TLS handshake
59           */
60          do {
61                  ret = gnutls_handshake(session);
62          }
63          while (ret < 0 && gnutls_error_is_fatal(ret) == 0);
64
65          if (ret < 0) {
66                  fprintf(stderr, "*** Handshake failed\n");
67                  gnutls_perror(ret);
68                  goto end;
69          } else {
70                  char *desc;
71
72                  desc = gnutls_session_get_desc(session);
73                  printf("- Session info: %s\n", desc);
74                  gnutls_free(desc);
75          }
76
77          gnutls_record_send(session, MSG, strlen(MSG));
78
79          ret = gnutls_record_recv(session, buffer, MAX_BUF);
80          if (ret == 0) {
81                  printf("- Peer has closed the TLS connection\n");
82                  goto end;
83          } else if (ret < 0 && gnutls_error_is_fatal(ret) == 0) {
84                  fprintf(stderr, "*** Warning: %s\n", gnutls_strerror(ret));
85          } else if (ret < 0) {
86                  fprintf(stderr, "*** Error: %s\n", gnutls_strerror(ret));
87                  goto end;
88          }
89
90          if (ret > 0) {
91                  printf("- Received %d bytes: ", ret);
92                  for (ii = 0; ii < ret; ii++) {
93                          fputc(buffer[ii], stdout);
94                  }
95                  fputs("\n", stdout);
96          }
97
98          gnutls_bye(session, GNUTLS_SHUT_RDWR);
99
100     end:
101
102         tcp_close(sd);
103
104         gnutls_deinit(session);
105
106         gnutls_anon_free_client_credentials(anoncred);
```

```
107
108         gnutls_global_deinit();
109
110         return 0;
111  }
```

6.1.4. Simple datagram TLS client example

This is a client that uses UDP to connect to a server. This is the DTLS equivalent to the TLS example with X.509 certificates.

```
1   /* This example code is placed in the public domain. */
2
3   #ifdef HAVE_CONFIG_H
4   #include <config.h>
5   #endif
6
7   #include <stdio.h>
8   #include <stdlib.h>
9   #include <string.h>
10  #include <sys/types.h>
11  #include <sys/socket.h>
12  #include <arpa/inet.h>
13  #include <assert.h>
14  #include <unistd.h>
15  #include <gnutls/gnutls.h>
16  #include <gnutls/dtls.h>
17
18  /* A very basic Datagram TLS client, over UDP with X.509 authentication.
19   */
20
21  #define CHECK(x) assert((x)>=0)
22
23  #define MAX_BUF 1024
24  #define MSG "GET / HTTP/1.0\r\n\r\n"
25
26  extern int udp_connect(void);
27  extern void udp_close(int sd);
28  extern int verify_certificate_callback(gnutls_session_t session);
29
30  int main(void)
31  {
32          int ret, sd, ii;
33          gnutls_session_t session;
34          char buffer[MAX_BUF + 1];
35          gnutls_certificate_credentials_t xcred;
36
37          if (gnutls_check_version("3.1.4") == NULL) {
38                  fprintf(stderr, "GnuTLS 3.1.4 or later is required for this example\n");
39                  exit(1);
40          }
41
42          /* for backwards compatibility with gnutls < 3.3.0 */
43          CHECK(gnutls_global_init());
44
```

```
45     /* X509 stuff */
46     CHECK(gnutls_certificate_allocate_credentials(&xcred));
47
48     /* sets the system trusted CAs for Internet PKI */
49     CHECK(gnutls_certificate_set_x509_system_trust(xcred));
50
51     /* Initialize TLS session */
52     CHECK(gnutls_init(&session, GNUTLS_CLIENT | GNUTLS_DATAGRAM));
53
54     /* Use default priorities */
55     CHECK(gnutls_set_default_priority(session));
56
57     /* put the x509 credentials to the current session */
58     CHECK(gnutls_credentials_set(session, GNUTLS_CRD_CERTIFICATE, xcred));
59     CHECK(gnutls_server_name_set(session, GNUTLS_NAME_DNS, "my_host_name",
60                                  strlen("my_host_name")));
61
62     gnutls_session_set_verify_cert(session, "my_host_name", 0);
63
64     /* connect to the peer */
65     sd = udp_connect();
66
67     gnutls_transport_set_int(session, sd);
68
69     /* set the connection MTU */
70     gnutls_dtls_set_mtu(session, 1000);
71     /* gnutls_dtls_set_timeouts(session, 1000, 60000); */
72
73     /* Perform the TLS handshake */
74     do {
75             ret = gnutls_handshake(session);
76     }
77     while (ret == GNUTLS_E_INTERRUPTED || ret == GNUTLS_E_AGAIN);
78     /* Note that DTLS may also receive GNUTLS_E_LARGE_PACKET */
79
80     if (ret < 0) {
81             fprintf(stderr, "*** Handshake failed\n");
82             gnutls_perror(ret);
83             goto end;
84     } else {
85             char *desc;
86
87             desc = gnutls_session_get_desc(session);
88             printf("- Session info: %s\n", desc);
89             gnutls_free(desc);
90     }
91
92     CHECK(gnutls_record_send(session, MSG, strlen(MSG)));
93
94     ret = gnutls_record_recv(session, buffer, MAX_BUF);
95     if (ret == 0) {
96             printf("- Peer has closed the TLS connection\n");
97             goto end;
98     } else if (ret < 0 && gnutls_error_is_fatal(ret) == 0) {
99             fprintf(stderr, "*** Warning: %s\n", gnutls_strerror(ret));
100    } else if (ret < 0) {
101            fprintf(stderr, "*** Error: %s\n", gnutls_strerror(ret));
102            goto end;
```

```
103          }
104
105          if (ret > 0) {
106                  printf("- Received %d bytes: ", ret);
107                  for (ii = 0; ii < ret; ii++) {
108                          fputc(buffer[ii], stdout);
109                  }
110                  fputs("\n", stdout);
111          }
112
113          /* It is suggested not to use GNUTLS_SHUT_RDWR in DTLS
114           * connections because the peer's closure message might
115           * be lost */
116          CHECK(gnutls_bye(session, GNUTLS_SHUT_WR));
117
118      end:
119
120          udp_close(sd);
121
122          gnutls_deinit(session);
123
124          gnutls_certificate_free_credentials(xcred);
125
126          gnutls_global_deinit();
127
128          return 0;
129 }
```

6.1.5. Obtaining session information

Most of the times it is desirable to know the security properties of the current established session. This includes the underlying ciphers and the protocols involved. That is the purpose of the following function. Note that this function will print meaningful values only if called after a successful **gnutls_handshake**.

```
1  /* This example code is placed in the public domain. */
2
3  #ifdef HAVE_CONFIG_H
4  #include <config.h>
5  #endif
6
7  #include <stdio.h>
8  #include <stdlib.h>
9  #include <gnutls/gnutls.h>
10 #include <gnutls/x509.h>
11
12 #include "examples.h"
13
14 /* This function will print some details of the
15  * given session.
16  */
17 int print_info(gnutls_session_t session)
18 {
19         const char *tmp;
```

```
20          gnutls_credentials_type_t cred;
21          gnutls_kx_algorithm_t kx;
22          int dhe, ecdh;
23
24          dhe = ecdh = 0;
25
26          /* print the key exchange's algorithm name
27           */
28          kx = gnutls_kx_get(session);
29          tmp = gnutls_kx_get_name(kx);
30          printf("- Key Exchange: %s\n", tmp);
31
32          /* Check the authentication type used and switch
33           * to the appropriate.
34           */
35          cred = gnutls_auth_get_type(session);
36          switch (cred) {
37          case GNUTLS_CRD_IA:
38                  printf("- TLS/IA session\n");
39                  break;
40
41
42  #ifdef ENABLE_SRP
43          case GNUTLS_CRD_SRP:
44                  printf("- SRP session with username %s\n",
45                          gnutls_srp_server_get_username(session));
46                  break;
47  #endif
48
49          case GNUTLS_CRD_PSK:
50                  /* This returns NULL in server side.
51                   */
52                  if (gnutls_psk_client_get_hint(session) != NULL)
53                          printf("- PSK authentication. PSK hint '%s'\n",
54                                  gnutls_psk_client_get_hint(session));
55                  /* This returns NULL in client side.
56                   */
57                  if (gnutls_psk_server_get_username(session) != NULL)
58                          printf("- PSK authentication. Connected as '%s'\n",
59                                  gnutls_psk_server_get_username(session));
60
61                  if (kx == GNUTLS_KX_ECDHE_PSK)
62                          ecdh = 1;
63                  else if (kx == GNUTLS_KX_DHE_PSK)
64                          dhe = 1;
65                  break;
66
67          case GNUTLS_CRD_ANON:  /* anonymous authentication */
68
69                  printf("- Anonymous authentication.\n");
70                  if (kx == GNUTLS_KX_ANON_ECDH)
71                          ecdh = 1;
72                  else if (kx == GNUTLS_KX_ANON_DH)
73                          dhe = 1;
74                  break;
75
76          case GNUTLS_CRD_CERTIFICATE:   /* certificate authentication */
77
```

205

```
78              /* Check if we have been using ephemeral Diffie-Hellman.
79               */
80              if (kx == GNUTLS_KX_DHE_RSA || kx == GNUTLS_KX_DHE_DSS)
81                      dhe = 1;
82              else if (kx == GNUTLS_KX_ECDHE_RSA
83                       || kx == GNUTLS_KX_ECDHE_ECDSA)
84                      ecdh = 1;
85
86              /* if the certificate list is available, then
87               * print some information about it.
88               */
89              print_x509_certificate_info(session);
90
91      }                       /* switch */
92
93      if (ecdh != 0)
94              printf("- Ephemeral ECDH using curve %s\n",
95                      gnutls_ecc_curve_get_name(gnutls_ecc_curve_get
96                                              (session)));
97      else if (dhe != 0)
98              printf("- Ephemeral DH using prime of %d bits\n",
99                      gnutls_dh_get_prime_bits(session));
100
101     /* print the protocol's name (ie TLS 1.0)
102      */
103     tmp =
104         gnutls_protocol_get_name(gnutls_protocol_get_version(session));
105     printf("- Protocol: %s\n", tmp);
106
107     /* print the certificate type of the peer.
108      * ie X.509
109      */
110     tmp =
111         gnutls_certificate_type_get_name(gnutls_certificate_type_get
112                                             (session));
113
114     printf("- Certificate Type: %s\n", tmp);
115
116     /* print the compression algorithm (if any)
117      */
118     tmp = gnutls_compression_get_name(gnutls_compression_get(session));
119     printf("- Compression: %s\n", tmp);
120
121     /* print the name of the cipher used.
122      * ie 3DES.
123      */
124     tmp = gnutls_cipher_get_name(gnutls_cipher_get(session));
125     printf("- Cipher: %s\n", tmp);
126
127     /* Print the MAC algorithms name.
128      * ie SHA1
129      */
130     tmp = gnutls_mac_get_name(gnutls_mac_get(session));
131     printf("- MAC: %s\n", tmp);
132
133     return 0;
134 }
```

6.1.6. Using a callback to select the certificate to use

There are cases where a client holds several certificate and key pairs, and may not want to load all of them in the credentials structure. The following example demonstrates the use of the certificate selection callback.

```
1   /* This example code is placed in the public domain. */
2
3   #ifdef HAVE_CONFIG_H
4   #include <config.h>
5   #endif
6
7   #include <stdio.h>
8   #include <stdlib.h>
9   #include <string.h>
10  #include <sys/types.h>
11  #include <sys/socket.h>
12  #include <arpa/inet.h>
13  #include <unistd.h>
14  #include <assert.h>
15  #include <gnutls/gnutls.h>
16  #include <gnutls/x509.h>
17  #include <gnutls/abstract.h>
18  #include <sys/types.h>
19  #include <sys/stat.h>
20  #include <fcntl.h>
21
22  /* A TLS client that loads the certificate and key.
23   */
24
25  #define CHECK(x) assert((x)>=0)
26
27  #define MAX_BUF 1024
28  #define MSG "GET / HTTP/1.0\r\n\r\n"
29
30  #define CERT_FILE "cert.pem"
31  #define KEY_FILE "key.pem"
32  #define CAFILE "/etc/ssl/certs/ca-certificates.crt"
33
34  extern int tcp_connect(void);
35  extern void tcp_close(int sd);
36
37  static int
38  cert_callback(gnutls_session_t session,
39               const gnutls_datum_t * req_ca_rdn, int nreqs,
40               const gnutls_pk_algorithm_t * sign_algos,
41               int sign_algos_length, gnutls_pcert_st ** pcert,
42               unsigned int *pcert_length, gnutls_privkey_t * pkey);
43
44  gnutls_pcert_st pcrt;
45  gnutls_privkey_t key;
46
47  /* Load the certificate and the private key.
48   */
49  static void load_keys(void)
50  {
51          gnutls_datum_t data;
```

```
52
53          CHECK(gnutls_load_file(CERT_FILE, &data));
54
55          CHECK(gnutls_pcert_import_x509_raw(&pcert, &data,
56                                             GNUTLS_X509_FMT_PEM, 0));
57
58          gnutls_free(data.data);
59
60          CHECK(gnutls_load_file(KEY_FILE, &data));
61
62          CHECK(gnutls_privkey_init(&key));
63
64          CHECK(gnutls_privkey_import_x509_raw(key, &data,
65                                               GNUTLS_X509_FMT_PEM,
66                                               NULL, 0));
67          gnutls_free(data.data);
68   }
69
70   int main(void)
71   {
72          int ret, sd, ii;
73          gnutls_session_t session;
74          char buffer[MAX_BUF + 1];
75          gnutls_certificate_credentials_t xcred;
76
77          if (gnutls_check_version("3.1.4") == NULL) {
78                  fprintf(stderr, "GnuTLS 3.1.4 or later is required for this example\n");
79                  exit(1);
80          }
81
82          /* for backwards compatibility with gnutls < 3.3.0 */
83          CHECK(gnutls_global_init());
84
85          load_keys();
86
87          /* X509 stuff */
88          CHECK(gnutls_certificate_allocate_credentials(&xcred));
89
90          /* sets the trusted cas file
91           */
92          CHECK(gnutls_certificate_set_x509_trust_file(xcred, CAFILE,
93                                                       GNUTLS_X509_FMT_PEM));
94
95          gnutls_certificate_set_retrieve_function2(xcred, cert_callback);
96
97          /* Initialize TLS session
98           */
99          CHECK(gnutls_init(&session, GNUTLS_CLIENT));
100
101          /* Use default priorities */
102          CHECK(gnutls_set_default_priority(session));
103
104          /* put the x509 credentials to the current session
105           */
106          CHECK(gnutls_credentials_set(session, GNUTLS_CRD_CERTIFICATE, xcred));
107
108          /* connect to the peer
109           */
```

208

```
110        sd = tcp_connect();
111
112        gnutls_transport_set_int(session, sd);
113
114        /* Perform the TLS handshake
115         */
116        ret = gnutls_handshake(session);
117
118        if (ret < 0) {
119                fprintf(stderr, "*** Handshake failed\n");
120                gnutls_perror(ret);
121                goto end;
122        } else {
123                char *desc;
124
125                desc = gnutls_session_get_desc(session);
126                printf("- Session info: %s\n", desc);
127                gnutls_free(desc);
128        }
129
130        CHECK(gnutls_record_send(session, MSG, strlen(MSG)));
131
132        ret = gnutls_record_recv(session, buffer, MAX_BUF);
133        if (ret == 0) {
134                printf("- Peer has closed the TLS connection\n");
135                goto end;
136        } else if (ret < 0) {
137                fprintf(stderr, "*** Error: %s\n", gnutls_strerror(ret));
138                goto end;
139        }
140
141        printf("- Received %d bytes: ", ret);
142        for (ii = 0; ii < ret; ii++) {
143                fputc(buffer[ii], stdout);
144        }
145        fputs("\n", stdout);
146
147        CHECK(gnutls_bye(session, GNUTLS_SHUT_RDWR));
148
149    end:
150
151        tcp_close(sd);
152
153        gnutls_deinit(session);
154
155        gnutls_certificate_free_credentials(xcred);
156
157        gnutls_global_deinit();
158
159        return 0;
160 }
161
162
163
164 /* This callback should be associated with a session by calling
165  * gnutls_certificate_client_set_retrieve_function( session, cert_callback),
166  * before a handshake.
167  */
```

```
168
169  static int
170  cert_callback(gnutls_session_t session,
171                const gnutls_datum_t * req_ca_rdn, int nreqs,
172                const gnutls_pk_algorithm_t * sign_algos,
173                int sign_algos_length, gnutls_pcert_st ** pcert,
174                unsigned int *pcert_length, gnutls_privkey_t * pkey)
175  {
176          char issuer_dn[256];
177          int i, ret;
178          size_t len;
179          gnutls_certificate_type_t type;
180
181          /* Print the server's trusted CAs
182           */
183          if (nreqs > 0)
184                  printf("- Server's trusted authorities:\n");
185          else
186                  printf
187                      ("- Server did not send us any trusted authorities names.\n");
188
189          /* print the names (if any) */
190          for (i = 0; i < nreqs; i++) {
191                  len = sizeof(issuer_dn);
192                  ret = gnutls_x509_rdn_get(&req_ca_rdn[i], issuer_dn, &len);
193                  if (ret >= 0) {
194                          printf("   [%d]: ", i);
195                          printf("%s\n", issuer_dn);
196                  }
197          }
198
199          /* Select a certificate and return it.
200           * The certificate must be of any of the "sign algorithms"
201           * supported by the server.
202           */
203          type = gnutls_certificate_type_get(session);
204          if (type == GNUTLS_CRT_X509) {
205                  *pcert_length = 1;
206                  *pcert = &pcrt;
207                  *pkey = key;
208          } else {
209                  return -1;
210          }
211
212          return 0;
213
214  }
```

6.1.7. Verifying a certificate

An example is listed below which uses the high level verification functions to verify a given certificate list.

```
1  /* This example code is placed in the public domain. */
2
```

```
3   #ifdef HAVE_CONFIG_H
4   #include <config.h>
5   #endif
6
7   #include <stdio.h>
8   #include <stdlib.h>
9   #include <string.h>
10  #include <assert.h>
11  #include <gnutls/gnutls.h>
12  #include <gnutls/x509.h>
13
14  #include "examples.h"
15
16  #define CHECK(x) assert((x)>=0)
17
18  /* All the available CRLs
19   */
20  gnutls_x509_crl_t *crl_list;
21  int crl_list_size;
22
23  /* All the available trusted CAs
24   */
25  gnutls_x509_crt_t *ca_list;
26  int ca_list_size;
27
28  static int print_details_func(gnutls_x509_crt_t cert,
29                                gnutls_x509_crt_t issuer,
30                                gnutls_x509_crl_t crl,
31                                unsigned int verification_output);
32
33  /* This function will try to verify the peer's certificate chain, and
34   * also check if the hostname matches.
35   */
36  void
37  verify_certificate_chain(const char *hostname,
38                           const gnutls_datum_t * cert_chain,
39                           int cert_chain_length)
40  {
41          int i;
42          gnutls_x509_trust_list_t tlist;
43          gnutls_x509_crt_t *cert;
44          gnutls_datum_t txt;
45          unsigned int output;
46
47          /* Initialize the trusted certificate list. This should be done
48           * once on initialization. gnutls_x509_crt_list_import2() and
49           * gnutls_x509_crl_list_import2() can be used to load them.
50           */
51          CHECK(gnutls_x509_trust_list_init(&tlist, 0));
52
53          CHECK(gnutls_x509_trust_list_add_cas(tlist, ca_list, ca_list_size, 0));
54          CHECK(gnutls_x509_trust_list_add_crls(tlist, crl_list, crl_list_size,
55                                        GNUTLS_TL_VERIFY_CRL, 0));
56
57          cert = malloc(sizeof(*cert) * cert_chain_length);
58
59          /* Import all the certificates in the chain to
60           * native certificate format.
```

```
61              */
62          for (i = 0; i < cert_chain_length; i++) {
63                  CHECK(gnutls_x509_crt_init(&cert[i]));
64                  CHECK(gnutls_x509_crt_import(cert[i], &cert_chain[i],
65                                      GNUTLS_X509_FMT_DER));
66          }
67
68          CHECK(gnutls_x509_trust_list_verify_named_crt(tlist, cert[0],
69                                              hostname,
70                                              strlen(hostname),
71                                              GNUTLS_VERIFY_DISABLE_CRL_CHECKS,
72                                              &output,
73                                              print_details_func));
74
75          /* if this certificate is not explicitly trusted verify against CAs
76           */
77          if (output != 0) {
78                  CHECK(gnutls_x509_trust_list_verify_crt(tlist, cert,
79                                              cert_chain_length, 0,
80                                              &output,
81                                              print_details_func));
82          }
83
84
85
86          if (output & GNUTLS_CERT_INVALID) {
87                  fprintf(stderr, "Not trusted\n");
88                  CHECK(gnutls_certificate_verification_status_print(
89                                              output,
90                                              GNUTLS_CRT_X509,
91                                              &txt, 0));
92
93                  fprintf(stderr, "Error: %s\n", txt.data);
94                  gnutls_free(txt.data);
95          } else
96                  fprintf(stderr, "Trusted\n");
97
98          /* Check if the name in the first certificate matches our destination!
99           */
100         if (!gnutls_x509_crt_check_hostname(cert[0], hostname)) {
101                 printf
102                     ("The certificate's owner does not match hostname '%s'\n",
103                      hostname);
104         }
105
106         gnutls_x509_trust_list_deinit(tlist, 1);
107
108         return;
109 }
110
111 static int
112 print_details_func(gnutls_x509_crt_t cert,
113                 gnutls_x509_crt_t issuer, gnutls_x509_crl_t crl,
114                 unsigned int verification_output)
115 {
116         char name[512];
117         char issuer_name[512];
118         size_t name_size;
```

212

```
119        size_t issuer_name_size;
120
121        issuer_name_size = sizeof(issuer_name);
122        gnutls_x509_crt_get_issuer_dn(cert, issuer_name,
123                                      &issuer_name_size);
124
125        name_size = sizeof(name);
126        gnutls_x509_crt_get_dn(cert, name, &name_size);
127
128        fprintf(stdout, "\tSubject: %s\n", name);
129        fprintf(stdout, "\tIssuer: %s\n", issuer_name);
130
131        if (issuer != NULL) {
132                issuer_name_size = sizeof(issuer_name);
133                gnutls_x509_crt_get_dn(issuer, issuer_name,
134                                       &issuer_name_size);
135
136                fprintf(stdout, "\tVerified against: %s\n", issuer_name);
137        }
138
139        if (crl != NULL) {
140                issuer_name_size = sizeof(issuer_name);
141                gnutls_x509_crl_get_issuer_dn(crl, issuer_name,
142                                              &issuer_name_size);
143
144                fprintf(stdout, "\tVerified against CRL of: %s\n",
145                        issuer_name);
146        }
147
148        fprintf(stdout, "\tVerification output: %x\n\n",
149                verification_output);
150
151        return 0;
152 }
```

6.1.8. Using a smart card with TLS

This example will demonstrate how to load keys and certificates from a smart-card or any other PKCS #11 token, and use it in a TLS connection.

```
1  /* This example code is placed in the public domain. */
2
3  #ifdef HAVE_CONFIG_H
4  #include <config.h>
5  #endif
6
7  #include <stdio.h>
8  #include <stdlib.h>
9  #include <string.h>
10 #include <sys/types.h>
11 #include <sys/socket.h>
12 #include <arpa/inet.h>
13 #include <unistd.h>
14 #include <gnutls/gnutls.h>
15 #include <gnutls/x509.h>
```

```
16  #include <gnutls/pkcs11.h>
17  #include <assert.h>
18  #include <sys/types.h>
19  #include <sys/stat.h>
20  #include <fcntl.h>
21  #include <getpass.h>                /* for getpass() */
22
23  /* A TLS client that loads the certificate and key.
24   */
25
26  #define CHECK(x) assert((x)>=0)
27
28  #define MAX_BUF 1024
29  #define MSG "GET / HTTP/1.0\r\n\r\n"
30  #define MIN(x,y) (((x)<(y))?(x):(y))
31
32  #define CAFILE "/etc/ssl/certs/ca-certificates.crt"
33
34  /* The URLs of the objects can be obtained
35   * using p11tool --list-all --login
36   */
37  #define KEY_URL "pkcs11:manufacturer=SomeManufacturer;object=Private%20Key" \
38    ";objecttype=private;id=%db%5b%3e%b5%72%33"
39  #define CERT_URL "pkcs11:manufacturer=SomeManufacturer;object=Certificate;" \
40    "objecttype=cert;id=db%5b%3e%b5%72%33"
41
42  extern int tcp_connect(void);
43  extern void tcp_close(int sd);
44
45  static int
46  pin_callback(void *user, int attempt, const char *token_url,
47              const char *token_label, unsigned int flags, char *pin,
48              size_t pin_max)
49  {
50          const char *password;
51          int len;
52
53          printf("PIN required for token '%s' with URL '%s'\n", token_label,
54                  token_url);
55          if (flags & GNUTLS_PIN_FINAL_TRY)
56                  printf("*** This is the final try before locking!\n");
57          if (flags & GNUTLS_PIN_COUNT_LOW)
58                  printf("*** Only few tries left before locking!\n");
59          if (flags & GNUTLS_PIN_WRONG)
60                  printf("*** Wrong PIN\n");
61
62          password = getpass("Enter pin: ");
63          /* FIXME: ensure that we are in UTF-8 locale */
64          if (password == NULL || password[0] == 0) {
65                  fprintf(stderr, "No password given\n");
66                  exit(1);
67          }
68
69          len = MIN(pin_max - 1, strlen(password));
70          memcpy(pin, password, len);
71          pin[len] = 0;
72
73          return 0;
```

```
74  }
75
76  int main(void)
77  {
78          int ret, sd, ii;
79          gnutls_session_t session;
80          char buffer[MAX_BUF + 1];
81          gnutls_certificate_credentials_t xcred;
82          /* Allow connections to servers that have OpenPGP keys as well.
83           */
84
85          if (gnutls_check_version("3.1.4") == NULL) {
86                  fprintf(stderr, "GnuTLS 3.1.4 or later is required for this example\n");
87                  exit(1);
88          }
89
90          /* for backwards compatibility with gnutls < 3.3.0 */
91          CHECK(gnutls_global_init());
92
93          /* The PKCS11 private key operations may require PIN.
94           * Register a callback. */
95          gnutls_pkcs11_set_pin_function(pin_callback, NULL);
96
97          /* X509 stuff */
98          CHECK(gnutls_certificate_allocate_credentials(&xcred));
99
100         /* sets the trusted cas file
101          */
102         CHECK(gnutls_certificate_set_x509_trust_file(xcred, CAFILE,
103                                                 GNUTLS_X509_FMT_PEM));
104
105         CHECK(gnutls_certificate_set_x509_key_file(xcred, CERT_URL, KEY_URL,
106                                                 GNUTLS_X509_FMT_DER));
107
108         /* Note that there is no server certificate verification in this example
109          */
110
111
112         /* Initialize TLS session
113          */
114         CHECK(gnutls_init(&session, GNUTLS_CLIENT));
115
116         /* Use default priorities */
117         CHECK(gnutls_set_default_priority(session));
118
119         /* put the x509 credentials to the current session
120          */
121         CHECK(gnutls_credentials_set(session, GNUTLS_CRD_CERTIFICATE, xcred));
122
123         /* connect to the peer
124          */
125         sd = tcp_connect();
126
127         gnutls_transport_set_int(session, sd);
128
129         /* Perform the TLS handshake
130          */
131         ret = gnutls_handshake(session);
```

```
132
133        if (ret < 0) {
134                fprintf(stderr, "*** Handshake failed\n");
135                gnutls_perror(ret);
136                goto end;
137        } else {
138                char *desc;
139
140                desc = gnutls_session_get_desc(session);
141                printf("- Session info: %s\n", desc);
142                gnutls_free(desc);
143        }
144
145        CHECK(gnutls_record_send(session, MSG, strlen(MSG)));
146
147        ret = gnutls_record_recv(session, buffer, MAX_BUF);
148        if (ret == 0) {
149                printf("- Peer has closed the TLS connection\n");
150                goto end;
151        } else if (ret < 0) {
152                fprintf(stderr, "*** Error: %s\n", gnutls_strerror(ret));
153                goto end;
154        }
155
156        printf("- Received %d bytes: ", ret);
157        for (ii = 0; ii < ret; ii++) {
158                fputc(buffer[ii], stdout);
159        }
160        fputs("\n", stdout);
161
162        CHECK(gnutls_bye(session, GNUTLS_SHUT_RDWR));
163
164   end:
165
166        tcp_close(sd);
167
168        gnutls_deinit(session);
169
170        gnutls_certificate_free_credentials(xcred);
171
172        gnutls_global_deinit();
173
174        return 0;
175 }
```

6.1.9. Client with resume capability example

This is a modification of the simple client example. Here we demonstrate the use of session resumption. The client tries to connect once using TLS, close the connection and then try to establish a new connection using the previously negotiated data.

```
1 /* This example code is placed in the public domain. */
2
3 #ifdef HAVE_CONFIG_H
4 #include <config.h>
```

```
 5  #endif
 6
 7  #include <string.h>
 8  #include <stdio.h>
 9  #include <stdlib.h>
10  #include <gnutls/gnutls.h>
11
12  /* Those functions are defined in other examples.
13   */
14  extern void check_alert(gnutls_session_t session, int ret);
15  extern int tcp_connect(void);
16  extern void tcp_close(int sd);
17
18  #define MAX_BUF 1024
19  #define CAFILE "/etc/ssl/certs/ca-certificates.crt"
20  #define MSG "GET / HTTP/1.0\r\n\r\n"
21
22  int main(void)
23  {
24          int ret;
25          int sd, ii;
26          gnutls_session_t session;
27          char buffer[MAX_BUF + 1];
28          gnutls_certificate_credentials_t xcred;
29
30          /* variables used in session resuming
31           */
32          int t;
33          char *session_data = NULL;
34          size_t session_data_size = 0;
35
36          gnutls_global_init();
37
38          /* X509 stuff */
39          gnutls_certificate_allocate_credentials(&xcred);
40
41          gnutls_certificate_set_x509_trust_file(xcred, CAFILE,
42                                              GNUTLS_X509_FMT_PEM);
43
44          for (t = 0; t < 2; t++) {       /* connect 2 times to the server */
45
46                  sd = tcp_connect();
47
48                  gnutls_init(&session, GNUTLS_CLIENT);
49
50                  gnutls_priority_set_direct(session,
51                                              "PERFORMANCE:!ARCFOUR-128",
52                                              NULL);
53
54                  gnutls_credentials_set(session, GNUTLS_CRD_CERTIFICATE,
55                                          xcred);
56
57                  if (t > 0) {
58                          /* if this is not the first time we connect */
59                          gnutls_session_set_data(session, session_data,
60                                                  session_data_size);
61                          free(session_data);
62                  }
```

```
63
64              gnutls_transport_set_int(session, sd);
65              gnutls_handshake_set_timeout(session,
66                                    GNUTLS_DEFAULT_HANDSHAKE_TIMEOUT);
67
68              /* Perform the TLS handshake
69               */
70              do {
71                      ret = gnutls_handshake(session);
72              }
73              while (ret < 0 && gnutls_error_is_fatal(ret) == 0);
74
75              if (ret < 0) {
76                      fprintf(stderr, "*** Handshake failed\n");
77                      gnutls_perror(ret);
78                      goto end;
79              } else {
80                      printf("- Handshake was completed\n");
81              }
82
83              if (t == 0) {    /* the first time we connect */
84                      /* get the session data size */
85                      gnutls_session_get_data(session, NULL,
86                                          &session_data_size);
87                      session_data = malloc(session_data_size);
88
89                      /* put session data to the session variable */
90                      gnutls_session_get_data(session, session_data,
91                                          &session_data_size);
92
93              } else {         /* the second time we connect */
94
95                      /* check if we actually resumed the previous session */
96                      if (gnutls_session_is_resumed(session) != 0) {
97                              printf("- Previous session was resumed\n");
98                      } else {
99                              fprintf(stderr,
100                                       "*** Previous session was NOT resumed\n");
101                      }
102              }
103
104              /* This function was defined in a previous example
105               */
106              /* print_info(session); */
107
108              gnutls_record_send(session, MSG, strlen(MSG));
109
110              ret = gnutls_record_recv(session, buffer, MAX_BUF);
111              if (ret == 0) {
112                      printf("- Peer has closed the TLS connection\n");
113                      goto end;
114              } else if (ret < 0 && gnutls_error_is_fatal(ret) == 0) {
115                      fprintf(stderr, "*** Warning: %s\n",
116                              gnutls_strerror(ret));
117              } else if (ret < 0) {
118                      fprintf(stderr, "*** Error: %s\n",
119                              gnutls_strerror(ret));
120                      goto end;
```

```
121                }
122
123                if (ret > 0) {
124                        printf("- Received %d bytes: ", ret);
125                        for (ii = 0; ii < ret; ii++) {
126                                fputc(buffer[ii], stdout);
127                        }
128                        fputs("\n", stdout);
129                }
130
131                gnutls_bye(session, GNUTLS_SHUT_RDWR);
132
133            end:
134
135                tcp_close(sd);
136
137                gnutls_deinit(session);
138
139        }                        /* for() */
140
141        gnutls_certificate_free_credentials(xcred);
142
143        gnutls_global_deinit();
144
145        return 0;
146 }
```

6.1.10. Simple client example with SRP authentication

The following client is a very simple SRP TLS client which connects to a server and authenticates using a *username* and a *password*. The server may authenticate itself using a certificate, and in that case it has to be verified.

```
1  /* This example code is placed in the public domain. */
2
3  #ifdef HAVE_CONFIG_H
4  #include <config.h>
5  #endif
6
7  #include <stdio.h>
8  #include <stdlib.h>
9  #include <string.h>
10 #include <gnutls/gnutls.h>
11
12 /* Those functions are defined in other examples.
13  */
14 extern void check_alert(gnutls_session_t session, int ret);
15 extern int tcp_connect(void);
16 extern void tcp_close(int sd);
17
18 #define MAX_BUF 1024
19 #define USERNAME "user"
20 #define PASSWORD "pass"
21 #define CAFILE "/etc/ssl/certs/ca-certificates.crt"
22 #define MSG "GET / HTTP/1.0\r\n\r\n"
```

```
23
24  int main(void)
25  {
26          int ret;
27          int sd, ii;
28          gnutls_session_t session;
29          char buffer[MAX_BUF + 1];
30          gnutls_srp_client_credentials_t srp_cred;
31          gnutls_certificate_credentials_t cert_cred;
32
33          if (gnutls_check_version("3.1.4") == NULL) {
34                  fprintf(stderr, "GnuTLS 3.1.4 or later is required for this example\n");
35                  exit(1);
36          }
37
38          /* for backwards compatibility with gnutls < 3.3.0 */
39          gnutls_global_init();
40
41          gnutls_srp_allocate_client_credentials(&srp_cred);
42          gnutls_certificate_allocate_credentials(&cert_cred);
43
44          gnutls_certificate_set_x509_trust_file(cert_cred, CAFILE,
45                                          GNUTLS_X509_FMT_PEM);
46          gnutls_srp_set_client_credentials(srp_cred, USERNAME, PASSWORD);
47
48          /* connects to server
49           */
50          sd = tcp_connect();
51
52          /* Initialize TLS session
53           */
54          gnutls_init(&session, GNUTLS_CLIENT);
55
56
57          /* Set the priorities.
58           */
59          gnutls_priority_set_direct(session,
60                                  "NORMAL:+SRP:+SRP-RSA:+SRP-DSS",
61                                  NULL);
62
63          /* put the SRP credentials to the current session
64           */
65          gnutls_credentials_set(session, GNUTLS_CRD_SRP, srp_cred);
66          gnutls_credentials_set(session, GNUTLS_CRD_CERTIFICATE, cert_cred);
67
68          gnutls_transport_set_int(session, sd);
69          gnutls_handshake_set_timeout(session,
70                                  GNUTLS_DEFAULT_HANDSHAKE_TIMEOUT);
71
72          /* Perform the TLS handshake
73           */
74          do {
75                  ret = gnutls_handshake(session);
76          }
77          while (ret < 0 && gnutls_error_is_fatal(ret) == 0);
78
79          if (ret < 0) {
80                  fprintf(stderr, "*** Handshake failed\n");
```

```
 81                    gnutls_perror(ret);
 82                    goto end;
 83            } else {
 84                    char *desc;
 85
 86                    desc = gnutls_session_get_desc(session);
 87                    printf("- Session info: %s\n", desc);
 88                    gnutls_free(desc);
 89            }
 90
 91            gnutls_record_send(session, MSG, strlen(MSG));
 92
 93            ret = gnutls_record_recv(session, buffer, MAX_BUF);
 94            if (gnutls_error_is_fatal(ret) != 0 || ret == 0) {
 95                    if (ret == 0) {
 96                            printf
 97                                ("- Peer has closed the GnuTLS connection\n");
 98                            goto end;
 99                    } else {
100                            fprintf(stderr, "*** Error: %s\n",
101                                    gnutls_strerror(ret));
102                            goto end;
103                    }
104            } else
105                    check_alert(session, ret);
106
107            if (ret > 0) {
108                    printf("- Received %d bytes: ", ret);
109                    for (ii = 0; ii < ret; ii++) {
110                            fputc(buffer[ii], stdout);
111                    }
112                    fputs("\n", stdout);
113            }
114            gnutls_bye(session, GNUTLS_SHUT_RDWR);
115
116      end:
117
118            tcp_close(sd);
119
120            gnutls_deinit(session);
121
122            gnutls_srp_free_client_credentials(srp_cred);
123            gnutls_certificate_free_credentials(cert_cred);
124
125            gnutls_global_deinit();
126
127            return 0;
128 }
```

6.1.11. Legacy client example with X.509 certificate support

For applications that need to maintain compatibility with the GnuTLS 3.1.x library, this client example is identical to subsection 6.1.1 but utilizes APIs that were available in GnuTLS 3.1.4.

221

```
1   /* This example code is placed in the public domain. */
2
3   #ifdef HAVE_CONFIG_H
4   #include <config.h>
5   #endif
6
7   #include <stdio.h>
8   #include <stdlib.h>
9   #include <string.h>
10  #include <assert.h>
11  #include <gnutls/gnutls.h>
12  #include <gnutls/x509.h>
13  #include "examples.h"
14
15  /* A very basic TLS client, with X.509 authentication and server certificate
16   * verification utilizing the GnuTLS 3.1.x API.
17   * Note that error recovery is minimal for simplicity.
18   */
19
20  #define CHECK(x) assert((x)>=0)
21
22  #define MAX_BUF 1024
23  #define CAFILE "/etc/ssl/certs/ca-certificates.crt"
24  #define MSG "GET / HTTP/1.0\r\n\r\n"
25
26  extern int tcp_connect(void);
27  extern void tcp_close(int sd);
28  static int _verify_certificate_callback(gnutls_session_t session);
29
30  int main(void)
31  {
32          int ret, sd, ii;
33          gnutls_session_t session;
34          char buffer[MAX_BUF + 1];
35          gnutls_certificate_credentials_t xcred;
36
37          if (gnutls_check_version("3.1.4") == NULL) {
38                  fprintf(stderr, "GnuTLS 3.1.4 or later is required for this example\n");
39                  exit(1);
40          }
41
42          CHECK(gnutls_global_init());
43
44          /* X509 stuff */
45          CHECK(gnutls_certificate_allocate_credentials(&xcred));
46
47          /* sets the trusted cas file
48           */
49          CHECK(gnutls_certificate_set_x509_trust_file(xcred, CAFILE,
50                                                      GNUTLS_X509_FMT_PEM));
51          gnutls_certificate_set_verify_function(xcred,
52                                                _verify_certificate_callback);
53
54          /* If client holds a certificate it can be set using the following:
55           *
56           gnutls_certificate_set_x509_key_file (xcred,
57           "cert.pem", "key.pem",
```

```
58              GNUTLS_X509_FMT_PEM);
59              */
60
61          /* Initialize TLS session
62           */
63          CHECK(gnutls_init(&session, GNUTLS_CLIENT));
64
65          gnutls_session_set_ptr(session, (void *) "my_host_name");
66
67          gnutls_server_name_set(session, GNUTLS_NAME_DNS, "my_host_name",
68                                  strlen("my_host_name"));
69
70          /* use default priorities */
71          CHECK(gnutls_set_default_priority(session));
72  #if 0
73          /* if more fine-graned control is required */
74          ret = gnutls_priority_set_direct(session,
75                                          "NORMAL", &err);
76          if (ret < 0) {
77                  if (ret == GNUTLS_E_INVALID_REQUEST) {
78                          fprintf(stderr, "Syntax error at: %s\n", err);
79                  }
80                  exit(1);
81          }
82  #endif
83
84          /* put the x509 credentials to the current session
85           */
86          CHECK(gnutls_credentials_set(session, GNUTLS_CRD_CERTIFICATE, xcred));
87
88          /* connect to the peer
89           */
90          sd = tcp_connect();
91
92          gnutls_transport_set_int(session, sd);
93          gnutls_handshake_set_timeout(session,
94                                          GNUTLS_DEFAULT_HANDSHAKE_TIMEOUT);
95
96          /* Perform the TLS handshake
97           */
98          do {
99                  ret = gnutls_handshake(session);
100         }
101         while (ret < 0 && gnutls_error_is_fatal(ret) == 0);
102
103         if (ret < 0) {
104                 fprintf(stderr, "*** Handshake failed\n");
105                 gnutls_perror(ret);
106                 goto end;
107         } else {
108                 char *desc;
109
110                 desc = gnutls_session_get_desc(session);
111                 printf("- Session info: %s\n", desc);
112                 gnutls_free(desc);
113         }
114
115         CHECK(gnutls_record_send(session, MSG, strlen(MSG)));
```

```
116
117         ret = gnutls_record_recv(session, buffer, MAX_BUF);
118         if (ret == 0) {
119                 printf("- Peer has closed the TLS connection\n");
120                 goto end;
121         } else if (ret < 0 && gnutls_error_is_fatal(ret) == 0) {
122                 fprintf(stderr, "*** Warning: %s\n", gnutls_strerror(ret));
123         } else if (ret < 0) {
124                 fprintf(stderr, "*** Error: %s\n", gnutls_strerror(ret));
125                 goto end;
126         }
127
128         if (ret > 0) {
129                 printf("- Received %d bytes: ", ret);
130                 for (ii = 0; ii < ret; ii++) {
131                         fputc(buffer[ii], stdout);
132                 }
133                 fputs("\n", stdout);
134         }
135
136         CHECK(gnutls_bye(session, GNUTLS_SHUT_RDWR));
137
138     end:
139
140         tcp_close(sd);
141
142         gnutls_deinit(session);
143
144         gnutls_certificate_free_credentials(xcred);
145
146         gnutls_global_deinit();
147
148         return 0;
149 }
150
151 /* This function will verify the peer's certificate, and check
152  * if the hostname matches, as well as the activation, expiration dates.
153  */
154 static int _verify_certificate_callback(gnutls_session_t session)
155 {
156         unsigned int status;
157         int type;
158         const char *hostname;
159         gnutls_datum_t out;
160
161         /* read hostname */
162         hostname = gnutls_session_get_ptr(session);
163
164         /* This verification function uses the trusted CAs in the credentials
165          * structure. So you must have installed one or more CA certificates.
166          */
167
168         CHECK(gnutls_certificate_verify_peers3(session, hostname,
169                                                &status));
170
171         type = gnutls_certificate_type_get(session);
172
173         CHECK(gnutls_certificate_verification_status_print(status, type,
```

```
174                                                    &out, 0));
175
176        printf("%s", out.data);
177
178        gnutls_free(out.data);
179
180        if (status != 0)          /* Certificate is not trusted */
181                return GNUTLS_E_CERTIFICATE_ERROR;
182
183        /* notify gnutls to continue handshake normally */
184        return 0;
185 }
```

6.1.12. Simple client example using the C++ API

The following client is a simple example of a client client utilizing the GnuTLS C++ API.

```
1  #include <config.h>
2  #include <iostream>
3  #include <stdexcept>
4  #include <gnutls/gnutls.h>
5  #include <gnutls/gnutlsxx.h>
6  #include <cstring> /* for strlen */
7
8  /* A very basic TLS client, with anonymous authentication.
9   * written by Eduardo Villanueva Che.
10  */
11
12 #define MAX_BUF 1024
13 #define SA struct sockaddr
14
15 #define CAFILE "ca.pem"
16 #define MSG "GET / HTTP/1.0\r\n\r\n"
17
18 extern "C"
19 {
20     int tcp_connect(void);
21     void tcp_close(int sd);
22 }
23
24
25 int main(void)
26 {
27     int sd = -1;
28     gnutls_global_init();
29
30     try
31     {
32
33         /* Allow connections to servers that have OpenPGP keys as well.
34          */
35         gnutls::client_session session;
36
37         /* X509 stuff */
38         gnutls::certificate_credentials credentials;
```

```
39
40
41         /* sets the trusted cas file
42          */
43         credentials.set_x509_trust_file(CAFILE, GNUTLS_X509_FMT_PEM);
44         /* put the x509 credentials to the current session
45          */
46         session.set_credentials(credentials);
47
48         /* Use default priorities */
49         session.set_priority ("NORMAL", NULL);
50
51         /* connect to the peer
52          */
53         sd = tcp_connect();
54         session.set_transport_ptr((gnutls_transport_ptr_t) (ptrdiff_t)sd);
55
56         /* Perform the TLS handshake
57          */
58         int ret = session.handshake();
59         if (ret < 0)
60         {
61             throw std::runtime_error("Handshake failed");
62         }
63         else
64         {
65             std::cout << "- Handshake was completed" << std::endl;
66         }
67
68         session.send(MSG, strlen(MSG));
69         char buffer[MAX_BUF + 1];
70         ret = session.recv(buffer, MAX_BUF);
71         if (ret == 0)
72         {
73             throw std::runtime_error("Peer has closed the TLS connection");
74         }
75         else if (ret < 0)
76         {
77             throw std::runtime_error(gnutls_strerror(ret));
78         }
79
80         std::cout << "- Received " << ret << " bytes:" << std::endl;
81         std::cout.write(buffer, ret);
82         std::cout << std::endl;
83
84         session.bye(GNUTLS_SHUT_RDWR);
85     }
86     catch (std::exception &ex)
87     {
88         std::cerr << "Exception caught: " << ex.what() << std::endl;
89     }
90
91     if (sd != -1)
92         tcp_close(sd);
93
94     gnutls_global_deinit();
95
96     return 0;
```

```
97 | }
```

6.1.13. Helper functions for TCP connections

Those helper function abstract away TCP connection handling from the other examples. It is
required to build some examples.

```
 1 | /* This example code is placed in the public domain. */
 2 |
 3 | #ifdef HAVE_CONFIG_H
 4 | #include <config.h>
 5 | #endif
 6 |
 7 | #include <stdio.h>
 8 | #include <stdlib.h>
 9 | #include <string.h>
10 | #include <sys/types.h>
11 | #include <sys/socket.h>
12 | #include <arpa/inet.h>
13 | #include <netinet/in.h>
14 | #include <unistd.h>
15 |
16 | /* tcp.c */
17 | int tcp_connect(void);
18 | void tcp_close(int sd);
19 |
20 | /* Connects to the peer and returns a socket
21 |  * descriptor.
22 |  */
23 | extern int tcp_connect(void)
24 | {
25 |         const char *PORT = "5556";
26 |         const char *SERVER = "127.0.0.1";
27 |         int err, sd;
28 |         struct sockaddr_in sa;
29 |
30 |         /* connects to server
31 |          */
32 |         sd = socket(AF_INET, SOCK_STREAM, 0);
33 |
34 |         memset(&sa, '\0', sizeof(sa));
35 |         sa.sin_family = AF_INET;
36 |         sa.sin_port = htons(atoi(PORT));
37 |         inet_pton(AF_INET, SERVER, &sa.sin_addr);
38 |
39 |         err = connect(sd, (struct sockaddr *) &sa, sizeof(sa));
40 |         if (err < 0) {
41 |                 fprintf(stderr, "Connect error\n");
42 |                 exit(1);
43 |         }
44 |
45 |         return sd;
46 | }
47 |
48 | /* closes the given socket descriptor.
```

```
49   */
50   extern void tcp_close(int sd)
51   {
52           shutdown(sd, SHUT_RDWR);        /* no more receptions */
53           close(sd);
54   }
```

6.1.14. Helper functions for UDP connections

The UDP helper functions abstract away UDP connection handling from the other examples.
It is required to build the examples using UDP.

```
1    /* This example code is placed in the public domain. */
2
3    #ifdef HAVE_CONFIG_H
4    #include <config.h>
5    #endif
6
7    #include <stdio.h>
8    #include <stdlib.h>
9    #include <string.h>
10   #include <sys/types.h>
11   #include <sys/socket.h>
12   #include <arpa/inet.h>
13   #include <netinet/in.h>
14   #include <unistd.h>
15
16   /* udp.c */
17   int udp_connect(void);
18   void udp_close(int sd);
19
20   /* Connects to the peer and returns a socket
21    * descriptor.
22    */
23   extern int udp_connect(void)
24   {
25           const char *PORT = "5557";
26           const char *SERVER = "127.0.0.1";
27           int err, sd, optval;
28           struct sockaddr_in sa;
29
30           /* connects to server
31            */
32           sd = socket(AF_INET, SOCK_DGRAM, 0);
33
34           memset(&sa, '\0', sizeof(sa));
35           sa.sin_family = AF_INET;
36           sa.sin_port = htons(atoi(PORT));
37           inet_pton(AF_INET, SERVER, &sa.sin_addr);
38
39   #if defined(IP_DONTFRAG)
40           optval = 1;
41           setsockopt(sd, IPPROTO_IP, IP_DONTFRAG,
42                       (const void *) &optval, sizeof(optval));
43   #elif defined(IP_MTU_DISCOVER)
```

```
44        optval = IP_PMTUDISC_DO;
45        setsockopt(sd, IPPROTO_IP, IP_MTU_DISCOVER,
46                   (const void *) &optval, sizeof(optval));
47 #endif
48
49        err = connect(sd, (struct sockaddr *) &sa, sizeof(sa));
50        if (err < 0) {
51                fprintf(stderr, "Connect error\n");
52                exit(1);
53        }
54
55        return sd;
56 }
57
58 /* closes the given socket descriptor.
59  */
60 extern void udp_close(int sd)
61 {
62        close(sd);
63 }
```

6.2. Server examples

This section contains examples of TLS and SSL servers, using GnuTLS.

6.2.1. Echo server with X.509 authentication

This example is a very simple echo server which supports X.509 authentication.

```
1 /* This example code is placed in the public domain. */
2
3 #ifdef HAVE_CONFIG_H
4 #include <config.h>
5 #endif
6
7 #include <stdio.h>
8 #include <stdlib.h>
9 #include <errno.h>
10 #include <sys/types.h>
11 #include <sys/socket.h>
12 #include <arpa/inet.h>
13 #include <netinet/in.h>
14 #include <string.h>
15 #include <unistd.h>
16 #include <gnutls/gnutls.h>
17 #include <assert.h>
18
19 #define KEYFILE "key.pem"
20 #define CERTFILE "cert.pem"
21 #define CAFILE "/etc/ssl/certs/ca-certificates.crt"
22 #define CRLFILE "crl.pem"
23
```

```
24  #define CHECK(x) assert((x)>=0)
25
26  /* The OCSP status file contains up to date information about revocation
27   * of the server's certificate. That can be periodically be updated
28   * using:
29   * $ ocsptool --ask --load-cert your_cert.pem --load-issuer your_issuer.pem
30   *            --load-signer your_issuer.pem --outfile ocsp-status.der
31   */
32  #define OCSP_STATUS_FILE "ocsp-status.der"
33
34  /* This is a sample TLS 1.0 echo server, using X.509 authentication and
35   * OCSP stapling support.
36   */
37
38  #define MAX_BUF 1024
39  #define PORT 5556                  /* listen to 5556 port */
40
41  int main(void)
42  {
43          int listen_sd;
44          int sd, ret;
45          gnutls_certificate_credentials_t x509_cred;
46          gnutls_priority_t priority_cache;
47          struct sockaddr_in sa_serv;
48          struct sockaddr_in sa_cli;
49          socklen_t client_len;
50          char topbuf[512];
51          gnutls_session_t session;
52          char buffer[MAX_BUF + 1];
53          int optval = 1;
54
55          /* for backwards compatibility with gnutls < 3.3.0 */
56          CHECK(gnutls_global_init());
57
58          CHECK(gnutls_certificate_allocate_credentials(&x509_cred));
59
60          CHECK(gnutls_certificate_set_x509_trust_file(x509_cred, CAFILE,
61                                              GNUTLS_X509_FMT_PEM));
62
63          CHECK(gnutls_certificate_set_x509_crl_file(x509_cred, CRLFILE,
64                                              GNUTLS_X509_FMT_PEM));
65
66          /* The following code sets the certificate key pair as well as,
67           * an OCSP response which corresponds to it. It is possible
68           * to set multiple key-pairs and multiple OCSP status responses
69           * (the latter since 3.5.6). See the manual pages of the individual
70           * functions for more information.
71           */
72          CHECK(gnutls_certificate_set_x509_key_file(x509_cred, CERTFILE,
73                                                  KEYFILE,
74                                                  GNUTLS_X509_FMT_PEM));
75
76          CHECK(gnutls_certificate_set_ocsp_status_request_file(x509_cred,
77                                                  OCSP_STATUS_FILE,
78                                                  0));
79
80          /* One could use specific priority strings such as "PERFORMANCE:%SERVER_PRECEDENCE"
81           * especially if they are read from a configuration file; otherwise, it
```

```
82          * is recommended to use the defaults as shown here. */
83         CHECK(gnutls_priority_init(&priority_cache, NULL, NULL));
84
85 #if GNUTLS_VERSION_NUMBER >= 0x030506
86         /* only available since GnuTLS 3.5.6, on previous versions see
87          * gnutls_certificate_set_dh_params(). */
88         gnutls_certificate_set_known_dh_params(x509_cred, GNUTLS_SEC_PARAM_MEDIUM);
89 #endif
90
91         /* Socket operations
92          */
93         listen_sd = socket(AF_INET, SOCK_STREAM, 0);
94
95         memset(&sa_serv, '\0', sizeof(sa_serv));
96         sa_serv.sin_family = AF_INET;
97         sa_serv.sin_addr.s_addr = INADDR_ANY;
98         sa_serv.sin_port = htons(PORT); /* Server Port number */
99
100        setsockopt(listen_sd, SOL_SOCKET, SO_REUSEADDR, (void *) &optval,
101                    sizeof(int));
102
103        bind(listen_sd, (struct sockaddr *) &sa_serv, sizeof(sa_serv));
104
105        listen(listen_sd, 1024);
106
107        printf("Server ready. Listening to port '%d'.\n\n", PORT);
108
109        client_len = sizeof(sa_cli);
110        for (;;) {
111                CHECK(gnutls_init(&session, GNUTLS_SERVER));
112                CHECK(gnutls_priority_set(session, priority_cache));
113                CHECK(gnutls_credentials_set(session, GNUTLS_CRD_CERTIFICATE,
114                                             x509_cred));
115
116                /* We don't request any certificate from the client.
117                 * If we did we would need to verify it. One way of
118                 * doing that is shown in the "Verifying a certificate"
119                 * example.
120                 */
121                gnutls_certificate_server_set_request(session,
122                                                      GNUTLS_CERT_IGNORE);
123                gnutls_handshake_set_timeout(session,
124                                             GNUTLS_DEFAULT_HANDSHAKE_TIMEOUT);
125
126                sd = accept(listen_sd, (struct sockaddr *) &sa_cli,
127                            &client_len);
128
129                printf("- connection from %s, port %d\n",
130                       inet_ntop(AF_INET, &sa_cli.sin_addr, topbuf,
131                                 sizeof(topbuf)), ntohs(sa_cli.sin_port));
132
133                gnutls_transport_set_int(session, sd);
134
135                do {
136                        ret = gnutls_handshake(session);
137                }
138                while (ret < 0 && gnutls_error_is_fatal(ret) == 0);
139
```

231

```
140            if (ret < 0) {
141                    close(sd);
142                    gnutls_deinit(session);
143                    fprintf(stderr,
144                            "*** Handshake has failed (%s)\n\n",
145                            gnutls_strerror(ret));
146                    continue;
147            }
148            printf("- Handshake was completed\n");
149
150            /* see the Getting peer's information example */
151            /* print_info(session); */
152
153            for (;;) {
154                    ret = gnutls_record_recv(session, buffer, MAX_BUF);
155
156                    if (ret == 0) {
157                            printf
158                                ("\n- Peer has closed the GnuTLS connection\n");
159                            break;
160                    } else if (ret < 0
161                            && gnutls_error_is_fatal(ret) == 0) {
162                            fprintf(stderr, "*** Warning: %s\n",
163                                    gnutls_strerror(ret));
164                    } else if (ret < 0) {
165                            fprintf(stderr, "\n*** Received corrupted "
166                                    "data(%d). Closing the connection.\n\n",
167                                    ret);
168                            break;
169                    } else if (ret > 0) {
170                            /* echo data back to the client
171                             */
172                            CHECK(gnutls_record_send(session, buffer, ret));
173                    }
174            }
175            printf("\n");
176            /* do not wait for the peer to close the connection.
177             */
178            CHECK(gnutls_bye(session, GNUTLS_SHUT_WR));
179
180            close(sd);
181            gnutls_deinit(session);
182
183    }
184    close(listen_sd);
185
186    gnutls_certificate_free_credentials(x509_cred);
187    gnutls_priority_deinit(priority_cache);
188
189    gnutls_global_deinit();
190
191    return 0;
192
193 }
```

6.2.2. Echo server with SRP authentication

This is a server which supports SRP authentication. It is also possible to combine this functionality with a certificate server. Here it is separate for simplicity.

```
1   /* This example code is placed in the public domain. */
2
3   #ifdef HAVE_CONFIG_H
4   #include <config.h>
5   #endif
6
7   #include <stdio.h>
8   #include <stdlib.h>
9   #include <errno.h>
10  #include <sys/types.h>
11  #include <sys/socket.h>
12  #include <arpa/inet.h>
13  #include <netinet/in.h>
14  #include <string.h>
15  #include <unistd.h>
16  #include <gnutls/gnutls.h>
17
18  #define SRP_PASSWD "tpasswd"
19  #define SRP_PASSWD_CONF "tpasswd.conf"
20
21  #define KEYFILE "key.pem"
22  #define CERTFILE "cert.pem"
23  #define CAFILE "/etc/ssl/certs/ca-certificates.crt"
24
25  /* This is a sample TLS-SRP echo server.
26   */
27
28  #define SOCKET_ERR(err,s) if(err==-1) {perror(s);return(1);}
29  #define MAX_BUF 1024
30  #define PORT 5556                   /* listen to 5556 port */
31
32  int main(void)
33  {
34          int err, listen_sd;
35          int sd, ret;
36          struct sockaddr_in sa_serv;
37          struct sockaddr_in sa_cli;
38          socklen_t client_len;
39          char topbuf[512];
40          gnutls_session_t session;
41          gnutls_srp_server_credentials_t srp_cred;
42          gnutls_certificate_credentials_t cert_cred;
43          char buffer[MAX_BUF + 1];
44          int optval = 1;
45          char name[256];
46
47          strcpy(name, "Echo Server");
48
49          if (gnutls_check_version("3.1.4") == NULL) {
50                  fprintf(stderr, "GnuTLS 3.1.4 or later is required for this example\n");
51                  exit(1);
52          }
```

```
53
54      /* for backwards compatibility with gnutls < 3.3.0 */
55      gnutls_global_init();
56
57      /* SRP_PASSWD a password file (created with the included srptool utility)
58       */
59      gnutls_srp_allocate_server_credentials(&srp_cred);
60      gnutls_srp_set_server_credentials_file(srp_cred, SRP_PASSWD,
61                                      SRP_PASSWD_CONF);
62
63      gnutls_certificate_allocate_credentials(&cert_cred);
64      gnutls_certificate_set_x509_trust_file(cert_cred, CAFILE,
65                                      GNUTLS_X509_FMT_PEM);
66      gnutls_certificate_set_x509_key_file(cert_cred, CERTFILE, KEYFILE,
67                                      GNUTLS_X509_FMT_PEM);
68
69      /* TCP socket operations
70       */
71      listen_sd = socket(AF_INET, SOCK_STREAM, 0);
72      SOCKET_ERR(listen_sd, "socket");
73
74      memset(&sa_serv, '\0', sizeof(sa_serv));
75      sa_serv.sin_family = AF_INET;
76      sa_serv.sin_addr.s_addr = INADDR_ANY;
77      sa_serv.sin_port = htons(PORT); /* Server Port number */
78
79      setsockopt(listen_sd, SOL_SOCKET, SO_REUSEADDR, (void *) &optval,
80                 sizeof(int));
81
82      err =
83          bind(listen_sd, (struct sockaddr *) &sa_serv, sizeof(sa_serv));
84      SOCKET_ERR(err, "bind");
85      err = listen(listen_sd, 1024);
86      SOCKET_ERR(err, "listen");
87
88      printf("%s ready. Listening to port '%d'.\n\n", name, PORT);
89
90      client_len = sizeof(sa_cli);
91      for (;;) {
92              gnutls_init(&session, GNUTLS_SERVER);
93              gnutls_priority_set_direct(session,
94                                      "NORMAL"
95                                      ":-KX-ALL:+SRP:+SRP-DSS:+SRP-RSA",
96                                      NULL);
97              gnutls_credentials_set(session, GNUTLS_CRD_SRP, srp_cred);
98              /* for the certificate authenticated ciphersuites.
99               */
100             gnutls_credentials_set(session, GNUTLS_CRD_CERTIFICATE,
101                                     cert_cred);
102
103             /* We don't request any certificate from the client.
104              * If we did we would need to verify it. One way of
105              * doing that is shown in the "Verifying a certificate"
106              * example.
107              */
108             gnutls_certificate_server_set_request(session,
109                                             GNUTLS_CERT_IGNORE);
110
```

```
111         sd = accept(listen_sd, (struct sockaddr *) &sa_cli,
112                     &client_len);
113
114         printf("- connection from %s, port %d\n",
115                 inet_ntop(AF_INET, &sa_cli.sin_addr, topbuf,
116                         sizeof(topbuf)), ntohs(sa_cli.sin_port));
117
118         gnutls_transport_set_int(session, sd);
119
120         do {
121                 ret = gnutls_handshake(session);
122         }
123         while (ret < 0 && gnutls_error_is_fatal(ret) == 0);
124
125         if (ret < 0) {
126                 close(sd);
127                 gnutls_deinit(session);
128                 fprintf(stderr,
129                         "*** Handshake has failed (%s)\n\n",
130                         gnutls_strerror(ret));
131                 continue;
132         }
133         printf("- Handshake was completed\n");
134         printf("- User %s was connected\n",
135                 gnutls_srp_server_get_username(session));
136
137         /* print_info(session); */
138
139         for (;;) {
140                 ret = gnutls_record_recv(session, buffer, MAX_BUF);
141
142                 if (ret == 0) {
143                         printf
144                             ("\n- Peer has closed the GnuTLS connection\n");
145                         break;
146                 } else if (ret < 0
147                         && gnutls_error_is_fatal(ret) == 0) {
148                         fprintf(stderr, "*** Warning: %s\n",
149                                 gnutls_strerror(ret));
150                 } else if (ret < 0) {
151                         fprintf(stderr, "\n*** Received corrupted "
152                                 "data(%d). Closing the connection.\n\n",
153                                 ret);
154                         break;
155                 } else if (ret > 0) {
156                         /* echo data back to the client
157                          */
158                         gnutls_record_send(session, buffer, ret);
159                 }
160         }
161         printf("\n");
162         /* do not wait for the peer to close the connection. */
163         gnutls_bye(session, GNUTLS_SHUT_WR);
164
165         close(sd);
166         gnutls_deinit(session);
167
168     }
```

```
169         close(listen_sd);
170
171         gnutls_srp_free_server_credentials(srp_cred);
172         gnutls_certificate_free_credentials(cert_cred);
173
174         gnutls_global_deinit();
175
176         return 0;
177
178 }
```

6.2.3. Echo server with anonymous authentication

This example server supports anonymous authentication, and could be used to serve the example client for anonymous authentication.

```
1  /* This example code is placed in the public domain. */
2
3  #ifdef HAVE_CONFIG_H
4  #include <config.h>
5  #endif
6
7  #include <stdio.h>
8  #include <stdlib.h>
9  #include <errno.h>
10 #include <sys/types.h>
11 #include <sys/socket.h>
12 #include <arpa/inet.h>
13 #include <netinet/in.h>
14 #include <string.h>
15 #include <unistd.h>
16 #include <gnutls/gnutls.h>
17
18 /* This is a sample TLS 1.0 echo server, for anonymous authentication only.
19  */
20
21
22 #define SOCKET_ERR(err,s) if(err==-1) {perror(s);return(1);}
23 #define MAX_BUF 1024
24 #define PORT 5556                 /* listen to 5556 port */
25
26 int main(void)
27 {
28         int err, listen_sd;
29         int sd, ret;
30         struct sockaddr_in sa_serv;
31         struct sockaddr_in sa_cli;
32         socklen_t client_len;
33         char topbuf[512];
34         gnutls_session_t session;
35         gnutls_anon_server_credentials_t anoncred;
36         char buffer[MAX_BUF + 1];
37         int optval = 1;
38
39         if (gnutls_check_version("3.1.4") == NULL) {
```

```
40          fprintf(stderr, "GnuTLS 3.1.4 or later is required for this example\n");
41          exit(1);
42      }
43
44      /* for backwards compatibility with gnutls < 3.3.0 */
45      gnutls_global_init();
46
47      gnutls_anon_allocate_server_credentials(&anoncred);
48
49      gnutls_anon_set_server_known_dh_params(anoncred, GNUTLS_SEC_PARAM_MEDIUM);
50
51      /* Socket operations
52       */
53      listen_sd = socket(AF_INET, SOCK_STREAM, 0);
54      SOCKET_ERR(listen_sd, "socket");
55
56      memset(&sa_serv, '\0', sizeof(sa_serv));
57      sa_serv.sin_family = AF_INET;
58      sa_serv.sin_addr.s_addr = INADDR_ANY;
59      sa_serv.sin_port = htons(PORT); /* Server Port number */
60
61      setsockopt(listen_sd, SOL_SOCKET, SO_REUSEADDR, (void *) &optval,
62                  sizeof(int));
63
64      err =
65          bind(listen_sd, (struct sockaddr *) &sa_serv, sizeof(sa_serv));
66      SOCKET_ERR(err, "bind");
67      err = listen(listen_sd, 1024);
68      SOCKET_ERR(err, "listen");
69
70      printf("Server ready. Listening to port '%d'.\n\n", PORT);
71
72      client_len = sizeof(sa_cli);
73      for (;;) {
74              gnutls_init(&session, GNUTLS_SERVER);
75              gnutls_priority_set_direct(session,
76                                      "NORMAL:+ANON-ECDH:+ANON-DH",
77                                      NULL);
78              gnutls_credentials_set(session, GNUTLS_CRD_ANON, anoncred);
79
80              sd = accept(listen_sd, (struct sockaddr *) &sa_cli,
81                      &client_len);
82
83              printf("- connection from %s, port %d\n",
84                  inet_ntop(AF_INET, &sa_cli.sin_addr, topbuf,
85                          sizeof(topbuf)), ntohs(sa_cli.sin_port));
86
87              gnutls_transport_set_int(session, sd);
88
89              do {
90                      ret = gnutls_handshake(session);
91              }
92              while (ret < 0 && gnutls_error_is_fatal(ret) == 0);
93
94              if (ret < 0) {
95                      close(sd);
96                      gnutls_deinit(session);
97                      fprintf(stderr,
```

237

```
 98                              "*** Handshake has failed (%s)\n\n",
 99                              gnutls_strerror(ret));
100                      continue;
101              }
102              printf("- Handshake was completed\n");
103
104              /* see the Getting peer's information example */
105              /* print_info(session); */
106
107              for (;;) {
108                      ret = gnutls_record_recv(session, buffer, MAX_BUF);
109
110                      if (ret == 0) {
111                              printf
112                                  ("\n- Peer has closed the GnuTLS connection\n");
113                              break;
114                      } else if (ret < 0
115                              && gnutls_error_is_fatal(ret) == 0) {
116                              fprintf(stderr, "*** Warning: %s\n",
117                                      gnutls_strerror(ret));
118                      } else if (ret < 0) {
119                              fprintf(stderr, "\n*** Received corrupted "
120                                      "data(%d). Closing the connection.\n\n",
121                                      ret);
122                              break;
123                      } else if (ret > 0) {
124                              /* echo data back to the client
125                               */
126                              gnutls_record_send(session, buffer, ret);
127                      }
128              }
129              printf("\n");
130              /* do not wait for the peer to close the connection.
131               */
132              gnutls_bye(session, GNUTLS_SHUT_WR);
133
134              close(sd);
135              gnutls_deinit(session);
136
137      }
138      close(listen_sd);
139
140      gnutls_anon_free_server_credentials(anoncred);
141
142      gnutls_global_deinit();
143
144      return 0;
145
146 }
```

6.2.4. DTLS echo server with X.509 authentication

This example is a very simple echo server using Datagram TLS and X.509 authentication.

238

```
 1  /* This example code is placed in the public domain. */
 2
 3  #ifdef HAVE_CONFIG_H
 4  #include <config.h>
 5  #endif
 6
 7  #include <stdio.h>
 8  #include <stdlib.h>
 9  #include <errno.h>
10  #include <sys/types.h>
11  #include <sys/socket.h>
12  #include <arpa/inet.h>
13  #include <netinet/in.h>
14  #include <sys/select.h>
15  #include <netdb.h>
16  #include <string.h>
17  #include <unistd.h>
18  #include <gnutls/gnutls.h>
19  #include <gnutls/dtls.h>
20
21  #define KEYFILE "key.pem"
22  #define CERTFILE "cert.pem"
23  #define CAFILE "/etc/ssl/certs/ca-certificates.crt"
24  #define CRLFILE "crl.pem"
25
26  /* This is a sample DTLS echo server, using X.509 authentication.
27   * Note that error checking is minimal to simplify the example.
28   */
29
30  #define MAX_BUFFER 1024
31  #define PORT 5557
32
33  typedef struct {
34          gnutls_session_t session;
35          int fd;
36          struct sockaddr *cli_addr;
37          socklen_t cli_addr_size;
38  } priv_data_st;
39
40  static int pull_timeout_func(gnutls_transport_ptr_t ptr, unsigned int ms);
41  static ssize_t push_func(gnutls_transport_ptr_t p, const void *data,
42                          size_t size);
43  static ssize_t pull_func(gnutls_transport_ptr_t p, void *data,
44                          size_t size);
45  static const char *human_addr(const struct sockaddr *sa, socklen_t salen,
46                              char *buf, size_t buflen);
47  static int wait_for_connection(int fd);
48
49  /* Use global credentials and parameters to simplify
50   * the example. */
51  static gnutls_certificate_credentials_t x509_cred;
52  static gnutls_priority_t priority_cache;
53
54  int main(void)
55  {
56          int listen_sd;
57          int sock, ret;
```

```
58         struct sockaddr_in sa_serv;
59         struct sockaddr_in cli_addr;
60         socklen_t cli_addr_size;
61         gnutls_session_t session;
62         char buffer[MAX_BUFFER];
63         priv_data_st priv;
64         gnutls_datum_t cookie_key;
65         gnutls_dtls_prestate_st prestate;
66         int mtu = 1400;
67         unsigned char sequence[8];
68
69         /* this must be called once in the program
70          */
71         gnutls_global_init();
72
73         gnutls_certificate_allocate_credentials(&x509_cred);
74         gnutls_certificate_set_x509_trust_file(x509_cred, CAFILE,
75                                           GNUTLS_X509_FMT_PEM);
76
77         gnutls_certificate_set_x509_crl_file(x509_cred, CRLFILE,
78                                           GNUTLS_X509_FMT_PEM);
79
80         ret =
81             gnutls_certificate_set_x509_key_file(x509_cred, CERTFILE,
82                                                  KEYFILE,
83                                                  GNUTLS_X509_FMT_PEM);
84         if (ret < 0) {
85                 printf("No certificate or key were found\n");
86                 exit(1);
87         }
88
89         gnutls_certificate_set_known_dh_params(x509_cred, GNUTLS_SEC_PARAM_MEDIUM);
90
91         gnutls_priority_init(&priority_cache,
92                         "PERFORMANCE:-VERS-TLS-ALL:+VERS-DTLS1.0:%SERVER_PRECEDENCE",
93                         NULL);
94
95         gnutls_key_generate(&cookie_key, GNUTLS_COOKIE_KEY_SIZE);
96
97         /* Socket operations
98          */
99         listen_sd = socket(AF_INET, SOCK_DGRAM, 0);
100
101         memset(&sa_serv, '\0', sizeof(sa_serv));
102         sa_serv.sin_family = AF_INET;
103         sa_serv.sin_addr.s_addr = INADDR_ANY;
104         sa_serv.sin_port = htons(PORT);
105
106         {                           /* DTLS requires the IP don't fragment (DF) bit to be set */
107 #if defined(IP_DONTFRAG)
108                 int optval = 1;
109                 setsockopt(listen_sd, IPPROTO_IP, IP_DONTFRAG,
110                         (const void *) &optval, sizeof(optval));
111 #elif defined(IP_MTU_DISCOVER)
112                 int optval = IP_PMTUDISC_DO;
113                 setsockopt(listen_sd, IPPROTO_IP, IP_MTU_DISCOVER,
114                         (const void *) &optval, sizeof(optval));
115 #endif
```

```
116          }
117
118          bind(listen_sd, (struct sockaddr *) &sa_serv, sizeof(sa_serv));
119
120          printf("UDP server ready. Listening to port '%d'.\n\n", PORT);
121
122          for (;;) {
123                  printf("Waiting for connection...\n");
124                  sock = wait_for_connection(listen_sd);
125                  if (sock < 0)
126                          continue;
127
128                  cli_addr_size = sizeof(cli_addr);
129                  ret = recvfrom(sock, buffer, sizeof(buffer), MSG_PEEK,
130                                  (struct sockaddr *) &cli_addr,
131                                  &cli_addr_size);
132                  if (ret > 0) {
133                          memset(&prestate, 0, sizeof(prestate));
134                          ret =
135                              gnutls_dtls_cookie_verify(&cookie_key,
136                                                        &cli_addr,
137                                                        sizeof(cli_addr),
138                                                        buffer, ret,
139                                                        &prestate);
140                          if (ret < 0) {  /* cookie not valid */
141                                  priv_data_st s;
142
143                                  memset(&s, 0, sizeof(s));
144                                  s.fd = sock;
145                                  s.cli_addr = (void *) &cli_addr;
146                                  s.cli_addr_size = sizeof(cli_addr);
147
148                                  printf
149                                      ("Sending hello verify request to %s\n",
150                                        human_addr((struct sockaddr *)
151                                                   &cli_addr,
152                                                   sizeof(cli_addr), buffer,
153                                                   sizeof(buffer)));
154
155                                  gnutls_dtls_cookie_send(&cookie_key,
156                                                          &cli_addr,
157                                                          sizeof(cli_addr),
158                                                          &prestate,
159                                                          (gnutls_transport_ptr_t)
160                                                          & s, push_func);
161
162                                  /* discard peeked data */
163                                  recvfrom(sock, buffer, sizeof(buffer), 0,
164                                          (struct sockaddr *) &cli_addr,
165                                          &cli_addr_size);
166                                  usleep(100);
167                                  continue;
168                          }
169                          printf("Accepted connection from %s\n",
170                                  human_addr((struct sockaddr *)
171                                             &cli_addr, sizeof(cli_addr),
172                                             buffer, sizeof(buffer)));
173                  } else
```

241

```
174              continue;
175
176      gnutls_init(&session, GNUTLS_SERVER | GNUTLS_DATAGRAM);
177      gnutls_priority_set(session, priority_cache);
178      gnutls_credentials_set(session, GNUTLS_CRD_CERTIFICATE,
179                             x509_cred);
180
181      gnutls_dtls_prestate_set(session, &prestate);
182      gnutls_dtls_set_mtu(session, mtu);
183
184      priv.session = session;
185      priv.fd = sock;
186      priv.cli_addr = (struct sockaddr *) &cli_addr;
187      priv.cli_addr_size = sizeof(cli_addr);
188
189      gnutls_transport_set_ptr(session, &priv);
190      gnutls_transport_set_push_function(session, push_func);
191      gnutls_transport_set_pull_function(session, pull_func);
192      gnutls_transport_set_pull_timeout_function(session,
193                                        pull_timeout_func);
194
195      do {
196              ret = gnutls_handshake(session);
197      }
198      while (ret == GNUTLS_E_INTERRUPTED
199             || ret == GNUTLS_E_AGAIN);
200      /* Note that DTLS may also receive GNUTLS_E_LARGE_PACKET.
201       * In that case the MTU should be adjusted.
202       */
203
204      if (ret < 0) {
205              fprintf(stderr, "Error in handshake(): %s\n",
206                      gnutls_strerror(ret));
207              gnutls_deinit(session);
208              continue;
209      }
210
211      printf("- Handshake was completed\n");
212
213      for (;;) {
214              do {
215                      ret =
216                      gnutls_record_recv_seq(session, buffer,
217                                        MAX_BUFFER,
218                                        sequence);
219              }
220              while (ret == GNUTLS_E_AGAIN
221                     || ret == GNUTLS_E_INTERRUPTED);
222
223              if (ret < 0 && gnutls_error_is_fatal(ret) == 0) {
224                      fprintf(stderr, "*** Warning: %s\n",
225                              gnutls_strerror(ret));
226                      continue;
227              } else if (ret < 0) {
228                      fprintf(stderr, "Error in recv(): %s\n",
229                              gnutls_strerror(ret));
230                      break;
231              }
```

242

```
232
233                           if (ret == 0) {
234                                   printf("EOF\n\n");
235                                   break;
236                           }
237
238                           buffer[ret] = 0;
239                           printf
240                               ("received[%.2x%.2x%.2x%.2x%.2x%.2x%.2x%.2x]: %s\n",
241                                   sequence[0], sequence[1], sequence[2],
242                                   sequence[3], sequence[4], sequence[5],
243                                   sequence[6], sequence[7], buffer);
244
245                           /* reply back */
246                           ret = gnutls_record_send(session, buffer, ret);
247                           if (ret < 0) {
248                                   fprintf(stderr, "Error in send(): %s\n",
249                                           gnutls_strerror(ret));
250                                   break;
251                           }
252                   }
253
254               gnutls_bye(session, GNUTLS_SHUT_WR);
255               gnutls_deinit(session);
256
257           }
258       close(listen_sd);
259
260       gnutls_certificate_free_credentials(x509_cred);
261       gnutls_priority_deinit(priority_cache);
262
263       gnutls_global_deinit();
264
265       return 0;
266
267   }
268
269   static int wait_for_connection(int fd)
270   {
271       fd_set rd, wr;
272       int n;
273
274       FD_ZERO(&rd);
275       FD_ZERO(&wr);
276
277       FD_SET(fd, &rd);
278
279       /* waiting part */
280       n = select(fd + 1, &rd, &wr, NULL, NULL);
281       if (n == -1 && errno == EINTR)
282               return -1;
283       if (n < 0) {
284               perror("select()");
285               exit(1);
286       }
287
288       return fd;
289   }
```

243

```
290
291  /* Wait for data to be received within a timeout period in milliseconds
292   */
293  static int pull_timeout_func(gnutls_transport_ptr_t ptr, unsigned int ms)
294  {
295          fd_set rfds;
296          struct timeval tv;
297          priv_data_st *priv = ptr;
298          struct sockaddr_in cli_addr;
299          socklen_t cli_addr_size;
300          int ret;
301          char c;
302
303          FD_ZERO(&rfds);
304          FD_SET(priv->fd, &rfds);
305
306          tv.tv_sec = 0;
307          tv.tv_usec = ms * 1000;
308
309          while (tv.tv_usec >= 1000000) {
310                  tv.tv_usec -= 1000000;
311                  tv.tv_sec++;
312          }
313
314          ret = select(priv->fd + 1, &rfds, NULL, NULL, &tv);
315
316          if (ret <= 0)
317                  return ret;
318
319          /* only report ok if the next message is from the peer we expect
320           * from
321           */
322          cli_addr_size = sizeof(cli_addr);
323          ret =
324              recvfrom(priv->fd, &c, 1, MSG_PEEK,
325                       (struct sockaddr *) &cli_addr, &cli_addr_size);
326          if (ret > 0) {
327                  if (cli_addr_size == priv->cli_addr_size
328                      && memcmp(&cli_addr, priv->cli_addr,
329                               sizeof(cli_addr)) == 0)
330                          return 1;
331          }
332
333          return 0;
334  }
335
336  static ssize_t
337  push_func(gnutls_transport_ptr_t p, const void *data, size_t size)
338  {
339          priv_data_st *priv = p;
340
341          return sendto(priv->fd, data, size, 0, priv->cli_addr,
342                        priv->cli_addr_size);
343  }
344
345  static ssize_t pull_func(gnutls_transport_ptr_t p, void *data, size_t size)
346  {
347          priv_data_st *priv = p;
```

```
348            struct sockaddr_in cli_addr;
349            socklen_t cli_addr_size;
350            char buffer[64];
351            int ret;
352
353            cli_addr_size = sizeof(cli_addr);
354            ret =
355                recvfrom(priv->fd, data, size, 0,
356                        (struct sockaddr *) &cli_addr, &cli_addr_size);
357            if (ret == -1)
358                    return ret;
359
360            if (cli_addr_size == priv->cli_addr_size
361                && memcmp(&cli_addr, priv->cli_addr, sizeof(cli_addr)) == 0)
362                    return ret;
363
364            printf("Denied connection from %s\n",
365                    human_addr((struct sockaddr *)
366                            &cli_addr, sizeof(cli_addr), buffer,
367                            sizeof(buffer)));
368
369            gnutls_transport_set_errno(priv->session, EAGAIN);
370            return -1;
371 }
372
373 static const char *human_addr(const struct sockaddr *sa, socklen_t salen,
374                                char *buf, size_t buflen)
375 {
376            const char *save_buf = buf;
377            size_t l;
378
379            if (!buf || !buflen)
380                    return NULL;
381
382            *buf = '\0';
383
384            switch (sa->sa_family) {
385 #if HAVE_IPV6
386            case AF_INET6:
387                    snprintf(buf, buflen, "IPv6 ");
388                    break;
389 #endif
390
391            case AF_INET:
392                    snprintf(buf, buflen, "IPv4 ");
393                    break;
394            }
395
396            l = strlen(buf);
397            buf += l;
398            buflen -= l;
399
400            if (getnameinfo(sa, salen, buf, buflen, NULL, 0, NI_NUMERICHOST) !=
401                0)
402                    return NULL;
403
404            l = strlen(buf);
405            buf += l;
```

```
406        buflen -= 1;
407
408        strncat(buf, " port ", buflen);
409
410        l = strlen(buf);
411        buf += l;
412        buflen -= l;
413
414        if (getnameinfo(sa, salen, NULL, 0, buf, buflen, NI_NUMERICSERV) !=
415            0)
416                return NULL;
417
418        return save_buf;
419 }
420
```

6.3. OCSP example

Generate OCSP request

A small tool to generate OCSP requests.

```
1  /* This example code is placed in the public domain. */
2
3  #ifdef HAVE_CONFIG_H
4  #include <config.h>
5  #endif
6
7  #include <stdio.h>
8  #include <stdlib.h>
9  #include <string.h>
10 #include <gnutls/gnutls.h>
11 #include <gnutls/crypto.h>
12 #include <gnutls/ocsp.h>
13 #ifndef NO_LIBCURL
14 #include <curl/curl.h>
15 #endif
16 #include "read-file.h"
17
18 size_t get_data(void *buffer, size_t size, size_t nmemb, void *userp);
19 static gnutls_x509_crt_t load_cert(const char *cert_file);
20 static void _response_info(const gnutls_datum_t * data);
21 static void
22 _generate_request(gnutls_datum_t * rdata, gnutls_x509_crt_t cert,
23                   gnutls_x509_crt_t issuer, gnutls_datum_t *nonce);
24 static int
25 _verify_response(gnutls_datum_t * data, gnutls_x509_crt_t cert,
26                  gnutls_x509_crt_t signer, gnutls_datum_t *nonce);
27
28 /* This program queries an OCSP server.
29    It expects three files. argv[1] containing the certificate to
30    be checked, argv[2] holding the issuer for this certificate,
31    and argv[3] holding a trusted certificate to verify OCSP's response.
```

```
32      argv[4] is optional and should hold the server host name.
33
34      For simplicity the libcurl library is used.
35   */
36
37   int main(int argc, char *argv[])
38   {
39           gnutls_datum_t ud, tmp;
40           int ret;
41           gnutls_datum_t req;
42           gnutls_x509_crt_t cert, issuer, signer;
43   #ifndef NO_LIBCURL
44           CURL *handle;
45           struct curl_slist *headers = NULL;
46   #endif
47           int v, seq;
48           const char *cert_file = argv[1];
49           const char *issuer_file = argv[2];
50           const char *signer_file = argv[3];
51           char *hostname = NULL;
52           unsigned char noncebuf[23];
53           gnutls_datum_t nonce = { noncebuf, sizeof(noncebuf) };
54
55           gnutls_global_init();
56
57           if (argc > 4)
58                   hostname = argv[4];
59
60           ret = gnutls_rnd(GNUTLS_RND_NONCE, nonce.data, nonce.size);
61           if (ret < 0)
62                   exit(1);
63
64           cert = load_cert(cert_file);
65           issuer = load_cert(issuer_file);
66           signer = load_cert(signer_file);
67
68           if (hostname == NULL) {
69
70                   for (seq = 0;; seq++) {
71                           ret =
72                               gnutls_x509_crt_get_authority_info_access(cert,
73                                                                         seq,
74                                                                         GNUTLS_IA_OCSP_URI,
75                                                                         &tmp,
76                                                                         NULL);
77                           if (ret == GNUTLS_E_UNKNOWN_ALGORITHM)
78                                   continue;
79                           if (ret == GNUTLS_E_REQUESTED_DATA_NOT_AVAILABLE) {
80                                   fprintf(stderr,
81                                           "No URI was found in the certificate.\n");
82                                   exit(1);
83                           }
84                           if (ret < 0) {
85                                   fprintf(stderr, "error: %s\n",
86                                           gnutls_strerror(ret));
87                                   exit(1);
88                           }
89
```

```
90                        printf("CA issuers URI: %.*s\n", tmp.size,
91                               tmp.data);
92
93                        hostname = malloc(tmp.size + 1);
94                        memcpy(hostname, tmp.data, tmp.size);
95                        hostname[tmp.size] = 0;
96
97                        gnutls_free(tmp.data);
98                        break;
99                    }
100
101            }
102
103            /* Note that the OCSP servers hostname might be available
104             * using gnutls_x509_crt_get_authority_info_access() in the issuer's
105             * certificate */
106
107            memset(&ud, 0, sizeof(ud));
108            fprintf(stderr, "Connecting to %s\n", hostname);
109
110            _generate_request(&req, cert, issuer, &nonce);
111
112    #ifndef NO_LIBCURL
113            curl_global_init(CURL_GLOBAL_ALL);
114
115            handle = curl_easy_init();
116            if (handle == NULL)
117                    exit(1);
118
119            headers =
120                curl_slist_append(headers,
121                                  "Content-Type: application/ocsp-request");
122
123            curl_easy_setopt(handle, CURLOPT_HTTPHEADER, headers);
124            curl_easy_setopt(handle, CURLOPT_POSTFIELDS, (void *) req.data);
125            curl_easy_setopt(handle, CURLOPT_POSTFIELDSIZE, req.size);
126            curl_easy_setopt(handle, CURLOPT_URL, hostname);
127            curl_easy_setopt(handle, CURLOPT_WRITEFUNCTION, get_data);
128            curl_easy_setopt(handle, CURLOPT_WRITEDATA, &ud);
129
130            ret = curl_easy_perform(handle);
131            if (ret != 0) {
132                    fprintf(stderr, "curl[%d] error %d\n", __LINE__, ret);
133                    exit(1);
134            }
135
136            curl_easy_cleanup(handle);
137    #endif
138
139            _response_info(&ud);
140
141            v = _verify_response(&ud, cert, signer, &nonce);
142
143            gnutls_x509_crt_deinit(cert);
144            gnutls_x509_crt_deinit(issuer);
145            gnutls_x509_crt_deinit(signer);
146            gnutls_global_deinit();
147
```

```
148        return v;
149  }
150
151  static void _response_info(const gnutls_datum_t * data)
152  {
153        gnutls_ocsp_resp_t resp;
154        int ret;
155        gnutls_datum buf;
156
157        ret = gnutls_ocsp_resp_init(&resp);
158        if (ret < 0)
159                exit(1);
160
161        ret = gnutls_ocsp_resp_import(resp, data);
162        if (ret < 0)
163                exit(1);
164
165        ret = gnutls_ocsp_resp_print(resp, GNUTLS_OCSP_PRINT_FULL, &buf);
166        if (ret != 0)
167                exit(1);
168
169        printf("%.*s", buf.size, buf.data);
170        gnutls_free(buf.data);
171
172        gnutls_ocsp_resp_deinit(resp);
173  }
174
175  static gnutls_x509_crt_t load_cert(const char *cert_file)
176  {
177        gnutls_x509_crt_t crt;
178        int ret;
179        gnutls_datum_t data;
180        size_t size;
181
182        ret = gnutls_x509_crt_init(&crt);
183        if (ret < 0)
184                exit(1);
185
186        data.data = (void *) read_binary_file(cert_file, &size);
187        data.size = size;
188
189        if (!data.data) {
190                fprintf(stderr, "Cannot open file: %s\n", cert_file);
191                exit(1);
192        }
193
194        ret = gnutls_x509_crt_import(crt, &data, GNUTLS_X509_FMT_PEM);
195        free(data.data);
196        if (ret < 0) {
197                fprintf(stderr, "Cannot import certificate in %s: %s\n",
198                        cert_file, gnutls_strerror(ret));
199                exit(1);
200        }
201
202        return crt;
203  }
204
205  static void
```

```
206  _generate_request(gnutls_datum_t * rdata, gnutls_x509_crt_t cert,
207                   gnutls_x509_crt_t issuer, gnutls_datum_t *nonce)
208  {
209          gnutls_ocsp_req_t req;
210          int ret;
211
212          ret = gnutls_ocsp_req_init(&req);
213          if (ret < 0)
214                  exit(1);
215
216          ret = gnutls_ocsp_req_add_cert(req, GNUTLS_DIG_SHA1, issuer, cert);
217          if (ret < 0)
218                  exit(1);
219
220
221          ret = gnutls_ocsp_req_set_nonce(req, 0, nonce);
222          if (ret < 0)
223                  exit(1);
224
225          ret = gnutls_ocsp_req_export(req, rdata);
226          if (ret != 0)
227                  exit(1);
228
229          gnutls_ocsp_req_deinit(req);
230
231          return;
232  }
233
234  static int
235  _verify_response(gnutls_datum_t * data, gnutls_x509_crt_t cert,
236                   gnutls_x509_crt_t signer, gnutls_datum_t *nonce)
237  {
238          gnutls_ocsp_resp_t resp;
239          int ret;
240          unsigned verify;
241          gnutls_datum_t rnonce;
242
243          ret = gnutls_ocsp_resp_init(&resp);
244          if (ret < 0)
245                  exit(1);
246
247          ret = gnutls_ocsp_resp_import(resp, data);
248          if (ret < 0)
249                  exit(1);
250
251          ret = gnutls_ocsp_resp_check_crt(resp, 0, cert);
252          if (ret < 0)
253                  exit(1);
254
255          ret = gnutls_ocsp_resp_get_nonce(resp, NULL, &rnonce);
256          if (ret < 0)
257                  exit(1);
258
259          if (rnonce.size != nonce->size || memcmp(nonce->data, rnonce.data,
260              nonce->size) != 0) {
261                  exit(1);
262          }
263
```

```
264        ret = gnutls_ocsp_resp_verify_direct(resp, signer, &verify, 0);
265        if (ret < 0)
266                exit(1);
267
268        printf("Verifying OCSP Response: ");
269        if (verify == 0)
270                printf("Verification success!\n");
271        else
272                printf("Verification error!\n");
273
274        if (verify & GNUTLS_OCSP_VERIFY_SIGNER_NOT_FOUND)
275                printf("Signer cert not found\n");
276
277        if (verify & GNUTLS_OCSP_VERIFY_SIGNER_KEYUSAGE_ERROR)
278                printf("Signer cert keyusage error\n");
279
280        if (verify & GNUTLS_OCSP_VERIFY_UNTRUSTED_SIGNER)
281                printf("Signer cert is not trusted\n");
282
283        if (verify & GNUTLS_OCSP_VERIFY_INSECURE_ALGORITHM)
284                printf("Insecure algorithm\n");
285
286        if (verify & GNUTLS_OCSP_VERIFY_SIGNATURE_FAILURE)
287                printf("Signature failure\n");
288
289        if (verify & GNUTLS_OCSP_VERIFY_CERT_NOT_ACTIVATED)
290                printf("Signer cert not yet activated\n");
291
292        if (verify & GNUTLS_OCSP_VERIFY_CERT_EXPIRED)
293                printf("Signer cert expired\n");
294
295        gnutls_free(rnonce.data);
296        gnutls_ocsp_resp_deinit(resp);
297
298        return verify;
299 }
300
301 size_t get_data(void *buffer, size_t size, size_t nmemb, void *userp)
302 {
303        gnutls_datum_t *ud = userp;
304
305        size *= nmemb;
306
307        ud->data = realloc(ud->data, size + ud->size);
308        if (ud->data == NULL) {
309                fprintf(stderr, "Not enough memory for the request\n");
310                exit(1);
311        }
312
313        memcpy(&ud->data[ud->size], buffer, size);
314        ud->size += size;
315
316        return size;
317 }
```

6.4. Miscellaneous examples

6.4.1. Checking for an alert

This is a function that checks if an alert has been received in the current session.

```
/* This example code is placed in the public domain. */

#ifdef HAVE_CONFIG_H
#include <config.h>
#endif

#include <stdio.h>
#include <stdlib.h>
#include <gnutls/gnutls.h>

#include "examples.h"

/* This function will check whether the given return code from
 * a gnutls function (recv/send), is an alert, and will print
 * that alert.
 */
void check_alert(gnutls_session_t session, int ret)
{
        int last_alert;

        if (ret == GNUTLS_E_WARNING_ALERT_RECEIVED
            || ret == GNUTLS_E_FATAL_ALERT_RECEIVED) {
                last_alert = gnutls_alert_get(session);

                /* The check for renegotiation is only useful if we are
                 * a server, and we had requested a rehandshake.
                 */
                if (last_alert == GNUTLS_A_NO_RENEGOTIATION &&
                    ret == GNUTLS_E_WARNING_ALERT_RECEIVED)
                        printf("* Received NO_RENEGOTIATION alert. "
                                "Client Does not support renegotiation.\n");
                else
                        printf("* Received alert '%d': %s.\n", last_alert,
                                gnutls_alert_get_name(last_alert));
        }
}
```

6.4.2. X.509 certificate parsing example

To demonstrate the X.509 parsing capabilities an example program is listed below. That program reads the peer's certificate, and prints information about it.

```
/* This example code is placed in the public domain. */

#ifdef HAVE_CONFIG_H
#include <config.h>
#endif
```

```
 6
 7   #include <stdio.h>
 8   #include <stdlib.h>
 9   #include <gnutls/gnutls.h>
10   #include <gnutls/x509.h>
11
12   #include "examples.h"
13
14   static const char *bin2hex(const void *bin, size_t bin_size)
15   {
16           static char printable[110];
17           const unsigned char *_bin = bin;
18           char *print;
19           size_t i;
20
21           if (bin_size > 50)
22                   bin_size = 50;
23
24           print = printable;
25           for (i = 0; i < bin_size; i++) {
26                   sprintf(print, "%.2x ", _bin[i]);
27                   print += 2;
28           }
29
30           return printable;
31   }
32
33   /* This function will print information about this session's peer
34    * certificate.
35    */
36   void print_x509_certificate_info(gnutls_session_t session)
37   {
38           char serial[40];
39           char dn[256];
40           size_t size;
41           unsigned int algo, bits;
42           time_t expiration_time, activation_time;
43           const gnutls_datum_t *cert_list;
44           unsigned int cert_list_size = 0;
45           gnutls_x509_crt_t cert;
46           gnutls_datum_t cinfo;
47
48           /* This function only works for X.509 certificates.
49            */
50           if (gnutls_certificate_type_get(session) != GNUTLS_CRT_X509)
51                   return;
52
53           cert_list = gnutls_certificate_get_peers(session, &cert_list_size);
54
55           printf("Peer provided %d certificates.\n", cert_list_size);
56
57           if (cert_list_size > 0) {
58                   int ret;
59
60                   /* we only print information about the first certificate.
61                    */
62                   gnutls_x509_crt_init(&cert);
63
```

```
64        gnutls_x509_crt_import(cert, &cert_list[0],
65                               GNUTLS_X509_FMT_DER);
66
67        printf("Certificate info:\n");
68
69        /* This is the preferred way of printing short information about
70           a certificate. */
71
72        ret =
73            gnutls_x509_crt_print(cert, GNUTLS_CRT_PRINT_ONELINE,
74                                  &cinfo);
75        if (ret == 0) {
76                printf("\t%s\n", cinfo.data);
77                gnutls_free(cinfo.data);
78        }
79
80        /* If you want to extract fields manually for some other reason,
81           below are popular example calls. */
82
83        expiration_time =
84            gnutls_x509_crt_get_expiration_time(cert);
85        activation_time =
86            gnutls_x509_crt_get_activation_time(cert);
87
88        printf("\tCertificate is valid since: %s",
89                ctime(&activation_time));
90        printf("\tCertificate expires: %s",
91                ctime(&expiration_time));
92
93        /* Print the serial number of the certificate.
94         */
95        size = sizeof(serial);
96        gnutls_x509_crt_get_serial(cert, serial, &size);
97
98        printf("\tCertificate serial number: %s\n",
99                bin2hex(serial, size));
100
101        /* Extract some of the public key algorithm's parameters
102         */
103        algo = gnutls_x509_crt_get_pk_algorithm(cert, &bits);
104
105        printf("Certificate public key: %s",
106                gnutls_pk_algorithm_get_name(algo));
107
108        /* Print the version of the X.509
109         * certificate.
110         */
111        printf("\tCertificate version: #%d\n",
112                gnutls_x509_crt_get_version(cert));
113
114        size = sizeof(dn);
115        gnutls_x509_crt_get_dn(cert, dn, &size);
116        printf("\tDN: %s\n", dn);
117
118        size = sizeof(dn);
119        gnutls_x509_crt_get_issuer_dn(cert, dn, &size);
120        printf("\tIssuer's DN: %s\n", dn);
121
```

```
122             gnutls_x509_crt_deinit(cert);
123
124        }
125 }
```

6.4.3. Listing the ciphersuites in a priority string

This is a small program to list the enabled ciphersuites by a priority string.

```
1  /* This example code is placed in the public domain. */
2
3  #include <config.h>
4  #include <stdio.h>
5  #include <stdlib.h>
6  #include <string.h>
7  #include <gnutls/gnutls.h>
8
9  static void print_cipher_suite_list(const char *priorities)
10 {
11         size_t i;
12         int ret;
13         unsigned int idx;
14         const char *name;
15         const char *err;
16         unsigned char id[2];
17         gnutls_protocol_t version;
18         gnutls_priority_t pcache;
19
20         if (priorities != NULL) {
21                 printf("Cipher suites for %s\n", priorities);
22
23                 ret = gnutls_priority_init(&pcache, priorities, &err);
24                 if (ret < 0) {
25                         fprintf(stderr, "Syntax error at: %s\n", err);
26                         exit(1);
27                 }
28
29                 for (i = 0;; i++) {
30                         ret =
31                             gnutls_priority_get_cipher_suite_index(pcache,
32                                                                    i,
33                                                                    &idx);
34                         if (ret == GNUTLS_E_REQUESTED_DATA_NOT_AVAILABLE)
35                                 break;
36                         if (ret == GNUTLS_E_UNKNOWN_CIPHER_SUITE)
37                                 continue;
38
39                         name =
40                             gnutls_cipher_suite_info(idx, id, NULL, NULL,
41                                                      NULL, &version);
42
43                         if (name != NULL)
44                                 printf("%-50s\t0x%02x, 0x%02x\t%s\n",
45                                        name, (unsigned char) id[0],
46                                        (unsigned char) id[1],
```

```
47                                  gnutls_protocol_get_name(version));
48                    }
49
50              return;
51        }
52  }
53
54  int main(int argc, char **argv)
55  {
56        if (argc > 1)
57                print_cipher_suite_list(argv[1]);
58        return 0;
59  }
```

6.4.4. PKCS #12 structure generation example

This small program demonstrates the usage of the PKCS #12 API, by generating such a structure.

```
1   /* This example code is placed in the public domain. */
2
3   #ifdef HAVE_CONFIG_H
4   #include <config.h>
5   #endif
6
7   #include <stdio.h>
8   #include <stdlib.h>
9   #include <gnutls/gnutls.h>
10  #include <gnutls/pkcs12.h>
11
12  #include "examples.h"
13
14  #define OUTFILE "out.p12"
15
16  /* This function will write a pkcs12 structure into a file.
17   * cert: is a DER encoded certificate
18   * pkcs8_key: is a PKCS #8 encrypted key (note that this must be
19   *  encrypted using a PKCS #12 cipher, or some browsers will crash)
20   * password: is the password used to encrypt the PKCS #12 packet.
21   */
22  int
23  write_pkcs12(const gnutls_datum_t * cert,
24               const gnutls_datum_t * pkcs8_key, const char *password)
25  {
26        gnutls_pkcs12_t pkcs12;
27        int ret, bag_index;
28        gnutls_pkcs12_bag_t bag, key_bag;
29        char pkcs12_struct[10 * 1024];
30        size_t pkcs12_struct_size;
31        FILE *fd;
32
33        /* A good idea might be to use gnutls_x509_privkey_get_key_id()
34         * to obtain a unique ID.
35         */
36        gnutls_datum_t key_id = { (void *) "\x00\x00\x07", 3 };
```

256

```
37
38          gnutls_global_init();
39
40          /* Firstly we create two helper bags, which hold the certificate,
41           * and the (encrypted) key.
42           */
43
44          gnutls_pkcs12_bag_init(&bag);
45          gnutls_pkcs12_bag_init(&key_bag);
46
47          ret =
48              gnutls_pkcs12_bag_set_data(bag, GNUTLS_BAG_CERTIFICATE, cert);
49          if (ret < 0) {
50                  fprintf(stderr, "ret: %s\n", gnutls_strerror(ret));
51                  return 1;
52          }
53
54          /* ret now holds the bag's index.
55           */
56          bag_index = ret;
57
58          /* Associate a friendly name with the given certificate. Used
59           * by browsers.
60           */
61          gnutls_pkcs12_bag_set_friendly_name(bag, bag_index, "My name");
62
63          /* Associate the certificate with the key using a unique key
64           * ID.
65           */
66          gnutls_pkcs12_bag_set_key_id(bag, bag_index, &key_id);
67
68          /* use weak encryption for the certificate.
69           */
70          gnutls_pkcs12_bag_encrypt(bag, password,
71                                  GNUTLS_PKCS_USE_PKCS12_RC2_40);
72
73          /* Now the key.
74           */
75
76          ret = gnutls_pkcs12_bag_set_data(key_bag,
77                                        GNUTLS_BAG_PKCS8_ENCRYPTED_KEY,
78                                        pkcs8_key);
79          if (ret < 0) {
80                  fprintf(stderr, "ret: %s\n", gnutls_strerror(ret));
81                  return 1;
82          }
83
84          /* Note that since the PKCS #8 key is already encrypted we don't
85           * bother encrypting that bag.
86           */
87          bag_index = ret;
88
89          gnutls_pkcs12_bag_set_friendly_name(key_bag, bag_index, "My name");
90
91          gnutls_pkcs12_bag_set_key_id(key_bag, bag_index, &key_id);
92
93
94          /* The bags were filled. Now create the PKCS #12 structure.
```

```
 95        */
 96      gnutls_pkcs12_init(&pkcs12);
 97
 98      /* Insert the two bags in the PKCS #12 structure.
 99       */
100
101      gnutls_pkcs12_set_bag(pkcs12, bag);
102      gnutls_pkcs12_set_bag(pkcs12, key_bag);
103
104
105      /* Generate a message authentication code for the PKCS #12
106       * structure.
107       */
108      gnutls_pkcs12_generate_mac(pkcs12, password);
109
110      pkcs12_struct_size = sizeof(pkcs12_struct);
111      ret =
112          gnutls_pkcs12_export(pkcs12, GNUTLS_X509_FMT_DER,
113                              pkcs12_struct, &pkcs12_struct_size);
114      if (ret < 0) {
115              fprintf(stderr, "ret: %s\n", gnutls_strerror(ret));
116              return 1;
117      }
118
119      fd = fopen(OUTFILE, "w");
120      if (fd == NULL) {
121              fprintf(stderr, "cannot open file\n");
122              return 1;
123      }
124      fwrite(pkcs12_struct, 1, pkcs12_struct_size, fd);
125      fclose(fd);
126
127      gnutls_pkcs12_bag_deinit(bag);
128      gnutls_pkcs12_bag_deinit(key_bag);
129      gnutls_pkcs12_deinit(pkcs12);
130
131      return 0;
132  }
```

7

Other included programs

Included with GnuTLS are also a few command line tools that let you use the library for common tasks without writing an application. The applications are discussed in this chapter.

7.1. Invoking gnutls-cli

Simple client program to set up a TLS connection to some other computer. It sets up a TLS connection and forwards data from the standard input to the secured socket and vice versa.

This section was generated by **AutoGen**, using the `agtexi-cmd` template and the option descriptions for the `gnutls-cli` program. This software is released under the GNU General Public License, version 3 or later.

gnutls-cli help/usage ("`--help`")

This is the automatically generated usage text for gnutls-cli.

The text printed is the same whether selected with the **help** option ("`--help`") or the **more-help** option ("`--more-help`"). **more-help** will print the usage text by passing it through a pager program. **more-help** is disabled on platforms without a working `fork(2)` function. The `PAGER` environment variable is used to select the program, defaulting to "`more`". Both will exit with a status code of 0.

```
1  gnutls-cli - GnuTLS client
2  Usage:  gnutls-cli [ -<flag> [<val>] | --<name>[{=| }<val>] ]... [hostname]
3
4     -d, --debug=num            Enable debugging
5                                  - it must be in the range:
6                                    0 to 9999
7     -V, --verbose              More verbose output
8                                  - may appear multiple times
9         --tofu                 Enable trust on first use authentication
10                                 - disabled as '--no-tofu'
11        --strict-tofu          Fail to connect if a known certificate has changed
12                                 - disabled as '--no-strict-tofu'
13        --dane                 Enable DANE certificate verification (DNSSEC)
14                                 - disabled as '--no-dane'
15        --local-dns            Use the local DNS server for DNSSEC resolving
```

```
16                                  - disabled as '--no-local-dns'
17       --ca-verification          Enable CA certificate verification
18                                  - disabled as '--no-ca-verification'
19                                  - enabled by default
20       --ocsp                     Enable OCSP certificate verification
21                                  - disabled as '--no-ocsp'
22   -r, --resume                   Establish a session and resume
23   -e, --rehandshake              Establish a session and rehandshake
24       --sni-hostname=str         Server's hostname for server name indication extension
25   -s, --starttls                 Connect, establish a plain session and start TLS
26       --app-proto=str            an alias for the 'starttls-proto' option
27       --starttls-proto=str       The application protocol to be used to obtain the server's certificate
28 (https, ftp, smtp, imap, ldap, xmpp, lmtp, pop3, nntp, sieve, postgres)
29                                  - prohibits the option 'starttls'
30   -u, --udp                      Use DTLS (datagram TLS) over UDP
31       --mtu=num                  Set MTU for datagram TLS
32                                  - it must be in the range:
33                                    0 to 17000
34       --crlf                     Send CR LF instead of LF
35       --fastopen                 Enable TCP Fast Open
36       --x509fmtder               Use DER format for certificates to read from
37       --print-cert               Print peer's certificate in PEM format
38       --save-cert=str            Save the peer's certificate chain in the specified file in PEM format
39       --save-ocsp=str            Save the peer's OCSP status response in the provided file
40       --save-server-trace=str Save the server-side TLS message trace in the provided file
41       --save-client-trace=str Save the client-side TLS message trace in the provided file
42       --dh-bits=num              The minimum number of bits allowed for DH
43       --priority=str             Priorities string
44       --x509cafile=str           Certificate file or PKCS #11 URL to use
45       --x509crlfile=file         CRL file to use
46                                  - file must pre-exist
47       --x509keyfile=str          X.509 key file or PKCS #11 URL to use
48       --x509certfile=str         X.509 Certificate file or PKCS #11 URL to use
49                                  - requires the option 'x509keyfile'
50       --srpusername=str          SRP username to use
51       --srppasswd=str            SRP password to use
52       --pskusername=str          PSK username to use
53       --pskkey=str               PSK key (in hex) to use
54   -p, --port=str                 The port or service to connect to
55       --insecure                 Don't abort program if server certificate can't be validated
56       --verify-allow-broken      Allow broken algorithms, such as MD5 for certificate verification
57       --ranges                   Use length-hiding padding to prevent traffic analysis
58       --benchmark-ciphers        Benchmark individual ciphers
59       --benchmark-tls-kx         Benchmark TLS key exchange methods
60       --benchmark-tls-ciphers  Benchmark TLS ciphers
61   -l, --list                     Print a list of the supported algorithms and modes
62                                  - prohibits the option 'port'
63       --priority-list            Print a list of the supported priority strings
64       --noticket                 Don't allow session tickets
65       --srtp-profiles=str        Offer SRTP profiles
66       --alpn=str                 Application layer protocol
67                                  - may appear multiple times
68   -b, --heartbeat                Activate heartbeat support
69       --recordsize=num           The maximum record size to advertize
70                                  - it must be in the range:
71                                    0 to 4096
72       --disable-sni              Do not send a Server Name Indication (SNI)
73       --disable-extensions       Disable all the TLS extensions
```

```
74        --inline-commands       Inline commands of the form ^<cmd>^
75        --inline-commands-prefix=str Change the default delimiter for inline commands.
76        --provider=file         Specify the PKCS #11 provider library
77                                  - file must pre-exist
78        --fips140-mode          Reports the status of the FIPS140-2 mode in gnutls library
79    -v, --version[=arg]         output version information and exit
80    -h, --help                  display extended usage information and exit
81    -!, --more-help             extended usage information passed thru pager
82
83 Options are specified by doubled hyphens and their name or by a single
84 hyphen and the flag character.
85 Operands and options may be intermixed.  They will be reordered.
86
87 Simple client program to set up a TLS connection to some other computer.  It
88 sets up a TLS connection and forwards data from the standard input to the
89 secured socket and vice versa.
90
```

debug option (-d)

This is the "enable debugging" option. This option takes a number argument. Specifies the debug level.

tofu option

This is the "enable trust on first use authentication" option.

This option has some usage constraints. It:

- can be disabled with –no-tofu.

This option will, in addition to certificate authentication, perform authentication based on previously seen public keys, a model similar to SSH authentication. Note that when tofu is specified (PKI) and DANE authentication will become advisory to assist the public key acceptance process.

strict-tofu option

This is the "fail to connect if a known certificate has changed" option.

This option has some usage constraints. It:

- can be disabled with –no-strict-tofu.

This option will perform authentication as with option –tofu; however, while –tofu asks whether to trust a changed public key, this option will fail in case of public key changes.

dane option

This is the "enable dane certificate verification (dnssec)" option.

This option has some usage constraints. It:

- can be disabled with –no-dane.

This option will, in addition to certificate authentication using the trusted CAs, verify the server certificates using on the DANE information available via DNSSEC.

local-dns option

This is the "use the local dns server for dnssec resolving" option.

This option has some usage constraints. It:

- can be disabled with –no-local-dns.

This option will use the local DNS server for DNSSEC. This is disabled by default due to many servers not allowing DNSSEC.

ca-verification option

This is the "enable ca certificate verification" option.

This option has some usage constraints. It:

- can be disabled with –no-ca-verification.
- It is enabled by default.

This option can be used to enable or disable CA certificate verification. It is to be used with the –dane or –tofu options.

ocsp option

This is the "enable ocsp certificate verification" option.

This option has some usage constraints. It:

- can be disabled with –no-ocsp.

This option will enable verification of the peer's certificate using ocsp

resume option (-r)

This is the "establish a session and resume" option. Connect, establish a session, reconnect and resume.

rehandshake option (-e)

This is the "establish a session and rehandshake" option. Connect, establish a session and rehandshake immediately.

sni-hostname option

This is the "server's hostname for server name indication extension" option. This option takes a string argument. Set explicitly the server name used in the TLS server name indication extension. That is useful when testing with servers setup on different DNS name than the intended. If not specified, the provided hostname is used.

starttls option (-s)

This is the "connect, establish a plain session and start tls" option. The TLS session will be initiated when EOF or a SIGALRM is received.

app-proto option

This is an alias for the `starttls-proto` option, section 7.1.

starttls-proto option

This is the "the application protocol to be used to obtain the server's certificate (https, ftp, smtp, imap, ldap, xmpp, lmtp, pop3, nntp, sieve, postgres)" option. This option takes a string argument.

This option has some usage constraints. It:

- must not appear in combination with any of the following options: starttls.

Specify the application layer protocol for STARTTLS. If the protocol is supported, gnutls-cli will proceed to the TLS negotiation.

dh-bits option

This is the "the minimum number of bits allowed for dh" option. This option takes a number argument. This option sets the minimum number of bits allowed for a Diffie-Hellman key exchange. You may want to lower the default value if the peer sends a weak prime and you get an connection error with unacceptable prime.

priority option

This is the "priorities string" option. This option takes a string argument. TLS algorithms and protocols to enable. You can use predefined sets of ciphersuites such as PERFORMANCE, NORMAL, PFS, SECURE128, SECURE256. The default is NORMAL.

Check the GnuTLS manual on section "Priority strings" for more information on the allowed keywords

ranges option

This is the "use length-hiding padding to prevent traffic analysis" option. When possible (e.g., when using CBC ciphersuites), use length-hiding padding to prevent traffic analysis.

benchmark-ciphers option

This is the "benchmark individual ciphers" option. By default the benchmarked ciphers will utilize any capabilities of the local CPU to improve performance. To test against the raw software implementation set the environment variable GNUTLS_CPUID_OVERRIDE to 0x1.

benchmark-tls-ciphers option

This is the "benchmark tls ciphers" option. By default the benchmarked ciphers will utilize any capabilities of the local CPU to improve performance. To test against the raw software implementation set the environment variable GNUTLS_CPUID_OVERRIDE to 0x1.

list option (-l)

This is the "print a list of the supported algorithms and modes" option.

This option has some usage constraints. It:

- must not appear in combination with any of the following options: port.

Print a list of the supported algorithms and modes. If a priority string is given then only the enabled ciphersuites are shown.

priority-list option

This is the "print a list of the supported priority strings" option. Print a list of the supported priority strings. The ciphersuites corresponding to each priority string can be examined using -l -p.

alpn option

This is the "application layer protocol" option. This option takes a string argument.

This option has some usage constraints. It:

- may appear an unlimited number of times.

This option will set and enable the Application Layer Protocol Negotiation (ALPN) in the TLS protocol.

disable-extensions option

This is the "disable all the tls extensions" option. This option disables all TLS extensions. Deprecated option. Use the priority string.

inline-commands option

This is the "inline commands of the form
textasciicircum<cmd>
textasciicircum" option. Enable inline commands of the form
textasciicircum<cmd>
textasciicircum. The inline commands are expected to be in a line by themselves. The available commands are: resume and renegotiate.

inline-commands-prefix option

This is the "change the default delimiter for inline commands." option. This option takes a string argument. Change the default delimiter (
textasciicircum) used for inline commands. The delimiter is expected to be a single US-ASCII character (octets 0 - 127). This option is only relevant if inline commands are enabled via the inline-commands option

provider option

This is the "specify the pkcs #11 provider library" option. This option takes a file argument. This will override the default options in /etc/gnutls/pkcs11.conf

gnutls-cli exit status

One of the following exit values will be returned:

- 0 (EXIT_SUCCESS) Successful program execution.

- 1 (EXIT_FAILURE) The operation failed or the command syntax was not valid.

gnutls-cli See Also

gnutls-cli-debug(1), gnutls-serv(1)

gnutls-cli Examples

Connecting using PSK authentication

To connect to a server using PSK authentication, you need to enable the choice of PSK by using a cipher priority parameter such as in the example below.

```
1  $ ./gnutls-cli -p 5556 localhost --pskusername psk_identity \
2      --pskkey 88f3824b3e5659f52d00e959bacab954b6540344 \
3      --priority NORMAL:-KX-ALL:+ECDHE-PSK:+DHE-PSK:+PSK
4  Resolving 'localhost'...
5  Connecting to '127.0.0.1:5556'...
6  - PSK authentication.
7  - Version: TLS1.1
8  - Key Exchange: PSK
9  - Cipher: AES-128-CBC
10 - MAC: SHA1
11 - Compression: NULL
12 - Handshake was completed
13
14 - Simple Client Mode:
```

By keeping the –pskusername parameter and removing the –pskkey parameter, it will query only for the password during the handshake.

Connecting to STARTTLS services

You could also use the client to connect to services with starttls capability.

```
1  $ gnutls-cli --starttls-proto smtp --port 25 localhost
```

Listing ciphersuites in a priority string

To list the ciphersuites in a priority string:

```
1  $ ./gnutls-cli --priority SECURE192 -l
2  Cipher suites for SECURE192
3  TLS_ECDHE_ECDSA_AES_256_CBC_SHA384        0xc0, 0x24        TLS1.2
4  TLS_ECDHE_ECDSA_AES_256_GCM_SHA384        0xc0, 0x2e        TLS1.2
5  TLS_ECDHE_RSA_AES_256_GCM_SHA384          0xc0, 0x30        TLS1.2
6  TLS_DHE_RSA_AES_256_CBC_SHA256            0x00, 0x6b        TLS1.2
```

```
 7  TLS_DHE_DSS_AES_256_CBC_SHA256                  0x00, 0x6a        TLS1.2
 8  TLS_RSA_AES_256_CBC_SHA256                      0x00, 0x3d        TLS1.2
 9
10  Certificate types: CTYPE-X.509
11  Protocols: VERS-TLS1.2, VERS-TLS1.1, VERS-TLS1.0, VERS-SSL3.0, VERS-DTLS1.0
12  Compression: COMP-NULL
13  Elliptic curves: CURVE-SECP384R1, CURVE-SECP521R1
14  PK-signatures: SIGN-RSA-SHA384, SIGN-ECDSA-SHA384, SIGN-RSA-SHA512, SIGN-ECDSA-SHA512
```

Connecting using a PKCS #11 token

To connect to a server using a certificate and a private key present in a PKCS #11 token you need to substitute the PKCS 11 URLs in the x509certfile and x509keyfile parameters.

Those can be found using "p11tool –list-tokens" and then listing all the objects in the needed token, and using the appropriate.

```
 1  $ p11tool --list-tokens
 2
 3  Token 0:
 4  URL: pkcs11:model=PKCS15;manufacturer=MyMan;serial=1234;token=Test
 5  Label: Test
 6  Manufacturer: EnterSafe
 7  Model: PKCS15
 8  Serial: 1234
 9
10  $ p11tool --login --list-certs "pkcs11:model=PKCS15;manufacturer=MyMan;serial=1234;token=Test"
11
12  Object 0:
13  URL: pkcs11:model=PKCS15;manufacturer=MyMan;serial=1234;token=Test;object=client;type=cert
14  Type: X.509 Certificate
15  Label: client
16  ID: 2a:97:0d:58:d1:51:3c:23:07:ae:4e:0d:72:26:03:7d:99:06:02:6a
17
18  $ MYCERT="pkcs11:model=PKCS15;manufacturer=MyMan;serial=1234;token=Test;object=client;type=cert"
19  $ MYKEY="pkcs11:model=PKCS15;manufacturer=MyMan;serial=1234;token=Test;object=client;type=private"
20  $ export MYCERT MYKEY
21
22  $ gnutls-cli www.example.com --x509keyfile $MYKEY --x509certfile $MYCERT
```

Notice that the private key only differs from the certificate in the type.

7.2. Invoking gnutls-serv

Server program that listens to incoming TLS connections.

This section was generated by **AutoGen**, using the `agtexi-cmd` template and the option descriptions for the `gnutls-serv` program. This software is released under the GNU General Public License, version 3 or later.

gnutls-serv help/usage ("--help")

This is the automatically generated usage text for gnutls-serv.

The text printed is the same whether selected with the help option ("--help") or the more-help option ("--more-help"). more-help will print the usage text by passing it through a pager program. more-help is disabled on platforms without a working fork(2) function. The PAGER environment variable is used to select the program, defaulting to "more". Both will exit with a status code of 0.

```
1  gnutls-serv - GnuTLS server
2  Usage:  gnutls-serv [ -<flag> [<val>] | --<name>[{=| }<val>] ]...
3
4     -d, --debug=num            Enable debugging
5                                  - it must be in the range:
6                                    0 to 9999
7         --sni-hostname=str     Server's hostname for server name extension
8         --sni-hostname-fatal   Send fatal alert on sni-hostname mismatch
9         --alpn=str             Specify ALPN protocol to be enabled by the server
10                                 - may appear multiple times
11        --alpn-fatal           Send fatal alert on non-matching ALPN name
12        --noticket             Don't accept session tickets
13    -g, --generate             Generate Diffie-Hellman parameters
14    -q, --quiet                Suppress some messages
15        --nodb                 Do not use a resumption database
16        --http                 Act as an HTTP server
17        --echo                 Act as an Echo server
18    -u, --udp                  Use DTLS (datagram TLS) over UDP
19        --mtu=num              Set MTU for datagram TLS
20                                 - it must be in the range:
21                                   0 to 17000
22        --srtp-profiles=str    Offer SRTP profiles
23    -a, --disable-client-cert  Do not request a client certificate
24    -r, --require-client-cert  Require a client certificate
25        --verify-client-cert   If a client certificate is sent then verify it.
26    -b, --heartbeat            Activate heartbeat support
27        --x509fmtder           Use DER format for certificates to read from
28        --priority=str         Priorities string
29        --dhparams=file        DH params file to use
30                                 - file must pre-exist
31        --x509cafile=str       Certificate file or PKCS #11 URL to use
32        --x509crlfile=file     CRL file to use
33                                 - file must pre-exist
34        --x509keyfile=str      X.509 key file or PKCS #11 URL to use
35                                 - may appear multiple times
36        --x509certfile=str     X.509 Certificate file or PKCS #11 URL to use
37                                 - may appear multiple times
38        --srppasswd=file       SRP password file to use
39                                 - file must pre-exist
40        --srppasswdconf=file   SRP password configuration file to use
41                                 - file must pre-exist
42        --pskpasswd=file       PSK password file to use
43                                 - file must pre-exist
44        --pskhint=str          PSK identity hint to use
45        --ocsp-response=file   The OCSP response to send to client
46                                 - file must pre-exist
47    -p, --port=num             The port to connect to
```

```
48   -l, --list                 Print a list of the supported algorithms and modes
49       --provider=file         Specify the PKCS #11 provider library
50                                  - file must pre-exist
51   -v, --version[=arg]        output version information and exit
52   -h, --help                 display extended usage information and exit
53   -!, --more-help            extended usage information passed thru pager
54
55 Options are specified by doubled hyphens and their name or by a single
56 hyphen and the flag character.
57
58 Server program that listens to incoming TLS connections.
59
```

debug option (-d)

This is the "enable debugging" option. This option takes a number argument. Specifies the debug level.

sni-hostname option

This is the "server's hostname for server name extension" option. This option takes a string argument. Server name of type host_name that the server will recognise as its own. If the server receives client hello with different name, it will send a warning-level unrecognized_name alert.

alpn option

This is the "specify alpn protocol to be enabled by the server" option. This option takes a string argument.

This option has some usage constraints. It:

- may appear an unlimited number of times.

Specify the (textual) ALPN protocol for the server to use.

require-client-cert option (-r)

This is the "require a client certificate" option. This option before 3.6.0 used to imply –verify-client-cert. Since 3.6.0 it will no longer verify the certificate by default.

verify-client-cert option

This is the "if a client certificate is sent then verify it." option. Do not require, but if a client certificate is sent then verify it and close the connection if invalid.

heartbeat option (-b)

This is the "activate heartbeat support" option. Regularly ping client via heartbeat extension messages

priority option

This is the "priorities string" option. This option takes a string argument. TLS algorithms and protocols to enable. You can use predefined sets of ciphersuites such as PERFORMANCE, NORMAL, SECURE128, SECURE256. The default is NORMAL.

Check the GnuTLS manual on section "Priority strings" for more information on allowed keywords

x509keyfile option

This is the "x.509 key file or pkcs #11 url to use" option. This option takes a string argument.

This option has some usage constraints. It:

  • may appear an unlimited number of times.

Specify the private key file or URI to use; it must correspond to the certificate specified in –x509certfile. Multiple keys and certificates can be specified with this option and in that case each occurrence of keyfile must be followed by the corresponding x509certfile or vice-versa.

x509certfile option

This is the "x.509 certificate file or pkcs #11 url to use" option. This option takes a string argument.

This option has some usage constraints. It:

  • may appear an unlimited number of times.

Specify the certificate file or URI to use; it must correspond to the key specified in –x509keyfile. Multiple keys and certificates can be specified with this option and in that case each occurrence of keyfile must be followed by the corresponding x509certfile or vice-versa.

x509dsakeyfile option

This is an alias for the `x509keyfile` option, section 7.2.

x509dsacertfile option

This is an alias for the `x509certfile` option, section 7.2.

x509ecckeyfile option

This is an alias for the `x509keyfile` option, section 7.2.

x509ecccertfile option

This is an alias for the `x509certfile` option, section 7.2.

ocsp-response option

This is the "the ocsp response to send to client" option. This option takes a file argument. If the client requested an OCSP response, return data from this file to the client.

list option (-l)

This is the "print a list of the supported algorithms and modes" option. Print a list of the supported algorithms and modes. If a priority string is given then only the enabled ciphersuites are shown.

provider option

This is the "specify the pkcs #11 provider library" option. This option takes a file argument. This will override the default options in /etc/gnutls/pkcs11.conf

gnutls-serv exit status

One of the following exit values will be returned:

- 0 (EXIT_SUCCESS) Successful program execution.
- 1 (EXIT_FAILURE) The operation failed or the command syntax was not valid.

gnutls-serv See Also

gnutls-cli-debug(1), gnutls-cli(1)

gnutls-serv Examples

Running your own TLS server based on GnuTLS can be useful when debugging clients and/or GnuTLS itself. This section describes how to use **gnutls-serv** as a simple HTTPS server.

The most basic server can be started as:

```
gnutls-serv --http --priority "NORMAL:+ANON-ECDH:+ANON-DH"
```

It will only support anonymous ciphersuites, which many TLS clients refuse to use.

The next step is to add support for X.509. First we generate a CA:

```
$ certtool --generate-privkey > x509-ca-key.pem
$ echo 'cn = GnuTLS test CA' > ca.tmpl
$ echo 'ca' >> ca.tmpl
$ echo 'cert_signing_key' >> ca.tmpl
$ certtool --generate-self-signed --load-privkey x509-ca-key.pem \
    --template ca.tmpl --outfile x509-ca.pem
```

Then generate a server certificate. Remember to change the dns_name value to the name of your server host, or skip that command to avoid the field.

```
$ certtool --generate-privkey > x509-server-key.pem
$ echo 'organization = GnuTLS test server' > server.tmpl
$ echo 'cn = test.gnutls.org' >> server.tmpl
$ echo 'tls_www_server' >> server.tmpl
$ echo 'encryption_key' >> server.tmpl
$ echo 'signing_key' >> server.tmpl
$ echo 'dns_name = test.gnutls.org' >> server.tmpl
$ certtool --generate-certificate --load-privkey x509-server-key.pem \
    --load-ca-certificate x509-ca.pem --load-ca-privkey x509-ca-key.pem \
    --template server.tmpl --outfile x509-server.pem
```

For use in the client, you may want to generate a client certificate as well.

```
$ certtool --generate-privkey > x509-client-key.pem
$ echo 'cn = GnuTLS test client' > client.tmpl
$ echo 'tls_www_client' >> client.tmpl
$ echo 'encryption_key' >> client.tmpl
$ echo 'signing_key' >> client.tmpl
$ certtool --generate-certificate --load-privkey x509-client-key.pem \
    --load-ca-certificate x509-ca.pem --load-ca-privkey x509-ca-key.pem \
    --template client.tmpl --outfile x509-client.pem
```

To be able to import the client key/certificate into some applications, you will need to convert them into a PKCS#12 structure. This also encrypts the security sensitive key with a password.

```
$ certtool --to-p12 --load-ca-certificate x509-ca.pem \
    --load-privkey x509-client-key.pem --load-certificate x509-client.pem \
    --outder --outfile x509-client.p12
```

For icing, we'll create a proxy certificate for the client too.

272

```
1  $ certtool --generate-privkey > x509-proxy-key.pem
2  $ echo 'cn = GnuTLS test client proxy' > proxy.tmpl
3  $ certtool --generate-proxy --load-privkey x509-proxy-key.pem \
4    --load-ca-certificate x509-client.pem --load-ca-privkey x509-client-key.pem \
5    --load-certificate x509-client.pem --template proxy.tmpl \
6    --outfile x509-proxy.pem
```

Then start the server again:

```
1  $ gnutls-serv --http \
2            --x509cafile x509-ca.pem \
3            --x509keyfile x509-server-key.pem \
4            --x509certfile x509-server.pem
```

Try connecting to the server using your web browser. Note that the server listens to port 5556 by default.

While you are at it, to allow connections using ECDSA, you can also create a ECDSA key and certificate for the server. These credentials will be used in the final example below.

```
1  $ certtool --generate-privkey --ecdsa > x509-server-key-ecc.pem
2  $ certtool --generate-certificate --load-privkey x509-server-key-ecc.pem \
3    --load-ca-certificate x509-ca.pem --load-ca-privkey x509-ca-key.pem \
4    --template server.tmpl --outfile x509-server-ecc.pem
```

The next step is to add support for SRP authentication. This requires an SRP password file created with **srptool**. To start the server with SRP support:

```
1  gnutls-serv --http --priority NORMAL:+SRP-RSA:+SRP \
2            --srppasswdconf srp-tpasswd.conf \
3            --srppasswd srp-passwd.txt
```

Let's also start a server with support for PSK. This would require a password file created with **psktool**.

```
1  gnutls-serv --http --priority NORMAL:+ECDHE-PSK:+PSK \
2            --pskpasswd psk-passwd.txt
```

Finally, we start the server with all the earlier parameters and you get this command:

```
1  gnutls-serv --http --priority NORMAL:+PSK:+SRP \
2            --x509cafile x509-ca.pem \
3            --x509keyfile x509-server-key.pem \
4            --x509certfile x509-server.pem \
5            --x509keyfile x509-server-key-ecc.pem \
6            --x509certfile x509-server-ecc.pem \
7            --srppasswdconf srp-tpasswd.conf \
8            --srppasswd srp-passwd.txt \
9            --pskpasswd psk-passwd.txt
```

7.3. Invoking gnutls-cli-debug

TLS debug client. It sets up multiple TLS connections to a server and queries its capabilities. It was created to assist in debugging GnuTLS, but it might be useful to extract a TLS server's capabilities. It connects to a TLS server, performs tests and print the server's capabilities. If called with the '-V' parameter more checks will be performed. Can be used to check for servers with special needs or bugs.

This section was generated by **AutoGen**, using the `agtexi-cmd` template and the option descriptions for the `gnutls-cli-debug` program. This software is released under the GNU General Public License, version 3 or later.

gnutls-cli-debug help/usage ("`--help`")

This is the automatically generated usage text for gnutls-cli-debug.

The text printed is the same whether selected with the `help` option ("`--help`") or the `more-help` option ("`--more-help`"). `more-help` will print the usage text by passing it through a pager program. `more-help` is disabled on platforms without a working `fork(2)` function. The `PAGER` environment variable is used to select the program, defaulting to "`more`". Both will exit with a status code of 0.

```
 1  gnutls-cli-debug - GnuTLS debug client
 2  Usage:  gnutls-cli-debug [ -<flag> [<val>] | --<name>[{=| }<val>] ]...
 3
 4    -d, --debug=num            Enable debugging
 5                                - it must be in the range:
 6                                  0 to 9999
 7    -V, --verbose              More verbose output
 8                                - may appear multiple times
 9    -p, --port=num             The port to connect to
10                                - it must be in the range:
11                                  0 to 65536
12        --app-proto=str        an alias for the 'starttls-proto' option
13        --starttls-proto=str   The application protocol to be used to obtain the server's certificate
14  (https, ftp, smtp, imap, ldap, xmpp, lmtp, pop3, nntp, sieve, postgres)
15    -v, --version[=arg]        output version information and exit
16    -h, --help                 display extended usage information and exit
17    -!, --more-help            extended usage information passed thru pager
18
19  Options are specified by doubled hyphens and their name or by a single
20  hyphen and the flag character.
21  Operands and options may be intermixed.  They will be reordered.
22
23  TLS debug client.  It sets up multiple TLS connections to a server and
24  queries its capabilities.  It was created to assist in debugging GnuTLS,
25  but it might be useful to extract a TLS server's capabilities.  It connects
26  to a TLS server, performs tests and print the server's capabilities.  If
27  called with the '-V' parameter more checks will be performed.  Can be used
28  to check for servers with special needs or bugs.
29
```

debug option (-d)

This is the "enable debugging" option. This option takes a number argument. Specifies the debug level.

app-proto option

This is an alias for the `starttls-proto` option, section 7.3.

starttls-proto option

This is the "the application protocol to be used to obtain the server's certificate (https, ftp, smtp, imap, ldap, xmpp, lmtp, pop3, nntp, sieve, postgres)" option. This option takes a string argument. Specify the application layer protocol for STARTTLS. If the protocol is supported, gnutls-cli will proceed to the TLS negotiation.

gnutls-cli-debug exit status

One of the following exit values will be returned:

- 0 (EXIT_SUCCESS) Successful program execution.

- 1 (EXIT_FAILURE) The operation failed or the command syntax was not valid.

gnutls-cli-debug See Also

gnutls-cli(1), gnutls-serv(1)

gnutls-cli-debug Examples

```
1  $ gnutls-cli-debug localhost
2  GnuTLS debug client 3.5.0
3  Checking localhost:443
4                       for SSL 3.0 (RFC6101) support... yes
5            whether we need to disable TLS 1.2... no
6            whether we need to disable TLS 1.1... no
7            whether we need to disable TLS 1.0... no
8            whether %NO_EXTENSIONS is required... no
9                   whether %COMPAT is required... no
10                 for TLS 1.0 (RFC2246) support... yes
11                 for TLS 1.1 (RFC4346) support... yes
12                 for TLS 1.2 (RFC5246) support... yes
13                      fallback from TLS 1.6 to... TLS1.2
14             for RFC7507 inappropriate fallback... yes
15                       for HTTPS server name... Local
16                 for certificate chain order... sorted
```

```
17                for safe renegotiation (RFC5746) support... yes
18                for Safe renegotiation support (SCSV)... no
19                for encrypt-then-MAC (RFC7366) support... no
20                for ext master secret (RFC7627) support... no
21                        for heartbeat (RFC6520) support... no
22                    for version rollback bug in RSA PMS... dunno
23               for version rollback bug in Client Hello... no
24           whether the server ignores the RSA PMS version... yes
25 whether small records (512 bytes) are tolerated on handshake... yes
26      whether cipher suites not in SSL 3.0 spec are accepted... yes
27 whether a bogus TLS record version in the client hello is accepted... yes
28        whether the server understands TLS closure alerts... partially
29            whether the server supports session resumption... yes
30                 for anonymous authentication support... no
31                 for ephemeral Diffie-Hellman support... no
32             for ephemeral EC Diffie-Hellman support... yes
33             ephemeral EC Diffie-Hellman group info... SECP256R1
34            for AES-128-GCM cipher (RFC5288) support... yes
35            for AES-128-CCM cipher (RFC6655) support... no
36          for AES-128-CCM-8 cipher (RFC6655) support... no
37            for AES-128-CBC cipher (RFC3268) support... yes
38        for CAMELLIA-128-GCM cipher (RFC6367) support... no
39        for CAMELLIA-128-CBC cipher (RFC5932) support... no
40              for 3DES-CBC cipher (RFC2246) support... yes
41             for ARCFOUR 128 cipher (RFC2246) support... yes
42                            for MD5 MAC support... yes
43                           for SHA1 MAC support... yes
44                         for SHA256 MAC support... yes
45                 for ZLIB compression support... no
46              for max record size (RFC6066) support... no
47           for OCSP status response (RFC6066) support... no
48         for OpenPGP authentication (RFC6091) support... no
```

You could also use the client to debug services with starttls capability.

```
1 $ gnutls-cli-debug --starttls-proto smtp --port 25 localhost
```

8

Internal Architecture of GnuTLS

This chapter is to give a brief description of the way GnuTLS works. The focus is to give an idea to potential developers and those who want to know what happens inside the black box.

8.1. The TLS Protocol

The main use case for the TLS protocol is shown in Figure 8.1. A user of a library implementing the protocol expects no less than this functionality, i.e., to be able to set parameters such as the accepted security level, perform a negotiation with the peer and be able to exchange data.

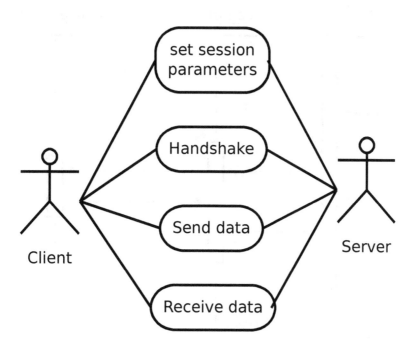

Figure 8.1.: TLS protocol use case.

8.2. TLS Handshake Protocol

The GnuTLS handshake protocol is implemented as a state machine that waits for input or returns immediately when the non-blocking transport layer functions are used. The main idea is shown in Figure 8.2.

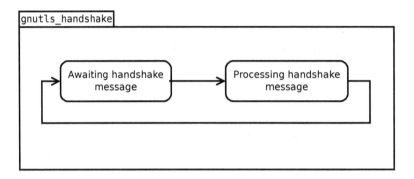

Figure 8.2.: GnuTLS handshake state machine.

Also the way the input is processed varies per ciphersuite. Several implementations of the internal handlers are available and **gnutls_handshake** only multiplexes the input to the appropriate handler. For example a PSK ciphersuite has a different implementation of the **process_client_key_exchange** than a certificate ciphersuite. We illustrate the idea in Figure 8.3.

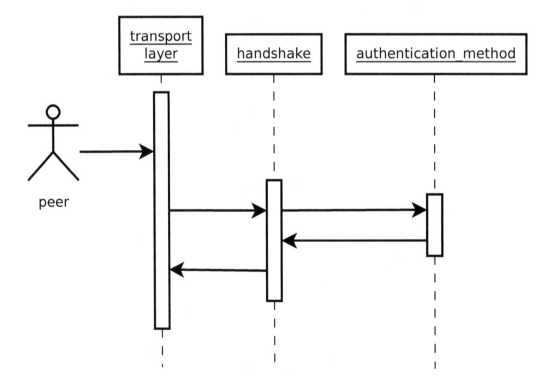

Figure 8.3.: GnuTLS handshake process sequence.

8.3. TLS Authentication Methods

In GnuTLS authentication methods can be implemented quite easily. Since the required changes to add a new authentication method affect only the handshake protocol, a simple interface is used. An authentication method needs to implement the functions shown below.

```
typedef struct
{
  const char *name;
  int (*gnutls_generate_server_certificate) (gnutls_session_t, gnutls_buffer_st*);
  int (*gnutls_generate_client_certificate) (gnutls_session_t, gnutls_buffer_st*);
  int (*gnutls_generate_server_kx) (gnutls_session_t, gnutls_buffer_st*);
  int (*gnutls_generate_client_kx) (gnutls_session_t, gnutls_buffer_st*);
  int (*gnutls_generate_client_cert_vrfy) (gnutls_session_t, gnutls_buffer_st *);
  int (*gnutls_generate_server_certificate_request) (gnutls_session_t,
                                             gnutls_buffer_st *);

  int (*gnutls_process_server_certificate) (gnutls_session_t, opaque *,
                                        size_t);
  int (*gnutls_process_client_certificate) (gnutls_session_t, opaque *,
                                        size_t);
  int (*gnutls_process_server_kx) (gnutls_session_t, opaque *, size_t);
  int (*gnutls_process_client_kx) (gnutls_session_t, opaque *, size_t);
  int (*gnutls_process_client_cert_vrfy) (gnutls_session_t, opaque *, size_t);
  int (*gnutls_process_server_certificate_request) (gnutls_session_t,
                                           opaque *, size_t);
} mod_auth_st;
```

Those functions are responsible for the interpretation of the handshake protocol messages. It is common for such functions to read data from one or more **credentials_t** structures[1] and write data, such as certificates, usernames etc. to **auth_info_t** structures.

Simple examples of existing authentication methods can be seen in **auth/psk.c** for PSK ciphersuites and **auth/srp.c** for SRP ciphersuites. After implementing these functions the structure holding its pointers has to be registered in **gnutls_algorithms.c** in the **_gnutls_-kx_algorithms** structure.

8.4. TLS Extension Handling

As with authentication methods, the TLS extensions handlers can be implemented using the interface shown below.

```
typedef int (*gnutls_ext_recv_func) (gnutls_session_t session,
                                   const unsigned char *data, size_t len);
typedef int (*gnutls_ext_send_func) (gnutls_session_t session,
```

---

[1]such as the **gnutls_certificate_credentials_t** structures

279

```
gnutls_buffer_st *extdata);
```

Here there are two functions, one for receiving the extension data and one for sending. These functions have to check internally whether they operate in client or server side.

A simple example of an extension handler can be seen in `ext/srp.c` in GnuTLS' source code. After implementing these functions, together with the extension number they handle, they have to be registered using `_gnutls_ext_register` in `gnutls_extensions.c` typically within `_gnutls_ext_init`.

Adding a new TLS extension

Adding support for a new TLS extension is done from time to time, and the process to do so is not difficult. Here are the steps you need to follow if you wish to do this yourself. For sake of discussion, let's consider adding support for the hypothetical TLS extension **foobar**. The following section is about adding an extension to GnuTLS, for custom application extensions you should check the exported functions **gnutls_session_ext_register** or **gnutls_ext_register**.

Add `configure` option like `--enable-foobar` or `--disable-foobar`.

This step is useful when the extension code is large and it might be desirable to disable the extension under some circumstances. Otherwise it can be safely skipped.

Whether to chose enable or disable depends on whether you intend to make the extension be enabled by default. Look at existing checks (i.e., SRP, authz) for how to model the code. For example:

```
1   AC_MSG_CHECKING([whether to disable foobar support])
2   AC_ARG_ENABLE(foobar,
3           AS_HELP_STRING([--disable-foobar],
4                   [disable foobar support]),
5           ac_enable_foobar=no)
6   if test x$ac_enable_foobar != xno; then
7     AC_MSG_RESULT(no)
8     AC_DEFINE(ENABLE_FOOBAR, 1, [enable foobar])
9   else
10    ac_full=0
11    AC_MSG_RESULT(yes)
12  fi
13  AM_CONDITIONAL(ENABLE_FOOBAR, test "$ac_enable_foobar" != "no")
```

These lines should go in `m4/hooks.m4`.

Add IANA extension value to `extensions_t` in `gnutls_int.h`.

A good name for the value would be GNUTLS_EXTENSION_FOOBAR. Check with http://www.iana.org/assignments/tls-extensiontype-values for allocated values. For experiments, you could pick a number but remember that some consider it a bad idea to deploy such modified version since it will lead to interoperability problems in the future when the IANA allocates that number to someone else, or when the foobar protocol is allocated another number.

Add an entry to _gnutls_extensions **in** gnutls_extensions.c.

A typical entry would be:

```
int ret;

#if ENABLE_FOOBAR
  ret = _gnutls_ext_register (&foobar_ext);
  if (ret != GNUTLS_E_SUCCESS)
    return ret;
#endif
```

Most likely you'll need to add an **#include "ext/foobar.h"**, that will contain something like like:

```
extension_entry_st foobar_ext = {
  .name = "FOOBAR",
  .type = GNUTLS_EXTENSION_FOOBAR,
  .parse_type = GNUTLS_EXT_TLS,
  .recv_func = _foobar_recv_params,
  .send_func = _foobar_send_params,
  .pack_func = _foobar_pack,
  .unpack_func = _foobar_unpack,
  .deinit_func = NULL
}
```

The GNUTLS_EXTENSION_FOOBAR is the integer value you added to **gnutls_int.h** earlier. In this structure you specify the functions to read the extension from the hello message, the function to send the reply to, and two more functions to pack and unpack from stored session data (e.g. when resumming a session). The **deinit** function will be called to deinitialize the extension's private parameters, if any.

Note that the conditional **ENABLE_FOOBAR** definition should only be used if step 1 with the **configure** options has taken place.

Add new files that implement the extension.

The functions you are responsible to add are those mentioned in the previous step. They should be added in a file such as **ext/foobar.c** and headers should be placed in **ext/foobar.h**. As a starter, you could add this:

```
int
_foobar_recv_params (gnutls_session_t session, const opaque * data,
                     size_t data_size)
{
  return 0;
}
```

```
7
8   int
9   _foobar_send_params (gnutls_session_t session, gnutls_buffer_st* data)
10  {
11    return 0;
12  }
13
14  int
15  _foobar_pack (extension_priv_data_t epriv, gnutls_buffer_st * ps)
16  {
17    /* Append the extension's internal state to buffer */
18    return 0;
19  }
20
21  int
22  _foobar_unpack (gnutls_buffer_st * ps, extension_priv_data_t * epriv)
23  {
24    /* Read the internal state from buffer */
25    return 0;
26  }
```

The _foobar_recv_params function is responsible for parsing incoming extension data (both in the client and server).

The _foobar_send_params function is responsible for sending extension data (both in the client and server). It should append data to provided buffer and return a positive (or zero) number on success or a negative error code. Previous to 3.6.0 versions of GnuTLS required that function to return the number of bytes that were written. If zero is returned and no bytes are appended the extension will not be sent. If a zero byte extension is to be sent this function must return GNUTLS_E_INT_RET_0.

If you receive length fields that don't match, return GNUTLS_E_UNEXPECTED_PACKET_LENGTH. If you receive invalid data, return GNUTLS_E_RECEIVED_ILLEGAL_PARAMETER. You can use other error codes from the list in Appendix D. Return 0 on success.

An extension typically stores private information in the **session** data for later usage. That can be done using the functions _gnutls_ext_set_session_data and _gnutls_ext_get_session_-data. You can check simple examples at ext/max_record.c and ext/server_name.c extensions. That private information can be saved and restored across session resumption if the following functions are set:

The _foobar_pack function is responsible for packing internal extension data to save them in the session resumption storage.

The _foobar_unpack function is responsible for restoring session data from the session resumption storage.

Recall that both the client and server, send and receive parameters, and your code most likely will need to do different things depending on which mode it is in. It may be useful to make this distinction explicit in the code. Thus, for example, a better template than above would be:

```
1   int
2   _gnutls_foobar_recv_params (gnutls_session_t session,
```

```
 3                               const opaque * data,
 4                               size_t data_size)
 5  {
 6    if (session->security_parameters.entity == GNUTLS_CLIENT)
 7      return foobar_recv_client (session, data, data_size);
 8    else
 9      return foobar_recv_server (session, data, data_size);
10  }
11
12  int
13  _gnutls_foobar_send_params (gnutls_session_t session,
14                              gnutls_buffer_st * data)
15  {
16    if (session->security_parameters.entity == GNUTLS_CLIENT)
17      return foobar_send_client (session, data);
18    else
19      return foobar_send_server (session, data);
20  }
```

The functions used would be declared as **static** functions, of the appropriate prototype, in the same file. When adding the files, you'll need to add them to **ext/Makefile.am** as well, for example:

```
1  if ENABLE_FOOBAR
2  libgnutls_ext_la_SOURCES += ext/foobar.c ext/foobar.h
3  endif
```

Add API functions to enable/disable the extension.

It might be desirable to allow users of the extension to request use of the extension, or set extension specific data. This can be implemented by adding extension specific function calls that can be added to **includes/gnutls/gnutls.h**, as long as the LGPLv2.1+ applies. The implementation of the function should lie in the **ext/foobar.c** file.

To make the API available in the shared library you need to add the symbol in **lib/-libgnutls.map**, so that the symbol is exported properly.

When writing GTK-DOC style documentation for your new APIs, don't forget to add **Since:** tags to indicate the GnuTLS version the API was introduced in.

Heartbeat extension.

One such extension is HeartBeat protocol (RFC6520: `https://tools.ietf.org/html/rfc6520`) implementation. To enable it use option –heartbeat with example client and server supplied with gnutls:

```
1  ./doc/credentials/gnutls-http-serv --priority "NORMAL:-CIPHER-ALL:+NULL" -d 100 \
2      --heartbeat --echo
3  ./src/gnutls-cli --priority "NORMAL:-CIPHER-ALL:+NULL" -d 100 localhost -p 5556 \
4      --insecure --heartbeat
```

After that pasting

```
1  **HEARTBEAT**
```

command into gnutls-cli will trigger corresponding command on the server and it will send
HeartBeat Request with random length to client.

Another way is to run capabilities check with:

```
1  ./doc/credentials/gnutls-http-serv -d 100 --heartbeat
2  ./src/gnutls-cli-debug localhost -p 5556
```

Adding a new Supplemental Data Handshake Message

TLS handshake extensions allow to send so called supplemental data handshake messages [39].
This short section explains how to implement a supplemental data handshake message for a
given TLS extension.

First of all, modify your extension foobar in the way, to instruct the handshake process to
send and receive supplemental data, as shown below.

```
1  int
2  _gnutls_foobar_recv_params (gnutls_session_t session, const opaque * data,
3                              size_t _data_size)
4  {
5      ...
6      gnutls_supplemental_recv(session, 1);
7      ...
8  }
9
10 int
11 _gnutls_foobar_send_params (gnutls_session_t session, gnutls_buffer_st *extdata)
12 {
13     ...
14     gnutls_supplemental_send(session, 1);
15     ...
16 }
```

Furthermore you'll need two new functions _foobar_supp_recv_params and _foobar_supp_-
send_params, which must conform to the following prototypes.

```
1  typedef int (*gnutls_supp_recv_func)(gnutls_session_t session,
2                                       const unsigned char *data,
3                                       size_t data_size);
4  typedef int (*gnutls_supp_send_func)(gnutls_session_t session,
5                                       gnutls_buffer_t buf);
```

The following example code shows how to send a "Hello World" string in the supplemental
data handshake message.

```
1  int
2  _foobar_supp_recv_params(gnutls_session_t session, const opaque *data, size_t _data_size)
3  {
```

```
4   uint8_t len = _data_size;
5   unsigned char *msg;
6
7   msg = gnutls_malloc(len);
8   if (msg == NULL) return GNUTLS_E_MEMORY_ERROR;
9
10  memcpy(msg, data, len);
11  msg[len]='\0';
12
13  /* do something with msg */
14  gnutls_free(msg);
15
16  return len;
17 }
18
19 int
20 _foobar_supp_send_params(gnutls_session_t session, gnutls_buffer_t buf)
21 {
22  unsigned char *msg = "hello world";
23  int len = strlen(msg);
24
25  if (gnutls_buffer_append_data(buf, msg, len) < 0)
26      abort();
27
28  return len;
29 }
```

Afterwards, register the new supplemental data using `gnutls_session_supplemental_register`, or `gnutls_supplemental_register` at some point in your program.

8.5. Cryptographic Backend

Today most new processors, either for embedded or desktop systems include either instructions intended to speed up cryptographic operations, or a co-processor with cryptographic capabilities. Taking advantage of those is a challenging task for every cryptographic application or library. GnuTLS handles the cryptographic provider in a modular way, following a layered approach to access cryptographic operations as in Figure 8.4.

The TLS layer uses a cryptographic provider layer, that will in turn either use the default crypto provider – a software crypto library, or use an external crypto provider, if available in the local system. The reason of handling the external cryptographic provider in GnuTLS and not delegating it to the cryptographic libraries, is that none of the supported cryptographic libraries support /dev/crypto or CPU-optimized cryptography in an efficient way.

Cryptographic library layer

The Cryptographic library layer, currently supports only libnettle. Older versions of GnuTLS used to support libgcrypt, but it was switched with nettle mainly for performance reasons[2]

---

[2]See http://lists.gnu.org/archive/html/gnutls-devel/2011-02/msg00079.html.

Figure 8.4.: GnuTLS cryptographic back-end design.

and secondary because it is a simpler library to use. In the future other cryptographic libraries might be supported as well.

External cryptography provider

Systems that include a cryptographic co-processor, typically come with kernel drivers to utilize the operations from software. For this reason GnuTLS provides a layer where each individual algorithm used can be replaced by another implementation, i.e., the one provided by the driver. The FreeBSD, OpenBSD and Linux kernels[3] include already a number of hardware assisted implementations, and also provide an interface to access them, called /dev/crypto. GnuTLS will take advantage of this interface if compiled with special options. That is because in most systems where hardware-assisted cryptographic operations are not available, using this interface might actually harm performance.

In systems that include cryptographic instructions with the CPU's instructions set, using the kernel interface will introduce an unneeded layer. For this reason GnuTLS includes such optimizations found in popular processors such as the AES-NI or VIA PADLOCK instruction sets.

---

[3]Check http://home.gna.org/cryptodev-linux/ for the Linux kernel implementation of /dev/crypto.

This is achieved using a mechanism that detects CPU capabilities and overrides parts of crypto back-end at runtime. The next section discusses the registration of a detected algorithm optimization. For more information please consult the GnuTLS source code in `lib/accelerated/`.

Overriding specific algorithms

When an optimized implementation of a single algorithm is available, say a hardware assisted version of AES-CBC then the following functions, from `crypto.h`, can be used to register those algorithms.

- `gnutls_crypto_register_cipher`: To register a cipher algorithm.

- `gnutls_crypto_register_aead_cipher`: To register an AEAD cipher algorithm.

- `gnutls_crypto_register_mac`: To register a MAC algorithm.

- `gnutls_crypto_register_digest`: To register a hash algorithm.

Those registration functions will only replace the specified algorithm and leave the rest of subsystem intact.

Protecting keys through isolation

For asymmetric or public keys, GnuTLS supports PKCS #11 which allows operation without access to long term keys, in addition to CPU offloading. For more information see chapter 4.

8.6. Random Number Generators

About the generators

GnuTLS provides two random generators. The default, and the AES-DRBG random generator which is only used when the library is compiled with support for FIPS140-2 and the system is in FIPS140-2 mode.

The default generator - inner workings

The random number generator levels in `gnutls_rnd_level_t` map to two CHACHA-based random generators which are initially seeded using the OS random device, e.g., `/dev/urandom` or `getrandom()`. These random generators are unique per thread, and are automatically re-seeded when a fork is detected.

The reason the CHACHA cipher was selected for the GnuTLS' PRNG is the fact that CHACHA is considered a secure and fast stream cipher, and is already defined for use in TLS protocol. As such, the utilization of it would not stress the CPU caches, and would allow for better performance on busy servers, irrespective of their architecture (e.g., even if AES is not available with an optimized instruction set).

The generators are unique per thread to allow lock-free operation. That induces a cost of around 140-bytes for the state of the generators per thread, on threads that would utilize `gnutls_rnd`. At the same time it allows fast and lock-free access to the generators. The lock-free access benefits servers which utilize more than 4 threads, while imposes no cost on single threaded processes.

On the first call to `gnutls_rnd` the generators are seeded with two independent keys obtained from the OS random device. Their seed is used to output a fixed amount of bytes before re-seeding; the number of bytes output varies per generator.

One generator is dedicated for the `GNUTLS_RND_NONCE` level, and the second is shared for the `GNUTLS_RND_KEY` and `GNUTLS_RND_RANDOM` levels. For the rest of this section we refer to the first as the nonce generator and the second as the key generator.

The nonce generator will reseed after outputing a fixed amount of bytes (typically few megabytes), or after few hours of operation without reaching the limit has passed. It is being re-seed using the key generator to obtain a new key for the CHACHA cipher, which is mixed with its old one.

Similarly, the key generator, will also re-seed after a fixed amount of bytes is generated (typically less than the nonce), and will also re-seed based on time, i.e., after few hours of operation without reaching the limit for a re-seed. For its re-seed it mixes mixes data obtained from the OS random device with the previous key.

Although the key generator used to provide data for the `GNUTLS_RND_RANDOM` and `GNUTLS_RND_KEY` levels is identical, when used with the `GNUTLS_RND_KEY` level a re-key of the PRNG using its own output, is additionally performed. That ensures that the recovery of the PRNG state will not be sufficient to recover previously generated values.

The AES-DRBG generator - inner workings

Similar with the default generator, the random number generator levels in `gnutls_rnd_level_t` map to two AES-DRBG random generators which are initially seeded using the OS random device, e.g., `/dev/urandom` or `getrandom()`. These random generators are unique per thread, and are automatically re-seeded when a fork is detected.

The AES-DRBG generator is based on the AES cipher in counter mode and is re-seeded after a fixed amount of bytes are generated.

Defense against PRNG attacks

This section describes the counter-measures available in the Pseudo-random number generator (PRNG) of GnuTLS for known attacks as described in [18]. Note that, the attacks on a PRNG such as state-compromise, assume a quite powerful adversary which has in practice access to the PRNG state.

Cryptanalytic

To defend against cryptanalytic attacks GnuTLS' PRNG is a stream cipher designed to defend against the same attacks. As such, GnuTLS' PRNG strength with regards to this attack relies on the underlying crypto block, which at the time of writing is CHACHA. That is easily replaceable in the future if attacks are found to be possible in that cipher.

Input-based attacks

These attacks assume that the attacker can influence the input that is used to form the state of the PRNG. To counter these attacks GnuTLS does not gather input from the system environment but rather relies on the OS provided random generator. That is the /dev/urandom or getentropy/getrandom system calls. As such, GnuTLS' PRNG is as strong as the system random generator can assure with regards to input-based attacks.

State-compromise: Backtracking

A backtracking attack, assumes that an adversary obtains at some point of time access to the generator state, and wants to recover past bytes. As the GnuTLS generator is fine-tuned to provide multiple levels, such an attack mainly concerns levels GNUTLS_RND_RANDOM and GNUTLS_RND_KEY, since GNUTLS_RND_NONCE is intended to output non-secret data. The GNUTLS_RND_RANDOM generator at the time of writing can output 2MB prior to being re-seeded thus this is its upper bound for previously generated data recovered using this attack. That assumes that the state of the operating system random generator is unknown to the attacker, and we carry that assumption on the next paragraphs. The usage of GNUTLS_RND_KEY level ensures that no backtracking is possible for all output data, by re-keying the PRNG using its own output.

Such an attack reflects the real world scenario where application's memory is temporarily compromised, while the kernel's memory is inaccessible.

State-compromise: Permanent Compromise Attack

A permanent compromise attack implies that once an attacker compromises the state of GnuTLS' random generator at a specific time, future and past outputs from the generator are compromised. For past outputs the previous paragraph applies. For future outputs, both the GNUTLS_RND_RANDOM and the GNUTLS_RND_KEY will recover after 2MB of data have been generated or few hours have passed (two at the time of writing). Similarly the GNUTLS_RND_NONCE level generator will recover after several megabytes of output is generated, or its re-key time is reached.

State-compromise: Iterative guessing

This attack assumes that after an attacker obtained the PRNG state at some point, is able to recover the state at a later time by observing outputs of the PRNG. That is countered by switching the key to generators using a combination of a fresh key and the old one (using XOR), at re-seed time. All levels are immune to such attack after a re-seed.

State-compromise: Meet-in-the-Middle

This attack assumes that the attacker obtained the PRNG state at two distinct times, and being able to recover the state at the third time after observing the output of the PRNG. Given the approach described on the above paragraph, all levels are immune to such attack.

8.7. FIPS140-2 mode

GnuTLS can operate in a special mode for FIPS140-2. That mode of operation is for the conformance to NIST's FIPS140-2 publication, which consists of policies for cryptographic modules (such as software libraries). Its implementation in GnuTLS is designed for Red Hat Enterprise Linux, and can only be enabled when the library is explicitly compiled with the '–enable-fips140-mode' configure option. The operation of the library is then modified, as follows.

- FIPS140-2 mode is enabled when `/proc/sys/crypto/fips_enabled` contains '1' and `/etc/system-fips` is present.

- Only approved by FIPS140-2 algorithms are enabled

- Only approved by FIPS140-2 key lengths are allowed for key generation

- The random generator used switches to DRBG-AES

- The integrity of the GnuTLS and dependent libraries is checked on startup

- Algorithm self-tests are run on library load

- Any cryptographic operation will be refused if any of the self-tests failed

There is a 'zombie' FIPS140-2 mode which is enabled when only one of the files described in the first step is available. In that case the self tests will be performed without affecting the operation of the library.

The integrity checks for the dependent libraries and GnuTLS are performed using '.hmac' files which are present at the same path as the library. The key for the operations can be provided on compile-time with the configure option '–with-fips140-key'. The MAC algorithm used is HMAC-SHA256.

There are also few environment variables which modify that operation. The environment variable `GNUTLS_SKIP_FIPS_INTEGRITY_CHECKS` will disable the library integrity tests on startup, and the variable GNUTLS_FORCE_FIPS_MODE when set to '1' will enable the FIPS140-2 mode, when set to '0' will force a disable of it.

On runtime an application can verify whether the library is in FIPS140-2 using the gnutls_fips140_mode_enabled function.

Upgrading from previous versions

The GnuTLS library typically maintains binary and source code compatibility across versions. The releases that have the major version increased break binary compatibility but source compatibility is provided. This section lists exceptional cases where changes to existing code are required due to library changes.

Upgrading to 2.12.x from previous versions

GnuTLS 2.12.x is binary compatible with previous versions but changes the semantics of `gnutls_transport_set_lowat`, which might cause breakage in applications that relied on its default value be 1. Two fixes are proposed:

- Quick fix. Explicitly call `gnutls_transport_set_lowat (session, 1);` after `gnutls_init`.

- Long term fix. Because later versions of gnutls abolish the functionality of using the system call `select` to check for gnutls pending data, the function `gnutls_record_check_pending` has to be used to achieve the same functionality as described in subsection 5.5.1.

Upgrading to 3.0.x from 2.12.x

GnuTLS 3.0.x is source compatible with previous versions except for the functions listed below.

Old function	Replacement
`gnutls_transport_set_lowat`	To replace its functionality the function `gnutls_record_check_pending` has to be used, as described in subsection 5.5.1
`gnutls_session_get_server_random`, `gnutls_session_get_client_random`	They are replaced by the safer function `gnutls_session_get_random`
`gnutls_session_get_master_secret`	Replaced by the keying material exporters discussed in subsection 5.12.5
`gnutls_transport_set_global_errno`	Replaced by using the system's errno facility or `gnutls_transport_set_errno`.
`gnutls_x509_privkey_verify_data`	Replaced by `gnutls_pubkey_verify_data2`.
`gnutls_certificate_verify_peers`	Replaced by `gnutls_certificate_verify_peers2`.
`gnutls_psk_netconf_derive_key`	Removed. The key derivation function was never standardized.
`gnutls_session_set_finished_function`	Removed.
`gnutls_ext_register`	Removed. Extension registration API is now internal to allow easier changes in the API.
`gnutls_certificate_get_x509_crls`, `gnutls_certificate_get_x509_cas`	Removed to allow updating the internal structures. Replaced by `gnutls_certificate_get_issuer`.
`gnutls_certificate_get_openpgp_keyring`	Removed.
`gnutls_ia_`	Removed. The inner application extensions were completely removed (they failed to be standardized).

Upgrading to 3.1.x from 3.0.x

GnuTLS 3.1.x is source and binary compatible with GnuTLS 3.0.x releases. Few functions have been deprecated and are listed below.

Old function	Replacement
`gnutls_pubkey_verify_hash`	The function `gnutls_pubkey_verify_hash2` is provided and is functionally equivalent and safer to use.
`gnutls_pubkey_verify_data`	The function `gnutls_pubkey_verify_data2` is provided and is functionally equivalent and safer to use.

Upgrading to 3.2.x from 3.1.x

GnuTLS 3.2.x is source and binary compatible with GnuTLS 3.1.x releases. Few functions have been deprecated and are listed below.

Old function	Replacement
`gnutls_privkey_sign_-raw_data`	The function `gnutls_privkey_sign_hash` is equivalent when the flag `GNUTLS_PRIVKEY_SIGN_FLAG_TLS1_RSA` is specified.

Upgrading to 3.3.x from 3.2.x

GnuTLS 3.3.x is source and binary compatible with GnuTLS 3.2.x releases; however there few changes in semantics which are listed below.

Old function	Replacement
`gnutls_global_init`	No longer required. The library is initialized using a constructor.
`gnutls_global_deinit`	No longer required. The library is deinitialized using a destructor.

Upgrading to 3.4.x from 3.3.x

GnuTLS 3.4.x is source compatible with GnuTLS 3.3.x releases; however, several deprecated functions were removed, and are listed below.

Old function	Replacement
Priority string "NORMAL" has been modified	The following string emulates the 3.3.x behavior "NORMAL:+VERS-SSL3.0:+ARCFOUR-128:+DHE-DSS:+SIGN-DSA-SHA512:+SIGN-DSA-SHA256:+SIGN-DSA-SHA1"
gnutls_certificate_client_set_retrieve_function, gnutls_certificate_server_set_retrieve_function	gnutls_certificate_set_retrieve_function
gnutls_certificate_set_rsa_export_params, gnutls_rsa_export_get_modulus_bits, gnutls_rsa_export_get_pubkey, gnutls_rsa_params_cpy, gnutls_rsa_params_deinit, gnutls_rsa_params_export_pkcs1, gnutls_rsa_params_export_raw, gnutls_rsa_params_generate2, gnutls_rsa_params_import_pkcs1, gnutls_rsa_params_import_raw, gnutls_rsa_params_init	No replacement; the library does not support the RSA-EXPORT ciphersuites.
gnutls_pubkey_verify_hash,	gnutls_pubkey_verify_hash2.
gnutls_pubkey_verify_data,	gnutls_pubkey_verify_data2.
gnutls_x509_crt_get_verify_algorithm,	No replacement; a similar function is gnutls_x509_crt_get_signature_algorithm.
gnutls_pubkey_get_verify_algorithm,	No replacement; a similar function is gnutls_pubkey_get_preferred_hash_algorithm.
gnutls_certificate_type_set_priority, gnutls_cipher_set_priority, gnutls_compression_set_priority, gnutls_kx_set_priority, gnutls_mac_set_priority, gnutls_protocol_set_priority	gnutls_priority_set_direct.
gnutls_sign_callback_get, gnutls_sign_callback_set	gnutls_privkey_import_ext3
gnutls_x509_crt_verify_hash	gnutls_pubkey_verify_hash2
gnutls_x509_crt_verify_data	gnutls_pubkey_verify_data2
gnutls_privkey_sign_raw_data	gnutls_privkey_sign_hash with the flag GNUTLS_PRIVKEY_SIGN_FLAG_TLS1_RSA

Upgrading to 3.6.x from 3.5.x

GnuTLS 3.6.x is source and binary compatible with GnuTLS 3.5.x releases; however, there are minor differences, listed below.

Old functionality	Replacement
The priority strings "+COMP" are a no-op	TLS compression is no longer available.
The hash function SHA2-224 is a no-op for TLS1.2	TLS 1.3 no longer uses SHA2-224, and it was never a widespread hash algorithm. As such it was removed for simplicity.
The SRP key exchange accepted parameters outside the [41] spec	The SRP key exchange is restricted to [41] spec parameters to protect clients from MitM attacks.
The compression-related functions are deprecated	No longer use gnutls_compression_get, gnutls_compression_get_name, gnutls_compression_list, and gnutls_compression_get_id.
gnutls_x509_crt_sign, gnutls_x509_crl_sign, gnutls_x509_crq_sign	These signing functions will no longer sign using SHA1, but with a secure hash algorithm.

B

Support

B.1. Getting Help

A mailing list where users may help each other exists, and you can reach it by sending e-mail to gnutls-help@gnutls.org. Archives of the mailing list discussions, and an interface to manage subscriptions, is available through the World Wide Web at `http://lists.gnutls.org/pipermail/gnutls-help/`.

A mailing list for developers are also available, see `http://www.gnutls.org/lists.html`. Bug reports should be sent to bugs@gnutls.org, see section B.3.

B.2. Commercial Support

Commercial support is available for users of GnuTLS. See `http://www.gnutls.org/commercial.html` for more information.

B.3. Bug Reports

If you think you have found a bug in GnuTLS, please investigate it and report it.

- Please make sure that the bug is really in GnuTLS, and preferably also check that it hasn't already been fixed in the latest version.

- You have to send us a test case that makes it possible for us to reproduce the bug.

- You also have to explain what is wrong; if you get a crash, or if the results printed are not good and in that case, in what way. Make sure that the bug report includes all information you would need to fix this kind of bug for someone else.

Please make an effort to produce a self-contained report, with something definite that can be tested or debugged. Vague queries or piecemeal messages are difficult to act on and don't help the development effort.

If your bug report is good, we will do our best to help you to get a corrected version of the software; if the bug report is poor, we won't do anything about it (apart from asking you to send better bug reports).

If you think something in this manual is unclear, or downright incorrect, or if the language needs to be improved, please also send a note.

Send your bug report to:

bugs@gnutls.org

B.4. Contributing

If you want to submit a patch for inclusion – from solving a typo you discovered, up to adding support for a new feature – you should submit it as a bug report, using the process in section B.3. There are some things that you can do to increase the chances for it to be included in the official package.

Unless your patch is very small (say, under 10 lines) we require that you assign the copyright of your work to the Free Software Foundation. This is to protect the freedom of the project. If you have not already signed papers, we will send you the necessary information when you submit your contribution.

For contributions that doesn't consist of actual programming code, the only guidelines are common sense. For code contributions, a number of style guides will help you:

- Coding Style. Follow the GNU Standards document.

  If you normally code using another coding standard, there is no problem, but you should use indent to reformat the code before submitting your work.

- Use the unified diff format diff -u.

- Return errors. No reason whatsoever should abort the execution of the library. Even memory allocation errors, e.g. when malloc return NULL, should work although result in an error code.

- Design with thread safety in mind. Don't use global variables. Don't even write to per-handle global variables unless the documented behaviour of the function you write is to write to the per-handle global variable.

- Avoid using the C math library. It causes problems for embedded implementations, and in most situations it is very easy to avoid using it.

- Document your functions. Use comments before each function headers, that, if properly formatted, are extracted into Texinfo manuals and GTK-DOC web pages.

- Supply a ChangeLog and NEWS entries, where appropriate.

B.5. Certification

Many cryptographic libraries claim certifications from national or international bodies. These certifications are tied on a specific (and often restricted) version of the library or a specific product using the library, and typically in the case of software they assure that the algorithms implemented are correct. The major certifications known are:

- USA's FIPS 140-2 at Level 1 which certifies that approved algorithms are used (see `http://en.wikipedia.org/wiki/FIPS_140-2`);

- Common Criteria for Information Technology Security Evaluation (CC), an international standard for verification of elaborate security claims (see `http://en.wikipedia.org/wiki/Common_Criteria`).

GnuTLS has support for FIPS 140-2 under Red Hat Enterprise Linux. See section 8.7 for more information.

Supported Ciphersuites

Ciphersuite name	TLS ID	Since
TLS_RSA_NULL_MD5	0x00 0x01	SSL3.0
TLS_RSA_NULL_SHA1	0x00 0x02	SSL3.0
TLS_RSA_NULL_SHA256	0x00 0x3B	TLS1.2
TLS_RSA_ARCFOUR_128_SHA1	0x00 0x05	SSL3.0
TLS_RSA_ARCFOUR_128_MD5	0x00 0x04	SSL3.0
TLS_RSA_3DES_EDE_CBC_SHA1	0x00 0x0A	SSL3.0
TLS_RSA_AES_128_CBC_SHA1	0x00 0x2F	SSL3.0
TLS_RSA_AES_256_CBC_SHA1	0x00 0x35	SSL3.0
TLS_RSA_CAMELLIA_128_CBC_SHA256	0x00 0xBA	TLS1.2
TLS_RSA_CAMELLIA_256_CBC_SHA256	0x00 0xC0	TLS1.2
TLS_RSA_CAMELLIA_128_CBC_SHA1	0x00 0x41	SSL3.0
TLS_RSA_CAMELLIA_256_CBC_SHA1	0x00 0x84	SSL3.0
TLS_RSA_AES_128_CBC_SHA256	0x00 0x3C	TLS1.2
TLS_RSA_AES_256_CBC_SHA256	0x00 0x3D	TLS1.2
TLS_RSA_AES_128_GCM_SHA256	0x00 0x9C	TLS1.2
TLS_RSA_AES_256_GCM_SHA384	0x00 0x9D	TLS1.2
TLS_RSA_CAMELLIA_128_GCM_SHA256	0xC0 0x7A	TLS1.2
TLS_RSA_CAMELLIA_256_GCM_SHA384	0xC0 0x7B	TLS1.2
TLS_RSA_AES_128_CCM	0xC0 0x9C	TLS1.2
TLS_RSA_AES_256_CCM	0xC0 0x9D	TLS1.2
TLS_RSA_AES_128_CCM_8	0xC0 0xA0	TLS1.2
TLS_RSA_AES_256_CCM_8	0xC0 0xA1	TLS1.2
TLS_DHE_DSS_ARCFOUR_128_SHA1	0x00 0x66	SSL3.0
TLS_DHE_DSS_3DES_EDE_CBC_SHA1	0x00 0x13	SSL3.0
TLS_DHE_DSS_AES_128_CBC_SHA1	0x00 0x32	SSL3.0
TLS_DHE_DSS_AES_256_CBC_SHA1	0x00 0x38	SSL3.0
TLS_DHE_DSS_CAMELLIA_128_CBC_SHA256	0x00 0xBD	TLS1.2
TLS_DHE_DSS_CAMELLIA_256_CBC_SHA256	0x00 0xC3	TLS1.2
TLS_DHE_DSS_CAMELLIA_128_CBC_SHA1	0x00 0x44	SSL3.0
TLS_DHE_DSS_CAMELLIA_256_CBC_SHA1	0x00 0x87	SSL3.0

TLS_DHE_DSS_AES_128_CBC_SHA256	0x00	0x40	TLS1.2
TLS_DHE_DSS_AES_256_CBC_SHA256	0x00	0x6A	TLS1.2
TLS_DHE_DSS_AES_128_GCM_SHA256	0x00	0xA2	TLS1.2
TLS_DHE_DSS_AES_256_GCM_SHA384	0x00	0xA3	TLS1.2
TLS_DHE_DSS_CAMELLIA_128_GCM_SHA256	0xC0	0x80	TLS1.2
TLS_DHE_DSS_CAMELLIA_256_GCM_SHA384	0xC0	0x81	TLS1.2
TLS_DHE_RSA_3DES_EDE_CBC_SHA1	0x00	0x16	SSL3.0
TLS_DHE_RSA_AES_128_CBC_SHA1	0x00	0x33	SSL3.0
TLS_DHE_RSA_AES_256_CBC_SHA1	0x00	0x39	SSL3.0
TLS_DHE_RSA_CAMELLIA_128_CBC_SHA256	0x00	0xBE	TLS1.2
TLS_DHE_RSA_CAMELLIA_256_CBC_SHA256	0x00	0xC4	TLS1.2
TLS_DHE_RSA_CAMELLIA_128_CBC_SHA1	0x00	0x45	SSL3.0
TLS_DHE_RSA_CAMELLIA_256_CBC_SHA1	0x00	0x88	SSL3.0
TLS_DHE_RSA_AES_128_CBC_SHA256	0x00	0x67	TLS1.2
TLS_DHE_RSA_AES_256_CBC_SHA256	0x00	0x6B	TLS1.2
TLS_DHE_RSA_AES_128_GCM_SHA256	0x00	0x9E	TLS1.2
TLS_DHE_RSA_AES_256_GCM_SHA384	0x00	0x9F	TLS1.2
TLS_DHE_RSA_CAMELLIA_128_GCM_SHA256	0xC0	0x7C	TLS1.2
TLS_DHE_RSA_CAMELLIA_256_GCM_SHA384	0xC0	0x7D	TLS1.2
TLS_DHE_RSA_CHACHA20_POLY1305	0xCC	0xAA	TLS1.2
TLS_DHE_RSA_AES_128_CCM	0xC0	0x9E	TLS1.2
TLS_DHE_RSA_AES_256_CCM	0xC0	0x9F	TLS1.2
TLS_DHE_RSA_AES_128_CCM_8	0xC0	0xA2	TLS1.2
TLS_DHE_RSA_AES_256_CCM_8	0xC0	0xA3	TLS1.2
TLS_ECDHE_RSA_NULL_SHA1	0xC0	0x10	SSL3.0
TLS_ECDHE_RSA_3DES_EDE_CBC_SHA1	0xC0	0x12	SSL3.0
TLS_ECDHE_RSA_AES_128_CBC_SHA1	0xC0	0x13	SSL3.0
TLS_ECDHE_RSA_AES_256_CBC_SHA1	0xC0	0x14	SSL3.0
TLS_ECDHE_RSA_AES_256_CBC_SHA384	0xC0	0x28	TLS1.2
TLS_ECDHE_RSA_ARCFOUR_128_SHA1	0xC0	0x11	SSL3.0
TLS_ECDHE_RSA_CAMELLIA_128_CBC_SHA256	0xC0	0x76	TLS1.2
TLS_ECDHE_RSA_CAMELLIA_256_CBC_SHA384	0xC0	0x77	TLS1.2
TLS_ECDHE_ECDSA_NULL_SHA1	0xC0	0x06	SSL3.0
TLS_ECDHE_ECDSA_3DES_EDE_CBC_SHA1	0xC0	0x08	SSL3.0
TLS_ECDHE_ECDSA_AES_128_CBC_SHA1	0xC0	0x09	SSL3.0
TLS_ECDHE_ECDSA_AES_256_CBC_SHA1	0xC0	0x0A	SSL3.0
TLS_ECDHE_ECDSA_ARCFOUR_128_SHA1	0xC0	0x07	SSL3.0
TLS_ECDHE_ECDSA_CAMELLIA_128_CBC_SHA256	0xC0	0x72	TLS1.2
TLS_ECDHE_ECDSA_CAMELLIA_256_CBC_SHA384	0xC0	0x73	TLS1.2
TLS_ECDHE_ECDSA_AES_128_CBC_SHA256	0xC0	0x23	TLS1.2
TLS_ECDHE_RSA_AES_128_CBC_SHA256	0xC0	0x27	TLS1.2

TLS_ECDHE_ECDSA_CAMELLIA_128_GCM_SHA256	0xC0	0x86	TLS1.2
TLS_ECDHE_ECDSA_CAMELLIA_256_GCM_SHA384	0xC0	0x87	TLS1.2
TLS_ECDHE_ECDSA_AES_128_GCM_SHA256	0xC0	0x2B	TLS1.2
TLS_ECDHE_ECDSA_AES_256_GCM_SHA384	0xC0	0x2C	TLS1.2
TLS_ECDHE_RSA_AES_128_GCM_SHA256	0xC0	0x2F	TLS1.2
TLS_ECDHE_RSA_AES_256_GCM_SHA384	0xC0	0x30	TLS1.2
TLS_ECDHE_ECDSA_AES_256_CBC_SHA384	0xC0	0x24	TLS1.2
TLS_ECDHE_RSA_CAMELLIA_128_GCM_SHA256	0xC0	0x8A	TLS1.2
TLS_ECDHE_RSA_CAMELLIA_256_GCM_SHA384	0xC0	0x8B	TLS1.2
TLS_ECDHE_RSA_CHACHA20_POLY1305	0xCC	0xA8	TLS1.2
TLS_ECDHE_ECDSA_CHACHA20_POLY1305	0xCC	0xA9	TLS1.2
TLS_ECDHE_ECDSA_AES_128_CCM	0xC0	0xAC	TLS1.2
TLS_ECDHE_ECDSA_AES_256_CCM	0xC0	0xAD	TLS1.2
TLS_ECDHE_ECDSA_AES_128_CCM_8	0xC0	0xAE	TLS1.2
TLS_ECDHE_ECDSA_AES_256_CCM_8	0xC0	0xAF	TLS1.2
TLS_ECDHE_PSK_3DES_EDE_CBC_SHA1	0xC0	0x34	SSL3.0
TLS_ECDHE_PSK_AES_128_CBC_SHA1	0xC0	0x35	SSL3.0
TLS_ECDHE_PSK_AES_256_CBC_SHA1	0xC0	0x36	SSL3.0
TLS_ECDHE_PSK_AES_128_CBC_SHA256	0xC0	0x37	TLS1.2
TLS_ECDHE_PSK_AES_256_CBC_SHA384	0xC0	0x38	TLS1.2
TLS_ECDHE_PSK_ARCFOUR_128_SHA1	0xC0	0x33	SSL3.0
TLS_ECDHE_PSK_NULL_SHA1	0xC0	0x39	SSL3.0
TLS_ECDHE_PSK_NULL_SHA256	0xC0	0x3A	TLS1.2
TLS_ECDHE_PSK_NULL_SHA384	0xC0	0x3B	TLS1.0
TLS_ECDHE_PSK_CAMELLIA_128_CBC_SHA256	0xC0	0x9A	TLS1.2
TLS_ECDHE_PSK_CAMELLIA_256_CBC_SHA384	0xC0	0x9B	TLS1.2
TLS_PSK_ARCFOUR_128_SHA1	0x00	0x8A	SSL3.0
TLS_PSK_3DES_EDE_CBC_SHA1	0x00	0x8B	SSL3.0
TLS_PSK_AES_128_CBC_SHA1	0x00	0x8C	SSL3.0
TLS_PSK_AES_256_CBC_SHA1	0x00	0x8D	SSL3.0
TLS_PSK_AES_128_CBC_SHA256	0x00	0xAE	TLS1.2
TLS_PSK_AES_256_GCM_SHA384	0x00	0xA9	TLS1.2
TLS_PSK_CAMELLIA_128_GCM_SHA256	0xC0	0x8E	TLS1.2
TLS_PSK_CAMELLIA_256_GCM_SHA384	0xC0	0x8F	TLS1.2
TLS_PSK_AES_128_GCM_SHA256	0x00	0xA8	TLS1.2
TLS_PSK_NULL_SHA1	0x00	0x2C	SSL3.0
TLS_PSK_NULL_SHA256	0x00	0xB0	TLS1.2
TLS_PSK_CAMELLIA_128_CBC_SHA256	0xC0	0x94	TLS1.2
TLS_PSK_CAMELLIA_256_CBC_SHA384	0xC0	0x95	TLS1.2
TLS_PSK_AES_256_CBC_SHA384	0x00	0xAF	TLS1.2
TLS_PSK_NULL_SHA384	0x00	0xB1	TLS1.2

TLS_RSA_PSK_ARCFOUR_128_SHA1	0x00	0x92	TLS1.0
TLS_RSA_PSK_3DES_EDE_CBC_SHA1	0x00	0x93	TLS1.0
TLS_RSA_PSK_AES_128_CBC_SHA1	0x00	0x94	TLS1.0
TLS_RSA_PSK_AES_256_CBC_SHA1	0x00	0x95	TLS1.0
TLS_RSA_PSK_CAMELLIA_128_GCM_SHA256	0xC0	0x92	TLS1.2
TLS_RSA_PSK_CAMELLIA_256_GCM_SHA384	0xC0	0x93	TLS1.2
TLS_RSA_PSK_AES_128_GCM_SHA256	0x00	0xAC	TLS1.2
TLS_RSA_PSK_AES_128_CBC_SHA256	0x00	0xB6	TLS1.2
TLS_RSA_PSK_NULL_SHA1	0x00	0x2E	TLS1.0
TLS_RSA_PSK_NULL_SHA256	0x00	0xB8	TLS1.2
TLS_RSA_PSK_AES_256_GCM_SHA384	0x00	0xAD	TLS1.2
TLS_RSA_PSK_AES_256_CBC_SHA384	0x00	0xB7	TLS1.2
TLS_RSA_PSK_NULL_SHA384	0x00	0xB9	TLS1.2
TLS_RSA_PSK_CAMELLIA_128_CBC_SHA256	0xC0	0x98	TLS1.2
TLS_RSA_PSK_CAMELLIA_256_CBC_SHA384	0xC0	0x99	TLS1.2
TLS_DHE_PSK_ARCFOUR_128_SHA1	0x00	0x8E	SSL3.0
TLS_DHE_PSK_3DES_EDE_CBC_SHA1	0x00	0x8F	SSL3.0
TLS_DHE_PSK_AES_128_CBC_SHA1	0x00	0x90	SSL3.0
TLS_DHE_PSK_AES_256_CBC_SHA1	0x00	0x91	SSL3.0
TLS_DHE_PSK_AES_128_CBC_SHA256	0x00	0xB2	TLS1.2
TLS_DHE_PSK_AES_128_GCM_SHA256	0x00	0xAA	TLS1.2
TLS_DHE_PSK_NULL_SHA1	0x00	0x2D	SSL3.0
TLS_DHE_PSK_NULL_SHA256	0x00	0xB4	TLS1.2
TLS_DHE_PSK_NULL_SHA384	0x00	0xB5	TLS1.2
TLS_DHE_PSK_AES_256_CBC_SHA384	0x00	0xB3	TLS1.2
TLS_DHE_PSK_AES_256_GCM_SHA384	0x00	0xAB	TLS1.2
TLS_DHE_PSK_CAMELLIA_128_CBC_SHA256	0xC0	0x96	TLS1.2
TLS_DHE_PSK_CAMELLIA_256_CBC_SHA384	0xC0	0x97	TLS1.2
TLS_DHE_PSK_CAMELLIA_128_GCM_SHA256	0xC0	0x90	TLS1.2
TLS_DHE_PSK_CAMELLIA_256_GCM_SHA384	0xC0	0x91	TLS1.2
TLS_PSK_AES_128_CCM	0xC0	0xA4	TLS1.2
TLS_PSK_AES_256_CCM	0xC0	0xA5	TLS1.2
TLS_DHE_PSK_AES_128_CCM	0xC0	0xA6	TLS1.2
TLS_DHE_PSK_AES_256_CCM	0xC0	0xA7	TLS1.2
TLS_PSK_AES_128_CCM_8	0xC0	0xA8	TLS1.2
TLS_PSK_AES_256_CCM_8	0xC0	0xA9	TLS1.2
TLS_DHE_PSK_AES_128_CCM_8	0xC0	0xAA	TLS1.2
TLS_DHE_PSK_AES_256_CCM_8	0xC0	0xAB	TLS1.2
TLS_DHE_PSK_CHACHA20_POLY1305	0xCC	0xAD	TLS1.2
TLS_ECDHE_PSK_CHACHA20_POLY1305	0xCC	0xAC	TLS1.2
TLS_RSA_PSK_CHACHA20_POLY1305	0xCC	0xAE	TLS1.2

TLS_PSK_CHACHA20_POLY1305	0xCC	0xAB	TLS1.2
TLS_DH_ANON_ARCFOUR_128_MD5	0x00	0x18	SSL3.0
TLS_DH_ANON_3DES_EDE_CBC_SHA1	0x00	0x1B	SSL3.0
TLS_DH_ANON_AES_128_CBC_SHA1	0x00	0x34	SSL3.0
TLS_DH_ANON_AES_256_CBC_SHA1	0x00	0x3A	SSL3.0
TLS_DH_ANON_CAMELLIA_128_CBC_SHA256	0x00	0xBF	TLS1.2
TLS_DH_ANON_CAMELLIA_256_CBC_SHA256	0x00	0xC5	TLS1.2
TLS_DH_ANON_CAMELLIA_128_CBC_SHA1	0x00	0x46	SSL3.0
TLS_DH_ANON_CAMELLIA_256_CBC_SHA1	0x00	0x89	SSL3.0
TLS_DH_ANON_AES_128_CBC_SHA256	0x00	0x6C	TLS1.2
TLS_DH_ANON_AES_256_CBC_SHA256	0x00	0x6D	TLS1.2
TLS_DH_ANON_AES_128_GCM_SHA256	0x00	0xA6	TLS1.2
TLS_DH_ANON_AES_256_GCM_SHA384	0x00	0xA7	TLS1.2
TLS_DH_ANON_CAMELLIA_128_GCM_SHA256	0xC0	0x84	TLS1.2
TLS_DH_ANON_CAMELLIA_256_GCM_SHA384	0xC0	0x85	TLS1.2
TLS_ECDH_ANON_NULL_SHA1	0xC0	0x15	SSL3.0
TLS_ECDH_ANON_3DES_EDE_CBC_SHA1	0xC0	0x17	SSL3.0
TLS_ECDH_ANON_AES_128_CBC_SHA1	0xC0	0x18	SSL3.0
TLS_ECDH_ANON_AES_256_CBC_SHA1	0xC0	0x19	SSL3.0
TLS_ECDH_ANON_ARCFOUR_128_SHA1	0xC0	0x16	SSL3.0
TLS_SRP_SHA_3DES_EDE_CBC_SHA1	0xC0	0x1A	SSL3.0
TLS_SRP_SHA_AES_128_CBC_SHA1	0xC0	0x1D	SSL3.0
TLS_SRP_SHA_AES_256_CBC_SHA1	0xC0	0x20	SSL3.0
TLS_SRP_SHA_DSS_3DES_EDE_CBC_SHA1	0xC0	0x1C	SSL3.0
TLS_SRP_SHA_RSA_3DES_EDE_CBC_SHA1	0xC0	0x1B	SSL3.0
TLS_SRP_SHA_DSS_AES_128_CBC_SHA1	0xC0	0x1F	SSL3.0
TLS_SRP_SHA_RSA_AES_128_CBC_SHA1	0xC0	0x1E	SSL3.0
TLS_SRP_SHA_DSS_AES_256_CBC_SHA1	0xC0	0x22	SSL3.0
TLS_SRP_SHA_RSA_AES_256_CBC_SHA1	0xC0	0x21	SSL3.0

Table C.1.: The ciphersuites table

Error Codes and Descriptions

The error codes used throughout the library are described below. The return code GNUTLS_E_SUCCESS indicates a successful operation, and is guaranteed to have the value 0, so you can use it in logical expressions.

Code	Name	Description
0	GNUTLS_E_SUCCESS	Success.
-3	GNUTLS_E_UNKNOWN_COMPRESSION_ALGORITHM	Could not negotiate a supported compression method.
-6	GNUTLS_E_UNKNOWN_CIPHER_TYPE	The cipher type is unsupported.
-7	GNUTLS_E_LARGE_PACKET	The transmitted packet is too large (EMSGSIZE).
-8	GNUTLS_E_UNSUPPORTED_VERSION_PACKET	A packet with illegal or unsupported version was received.
-9	GNUTLS_E_UNEXPECTED_PACKET_LENGTH	Error decoding the received TLS packet.
-10	GNUTLS_E_INVALID_SESSION	The specified session has been invalidated for some reason.
-12	GNUTLS_E_FATAL_ALERT_RECEIVED	A TLS fatal alert has been received.
-15	GNUTLS_E_UNEXPECTED_PACKET	An unexpected TLS packet was received.
-16	GNUTLS_E_WARNING_ALERT_RECEIVED	A TLS warning alert has been received.
-18	GNUTLS_E_ERROR_IN_FINISHED_PACKET	An error was encountered at the TLS Finished packet calculation.
-19	GNUTLS_E_UNEXPECTED_HANDSHAKE_PACKET	An unexpected TLS handshake packet was received.
-21	GNUTLS_E_UNKNOWN_CIPHER_SUITE	Could not negotiate a supported cipher suite.
-22	GNUTLS_E_UNWANTED_ALGORITHM	An algorithm that is not enabled was negotiated.
-23	GNUTLS_E_MPI_SCAN_FAILED	The scanning of a large integer has failed.
-24	GNUTLS_E_DECRYPTION_FAILED	Decryption has failed.
-25	GNUTLS_E_MEMORY_ERROR	Internal error in memory allocation.
-26	GNUTLS_E_DECOMPRESSION_FAILED	Decompression of the TLS record packet has failed.

-27	GNUTLS_E_COMPRESSION_FAILED	Compression of the TLS record packet has failed.
-28	GNUTLS_E_AGAIN	Resource temporarily unavailable, try again.
-29	GNUTLS_E_EXPIRED	The session or certificate has expired.
-30	GNUTLS_E_DB_ERROR	Error in Database backend.
-31	GNUTLS_E_SRP_PWD_ERROR	Error in password file.
-32	GNUTLS_E_INSUFFICIENT_CREDENTIALS	Insufficient credentials for that request.
-33	GNUTLS_E_HASH_FAILED	Hashing has failed.
-34	GNUTLS_E_BASE64_DECODING_ERROR	Base64 decoding error.
-35	GNUTLS_E_MPI_PRINT_FAILED	Could not export a large integer.
-37	GNUTLS_E_REHANDSHAKE	Rehandshake was requested by the peer.
-38	GNUTLS_E_GOT_APPLICATION_DATA	TLS Application data were received, while expecting handshake data.
-39	GNUTLS_E_RECORD_LIMIT_REACHED	The upper limit of record packet sequence numbers has been reached. Wow!
-40	GNUTLS_E_ENCRYPTION_FAILED	Encryption has failed.
-43	GNUTLS_E_CERTIFICATE_ERROR	Error in the certificate.
-44	GNUTLS_E_PK_ENCRYPTION_FAILED	Public key encryption has failed.
-45	GNUTLS_E_PK_DECRYPTION_FAILED	Public key decryption has failed.
-46	GNUTLS_E_PK_SIGN_FAILED	Public key signing has failed.
-47	GNUTLS_E_X509_UNSUPPORTED_CRITICAL_EXTENSION	Unsupported critical extension in X.509 certificate.
-48	GNUTLS_E_KEY_USAGE_VIOLATION	Key usage violation in certificate has been detected.
-49	GNUTLS_E_NO_CERTIFICATE_FOUND	No certificate was found.
-50	GNUTLS_E_INVALID_REQUEST	The request is invalid.
-51	GNUTLS_E_SHORT_MEMORY_BUFFER	The given memory buffer is too short to hold parameters.
-52	GNUTLS_E_INTERRUPTED	Function was interrupted.
-53	GNUTLS_E_PUSH_ERROR	Error in the push function.
-54	GNUTLS_E_PULL_ERROR	Error in the pull function.
-55	GNUTLS_E_RECEIVED_ILLEGAL_PARAMETER	An illegal parameter has been received.
-56	GNUTLS_E_REQUESTED_DATA_NOT_AVAILABLE	The requested data were not available.
-57	GNUTLS_E_PKCS1_WRONG_PAD	Wrong padding in PKCS1 packet.
-58	GNUTLS_E_RECEIVED_ILLEGAL_EXTENSION	An illegal TLS extension was received.
-59	GNUTLS_E_INTERNAL_ERROR	GnuTLS internal error.
-60	GNUTLS_E_CERTIFICATE_KEY_MISMATCH	The certificate and the given key do not match.

-61	GNUTLS_E_UNSUPPORTED_-CERTIFICATE_TYPE	The certificate type is not supported.
-62	GNUTLS_E_X509_UNKNOWN_SAN	Unknown Subject Alternative name in X.509 certificate.
-63	GNUTLS_E_DH_PRIME_UNACCEPTABLE	The Diffie-Hellman prime sent by the server is not acceptable (not long enough).
-64	GNUTLS_E_FILE_ERROR	Error while reading file.
-67	GNUTLS_E_ASN1_ELEMENT_NOT_FOUND	ASN1 parser: Element was not found.
-68	GNUTLS_E_ASN1_IDENTIFIER_NOT_-FOUND	ASN1 parser: Identifier was not found
-69	GNUTLS_E_ASN1_DER_ERROR	ASN1 parser: Error in DER parsing.
-70	GNUTLS_E_ASN1_VALUE_NOT_FOUND	ASN1 parser: Value was not found.
-71	GNUTLS_E_ASN1_GENERIC_ERROR	ASN1 parser: Generic parsing error.
-72	GNUTLS_E_ASN1_VALUE_NOT_VALID	ASN1 parser: Value is not valid.
-73	GNUTLS_E_ASN1_TAG_ERROR	ASN1 parser: Error in TAG.
-74	GNUTLS_E_ASN1_TAG_IMPLICIT	ASN1 parser: error in implicit tag
-75	GNUTLS_E_ASN1_TYPE_ANY_ERROR	ASN1 parser: Error in type 'ANY'.
-76	GNUTLS_E_ASN1_SYNTAX_ERROR	ASN1 parser: Syntax error.
-77	GNUTLS_E_ASN1_DER_OVERFLOW	ASN1 parser: Overflow in DER parsing.
-78	GNUTLS_E_TOO_MANY_EMPTY_PACKETS	Too many empty record packets have been received.
-79	GNUTLS_E_OPENPGP_UID_REVOKED	The OpenPGP User ID is revoked.
-80	GNUTLS_E_UNKNOWN_PK_ALGORITHM	An unknown public key algorithm was encountered.
-81	GNUTLS_E_TOO_MANY_HANDSHAKE_-PACKETS	Too many handshake packets have been received.
-84	GNUTLS_E_NO_TEMPORARY_RSA_-PARAMS	No temporary RSA parameters were found.
-86	GNUTLS_E_NO_COMPRESSION_-ALGORITHMS	No supported compression algorithms have been found.
-87	GNUTLS_E_NO_CIPHER_SUITES	No supported cipher suites have been found.
-88	GNUTLS_E_OPENPGP_GETKEY_FAILED	Could not get OpenPGP key.
-89	GNUTLS_E_PK_SIG_VERIFY_FAILED	Public key signature verification has failed.
-90	GNUTLS_E_ILLEGAL_SRP_USERNAME	The SRP username supplied is illegal.
-91	GNUTLS_E_SRP_PWD_PARSING_ERROR	Parsing error in password file.
-93	GNUTLS_E_NO_TEMPORARY_DH_PARAMS	No temporary DH parameters were found.
-94	GNUTLS_E_OPENPGP_FINGERPRINT_-UNSUPPORTED	The OpenPGP fingerprint is not supported.
-95	GNUTLS_E_X509_UNSUPPORTED_-ATTRIBUTE	The certificate has unsupported attributes.

-96	GNUTLS_E_UNKNOWN_HASH_-ALGORITHM	The hash algorithm is unknown.
-97	GNUTLS_E_UNKNOWN_PKCS_CONTENT_-TYPE	The PKCS structure's content type is unknown.
-98	GNUTLS_E_UNKNOWN_PKCS_BAG_TYPE	The PKCS structure's bag type is unknown.
-99	GNUTLS_E_INVALID_PASSWORD	The given password contains invalid characters.
-100	GNUTLS_E_MAC_VERIFY_FAILED	The Message Authentication Code verification failed.
-101	GNUTLS_E_CONSTRAINT_ERROR	Some constraint limits were reached.
-104	GNUTLS_E_IA_VERIFY_FAILED	Verifying TLS/IA phase checksum failed
-105	GNUTLS_E_UNKNOWN_ALGORITHM	The specified algorithm or protocol is unknown.
-106	GNUTLS_E_UNSUPPORTED_SIGNATURE_-ALGORITHM	The signature algorithm is not supported.
-107	GNUTLS_E_SAFE_RENEGOTIATION_-FAILED	Safe renegotiation failed.
-108	GNUTLS_E_UNSAFE_RENEGOTIATION_-DENIED	Unsafe renegotiation denied.
-109	GNUTLS_E_UNKNOWN_SRP_USERNAME	The SRP username supplied is unknown.
-110	GNUTLS_E_PREMATURE_TERMINATION	The TLS connection was non-properly terminated.
-111	GNUTLS_E_MALFORMED_CIDR	CIDR name constraint is malformed in size or structure.
-201	GNUTLS_E_BASE64_ENCODING_ERROR	Base64 encoding error.
-202	GNUTLS_E_INCOMPATIBLE_GCRYPT_-LIBRARY	The crypto library version is too old.
-203	GNUTLS_E_INCOMPATIBLE_LIBTASN1_-LIBRARY	The tasn1 library version is too old.
-204	GNUTLS_E_OPENPGP_KEYRING_ERROR	Error loading the keyring.
-205	GNUTLS_E_X509_UNSUPPORTED_OID	The OID is not supported.
-206	GNUTLS_E_RANDOM_FAILED	Failed to acquire random data.
-207	GNUTLS_E_BASE64_UNEXPECTED_-HEADER_ERROR	Base64 unexpected header error.
-208	GNUTLS_E_OPENPGP_SUBKEY_ERROR	Could not find OpenPGP subkey.
-209	GNUTLS_E_CRYPTO_ALREADY_-REGISTERED	There is already a crypto algorithm with lower priority.
-210	GNUTLS_E_HANDSHAKE_TOO_LARGE	The handshake data size is too large.
-211	GNUTLS_E_CRYPTODEV_IOCTL_ERROR	Error interfacing with /dev/crypto
-212	GNUTLS_E_CRYPTODEV_DEVICE_ERROR	Error opening /dev/crypto
-213	GNUTLS_E_CHANNEL_BINDING_NOT_-AVAILABLE	Channel binding data not available

-214	GNUTLS_E_BAD_COOKIE	The cookie was bad.
-215	GNUTLS_E_OPENPGP_PREFERRED_KEY_-ERROR	The OpenPGP key has not a preferred key set.
-216	GNUTLS_E_INCOMPAT_DSA_KEY_WITH_-TLS_PROTOCOL	The given DSA key is incompatible with the selected TLS protocol.
-217	GNUTLS_E_INSUFFICIENT_SECURITY	One of the involved algorithms has insufficient security level.
-292	GNUTLS_E_HEARTBEAT_PONG_-RECEIVED	A heartbeat pong message was received.
-293	GNUTLS_E_HEARTBEAT_PING_RECEIVED	A heartbeat ping message was received.
-294	GNUTLS_E_UNRECOGNIZED_NAME	The SNI host name not recognised.
-300	GNUTLS_E_PKCS11_ERROR	PKCS #11 error.
-301	GNUTLS_E_PKCS11_LOAD_ERROR	PKCS #11 initialization error.
-302	GNUTLS_E_PARSING_ERROR	Error in parsing.
-303	GNUTLS_E_PKCS11_PIN_ERROR	Error in provided PIN.
-305	GNUTLS_E_PKCS11_SLOT_ERROR	PKCS #11 error in slot
-306	GNUTLS_E_LOCKING_ERROR	Thread locking error
-307	GNUTLS_E_PKCS11_ATTRIBUTE_ERROR	PKCS #11 error in attribute
-308	GNUTLS_E_PKCS11_DEVICE_ERROR	PKCS #11 error in device
-309	GNUTLS_E_PKCS11_DATA_ERROR	PKCS #11 error in data
-310	GNUTLS_E_PKCS11_UNSUPPORTED_-FEATURE_ERROR	PKCS #11 unsupported feature
-311	GNUTLS_E_PKCS11_KEY_ERROR	PKCS #11 error in key
-312	GNUTLS_E_PKCS11_PIN_EXPIRED	PKCS #11 PIN expired
-313	GNUTLS_E_PKCS11_PIN_LOCKED	PKCS #11 PIN locked
-314	GNUTLS_E_PKCS11_SESSION_ERROR	PKCS #11 error in session
-315	GNUTLS_E_PKCS11_SIGNATURE_ERROR	PKCS #11 error in signature
-316	GNUTLS_E_PKCS11_TOKEN_ERROR	PKCS #11 error in token
-317	GNUTLS_E_PKCS11_USER_ERROR	PKCS #11 user error
-318	GNUTLS_E_CRYPTO_INIT_FAILED	The initialization of crypto backend has failed.
-319	GNUTLS_E_TIMEDOUT	The operation timed out
-320	GNUTLS_E_USER_ERROR	The operation was cancelled due to user error
-321	GNUTLS_E_ECC_NO_SUPPORTED_CURVES	No supported ECC curves were found
-322	GNUTLS_E_ECC_UNSUPPORTED_CURVE	The curve is unsupported
-323	GNUTLS_E_PKCS11_REQUESTED_-OBJECT_NOT_AVAILBLE	The requested PKCS #11 object is not available
-324	GNUTLS_E_CERTIFICATE_LIST_-UNSORTED	The provided X.509 certificate list is not sorted (in subject to issuer order)
-325	GNUTLS_E_ILLEGAL_PARAMETER	An illegal parameter was found.

-326	GNUTLS_E_NO_PRIORITIES_WERE_SET	No or insufficient priorities were set.
-327	GNUTLS_E_X509_UNSUPPORTED_-EXTENSION	Unsupported extension in X.509 certificate.
-328	GNUTLS_E_SESSION_EOF	Peer has terminated the connection
-329	GNUTLS_E_TPM_ERROR	TPM error.
-330	GNUTLS_E_TPM_KEY_PASSWORD_ERROR	Error in provided password for key to be loaded in TPM.
-331	GNUTLS_E_TPM_SRK_PASSWORD_ERROR	Error in provided SRK password for TPM.
-332	GNUTLS_E_TPM_SESSION_ERROR	Cannot initialize a session with the TPM.
-333	GNUTLS_E_TPM_KEY_NOT_FOUND	TPM key was not found in persistent storage.
-334	GNUTLS_E_TPM_UNINITIALIZED	TPM is not initialized.
-335	GNUTLS_E_TPM_NO_LIB	The TPM library (trousers) cannot be found.
-340	GNUTLS_E_NO_CERTIFICATE_STATUS	There is no certificate status (OCSP).
-341	GNUTLS_E_OCSP_RESPONSE_ERROR	The OCSP response is invalid
-342	GNUTLS_E_RANDOM_DEVICE_ERROR	Error in the system's randomness device.
-343	GNUTLS_E_AUTH_ERROR	Could not authenticate peer.
-344	GNUTLS_E_NO_APPLICATION_PROTOCOL	No common application protocol could be negotiated.
-345	GNUTLS_E_SOCKETS_INIT_ERROR	Error in sockets initialization.
-346	GNUTLS_E_KEY_IMPORT_FAILED	Failed to import the key into store.
-347	GNUTLS_E_INAPPROPRIATE_FALLBACK	A connection with inappropriate fallback was attempted.
-348	GNUTLS_E_CERTIFICATE_-VERIFICATION_ERROR	Error in the certificate verification.
-349	GNUTLS_E_PRIVKEY_VERIFICATION_-ERROR	Error in the private key verification; seed doesn't match.
-350	GNUTLS_E_UNEXPECTED_EXTENSIONS_-LENGTH	Invalid TLS extensions length field.
-351	GNUTLS_E_ASN1_EMBEDDED_NULL_IN_-STRING	The provided string has an embedded null.
-400	GNUTLS_E_SELF_TEST_ERROR	Error while performing self checks.
-401	GNUTLS_E_NO_SELF_TEST	There is no self test for this algorithm.
-402	GNUTLS_E_LIB_IN_ERROR_STATE	An error has been detected in the library and cannot continue operations.
-403	GNUTLS_E_PK_GENERATION_ERROR	Error in public key generation.
-404	GNUTLS_E_IDNA_ERROR	There was an issue converting to or from UTF8.
-406	GNUTLS_E_SESSION_USER_ID_CHANGED	Peer's certificate or username has changed during a rehandshake.

-407	GNUTLS_E_HANDSHAKE_DURING_-FALSE_START	Attempted handshake during false start.
-408	GNUTLS_E_UNAVAILABLE_DURING_-HANDSHAKE	Cannot perform this action while hand-shake is in progress.
-409	GNUTLS_E_PK_INVALID_PUBKEY	The public key is invalid.
-410	GNUTLS_E_PK_INVALID_PRIVKEY	The private key is invalid.
-411	GNUTLS_E_NOT_YET_ACTIVATED	The certificate is not yet activated.
-412	GNUTLS_E_INVALID_UTF8_STRING	The given string contains invalid UTF-8 characters.
-413	GNUTLS_E_NO_EMBEDDED_DATA	There are no embedded data in the structure.
-414	GNUTLS_E_INVALID_UTF8_EMAIL	The given email string contains non-ASCII characters before '@'.
-415	GNUTLS_E_INVALID_PASSWORD_STRING	The given password contains invalid characters.
-416	GNUTLS_E_CERTIFICATE_TIME_ERROR	Error in the time fields of certificate.
-417	GNUTLS_E_RECORD_OVERFLOW	A TLS record packet with invalid length was received.
-418	GNUTLS_E_ASN1_TIME_ERROR	The DER time encoding is invalid.
-419	GNUTLS_E_INCOMPATIBLE_SIG_WITH_-KEY	The signature is incompatible with the public key.
-420	GNUTLS_E_PK_INVALID_PUBKEY_-PARAMS	The public key parameters are invalid.
-421	GNUTLS_E_PK_NO_VALIDATION_PARAMS	There are no validation parameters present.

Table D.1.: The error codes table

GNU Free Documentation License

Version 1.3, 3 November 2008

Copyright © 2000, 2001, 2002, 2007, 2008 Free Software Foundation, Inc.

http://fsf.org/

Preamble

The purpose of this License is to make a manual, textbook, or other functional and useful document "free" in the sense of freedom: to assure everyone the effective freedom to copy and redistribute it, with or without modifying it, either commercially or noncommercially. Secondarily, this License preserves for the author and publisher a way to get credit for their work, while not being considered responsible for modifications made by others.

This License is a kind of "copyleft", which means that derivative works of the document must themselves be free in the same sense. It complements the GNU General Public License, which is a copyleft license designed for free software.

We have designed this License in order to use it for manuals for free software, because free software needs free documentation: a free program should come with manuals providing the same freedoms that the software does. But this License is not limited to software manuals; it can be used for any textual work, regardless of subject matter or whether it is published as a printed book. We recommend this License principally for works whose purpose is instruction or reference.

1. APPLICABILITY AND DEFINITIONS

This License applies to any manual or other work, in any medium, that contains a notice placed by the copyright holder saying it can be distributed under the terms of this License. Such a notice grants a world-wide, royalty-free license, unlimited in duration, to use that work under the conditions stated herein. The "**Document**", below, refers to any such manual or work. Any member of the public is a licensee, and is addressed as "**you**". You accept the license if you copy, modify or distribute the work in a way requiring permission under copyright law.

A "**Modified Version**" of the Document means any work containing the Document or a portion of it, either copied verbatim, or with modifications and/or translated into another language.

A "**Secondary Section**" is a named appendix or a front-matter section of the Document that deals exclusively with the relationship of the publishers or authors of the Document to the Document's overall subject (or to related matters) and contains nothing that could fall directly within that overall subject. (Thus, if the Document is in part a textbook of mathematics, a Secondary Section may not explain any mathematics.) The relationship could be a matter of historical connection with the subject or with related matters, or of legal, commercial, philosophical, ethical or political position regarding them.

The "**Invariant Sections**" are certain Secondary Sections whose titles are designated, as being those of Invariant Sections, in the notice that says that the Document is released under this License. If a section does not fit the above definition of Secondary then it is not allowed to be designated as Invariant. The Document may contain zero Invariant Sections. If the Document does not identify any Invariant Sections then there are none.

The "**Cover Texts**" are certain short passages of text that are listed, as Front-Cover Texts or Back-Cover Texts, in the notice that says that the Document is released under this License. A Front-Cover Text may be at most 5 words, and a Back-Cover Text may be at most 25 words.

A "**Transparent**" copy of the Document means a machine-readable copy, represented in a format whose specification is available to the general public, that is suitable for revising the document straightforwardly with generic text editors or (for images composed of pixels) generic paint programs or (for drawings) some widely available drawing editor, and that is suitable for input to text formatters or for automatic translation to a variety of formats suitable for input to text formatters. A copy made in an otherwise Transparent file format whose markup, or absence of markup, has been arranged to thwart or discourage subsequent modification by readers is not Transparent. An image format is not Transparent if used for any substantial amount of text. A copy that is not "Transparent" is called "**Opaque**".

Examples of suitable formats for Transparent copies include plain ASCII without markup, Texinfo input format, LaTeX input format, SGML or XML using a publicly available DTD, and standard-conforming simple HTML, PostScript or PDF designed for human modification. Examples of transparent image formats include PNG, XCF and JPG. Opaque formats include proprietary formats that can be read and edited only by proprietary word processors, SGML or XML for which the DTD and/or processing tools are not generally available, and the machine-generated HTML, PostScript or PDF produced by some word processors for output purposes only.

The "**Title Page**" means, for a printed book, the title page itself, plus such following pages as are needed to hold, legibly, the material this License requires to appear in the title page. For works in formats which do not have any title page as such, "Title Page" means the text near the most prominent appearance of the work's title, preceding the beginning of the body of the text.

The "**publisher**" means any person or entity that distributes copies of the Document to the public.

A section "**Entitled XYZ**" means a named subunit of the Document whose title either is precisely XYZ or contains XYZ in parentheses following text that translates XYZ in another language. (Here XYZ stands for a specific section name mentioned below, such as "**Acknowledgements**", "**Dedications**", "**Endorsements**", or "**History**".) To "**Preserve the Title**" of such a section when you modify the Document means that it remains a section "Entitled XYZ" according to this definition.

The Document may include Warranty Disclaimers next to the notice which states that this License applies to the Document. These Warranty Disclaimers are considered to be included by reference in this License, but only as regards disclaiming warranties: any other implication that these Warranty Disclaimers may have is void and has no effect on the meaning of this License.

2. VERBATIM COPYING

You may copy and distribute the Document in any medium, either commercially or noncommercially, provided that this License, the copyright notices, and the license notice saying this License applies to the Document are reproduced in all copies, and that you add no other conditions whatsoever to those of this License. You may not use technical measures to obstruct or control the reading or further copying of the copies you make or distribute. However, you may accept compensation in exchange for copies. If you distribute a large enough number of copies you must also follow the conditions in section 3.

You may also lend copies, under the same conditions stated above, and you may publicly display copies.

3. COPYING IN QUANTITY

If you publish printed copies (or copies in media that commonly have printed covers) of the Document, numbering more than 100, and the Document's license notice requires Cover Texts, you must enclose the copies in covers that carry, clearly and legibly, all these Cover Texts: Front-Cover Texts on the front cover, and Back-Cover Texts on the back cover. Both covers must also clearly and legibly identify you as the publisher of these copies. The front cover must present the full title with all words of the title equally prominent and visible. You may add other material on the covers in addition. Copying with changes limited to the covers, as long as they preserve the title of the Document and satisfy these conditions, can be treated as verbatim copying in other respects.

If the required texts for either cover are too voluminous to fit legibly, you should put the first ones listed (as many as fit reasonably) on the actual cover, and continue the rest onto adjacent pages.

If you publish or distribute Opaque copies of the Document numbering more than 100, you must either include a machine-readable Transparent copy along with each Opaque copy, or state in or with each Opaque copy a computer-network location from which the general network-using public has access to download using public-standard network protocols a complete Transparent copy of the Document, free of added material. If you use the latter option, you must take reasonably prudent steps, when you begin distribution of Opaque copies in quantity, to ensure that this Transparent copy will remain thus accessible at the stated location until at least one year after the last time you distribute an Opaque copy (directly or through your agents or retailers) of that edition to the public.

It is requested, but not required, that you contact the authors of the Document well before redistributing any large number of copies, to give them a chance to provide you with an updated version of the Document.

4. MODIFICATIONS

You may copy and distribute a Modified Version of the Document under the conditions of sections 2 and 3 above, provided that you release the Modified Version under precisely this License, with the Modified Version filling the role of the Document, thus licensing distribution and modification of the Modified Version to whoever possesses a copy of it. In addition, you must do these things in the Modified Version:

A. Use in the Title Page (and on the covers, if any) a title distinct from that of the Document, and from those of previous versions (which should, if there were any, be listed in the History section of the Document). You may use the same title as a previous version if the original publisher of that version gives permission.

B. List on the Title Page, as authors, one or more persons or entities responsible for authorship of the modifications in the Modified Version, together with at least five of the principal authors of the Document (all of its principal authors, if it has fewer than five), unless they release you from this requirement.

C. State on the Title page the name of the publisher of the Modified Version, as the publisher.

D. Preserve all the copyright notices of the Document.

E. Add an appropriate copyright notice for your modifications adjacent to the other copyright notices.

F. Include, immediately after the copyright notices, a license notice giving the public permission to use the Modified Version under the terms of this License, in the form shown in the Addendum below.

G. Preserve in that license notice the full lists of Invariant Sections and required Cover Texts given in the Document's license notice.

H. Include an unaltered copy of this License.

I. Preserve the section Entitled "History", Preserve its Title, and add to it an item stating at least the title, year, new authors, and publisher of the Modified Version as given on the Title Page. If there is no section Entitled "History" in the Document, create one stating the title, year, authors, and publisher of the Document as given on its Title Page, then add an item describing the Modified Version as stated in the previous sentence.

J. Preserve the network location, if any, given in the Document for public access to a Transparent copy of the Document, and likewise the network locations given in the Document for previous versions it was based on. These may be placed in the "History" section. You may omit a network location for a work that was published at least four years before the Document itself, or if the original publisher of the version it refers to gives permission.

K. For any section Entitled "Acknowledgements" or "Dedications", Preserve the Title of the section, and preserve in the section all the substance and tone of each of the contributor acknowledgements and/or dedications given therein.

L. Preserve all the Invariant Sections of the Document, unaltered in their text and in their titles. Section numbers or the equivalent are not considered part of the section titles.

M. Delete any section Entitled "Endorsements". Such a section may not be included in the Modified Version.

N. Do not retitle any existing section to be Entitled "Endorsements" or to conflict in title with any Invariant Section.

O. Preserve any Warranty Disclaimers.

If the Modified Version includes new front-matter sections or appendices that qualify as Secondary Sections and contain no material copied from the Document, you may at your option designate some or all of these sections as invariant. To do this, add their titles to the list of Invariant Sections in the Modified Version's license notice. These titles must be distinct from any other section titles.

You may add a section Entitled "Endorsements", provided it contains nothing but endorsements of your Modified Version by various parties—for example, statements of peer review or that the text has been approved by an organization as the authoritative definition of a standard.

You may add a passage of up to five words as a Front-Cover Text, and a passage of up to 25 words as a Back-Cover Text, to the end of the list of Cover Texts in the Modified Version. Only one passage of Front-Cover Text and one of Back-Cover Text may be added by (or through arrangements made by) any one entity. If the Document already includes a cover text for the same cover, previously added by you or by arrangement made by the same entity you are acting on behalf of, you may not add another; but you may replace the old one, on explicit permission from the previous publisher that added the old one.

The author(s) and publisher(s) of the Document do not by this License give permission to use their names for publicity for or to assert or imply endorsement of any Modified Version.

5. COMBINING DOCUMENTS

You may combine the Document with other documents released under this License, under the terms defined in section 4 above for modified versions, provided that you include in the combination all of the Invariant Sections of all of the original documents, unmodified, and list them all as Invariant Sections of your combined work in its license notice, and that you preserve all their Warranty Disclaimers.

The combined work need only contain one copy of this License, and multiple identical Invariant Sections may be replaced with a single copy. If there are multiple Invariant Sections with the same name but different contents, make the title of each such section unique by adding at the end of it, in parentheses, the name of the original author or publisher of that section if known, or else a unique number. Make the same adjustment to the section titles in the list of Invariant Sections in the license notice of the combined work.

In the combination, you must combine any sections Entitled "History" in the various original documents, forming one section Entitled "History"; likewise combine any sections Entitled "Acknowledgements", and any sections Entitled "Dedications". You must delete all sections Entitled "Endorsements".

6. COLLECTIONS OF DOCUMENTS

You may make a collection consisting of the Document and other documents released under this License, and replace the individual copies of this License in the various documents with a single copy that is included in the collection, provided that you follow the rules of this License for verbatim copying of each of the documents in all other respects.

You may extract a single document from such a collection, and distribute it individually under this License, provided you insert a copy of this License into the extracted document, and follow this License in all other respects regarding verbatim copying of that document.

7. AGGREGATION WITH INDEPENDENT WORKS

A compilation of the Document or its derivatives with other separate and independent documents or works, in or on a volume of a storage or distribution medium, is called an "aggregate" if the copyright resulting from the compilation is not used to limit the legal rights of the compilation's users beyond what the individual works permit. When the Document is included in an aggregate, this License does not apply to the other works in the aggregate which are not themselves derivative works of the Document.

If the Cover Text requirement of section 3 is applicable to these copies of the Document, then if the Document is less than one half of the entire aggregate, the Document's Cover Texts may be placed on covers that bracket the Document within the aggregate, or the electronic equivalent of covers if the Document is in electronic form. Otherwise they must appear on printed covers that bracket the whole aggregate.

8. TRANSLATION

Translation is considered a kind of modification, so you may distribute translations of the Document under the terms of section 4. Replacing Invariant Sections with translations requires special permission from their copyright holders, but you may include translations of some or all Invariant Sections in addition to the original versions of these Invariant Sections. You may include a translation of this License, and all the license notices in the Document, and any Warranty Disclaimers, provided that you also include the original English version of this License and the original versions of those notices and disclaimers. In case of a disagreement between the translation and the original version of this License or a notice or disclaimer, the original version will prevail.

If a section in the Document is Entitled "Acknowledgements", "Dedications", or "History", the requirement (section 4) to Preserve its Title (section 1) will typically require changing the actual title.

9. TERMINATION

You may not copy, modify, sublicense, or distribute the Document except as expressly provided under this License. Any attempt otherwise to copy, modify, sublicense, or distribute it is void, and will automatically terminate your rights under this License.

However, if you cease all violation of this License, then your license from a particular copyright holder is reinstated (a) provisionally, unless and until the copyright holder explicitly and finally terminates your license, and (b) permanently, if the copyright holder fails to notify you of the violation by some reasonable means prior to 60 days after the cessation.

Moreover, your license from a particular copyright holder is reinstated permanently if the copyright holder notifies you of the violation by some reasonable means, this is the first time you have received notice of violation of this License (for any work) from that copyright holder, and you cure the violation prior to 30 days after your receipt of the notice.

Termination of your rights under this section does not terminate the licenses of parties who have received copies or rights from you under this License. If your rights have been terminated and not permanently reinstated, receipt of a copy of some or all of the same material does not give you any rights to use it.

10. FUTURE REVISIONS OF THIS LICENSE

The Free Software Foundation may publish new, revised versions of the GNU Free Documentation License from time to time. Such new versions will be similar in spirit to the present version, but may differ in detail to address new problems or concerns. See http://www.gnu.org/copyleft/.

Each version of the License is given a distinguishing version number. If the Document specifies that a particular numbered version of this License "or any later version" applies to it, you have the option of following the terms and conditions either of that specified version or of any later version that has been published (not as a draft) by the Free Software Foundation. If the Document does not specify a version number of this License, you may choose any version ever published (not as a draft) by the Free Software Foundation. If the Document specifies that a proxy can decide which future versions of this License can be used, that proxy's public statement of acceptance of a version permanently authorizes you to choose that version for the Document.

11. RELICENSING

"Massive Multiauthor Collaboration Site" (or "MMC Site") means any World Wide Web server that publishes copyrightable works and also provides prominent facilities for anybody to edit those works. A public wiki that anybody can edit is an example of such a server. A "Massive Multiauthor Collaboration" (or "MMC") contained in the site means any set of copyrightable works thus published on the MMC site.

"CC-BY-SA" means the Creative Commons Attribution-Share Alike 3.0 license published by Creative Commons Corporation, a not-for-profit corporation with a principal place of business in San Francisco, California, as well as future copyleft versions of that license published by that same organization.

"Incorporate" means to publish or republish a Document, in whole or in part, as part of another Document.

An MMC is "eligible for relicensing" if it is licensed under this License, and if all works that were first published under this License somewhere other than this MMC, and subsequently incorporated in whole or in part into the MMC, (1) had no cover texts or invariant sections, and (2) were thus incorporated prior to November 1, 2008.

The operator of an MMC Site may republish an MMC contained in the site under CC-BY-SA on the same site at any time before August 1, 2009, provided the MMC is eligible for relicensing.

ADDENDUM: How to use this License for your documents

To use this License in a document you have written, include a copy of the License in the document and put the following copyright and license notices just after the title page:

> Copyright © YEAR YOUR NAME. Permission is granted to copy, distribute and/or modify this document under the terms of the GNU Free Documentation License, Version 1.3 or any later version published by the Free Software Foundation; with no Invariant Sections, no Front-Cover Texts, and no Back-Cover Texts. A copy of the license is included in the section entitled "GNU Free Documentation License".

If you have Invariant Sections, Front-Cover Texts and Back-Cover Texts, replace the "with ... Texts." line with this:

> with the Invariant Sections being LIST THEIR TITLES, with the Front-Cover Texts being LIST, and with the Back-Cover Texts being LIST.

If you have Invariant Sections without Cover Texts, or some other combination of the three, merge those two alternatives to suit the situation.

If your document contains nontrivial examples of program code, we recommend releasing these examples in parallel under your choice of free software license, such as the GNU General Public License, to permit their use in free software.

Bibliography

[1] NIST Special Publication 800-57, Recommendation for Key Management - Part 1: General (Revised), March 2007.

[2] PKCS #11 Base Functionality v2.30: Cryptoki Draft 4, July 2009.

[3] ECRYPT II Yearly Report on Algorithms and Keysizes (2009-2010), 2010.

[4] J. Altman, N. Williams, and L. Zhu. Channel bindings for TLS, July 2010. Available from http://www.ietf.org/rfc/rfc5929.

[5] R. J. Anderson. *Security Engineering: A Guide to Building Dependable Distributed Systems*. John Wiley & Sons, Inc., New York, NY, USA, 1st edition, 2001.

[6] S. Blake-Wilson, M. Nystrom, D. Hopwood, J. Mikkelsen, and T. Wright. Transport layer security (TLS) extensions, June 2003. Available from http://www.ietf.org/rfc/rfc3546.

[7] Y. Cheng, J. Chu, S. Radhakrishnan, and A. Jain. Tcp fast open. RFC 7413, December 2014.

[8] D. Cooper, S. Santesson, S. Farrell, S. Boeyen, R. Housley, and W. Polk. Internet X.509 Public Key Infrastructure Certificate and Certificate Revocation List (CRL) Profile. RFC 5280 (Proposed Standard), May 2008. Available from http://www.ietf.org/rfc/rfc5280.

[9] T. Dierks and E. Rescorla. The TLS protocol version 1.1, April 2006. Available from http://www.ietf.org/rfc/rfc4346.

[10] T. Dierks and E. Rescorla. The TLS Protocol Version 1.2, August 2008. Available from http://www.ietf.org/rfc/rfc5246.

[11] P. Eronen and H. Tschofenig. Pre-shared key ciphersuites for TLS, December 2005. Available from http://www.ietf.org/rfc/rfc4279.

[12] C. Evans and C. Palmer. Public Key Pinning Extension for HTTP, December 2011. Available from http://tools.ietf.org/html/draft-ietf-websec-key-pinning-01.

[13] A. Freier, P. Karlton, and P. Kocher. The secure sockets layer (ssl) protocol version 3.0, August 2011. Available from http://www.ietf.org/rfc/rfc6101.

[14] D. Gillmor. Negotiated Finite Field Diffie-Hellman Ephemeral Parameters for Transport Layer Security (TLS). RFC 7919 (Proposed Standard), Aug. 2016.

[15] P. Gutmann. Everything you never wanted to know about PKI but were forced to find out, 2002. Available from http://www.cs.auckland.ac.nz/~pgut001/pubs/pkitutorial.pdf.

[16] P. Hallam-Baker. X.509v3 transport layer security (tls) feature extension. RFC 7633, October 2015.

[17] R. Housley, T. Polk, W. Ford, and D. Solo. Internet X.509 public key infrastructure certificate and certificate revocation list (CRL) profile, April 2002. Available from `http://www.ietf.org/rfc/rfc3280`.

[18] J. Kelsey and B. Schneier. Cryptanalytic attacks on pseudorandom number generators. Available from `https://www.schneier.com/academic/paperfiles/paper-prngs.pdf`.

[19] R. Khare and S. Lawrence. Upgrading to TLS within HTTP/1.1, May 2000. Available from `http://www.ietf.org/rfc/rfc2817`.

[20] R. Laboratories. PKCS 12 v1.0: Personal information exchange syntax, June 1999.

[21] A. Langley. A Transport Layer Security (TLS) ClientHello Padding Extension, October 2015. Available from `http://www.ietf.org/rfc/rfc7685`.

[22] A. Langley, N. Modadugu, and B. Moeller. Transport layer security (tls) false start. RFC 7918, August 2016.

[23] C. Latze and N. Mavrogiannopoulos. The TPMKEY URI Scheme, January 2013. Work in progress, available from `http://tools.ietf.org/html/draft-mavrogiannopoulos-tpmuri-01`.

[24] A. Lenstra, X. Wang, and B. de Weger. Colliding X.509 Certificates, 2005. Available from `http://eprint.iacr.org/2005/067`.

[25] M. Mathis and J. Heffner. Packetization Layer Path MTU Discovery, March 2007. Available from `http://www.ietf.org/rfc/rfc4821`.

[26] D. McGrew and E. Rescorla. Datagram transport layer security (dtls) extension to establish keys for the secure real-time transport protocol (srtp). RFC 5764, May 2010.

[27] B. Moeller. Security of CBC ciphersuites in SSL/TLS: Problems and countermeasures, 2002. Available from `http://www.openssl.org/~bodo/tls-cbc.txt`.

[28] M. Myers, R. Ankney, A. Malpani, S. Galperin, and C. Adams. X.509 Internet Public Key Infrastructure Online Certificate Status Protocol - OCSP, June 1999. Available from `http://www.ietf.org/rfc/rfc2560`.

[29] M. Nystrom and B. Kaliski. PKCS 10 v1.7: certification request syntax specification, November 2000. Available from `http://www.ietf.org/rfc/rfc2986`.

[30] J. Pechanec and D. J. Moffat. The PKCS 11 URI Scheme. RFC 7512 (Standards Track), Apr. 2015.

[31] M. T. R. Seggelmann and M. Williams. Transport Layer Security (TLS) and Datagram Transport Layer Security (DTLS) Heartbeat Extension, February 2012. Available from `http://www.ietf.org/rfc/rfc6520`.

[32] E. Rescola. HTTP over TLS, May 2000. Available from `http://www.ietf.org/rfc/rfc2818`.

[33] E. Rescorla and N. Modadugu. Datagram transport layer security, April 2006. Available from `http://www.ietf.org/rfc/rfc4347`.

[34] E. Rescorla, M. Ray, S. Dispensa, and N. Oskov. Transport layer security (TLS) renegotiation indication extension, February 2010. Available from http://www.ietf.org/rfc/rfc5746.

[35] R. L. Rivest. Can We Eliminate Certificate Revocation Lists?, February 1998. Available from http://people.csail.mit.edu/rivest/Rivest-CanWeEliminateCertificateRevocationLists.pdf.

[36] P. Saint-Andre and J. Hodges. Representation and Verification of Domain-Based Application Service Identity within Internet Public Key Infrastructure Using X.509 (PKIX) Certificates in the Context of Transport Layer Security (TLS), March 2011. Available from http://www.ietf.org/rfc/rfc6125.

[37] P. Saint-Andre and A. Melnikov. Preparation, Enforcement, and Comparison of Internationalized Strings Representing Usernames and Passwords, August 2015. Available from http://www.ietf.org/rfc/rfc7613.

[38] J. Salowey, H. Zhou, P. Eronen, and H. Tschofenig. Transport layer security (TLS) session resumption without server-side state, January 2008. Available from http://www.ietf.org/rfc/rfc5077.

[39] S. Santesson. TLS Handshake Message for Supplemental Data, September 2006. Available from http://www.ietf.org/rfc/rfc4680.

[40] W. R. Stevens. *UNIX Network Programming, Volume 1*. Prentice Hall, 1998.

[41] D. Taylor, T. Perrin, T. Wu, and N. Mavrogiannopoulos. Using SRP for TLS authentication, November 2007. Available from http://www.ietf.org/rfc/rfc5054.

[42] S. Tuecke, V. Welch, D. Engert, L. Pearlman, and M. Thompson. Internet X.509 public key infrastructure (PKI) proxy certificate profile, June 2004. Available from http://www.ietf.org/rfc/rfc3820.

[43] M. Tuexen, R. Seggelmann, and E. Rescorla. Datagram transport layer security (dtls) for stream control transmission protocol (sctp). RFC 6083, January 2011. http://www.rfc-editor.org/rfc/rfc6083.txt.

[44] N. Williams. On the use of channel bindings to secure channels, November 2007. Available from http://www.ietf.org/rfc/rfc5056.

[45] T. Wu. The stanford SRP authentication project. Available from http://srp.stanford.edu/.

[46] T. Wu. The SRP authentication and key exchange system, September 2000. Available from http://www.ietf.org/rfc/rfc2945.

[47] K. D. Zeilenga. Lightweight Directory Access Protocol (LDAP): String Representation of Distinguished Names, June 2006. Available from http://www.ietf.org/rfc/rfc4514.

Index